COMMONWEALTH CARIBBEAN CONSTITUTIONAL LAW

COMMONWEALTH CARIBBEAN CONSTITUTIONAL LAW

Sir Fred Phillips
CVO, QC, LLB (Lon)
MCL (McGill Uni), LLD (Hon) UWI
former Governor, St Kitts/Nevis/Anguilla

Cavendish
Publishing
Limited

London • Sydney

First published in Great Britain 2002 by Cavendish Publishing Limited, The Glass House, Wharton Street, London WC1X 9PX, United Kingdom

Telephone: +44 (0)20 7278 8000   Facsimile: +44 (0)20 7278 8080

Email: info@cavendishpublishing.com

Website: www.cavendishpublishing.com

British Library Cataloguing in Publication Data

Phillips, Sir Fred

Commonwealth Caribbean constitutional law

1 Constitutional law – West Indies, British

I Title

342.7'29

ISBN 1 85941 691 8

Printed and bound in Great Britain

For Gloria my wife, without whose forbearance and encouragement this book would never have been completed.

PREFACE

Over the last 30–40 years, the former territories of the British Caribbean have been a laboratory in which the generally accepted 'Westminster System' is being adapted to suit the patterns of behaviour of the people of the area.

Sir Fred Phillips has played an active part in some of these processes of adaptation and in other cases he has been an informed observer whose advice has been sought by the participants themselves.

His record of the events of that period is invaluable for the people of the British Caribbean and their leaders. A thorough understanding of the past is the best safeguard against a repetition of the mistakes which may have been made.

The book will also prove a useful resource for students at all levels from the secondary schools to those engaged in post-graduate studies. By making the citizens of each country more acutely aware of the events which have taken place in neighbouring countries, it will also contribute to the creation of a Caribbean nation.

The objective of all constitutions is, undeniably, the preservation of the freedom of the individual and the enlargement of the area of his and her participation in the conduct of public affairs.

Sir Fred's analysis of the recent case law provides a convenient compilation of the legal developments over the period which will certainly be of assistance to practitioners whose advice will be sought, as new circumstances bring new problems to the fore.

The Right Honourable P Telford Georges

CONTENTS

PART II

CHAPTER 7: THE AGONY OF ST KITTS, NEVIS AND ANGUILLA   115

PART III

CHAPTER 13: THE JUDICIARY   265

TABLE OF CASES

TABLE OF LEGISLATION

United Kingdom

United States of America

TABLE OF STATUTORY INSTRUMENTS

TABLE OF ABBREVIATIONS

ADC	Aide-de-Camp
AG	Attorney General
ALP	Antigua Labour Party
ANT	Antigua
BAH	Bahamas
BAR	Barbados
BEL	Belize
BLP	Barbados Labour Party
CARICOM	Caribbean Community
CLB	Commonwealth Law Bulletin
CNS	Committee of National Salvation (Dominica)
DOM	Dominica
DDF	Dominica Defence Force
DDLP	Dominica Democratic Labour Party
DFP	Dominica Freedom Party
DLP	Democratic Labour Party (Barbados)
DLP	Dominica Labour Party
DPRK	Democratic People's Republic of Korea
DPP	Director of Public Prosecutions
FBI	Federal Bureau of Investigation
GDP	Grenada Democratic Party
GDR	German Democratic Republic
GNP	Grenada National Party
GREN	Grenada
GULP	Grenada United Labour Party
GUY	Guyana
HMG	Her Majesty's Government
ISER	Institute of Social and Economic Research
JAM	Jamaica
JA	Justice of Appeal
JLP	Jamaica Labour Party
MAP	Movement for Assemblies of the People (Grenada)

NDP	National Democratic Party (St Vincent)
NJM	New Jewel Movement (Grenada)
NLM	National Labour Movement (St Lucia)
NRP	Nevis Reformation Party
OAS	Organisation of American States
PAM	People's Action Movement (St Kitts)
PDM	People's Democratic Movement (Grenada and Turks)
PL	People's Laws (Grenada)
PLM	People's Liberation Movement (Antigua)
PLP	Progressive Labour Party (St Lucia and Bermuda)
PNM	People's National Movement
PNP	People's National Party (Jamaica and Turks)
PPP	People's Progressive Party (St Vincent and Guyana)
PRA	People's Revolutionary Army (Grenada)
PRG	People's Revolutionary Government (Grenada)
PSC	Public Service Commission
RMC	Revolutionary Military Council
St K	St Kitts
SLP	St Lucia Labour Party
St L	St Lucia
SRO	Statutory Rule and Order
St V	St Vincent
SVLP	St Vincent Labour Party
T & T	Trinidad and Tobago
UBP	United Bermuda Party
UN	United Nations
UNDP	United Nations Development Programme
UPP	United Political Party (Antigua and Barbuda)
UWI	University of the West Indies
UWP	United Workers Party (St Lucia)
WIR	West Indies Reports
WISA	West Indies Associated States

INTRODUCTION

I dealt in depth in Chapter I of the edition of this work published by Ocean Publications Inc, Dobbs Ferry, New York, in 1985 with the manner in which the People's Revolution of 1979 had affected the constitutional position of Grenada and with the initial arrangements for bringing the country back to normality after the Governor General had found it requisite on the basis of State necessity to intervene. In Chapter II, I considered the 1980 Republican Constitution of Guyana, outlining what had been achieved by that Instrument which was heavily influenced by socialist ideas. Chapter III examined some unique political events which affected the governance of Dominica, St Lucia, and (to a lesser extent) St Vincent and the Grenadines. Chapter IV reviewed the Trinidad and Tobago position while Chapter V was concerned with the rather unique union between St Kitts, Nevis and Anguilla. Chapter VI dealt with Antigua and Barbuda, Barbados, Jamaica and Belize. Chapter VII was a critique on the non-independent Caribbean territories. Chapter VIII touched very briefly on the Judiciary, while Chapter IX considered some important judgments of Caribbean courts in the field of human rights. Chapter X succinctly reviewed the position of Governors and Governor-General in their role of representatives of the Head of State (the Queen) and compared their situation with the Presidents of Guyana, Trinidad and Tobago and Dominica (Heads of State in their own right). Chapter XI provided an Epilogue.

I have felt a great sense of obligation to those lawyers and students who, having read the first edition, have been kind enough to write to commend me for having produced it and to suggest that I should now do a further edition, bringing it up to date. Many students in our University's Faculties of Law and Social Sciences, as well as in the United Kingdom and North America, found the book helpful in writing papers for higher degrees. Several legal practitioners who found the book useful in their professional work have written to me to say so.

In this second edition which is entitled *Commonwealth Caribbean Constitutional Law*, I have drastically changed the original format of the book.

Part I is written mainly for legal students and those who are being introduced to the subject for the first time (for example, students of political science) but might well be read by legal practitioners and law teachers who wish to refresh their memories. It covers such broad themes as the sources of our constitutional law and the reception of English Law; the Rule of Law; the Sovereignty of Parliament; the Separation of Powers; and the Conventions of the Constitution. In this Part I also deal in some detail with a number of recent decided cases affecting Bills of Right matters.

I have dealt in Part II with Guyana and St Kitts/Nevis as well as with Grenada, St Vincent and the Grenadines, St Lucia, Dominica, Antigua and Barbuda, Barbados, Jamaica, Belize and Trinidad and Tobago. In Chapter 11, I have inserted a section on another failed attempt at political union about which legal scholars have not yet written.

In Part III I have written a lengthy chapter on the Judiciary which at the beginning of the 21st century is a subject of much interest to lawyers and others. I have also dealt with the Public Service and with the type of Heads of State who should preside over our jurisdictions. The final chapter provides a short Epilogue.

In the chapters dealing with Grenada, Trinidad and Tobago, Barbados, St Lucia, St Vincent, Dominica, Guyana, St Kitts and Nevis, Jamaica, Antigua and Barbuda, I have deliberately included full details of political developments affecting the operation of the independence instruments. I have also discussed the various Constitution Commissions which have since 1984 been reviewing the constitutions of the respective jurisdictions. My object is twofold: to acquaint the general reader of what has been taking place in these vital matters and hopefully to prevent any government proposing to engage in constitutional changes from 're-inventing the wheel'. In this respect, it has surprised me greatly, having chaired three of the Commissions, how little the people of one territory know of what has been happening in another territory.

I must specially mention Professor Fiadjoe at the Faculty of Law at Cave Hill as well as former Senior Lecturer in Law, Dr Francis Alexis. I have derived much assistance from the writings of these two publicists.

I wish to commend the indulgence of Oceana Publications Inc, my former publishers, for permitting me to use the material in West Indian Constitutions Post-Independence Reform contained in the following pages of that volume: 3–7, 9–11,15–24, 53–66, 73–93, 95–104, 115–38, 141–57, 165–74, 205–16, 219–40, 242–68, 272–80, 301–17, 318–20, 328–30, 333–34 and 335.

Senator Velma Newton of the University of the West Indies Faculty of Law Library was extremely helpful in answer to my many requests and I convey my gratitude to her and her staff.

Mrs Sandra-Dawn Husbands-Patterson was kind enough as to assist with the research on the relation between the Barbados Executive and the Legislature in so far as the separation of powers is concerned. I wish to thank her very much.

Miss Doreen Applewhaite has borne the brunt of the typing and re-typing associated with the production of the book and I greatly appreciate her assistance.

My wife Gloria has been a veritable tower of strength, stoically accepting the lengthy periods of silence and non-communication that go with writing of this nature. She has encouraged me in every way to complete this book and I owe her a greater debt than I can repay.

Mr Justice Telford Georges has been once again kind enough to read the entire manuscript and to furnish his usually discerning comments. He has served as a High Court Judge in Trinidad and Tobago; as a Professor of Law and Dean of the Faculty of Law in the University of the West Indies; as Chief Justice in Tanzania, Zimbabwe and the Bahamas; as President of the Belize Court of Appeal; and as a Member of the Appeal Courts of the Seychelles, Bermuda and the Cayman Islands – in the course of which he has found time to sit on occasion on the Judicial Committee of the Privy Council in London. I cannot thank him too much for the generous words he has written in the Foreword to this volume.

My publishers, Cavendish Publishing, have been most efficient and helpful. They deserve highest commendation.

Finally, for any errors or other defects that may have found their way into the text, the responsibility is mine and mine alone. In true Trumanian language: 'The buck stops here.'

CHAPTER 1

SOURCES OF CARIBBEAN CONSTITUTIONAL LAW

In this chapter, we examine the sources of some of the most important aspects of our constitutional law. As is well established, the English Constitution has been largely uncoded, although it is to be found in such statutes as the Magna Carta, the Bill of Rights of 1689 and the Representation of the People Acts. Caribbean Constitutional Law shares these sources and it is to illustrate that fact that, in this chapter, we briefly outline, *seriatim*, the sources of due process of law; the status and powers of the Sovereign; how Parliament is regulated; the operation and status of the judicial system; and citizenship and nationality. We shall then consider the principles on which the reception of English Law is based.

A   DUE PROCESS OF LAW

No serious student of constitutional law can fully appreciate the subject unless he reads *Blackstone's Commentaries of the Laws of England*. In Book I, the learned writer outlines the sources of the rights of persons and illustrates the meaning of 'due process' by reference to Magna Carta. Blackstone avers that, with regard to the administration of justice, Magna Carta forbade the denial of justice and its delay to all citizens; fixed the court of common pleas to be held at Westminster; directed assizes to be held in the proper counties; directed the holding of inquests in matters of sudden and unnatural death; and prohibited ministers 'from holding pleas of the crown or trying any criminal charge, whereby many forfeitures might otherwise have unjustly accrued to the exchequer'. Magna Carta 'confirmed and established the liberties of the city of London, and all other cities, boroughs, towns and ports of the Kingdom ... And lastly (which alone would have merited the title that it bears, of the great charter) it protects every individual of the nation in the full enjoyment of his life, his liberty and his property, unless declared to be forfeited by the judgment of his peers or the law of the land'.[1]

Thus when one studies the terms of Magna Carta carefully, one finds that they lay the foundations for the protection of the right to life, the right to personal liberty, the right to the protection of property and the right not 'to be arrested, imprisoned, put out of (one's) freedom, outlawed, destroyed or put upon in any way except by the lawful judgment of (one's) peers or the law of the land'.

The declaration was confirmed by many subsequent laws including a statute, 28 Edw III c 3 (1354) where, for the first time we find the expression 'due process of law' in the following statement:

> ... no man of whatever estate or condition that he be, shall be put out of land or tenement, nor taken nor imprisoned, nor disinherited, nor put to death, without being brought in answer by due process of law.

---

1   *Blackstone's Commentaries on the Laws of England*, 1803, pp 423–24.

In 1628 in a commentary on Magna Carta, Sir Edward Coke identified 'due process of law' with 'law of the land' and, when the Star Chamber was abolished in 1640, the statute abolishing it included a recital that its actions were contrary to due process and out of harmony with the law of the land.

No other phrase of the US Constitution has been involved in more US litigation than this clause, which has recurred in not less than 2,000 cases during the 20th century and which, since 1926, has been referred to in more than 2,000 articles and case notes.[2]

B   STATUS AND POWERS OF THE SOVEREIGN

The Bill of Rights 1688 effectively debarred the Sovereign from suspending laws passed by Parliament or from executing laws not so passed. It deemed such action illegal and of no effect and enacted that no standing army in time of peace was to be maintained except by parliamentary authority. Provision was made under that Act for freedom of speech in debates in the House and for preventing the imposition of excessive bail and of cruel and inhuman punishment. The phrase 'cruel and inhuman', also much canvassed today, was, therefore, first used in Parliament more than 300 years ago and so was the expression 'Bill of Rights'.

The supreme law-making body also passed the Act of Settlement in 1701, providing for succession to the Throne. Laws for securing the liberties of the Church and the subject, together with laws to assist those unlawfully detained by illegal courts for offences other than criminal wrongs, were also passed at the time of Charles I, Charles II, and George III (for example, writ of habeas corpus). That prerogative writ is still much in use today.

The status and powers of the Crown have. over the years. been defined by statute. (See, for example, the Queen Regent's Prerogative Act 1554.) The Sovereign's position in the established Church is likewise provided by the House of Lords Precedence Act 1539 in which the Sovereign is stated to be 'justly and laufullie hed in erthe, under God, of the Churche of Englande'. The Sovereign is also by that same Act declared to be 'supreme governor of this realm ... as well as in all spiritual or ecclesiastical things or causes as temporal'. There is a 1661 Act expressing 'the sole right of the Militia to be in the King' and declaring that the Sovereign has the sole right of command of the armed forces. Thus, colonial governors were always described as Governor and Commander-in-Chief of the Armed Forces in the territory they administered at any given time.

C   REGULATION OF PARLIAMENT

How were laws to be made? Parliament decided by statute. By an Act of 1322, all laws were to be made by the Crown. On the regulatory side, a 1694 Act prescribed that Parliament was to meet once in every three years, but (even before that) the Petition of Right 1627 had prescribed that taxes could not be levied without its approval while an

---

2   See Tarnopolsky, 1974, pp 149–50.

Act of 1612 had laid down that parliamentary debates were to be privileged. The Parliamentary Privilege Act 1770 made members free from arrest or imprisonment in civil proceedings. The Meeting of Parliament Acts 1797 and 1799 covered duration, convening, dissolution and prorogation. It is from these Acts that we, in other parts of the Commonwealth, derive so much guidance in drawing up parliamentary rules affecting privilege and freedom from arrest or imprisonment in civil proceedings.

D   OPERATION OF THE JUDICIAL SYSTEM

The Judicial Committee Act 1833 not only brought the Privy Council into being but named the courts from which appeals could be brought while the Appellate Jurisdiction Acts of 1876 and 1913 established the composition of the Council. Also, the Judicial Committee (Amendment) Act 1895 made judges from the Dominions and India (who were Privy Councillors) eligible to sit. This position has not changed, except that more and more Commonwealth countries are establishing their own final Courts of Appeal.

The Supreme Court of Judicature (Consolidation) Act 1925 laid down the appointment requirement *for members of the higher judiciary who were disqualified from membership in the House of Commons*. This Act also provided that judges could only be dismissed by an address by both Houses of Parliament. The constitution of the Supreme Court of Judicature (the High Court and Appeal Court) is set out in the Supreme Court of Judicature (Consolidation) Act 1925 as amended from time to time. Reference has already been made to the Judicial Committee of the Privy Council and the position of the Law Lords in the House of Lords will be addressed in Chapter 5, below. But statutory provision was made for Courts Martial Appeals Courts by the Courts Martial (Appeal) Act 1951, in respect of which the judges are appointed by the Lord Chancellor and the courts have the right of appeal to the House of Lords as the final appeal tribunal. The principles implicit in these arrangements have helped to make our judiciary as independent as it has turned out to be.

E   CITIZENSHIP AND NATIONALITY

It was the *Calvin* case[3] which, following the union between England and Scotland, laid down in 1608 that those who were born in or were otherwise associated with the King's dominions owed allegiance to the King and were his 'subjects'. The principle was thereafter extended to the colonies, whether secured by settlement, conquest or cession. In this respect, a person born in a colony was in the same position as his or her counterpart born in Great Britain or otherwise associated therewith. So long as the doctrine subsisted that the Crown was one and indivisible throughout Her Majesty's domains, this citizenship doctrine held good. What brought about a change was the movement in the Commonwealth relationship away from the single indivisible institutionalised bonds.

The first codification of citizenship in the United Kingdom was attempted in the British Nationality and Status of Aliens Act 1914 which was put on the statute book after

---

3   The *Calvin* case (1608) 7 Co Rep 1a.

full discussion with representatives of the then Dominions – Canada, Australia, New Zealand and the Union of South Africa.

Eire was the first independent country to break rank with Britain in creating its own citizenship when it passed the Irish Nationality and Citizenship Act 1935 which repealed the 1914 Act and set out the persons who were Eire citizens. That was followed by the Canadian Citizenship Act 1946 which created a Canadian citizenship and opened the way for each Commonwealth country to pass legislation outlining who its citizens were henceforth to be.

In 1948, the British Government passed another British Nationality Act, the effect of which was to divide British citizenship into two divisions, viz, citizenship of the independent countries of the Commonwealth and citizenship of the United Kingdom and Colonies.

In 1962, the Commonwealth Immigration Act was passed with the object of limiting black immigration to Britain: the Act applying to citizens of independent countries and Colonies alike so long as their passports had been issued in the Colonies. But it did not control citizens of the United Kingdom and Colonies whose passports had been issued in England by the British Government.

When faced with the fact that a number of British East African immigrants (who found it untenable to live under Amin's regime) were coming to Britain, the United Kingdom Parliament passed a second Commonwealth Immigration Act with the object of depriving the (East African) British subjects of their citizenship. It was left to the European Commission and the European Court of Human Rights in 1973 to rule that the new Act constituted discrimination on racial grounds, relegating the British East Africans to the level of second class citizens and making them subject to an interference with their human dignity which amounted to degrading treatment under Art 3 of the European Convention on Human Rights which provided that: 'No one shall be subjected to torture or to inhuman treatment or punishment.'[4]

The victory of the East African Asians was, however, a pyrrhic one, since the Act was not revoked: their quota for entry simply being increased so as to permit an acceleration of their rate of entry. But, three years later, they were deemed non-patrials without a right of abode under the Immigration Act of 1971.[5] Further, in the words of Lord Lester, 'their second class status is reflected in their new definition as "British Overseas Citizens" in the British Nationality Act 1981'.

This 1981 British Nationality Act provided for the continuation of citizens of the United Kingdom and Colonies as well as for three categories of citizens, viz, British citizens, British dependent territories citizens and British overseas citizens. And the title of Commonwealth citizen is given to all these three classes as well as to the citizens of those Commonwealth countries whose Parliament makes provision for those entitled to Commonwealth citizenship.

In Lord Lester's view: 'Many of its provisions are so obscurely drafted that they are not fit to be on the statute book.'[6] But Lord Denning has painted a rosy picture: 'We are all

---

4   See *East African Asians v United Kingdom* (1973) 3 EHRR 76, E Com HR.
5   See Immigration Act 1971, s 1(1).
6   Lester, 1989, p 351. Much of the material in this section on Citizenship is drawn from an article by Lord Lester in Jowell, J and Oliver, D (eds), 1989, pp 345–69.

patrials. We are no longer in the eyes of the law Englishmen, Scotsmen or Welshmen. We are just patrials. Parliament gave this new man a fine set of clothes. It invested him with a new right. It called it "the right of abode in the United Kingdom". It is the most precious right that anyone can have.'[7] Whether this 'most precious right' has been enjoyed by black patrials is another question.

F   RECEPTION OF ENGLISH LAW

We must now examine how the new legal systems in the Caribbean came to be 'received' locally.

From the 17th century for about 100 years, colonisation was the order of the day in the region – the British, French, Spanish and Dutch fighting many naval battles to capture various territories. The British were the most successful and, since we are considering only former British colonies, it is to the English common law of colonisation that we must look for the basic rules of 'reception' or (as it is sometimes called) 'adoption'.

Even at that primitive stage, every colonial jurisdiction operated under some system of law and never in a vacuum. But such a system was not always a developed one. In such a case, whenever a settlement took place, English law applied.

In many of the Caribbean territories, there were Caribs and Arawaks who lived simple lives without any *recognised* legal systems. It is in such a situation that, in the first half of the 17th century, Barbados, Montserrat, St Kitts, Nevis, Antigua and Barbuda were all '*settled*' by Englishmen and Irish; while Trinidad, Jamaica, St Vincent, Grenada, Dominica and St Lucia were 'ceded' by treaty to the British Crown at the end of various wars.

The following common law rules became applicable.

G   IN THE CASE OF SETTLEMENT

If a country that was uninhabited or very sparsely inhabited became settled by the British, the common law rule was that those settlers were deemed to have imported English law with them. To quote Professor Peter Hogg: 'English law followed British subjects and filled the legal void in the new territory.'[8] However, the settlers took with them only such laws as were applicable to their situation – such importation dating from the date of settlement.[9] This date was in turn interpreted in the courts as the date of 'the institution of a local legislature in the colony'. The law imported included statute law, equity and the common law, but excluded all laws deemed unsuitable to the needs of the particular colony. In the condescendingly quaint words of Sir William Blackstone:[10]

---

7   See Lord Denning, 1980, p 168.
8   Hogg, 1985, p 23.
9   *Blankard v Galdy* (1693) 2 Salk 411. The law of mortmain did not apply to Grenada when it was conquered.
10   *Blackstone's Commentaries on the Laws of England*, 1803, Book 1, pp 106–07.

[Besides these adjacent islands] our most distant possessions in America, and elsewhere, are also in some respects subject to the English laws. If an uninhabited country be discovered and planted by English subjects, all the English laws then in being, which are the birthright of every subject, are immediately there in force.

However, in the view of Blackstone, those laws should be restricted to such as are 'applicable to their own situation and the condition of an infant colony'. What he refers to as 'the artificial refinements and distinctions incident to the property of a great and commercial people' are neither 'necessary nor convenient' for natives.[11] Thus, it has been held that the law of mortmain did not apply to Grenada at the time of settlement.[12]

H   IN THE CASE OF CESSION FROM ANOTHER POWER OR CONQUEST

Where a country is conquered or ceded, the *prevailing* law remained. As Blackstone puts it:

[In such a case] they have already laws of their own. The King may indeed alter and change those laws.

But, until the Sovereign takes that step, the ancient laws of the country remain 'unless such as are against the law of God as in the case of an infidel country'. When it is a case of conquest, the territory is subject to the control of Parliament which must pass new laws for the governance thereof under the Royal Prerogative. Thus, the pre-existing private (criminal) law remains in force whereas the Crown's prerogative power operates to pass legislation to provide governmental institutions (by way of public law).

The prerogative power, however, comes to an end as soon as a new legislative assembly is given to a conquered territory and, thereafter, Parliament in the United Kingdom would not legislate for such a colony.

Thus, in the famous case of *Campbell v Hall*,[13] the King issued a proclamation granting an assembly to the Island of Grenada, which had been conquered from France. Later, the King issued a further proclamation imposing an export tax on the inhabitants of the country. This tax was held to be invalid by the Court of Queen's Bench sitting in England: the prior grant of the assembly being held to terminate the King's prerogative to legislate (except with the authority of Parliament).

Our next chapter considers the rule of law.

---

11   *Ibid*, p 107.
12   *AG v Stewart* (1816) 2 Mer 143.
13   (1774) 1 Cow 204, 98 ER 1045.

CHAPTER 2

THE RULE OF LAW

In order to understand this concept, the context in which Professor Albert Venn Dicey first propounded his interpretation of it in 1885 must be examined. We shall then consider how, in Dicey's view, the rule of law was alleged to have controlled the legality of official action. Finally, we shall see how the doctrine has influenced Caribbean constitutional legal thinking to this day.

THE IDEA AS ORIGINALLY STATED

Dicey's thesis as originally stated was much too sweeping and doctrinaire. It was in fact based on a number of misconceptions as to the constitutional and administrative status quo.

In his now famous work – *The Law of the Constitution* – Dicey laid down three fundamental principles, viz:

- No citizen 'is punishable or can be lawfully made to suffer in body or goods except for a distinct breach of law established before the ordinary courts of the land. In this sense the rule of law is contrasted with every system of government based on the exercise by persons in authority of wide, arbitrary or discretionary powers of constraint'.[1]
- The 'equal subjection' of all classes to one law administered by the ordinary courts.
- 'The result of judicial decisions determining the rights of private persons' before the courts was what, in Dicey's view, was the non-codified rule of law.

But when the three elements are carefully considered, the fallacies implicit in them become manifest.

As regards the lack of arbitrary government, Dicey considered that the English regime provided certainty of the law, non-discretionary powers and equality before the law. In his own words:

> With us every official, from the Prime Minister down to a constable or a collector of taxes is under the same responsibility as any other citizen.

On the contrary, he insisted, the French *droit administratif* provided special provisions protecting officials. However, as Professor WA Robson has pointed out, the statement (about the French position) was based on a misinterpretation of French law which did not, in fact, *exempt* public officials, but simply *permitted* dignitaries versed in public administration to determine the extent to which officials were liable in any given case.

In answer to Dicey's second assertion that there was an equal subjection in England of all classes to the laws, Robson pointed to the 'colossal distinctions' between the rights and duties of private individuals and those of administrative cadres in England. Indeed, in

---

1   Dicey, 1965, p 188.

many vital cases, according to Robson, the individual was deprived of his rights against the State because of immunities claimed by the State.[2] Also, Robson stressed, even in Dicey's day, a number of special tribunals were already set up to deal with disputes outside the courts system.[3]

Surprisingly, Dicey found well known allies for his views in such distinguished thinkers as Lord Hewart,[4] Sir Henry Maine,[5] and FA Hayek.[6] His theories were, however, violently opposed by an equally eminent array of jurists. Sir Ivor Jennings objected strongly to his views that in English Law discretionary powers played little part in public administration.[7] Mr Justice Felix Frankfurter, a respected former member of the United States Supreme Court, made the pronouncement that 'the persistence of the misdirection that Dicey has given to the development of administrative law strikingly proves the elder Huxley's observation that many a theory survives long after its brains are knocked out'.[8]

In more recent times, Professor Jeffrey Jowell has shown the flaws in Dicey's thesis and posited that the rule of law should be seen as 'a principle of institutional morality' and that today it 'by no means precludes acceptance of the welfare and regulatory functions of government'. In Professor Jowell's view, the ghost 'has refused to rest. It rises still to haunt a minister who publishes guidelines that cut across a statute under which it operates, the minister who penalizes local authorities for overspending without giving them a fair hearing ... or a Prime Minister who seeks to deprive Civil Servants of their rights to remain members of a trade union'.[9]

Lord Lester has likewise added his erudite voice in outlining some of the pitfalls in Dicey's postulations. He has shown in a most convincing way how, despite the Crown Proceedings Act 1967, the Government and public authorities enjoy special immunities from ordinary legal process – so much so that neither the Ministry of Defence nor a member of the armed forces is liable in tort for the death of, or personal injury to, another member of the armed forces while on duty, even if it is in peace time.[10] Of Dicey's theory of equality of governors and the governed, he summarily states: 'In reality this is not and never was true.'[11]

THE POSITION TODAY

It is high time that the doctrine as expounded by Dicey should be buried with full military honours.

---

2   Robson, 1947, p 345.

3   See a very useful article on this aspect by Arthurs, 1979.

4   Lord Hewart, *The New Despotism*.

5   Sir Henry Maine, *Collected Papers*, Vol I, 1911, p 81.

6   Hayek, 1943.

7   Jennings, 1933, pp 309–10.

8   See Frankfurter, 1938, p 517.

9   See a discerning article by Jeffrey Jowell on the rule of law today: Jowell and Oliver, 1989, pp 22–23.

10   See Lord Lester's masterly contribution (Lester, 1989, p 356).

11   *Ibid*, p 346.

But a new rule of law, such as described by Paul Johnson in his book *A History of the Modern World*, should be installed to take its place. Under this new rule, it should be laid down that there is no law without order and no freedom without law. In other words, law, order and freedom must go together and work together.

Johnson characterises the rule of law as 'an abstract, sophisticated concept .... mightily difficult to achieve. Until it is attained and implanted in the public mind to the extent that large groups of people are prepared to sacrifice their lives to support it, progress will be uncertain. The essence of the rule,' he asserts, 'is its impersonality, omnipotence and ubiquity.' For him, the law must apply to every citizen with equal force – 'kings, emperors, high priests and the State itself' – this principle admitting of no exceptions. Indeed, he declares that: 'If exceptions are made, the rule of law begins to collapse – that was the grand lesson of antiquity.'[12]

It is striking how often it is stated today that, in giving themselves new constitutions, those people throwing off the colonial yoke in various parts of the world wish, in future, to have freedom protected by the rule of law. A few examples taken from recent Caribbean constitutions will illustrate how consistently draftsmen find it necessary nowadays to include references in new constitutions to the rule of law.

The Barbados Constitution[13] and its Grenada counterpart[14] both express in their respective Preambles 'respect for the rule of law'. The Constitutions of Dominica,[15] Belize[16] and Trinidad and Tobago:[17]

> ... recognise that men and institutions remain free only when freedom is founded upon respect for moral and spiritual values and upon the rule of law.

The St Lucia Preamble[18] contains this declaration:

> We the People of St Lucia – maintain that these freedoms can only be safeguarded by the rule of law.

The Bahamas Preamble[19] expresses the same sentiment in more fulsome and flowery terms, viz:

> Whereas The People of this Family of Islands recognise that the preservation of their Freedom will be guaranteed by a national commitment to Self Discipline, Industry, Loyalty, Unity and an abiding respect for Christian values and the rule of law.

It is on this note of freedom that we must end this discussion on the meaning of the term – for we must always bear in mind that the principle ceases to have any efficacy where the people are not truly free.

We next address the doctrine of the sovereignty of Parliament.

---

12   See Johnson, 1999, pp 23–23.
13   The Barbados Independence Order 1966 SI 1966/1455 UK.
14   The Grenada Constitution Order 1973 SI 1973/2155 UK.
15   The Dominica Independence Order 1978 SI 1978/1027 UK.
16   The Belize Independence Order 1981 SI 1981/1107 UK.
17   The Trinidad and Tobago Republic Constitution Act 1976, No 4 of 1996 – Trinidad and Tobago.
18   The St Lucia Constitution Order 1978 SI 1978/1901 UK.
19   The Bahamas Independence Order 1973 SI 1973/1000 UK.

CHAPTER 3

THE SOVEREIGNTY OF PARLIAMENT

This was a doctrine in its heyday in the days of Professor AV Dicey[1] who expressed it as the rule which conferred on Parliament the power 'to make or unmake any law whatever'. Up to the end of the Second World War, the doctrine was one of great constitutional significance which was not seriously questioned from any quarter. It was taken as axiomatic that Parliament could pass laws on any matter whatsoever and this applied to the many statutes and other laws constituting (in large measure) the British Constitution, to which reference has been made in Chapter 1 above.

After the Second World War, there were two powerful developments which called the doctrine into question and in this chapter we shall very briefly examine them. We shall also see later in the text the extent to which the British restrained themselves from exporting the principle of the supremacy of Parliament in the grant of new constitutions to many of its former colonies, including those in the Caribbean.

The first development affecting that sovereignty was the European Court of Justice which came into operation after Britain joined the European Economic Community (EEC), now the European Union. As will be shown hereunder, no doctrine of constitutional law – no matter how ancient or well entrenched – can ignore the reality of Britain's international obligations. It is for this reason we must now examine the impact of that fact upon the doctrine of the sovereignty of Parliament, in so far as the judicial organs of the European Union are concerned.

A   DEVELOPMENT IN THE DIRECTION OF QUALIFYING SOVEREIGNTY OF PARLIAMENT

The British Constitution has left the United Kingdom isolated from the rest of the Commonwealth because its protagonists have clung to the myth that its unwritten nature gives it flexibility to grow and evolve.[2] But Lord Lester has been relentless in pointing out that the most striking characteristic of the British Constitution is 'its failure to adapt to the changed needs of the nation'.[3] In this connection, he has referred to what he describes as 'the alienation of Northern Ireland',[4] to colour and citizenship in Britain,[5] to 'devolution in a vacuum',[6] to equality in parts of the United Kingdom. In Britain, it is unlawful to discriminate on racial grounds, but racial discrimination is not unlawful in Northern Ireland. At the same time, it is unlawful in Northern Ireland to discriminate on grounds

---

1 Dicey, 1965, p 39.
2 See Lester, 1989, pp 345–69. See, also, Lord Hailsham, 1978, pp 137–40.
3 See Lester, 1989, p 368.
4 *Ibid*, p 348.
5 *Ibid*, pp 349–52.
6 *Ibid*, pp 353–56.

of religion, whereas this is not the case in Britain.[7] 'Every major attempt at reform,' he asserted, in 1989, 'has been blocked or mismanaged':[8]

... incorporating of the European Convention;[9] the electoral system; the House of Lords; devolution; regional and local government; citizenship; public access to official information; administrative law.

At that time, too, he expressed the hope that the United Kingdom adherence to the European system would cause them to see the need for a new constitutional settlement.[10] This settlement would clearly include the need to recognise that Parliament is no longer sacrosanct.

In making such a pronouncement, he has come close to prophesy, when one looks at the programme of constitutional reform upon which the Labour Government, headed by Tony Blair, has embarked.

It has at last been agreed that the European Convention on Human Rights will be incorporated into the United Kingdom municipal law, thus enabling people in British courts to have the opportunity *in those courts* of enforcing their rights under the European Convention.[11]

What is odd is that the Government was not prepared, in the Human Rights Act of 1998, to permit the courts to strike down legislation which is in conflict with the Convention. Section 3 of the Act requires the court to interpret legislation as far as possible in accordance with the Convention. Where this is not possible, the Act gives the higher courts (as described below) the right, in s 4, to make a declaration of incompatibility, if the court is satisfied that a provision of *primary legislation* is incompatible with a Convention right (s 4(3)). There is, of course, a similar right where the court decides that a power conferred by *subordinate legislation* is incompatible with a Convention Right (s 4(4)).

The only courts capable of making such declarations are the House of Lords, the Judicial Committee of the Privy Council, the Courts Martial Appeal Courts (in Scotland), the High Court of Judiciary, (in England and Wales or Northern Ireland), the High Court and the Court of Appeal (s 4(5)).

Section 4(6) makes it clear that the validity of the legislation is not affected by a declaration of incompatibility.

Where a court is considering making a declaration, the Crown is entitled to notice and to be joined as a party to the proceedings (s 5(1)).

---

7   Lester, 1989, pp 352–53.
8   *Ibid*, pp 368–69.
9   It must be observed that Lord Lester introduced two bills (on incorporation) into the House of Lords in 1994 and 1996.
10   Lester, 1989, p 369.
11   See the United Kingdom Human Rights Act 1998 (Cap 42) which came into force on 2 October 2000.

The United Kingdom Government refuses to accept that the sovereignty of Parliament (as originally conceived) cannot stand for all time. One can only hope that the day is not far distant when they will heed these wise words of Lord Scarman:[12]

> It is the helplessness of the law in the face of the legislative sovereignty of Parliament which makes it difficult for the legal system to accommodate the concept of fundamental and inviolable human rights. Means therefore have to be found whereby: (1) there is incorporated into English law a declaration of such rights, (2) these rights are protected against all encroachments, including the power of the state, even when that power is exerted by a representative legislative institution such as Parliament.

The United Kingdom acceded to the EEC by the Treaty of Brussels 1972 which was given effect in the country by the European Communities Act 1972. One of the distinctive features of the treaty is that the relevant organs of the EEC have been vested with executive, legislative, judicial and fiscal powers: a specific example being the European Court of Justice which in 1964 settled the question of legislative supremacy by ruling that community law prevails over incompatible national law, irrespective of when the national legislation was enacted.[13]

To put the primacy of Community legislation beyond doubt, the European Court of Justice also ruled that the court's judgments take precedence, even when the national law is enacted *subsequent* to the court's ruling.[14] In a 1977 ruling, the European Court indicated that private parties may obtain a judgment in which a national judge denies enforcement of a domestic statute which does not conform with Community law. It was held that:

> A National Court which is called upon ... to apply provisions of Community law is under a duty to give full effect to those provisions, if necessary refusing its own motion to apply any conflicting provision of national legislation, even if adopted subsequently, and it is not necessary for the [national court] to request or wait the prior setting aside of such provisions by legislative or other constitutional means.

The Court referred, in the *Costa* case, to the treaty as 'an independent source of law (which) could not, because of its special and original nature, be overridden by domestic legal provisions, however formed, without being deprived of its character as Community law and without the legal basis of the Community itself being called into question'.

In 1972, Denmark, Eire and the United Kingdom signed the Treaty of Accession to the Treaty of Rome, whereupon Denmark and Eire proceeded to make the necessary constitutional amendments to accommodate the new legal arrangements. Britain passed the European Communities Act which empowered British courts to administer Community law and which permitted its reception.

The moot problem has always been: what of legislation affecting Community law passed after the 1972 enabling Act came into effect? It is a principle of British Law that the

---

12 Lord Scarman,1974, p 15. See, also, to the same effect, a speech given by Arthur Chaskalson (1989) (now President of the South African Constitutional Court) at a Bar dinner at the Harare Colloquium organised by the International Center for the Legal Protection of Human Rights (INTERIGHTS) and the Commonwealth Secretariat in 1989.

13 See *Costa v ENEL* [1964] ECR 585, European Court of Justice.

14 *Amministrazione delle Finanze dello Stato v Simmenthal Spa* (No 106/77) [1978] ECR 629.

courts will endeavour to interpret a statute to bring it in conformity with international law whenever they are called upon to interpret such a statute intended to give effect to a treaty obligation. But the issue has not yet neatly arisen as to whether a British court would refuse to interpret a *subsequent* Act affecting the Community as being in conflict with Community law. The matter came close to being raised before the English Court of Appeal in 1979[15] when the Court was divided as to whether Art 119 of the Treaty (which enunciates the broad principle that throughout the Community men and women should receive equal pay for the same work) should be referred for an opinion of the European Court. In this case, the majority of the Court, Lawton and Cumming-Bruce LJJ (Denning MR dissenting), ruled that the 1970 English Act under review was to be construed according to the ordinary canons of construction and, since according to its natural and ordinary meaning s 1(2)(a)(i) was confined to cases where a man and a woman were in the same employment, *at the same time*, the Court could not use the terms of Art 119 of the EEC Treaty as an aid to the construction of the section. Lord Denning dissented from the majority, but was, however, able to agree with them that, since there was doubt as to the ambit of Art 119 and since the Court was bound by the European Communities Act 1972 to give effect to the provisions of the EEC Treaty *in priority to a United Kingdom statute*, the matter of the true interpretation of Art 119 should be referred to the Court of Justice under Art 177 of the Treaty.

In the event, the European Court held that s 119 should be broadly interpreted so that the English court could hold that the English legislation was intended to include discrimination against a woman, even when such a woman *succeeded a male within a short time* in the same employment.

As we have seen, therefore, the European Court of Justice has consistently spoken with firmness and certainty in emphasizing the supremacy of Community law over the laws passed by the United Kingdom Parliament where Community issues are involved. No more summary language could be used than in the *Van Gend* case, in which the European Court expounded that 'the Community constitutes a new legal order of international law, for the benefits of which the states have limited their sovereign rights, albeit within limited fields, and the subjects of which comprise not only Member States but also their nationals'.[16]

It is also interesting to observe that there was no British dissent from the EEC Opinion published, concerning United Kingdom membership at the time of accession to the Treaty. In the document, the Commission expressed the view that British Acts of Parliament would effect a transfer of the relevant legislative powers 'with the consequences this entails for the legislative activity of Parliament, that is, the adoption of measures required by Community law'.[17]

---

15   See *Macarthy's Ltd v Smith* [1979] 3 All ER 325

16   See *Van Gend En Loos v Nederlande Tarief Commissie* [1963] CMLR 105, p 129.

17   See the Opinion of the EEC on Britain's application for membership on 29 September 1967 (80–81).

B DILUTION OF THE DOCTRINE

Unfortunately, both the United Kingdom House of Lords and the Court of Appeal appeared reluctant to come to grips with the obvious dilution of the doctrine of parliamentary sovereignty and continued to speak with a forked tongue on the matter. Thus, in one case, Lord Denning MR asserted that if a law was intentionally passed by Parliament in defiance of Community obligations, the treaty would have to be ignored.[18] Likewise, in the later case of *Garland v British Rail Engineering Ltd*,[19] Lord Diplock speaking for a unanimous House of Lords, was prepared to go no further than to assert that whenever a statute had to be construed involving treaty obligations and the words were capable of bearing a meaning consistent with such obligations, the words shall be accorded that meaning 'without undue straining of the ordinary meaning of language'. And, in making this pronouncement, Lord Diplock gave the Treaty of Rome as an example. The fact is that it would be a foolhardy English court who would follow an English statute running counter to a decision of the European Court and one would expect 'undue straining' if that became necessary. Plain judicial talk in England has so far been withheld.

The second development that has tended to undermine the myth of the sovereignty of Parliament was the worldwide recognition of the fundamental rights of the individual which arose out of the Second World War. This recognition found expression in the 1948 Universal Declaration of Human Rights to which all members of the United Nations Organisation deemed it expedient to subscribe.

The upshot is that all newly independent countries since 1949 have included protection for fundamental rights and freedoms in their constitutions, and such constitutions have in almost all cases been designated 'the supreme law'. Accordingly, any laws passed in derogation of the supreme law have been declared void to the extent of the inconsistency.

In this way, the sovereignty of Parliament – as understood in Britain – has been dealt a severe blow in most modern constitutions in the past 35 years, including those in the former British Caribbean. In the chapter dealing with civil liberties, we will show that many laws duly passed by Caribbean Legislatures have been declared *ultra vires*, void and of no effect.

Thus, in so far as West Indian Constitutions[20] are concerned, we now have *not* parliamentary sovereignty, but constitutional supremacy.

In this aspect of constitutional development, the British had unfortunately become 'timorous souls' until 2 October 2000, and the fear of dismantling the doctrine of the sovereignty of Parliament seemed to be ruling them from Dicey's grave.

---

18 *Felixstowe Dock and Railway Co v British Transport Docks Board* [1976] Lloyd's Rep 663.

19 [1983] 2 AC 751.

20 See Phillips, 1977, in Chapter V of which 31 cases involving judicial review of legislation and executive action between 1964 and 1975 were discussed, pp 124–65. See, also, Phillips, 1985, in Chapter IX of which a further 23 cases are considered calling for State redress, including the striking down of legislation.

Even though the present Labour Government in Britain expressed a wish on coming to office to introduce a Bill of Rights as part of the constitutional machinery for judicial review, they insisted that such an innovation must have no effect on this sacred cow – parliamentary supremacy.

We shall see in the next chapter to what extent (if at all) there exists a true separation of powers.

CHAPTER 4

THE SEPARATION OF POWERS

In his *L'Esprit de Lois*, Montesquieu expressed the view that liberty cannot exist when there is a merger between the executive and the legislature. He also quite appropriately maintained that liberty would be impossible if there was no division between the judicial arm on the one hand and the executive and legislative arms on the other.[1]

According to Lawson and Bentley,[2] this doctrine had a decisive influence upon those who framed the American Constitution and particularly on those who devised the Massachusetts Constitution and who made the famous declaration:

> In the Government of this Commonwealth the legislative department shall never exercise the executive and judicial powers or either of them; the executive shall never exercise the legislative and judicial powers or either of them; the judicial shall never exercise the executive and legislative powers or either of them.

But clear-cut as this statement may be, it is not a principle which has ever conformed with the facts of constitutional realities, as will be illustrated later. Britain has always witnessed some overlap between the three branches: the most glaring example being the way the House of Lords operates as the second chamber of the legislature and as the final Court of Appeal. Government ministers sit and vote with the Law Lords and the Lord Chancellor (who presides) is a member of the Cabinet, a legislator and a judge.

What is more, when the history of British colonial policy is examined one finds that, at the time Montesquieu was making his statement in the 17th century (and even beyond that time), such a separation was completely absent in countries abroad over which Britain claimed suzerainty or developed settlements. Thus, Chief Justice William Hey (the then Canadian Chief Justice), who was entrusted in 1773 with preparing the Quebec Act, was at the same time also the Member of Parliament for Kent at Westminster. While the Lord Chancellor of England avidly sought his advice, the then Governor of Canada did the same in so far as *Government policy* was concerned. The record shows that all the Chief Justices of Canada at the time were legislators, administrators and judicial officers rolled into one. It should also be recorded that, at the same time, governors in the rest of the then British Empire presided over the legislature and over courts of justice while administering the countries where they held commissions.

THE PROPER BASIS FOR THE SEPARATION CONCEPT

In his treatise on Caribbean Public Law, Professor Albert Fiadjoe goes to the root of the matter when he propounds that government activities cannot be compartmentalised. He writes:[3]

---

1   Montesquieu, 1989, Book XI, Chapter VI.
2   See Lawson and Bentley, 1961, Chapter 9, p 70.
3   See Fiadjoe, 1999, p 161.

It is submitted that the doctrine of the separation of powers no longer bears the meaning that the early writers conceived of. In the context of the times then, the doctrine addressed the legitimate concern of the day, which was the fear of arbitrary rule. In today's world, it is submitted that the new meaning of the doctrine may be stated in two senses. First, the doctrine helps us to appreciate that in the complexities of modern government, there can only be shared powers among separate and quasi-autonomous yet inter-dependent State organs. Secondly, the doctrine helps us to appreciate the truism that the system of government which we operate works on the assumption that there is a core function which can be classified as legislative, executive and judicial and that these core functions belong to their respective branches or organs. Thirdly, the doctrine helps us to recognise that government involves the blending of the respective powers of the principal organs of State. Experience shows that we cannot have watertight compartments in government.

Professor Fiadjoe's views are fully supported by another powerful jurist, the late Sir Allen Lewis, who expressed the application of the principle in the Caribbean in the following terms:[4]

In this Constitution, which has been described as 'evolutionary not revolutionary', provision is normally made for continuity of government through successor institutions, legislative, executive and judicial, and particularly for the separation and independence of the judicial power. The party system and Cabinet government are maintained. To the judiciary is entrusted the guardianship of the constitution, the preservation of the Rule of Law and the protection of certain fundamental rights and freedoms already well established in the law of the former colony. The division of governmental powers into three branches, the fundamental rights and freedoms, the electoral process and the independence of the judiciary (*inter alia*), all of which in theory are intended to be unchangeable, unless the safety of the State demands temporary suspension, are 'entrenched' in provisions which can only be altered by the legislature on compliance with specially prescribed procedures. Further provision is made for restricting the exercise of arbitrary power by institutionalizing the distinction between the office of Attorney-General with responsibility for administration of legal affairs of the State, including the preparation of legislation consistent with legal interpretation of the Constitution, and that of the Director of Public Prosecutions, a legal officer with the secured tenure and independent status of a judge with responsibility for the conducting of criminal proceedings. And in some constitutions Parliament is authorised to create the office of Ombudsman, a Parliamentary Commissioner with similarly independent status, whose duty is to investigate complaints of maladministration by government departments where no redress is obtainable through judicial proceedings. Though he is given wide powers of enquiry he has no power to alter departmental decisions and can only report to Parliament his findings as recommendations. And the section creating these offices are among the 'entrenched provisions'.

The principle of the separation of powers, deriving from our new constitutions, has since 1960 been articulated in some leading cases designed to highlight the fact that the executive and the legislature should not trench upon the preserves of the judiciary. Four of these cases will now be briefly examined.

---

4   See Sir Allen's article (Lewis, 1978).

Hinds

First came *Hinds*[5] which, in the words of Professor Fiadjoe,[6] 'settled the point that there is indeed a separation of the legislative and executive powers from the judicial power and that the Supreme Court's jurisdiction is especially protected'. The particular jurisdiction was expressed to comprise:

(a) unlimited original jurisdiction in all substantial civil cases;

(b) unlimited original jurisdiction in all serious criminal offences;

(c) supervisory jurisdiction over the proceedings of inferior courts, that is, of the kind which owes its origin to the prerogative writs of certiorari, mandamus and injunction.

The present writer agrees with Professor Fiadjoe that *Hinds* 're-affirms one of the constitutional fundamentals of West Indian Public Law with respect to the independence of the judiciary'. He does not necessarily agree that the case 'establishes' the principle, which in his submission is intrinsic to the terms of the constitutions themselves. The case admittedly enables the judges on the basis of *stare decisis* to emphasise the dichotomy with greater confidence and certainty.

Farrell

Since *Hinds* was decided, the courts have found it necessary to strike down a section of an Antigua law in the following circumstances.[7]

In 1976 the Industrial Courts Act was passed, s 17(4) of which purported to divest the Supreme Court of the West Indies Associated State Supreme Court of its supervisory jurisdiction over inferior courts.

The relevant section was in the following terms:

17(4) Subject to subsection (1), the hearing and determination of any proceedings before the Court, and an order or award or any finding or decision of the Court in any matter (including an order or award)–

shall not be challenged, appealed against, reviewed, quashed or called in question in any court on any account whatever; and

shall not be subject to prohibition, mandamus or injunction in any court on any account whatever.

In giving their judgment, the Court of Appeal ruled that the effect of that provision in the Act was to give the Industrial Court the status of a High Court and to create a superior court having jurisdiction normally vested in the High Court by completely divesting the Supreme Court of all supervisory powers over its proceedings.

The section was declared void and duly severed from the rest of the Act.

---

5   *Hinds v R* [1977] AC 175.
6   See Fiadjoe, 1999, p 159.
7   See *Farrell v AG of Antigua* (1979) 27 WIR 377.

J Astaphan and Co Ltd v Comptroller of Customs of Dominica[8]

In this case, which came before the Eastern Caribbean Court of Appeal, the appellant, a merchant in Dominica, imported vehicular spare parts which arrived in five separate consignments at different times during 1991 and 1992.

On arrival of each consignment the appellant, not having received the relevant shipping documents, could not make perfect entries of the goods. Because the appellant was anxious to take delivery, the Comptroller of Customs required him to pay amounts in excess of the estimated duty. The Comptroller later refused to refund the excess on the ground that the relevant law[9] sanctioned the forfeiture of the excess.

In delivering the judgment of the Court of Appeal, Sir Vincent Floissac CJ ruled that the legislature is not competent to delegate its law making powers to the executive and that any attempt so to do would amount to an abdication of its functions – which would be inconsistent with the basic principle of the separation of powers.[10]

The *Browne* case[11]

The head note best describes the facts and holding in this case:

> The defendant was convicted of murder when he was 16 years old and the judge sentenced him to be 'detained until the pleasure of the Governor-General be known'. In so sentencing him the judge had intended to apply the proviso to section 3(1) of the Offences against the Person Act and the words used should have been detention 'during the Governor-General's pleasure'. The Court of Appeal of the Eastern Caribbean States dismissed his appeal against conviction and sentence. The defendant challenged the legality of the sentence on the ground, *inter alia,* that it contravened the Constitution of Saint Christopher and Nevis:

> On the defendant's appeal to the Judicial Committee – *HELD* allowing the appeal (1) that detention at the Governor-General's pleasure was a discretionary sentence for which the duration, including its punitive element, was to be determined by the Governor-General and not by the court; that under the Constitution of Saint Christopher and Nevis the Governor-General was part of the executive and not the judiciary; that, therefore, the sentence prescribed by the proviso to section 3(1) of the Offences Against the Person Act was a deprivation of liberty otherwise than in execution of an order or sentence of the court and was contrary to the Constitution; and that, accordingly even after the correction of the judge's verbal error, the sentence was an unlawful one which the courts were not entitled to pass or uphold.

> (2) that it was the duty of the court to decide what modifications needed to be made to the proviso so as to give effect to the requirements of the Constitution and the defendant's constitutional rights: that the proviso could be made to comply with the Constitution by removing the unlawful part of the sentencing process and the objective of the proviso could be achieved by substituting a sentence at the court's pleasure: and that the case should be

---

8   (1996) 54 WIR 153.
9   The Customs (Control and Management) Act (Cap 69.01 of the Laws of Dominica).
10 See an exposition of the judgment in Fiadjoe, 1999, pp 162–65.
11 *Green Browne v R* (1999) 54 WIR 213.

remitted to the Court of Appeal for the exercise of its powers in accordance with the relevant statutes.

The appeal against the sentence was therefore allowed and the case remitted to the Court of Appeal to exercise its powers under the appropriate legislation.

THE SYMBIOSIS BETWEEN LEGISLATURE AND THE EXECUTIVE

Having briefly surveyed the constitutional position of the judiciary vis à vis these two other branches, we must now examine the extent to which the executive and the legislature interact. In practice, all legislation is first considered by the executive in Cabinet and then remitted to the legislature, where the same members along with others (where they exist) consider them in the open forum of Parliament. But it is to the same Cabinet or members thereof, that Parliament invariably entrusts the making of rules and regulations to give effect to the wishes of the legislative branch by way of delegated legislation.

The writer has carefully scrutinised the process in respect of nine Barbados statutes of recent vintage, to which he now proposes to refer, and he has found it difficult to resist the conclusion that in many of the cases there is an almost total abdication of powers by the law givers to the executive ministers.

Under the Cremation Act[12] *the Minister* may make regulations: (a) respecting the establishment of crematoria; (b) respecting the operating standards; (c) prescribing in what cases and under what conditions the burning of human remains may take place; (d) directing the disposition or interment of the ashes; (e) prescribing the forms of any notices, certificates, and declarations to be given or made before the commencement of any burning of human remains in a crematorium; (f) providing for the issue, supervision and cancellation of licences or permits to burn human remains in a crematorium; (g) *prescribing anything that is required by the Act to be prescribed;* and (h) *generally for giving effect to the provisions of the Act.*

In the Act to provide the establishment of a regulatory framework that would facilitate *the groups of the small business sector* in Barbados,[13] *the Minister* may: (a) make regulations to give effect to the operation of the Act; (b) by order, approve private sector organisations for the purpose of the Act; and (c) by order amend the relevant Schedules.

In respect of the Copyright Act,[14] *the Minister* may prescribe: (a) 'anything that is by this Act authorised or required to be prescribed'; and (b) 'anything that is necessary for the purpose of giving effect to this Act'.

In respect of the Firearms Act,[15] *the Minister* may make regulations: (a) prescribing the form of licences under the Act, returns and other documents; (b) prescribing the requirements to be satisfied in respect of a place where arms or ammunition *are to be stored or kept before such place may be approved of* by the Commissioner as being a place of safety

---

12   Cremation Act 1999, s 14.
13   Small Business Development Act, 1999-23, s 15.
14   Copyright Act 1998-4, s 148.
15   Firearms Act 1998-323, s 32.

for the purposes of s 23 and for the manner in which such place is to be secured; (c) prescribing the manner by which any notice under the Act may be given; (d) controlling and regulating the importation, sale, possession or use of hand grenades manufactured for the purpose of extinguishing fires and the application of the Act in relation to such bombs and hand grenades; (e) prescribing anything which by the Act is permitted or required to be prescribed; and (f) generally for carrying the Act into effect.

In so far as *Mutual Funds* are concerned, the Act[16] gives *the Minister* the power to make regulations respecting: (a) the role of trustees, custodians and mutual fund administrators in relation to mutual funds; (b) the operation of mutual funds; (c) the type and content of advertisement published by mutual funds; (d) the requirements of non-Barbadian based mutual funds; and (e) any other matter that is required to be prescribed under the Act.

There are two other instances where Ministers are empowered to make rules.

First, under the Act to provide for the appointment of a *Public Trustee* and to amend the law relating to the administration of trusts,[17] there is provision for *the Minister* to make rules for: (a) prescribing the trusts or duties the Public Trustee is authorised to accept or undertake and the security, if any, to be given by the Public Trustee and his officers; (b) the transfer to and from the Public Trustee of any property; (c) the accounts to be kept and the audit thereof; and (d) the form and manner in which notice under the Act is given.

Similarly, under the Prisons Act,[18] the power is granted to *the Minister* to make rules for any of the purposes of the Act and, by rule, to provide: (a) the classification of prisons; (b) the duties and responsibilities of prison officers including the duties and responsibilities of particular classes of such officers; (c) the duties and powers of the Board; (d) the duties and powers of visiting justices; and (e) the safe custody, management, organisation, hours and kinds of labour and employment, clothing maintenance, instruction, discipline and discharge of prisoners; and (f) execution of condemned prisoners.

There is even a case where *an authority is permitted to make rules or regulations with the approval of the Minister*. Thus, in *the Act to provide for the licensing of persons who wire buildings for the supply of electricity*,[19] the Board may, subject to the approval of the Minister, make rules for any of the following purposes: (a) the proper conduct of its affairs, including the time, manner and place of meetings and the proceedings thereof; (b) the maintaining of a high standard of practice among electrical wiremen; (c) the conduct of examinations and related matter, and the fees to be paid for such examinations; (d) the institution of disciplinary proceedings in relation to any charge made against a wireman and the manner in which proceedings relative to such charge are to be conducted.

The Minister may also make regulations to carry out the provisions of the Act and for any of the purposes, viz: (a) prescribing the fees, other than those fixed by the rules,

---

16 Mutual Funds Act 1998-45, s 49.
17 Public Trustee Act, Cap 248, s 14.
18 Prisons Act, Cap 168, s 66.
19 Electrical Wiremen (Licensing) Act, Cap 368 A, s 18(1).

which are by the Act required to be prescribed; and (b) providing for anything in respect of electrical installation not provided for in the rules.

Finally, there is the *Act to provide for the control and management of the public finances of Barbados*[20] under which the rule making s 39 provides for *the Cabinet to make rules* for all or any of the following matters:

(a) prescribing the duties of the Accountant General and accounting officers;

(b) prescribing the form and manner in which any of the public accounts are to be kept;

(c) prescribing the procedure for the reporting by the Auditor General of delays and irregularities; and prescribing the response and liabilities of all accounting officers;

(d) respecting the accounts of the Barbados Defence Force and the purchase of military stores, equipment and supplies therefor.

CONCLUSION

The conclusion that can be safely drawn from the relations which exist between the executive and the legislature is that to separate them would be to impede the smooth running of the government machine. This is the reality of the situation. On the other hand, the judiciary must remain 'a place apart' – always able and willing to stand between government (be it the legislative or the executive arm) and the citizen when the occasion arises.

The next chapter looks at Conventions of the Constitution.

---

20   Financial Administration and Audit Act, Cap 5, s 39.

CHAPTER 5

THE CONVENTIONS OF THE CONSTITUTION

These are the largely unwritten and non-legal political rules which govern and influence the powers of the State.

Much has been written on this subject, beginning with Dicey, who postulated that conventions were not part of constitutional law which, in his view, included only those rules which were enforceable in a court of law.[1]

Subsequent publicists took issue with Dicey's theory of exclusion since, as we shall show, conventions prove an important component of constitutional law. They pose political difficulties when they are disobeyed.[2]

DeSmith adopts the language of HLA Hart[3] in the following comprehensive definition:

> ... constitutional conventions, insofar as they impose duties, are primary rules of recognition unaccompanied by an adequate apparatus of secondary rules of recognition, interpretation (or adjudication) and change ...

> Most of the conventions are bonding usages, undertakings and practices. They are forms of political behaviour regarded as obligatory.

The attributes and purpose of Conventions have been neatly analysed by a distinguished writer on public law in this way:[4]

> In the United Kingdom, with no written constitutional text, conventions which have developed over time play a critical rôle in the process of identifying the meaning of various constitutional rules. These understandings, habits, customs and practices which are not written down in any authoritative sense are nevertheless obeyed by the political directorate although they are not enforceable in the Court or by Parliament. A reasonable explanation for this would lie in these unchanged usages qualifying for constitutional statutes. Of the attributes claimed for conventions, three may be singled out.

> First, they help in the interpretation of the law. Second, they help to regulate the relationships between the different branches of government. And third, they act as useful tools in adjusting the strict letter of the law to meet the imperatives of the times.

One writer has described Dicey's distinction as 'dogmatic' and 'the product of an outmoded jurisprudence'.[5] To an enlightened publicist his distinction is distinctly quaint.

---

1   See, generally, Dicey, 1959.
2   Jennings, 1959, p 134.
3   Hart, 1961, p 118.
4   Fiadjoe, 1999, p 167.
5   Jennings, 1959.

A   HOW EXTENSIVE ARE CONVENTIONS?

Although conventions are of more significance in the context of the uncodified nature of the English Constitution for reasons which will appear, they are to be found in the constitutional regimes of such countries as Denmark, Norway, Sweden, Holland, France and Belgium - not to mention the United States and Canada, Australia, New Zealand and the other countries of the Commonwealth.[6]

KC Wheare has pointed out that it is not true to say that 'the principal rules which govern the government in England' are non-legal and he cites the Representation of the People Acts 1932 to 1948 to be 'as important as the conventions which regulate cabinet government'[7] – a matter to be discussed shortly.

Even Dicey, says Wheare, was aware, too, that the 'conventional element in the Constitution of the United States is as large as in the English Constitution'. We now appreciate (for example) that one major convention of the US Constitution is that no member of the President's Cabinet can be a member of either House of Congress, just as it is an undisputed convention that no English Prime Minister can operate with a Cabinet Minister who is not either a Member of the House of Commons or of the Lords.

In the US constitutional regime, although no written law specifically so provides, the Speaker of the House of Representatives has always been regarded and recognised as the active organiser of the party's legislative programme. On the other hand, the Speaker of the British House of Commons takes no part in party matters and, while Speaker, is not usually opposed in the hustings at a general election.

Similarly, in the USA up to 1940, there was nothing enshrined in the Constitution about the re-election of a President, although a convention had developed for the President to offer himself only once for such re-election – until President Franklyn Delano Roosevelt offered himself for a third term in 1940 and a fourth in 1944. Although the convention was breached, the country did not suffer since, at the time, America had just entered the Second World War and it was felt that the President's two re-elections would provide the continuity considered necessary. It was only after the President's demise that Congress deemed it desirable by a constitutional amendment to debar future holders of the office from serving more than two terms. The position was the same in France up to 1939, by which time it had become a convention that the French President would serve only one seven year term. However, in that year the then President – M Lebrun – was re-elected for a second term as a result of which a constitutional change was enacted to restore the one term arrangement. The reason for his second term was the same as for President Roosevelt, viz, continuity in time of war.

One further American convention may be mentioned. The President has the right to appoint senior officials, but in the various States he exercises it by what is termed 'senatorial courtesy', viz, he consults with the State senators of his own party or (where there are no such senators) with other senior State political figures of his party.

---

6   See Wheare, 1951, pp 181–82.
7   *Ibid*, p 179.

B   CONVENTIONS AFFECTING THE EXECUTIVE

The conventions that have developed in the United Kingdom and the rest of the Commonwealth in the exercise of prerogative powers are many. Fundamental to the working of the system, however, is the convention that the Sovereign or his representative exercises the prerogative mainly through a Cabinet which is headed by a Prime Minister, supported by ministers of his or her choice. In the older Commonwealth countries, no specific reference was ever made to a Cabinet or to a Prime Minister. It is worth remembering that, in the 17th and 18th centuries, weighty matters of policy were decided in England by a small number of privy councillors referred to as 'confidential advisers' to the King or Queen who convened meetings of the group in his or her private chambers (referred to in French as the 'Cabinet'). Executive power was, however, said to be vested in the King or Queen.

Today, there are some foundation conventions of the British Convention, such as:

(a) the Queen will not retain as Prime Minister a person who cannot obtain the support of a majority in the House of Commons;

(b) the Queen accepts the advice of the Prime Minister in the appointment and dismissal of the ministers;

(c) the Queen must assent to legislation duly passed by the two Houses of Parliament;

(d) the Queen's powers in respect of the government of the country is exercised generally on the advice of the Cabinet, the Prime Minister or a minister delegated by Cabinet;

(e) the Cabinet is responsible collectively to Parliament;

(f) there is a collective responsibility in the Cabinet itself;

(g) the Queen usually grants a dissolution on the advice of the Prime Minister, but may in a suitable case exercise a discretion.

It is in the above context that, for instance, the Canadian Constitution Act of 1867 stated the executive authority of Canada in these terms, in s 9 of the British North America Act 1867 (as it was originally entitled):

> The Executive Government and authority of and over Canada is hereby declared to continue and be vested in the Queen.

Section 11 of the same Act is to the following effect:

> There shall be a Council to aid and advise in the Government of Canada, to be styled the Queen's Privy Council for Canada; and the Persons who are to be Members of that Council shall be from time to time chosen and summoned by the Governor-General and sworn in as Privy Councillors, and members thereof may be from time to time removed by the Governor-General.

Section 13 states:

> The Provisions of this Act referring to the Governor-General in Council shall be construed as referring to the Governor-General acting by and with the Advice of the Queen's Privy Council for Canada.

There is no reference to the Cabinet, nor to the Prime Minister, nor, *a fortiori*, to ministers or the Leader of the Opposition. These are all, in Canada, creatures of convention. Later in this chapter we shall see to what extent all these conventional creatures are statutorily recognised and enshrined in recent Caribbean Constitutions.

Sir Ivor Jennings has pointed out that conventions governed the distinction between self-governing Dominions and colonies in the second half of the 19th century. He has also pointed to the convention governing the relations between the United Kingdom Government and the Dominions and to the system of consultation and co-operation which evolved as the self-governing countries attained maturity.[8]

What we now recognise as self-government was not achieved by Canada, Australia, New Zealand and Eire by a constitutional instrument and an independence Order in Council. On the contrary, it was implanted as a convention borrowed from the United Kingdom and followed in that country.[9] The Governor General's position evolved by convention in a Constitution under which the Prime Minister and ministers were to be appointed, but the convention was that these appointments should be made on the bases of the 'Instructions' from the Crown that his ministers should be nominated by the Prime Minister who by convention was to be the member of the House of Representatives best able to command the support of a majority of the elected members of that House. But even when, eventually, constitutions were prepared for these Dominions, no specific reference was made therein to 'self-government' or 'self-determination' or 'independence'. These were left to be inferred.

To quote Sir Ivor Jennings:[10]

> The representative of the Crown was authorized to appoint a Council or a Cabinet of Ministers but it was left to formal or informal instructions to indicate that he must act on the advice of Ministers and that the Ministers were to be responsible to the legislature.

Finally, we must look at those conventions which governed the relations between Great Britain and the Dominions after the latter became self-governing. The wide powers exercised over them by Great Britain were gradually whittled away until, in the Balfour Declaration of 1926, all the parties involved could be defined (most generously) as 'autonomous communities in no way subordinate one to another in any aspect of their domestic and external affairs' – the remaining limits to Dominion autonomy being quietly swept away by the Statute of Westminster 1931: the 'Dominions' at the time constituting Canada, Australia, New Zealand, the Union of South Africa, the Irish Free State and Newfoundland.

The most vital section of the Act was s 4 which provided:

> No Act of Parliament of the United Kingdom shall extend, or be deemed to extend, to a Dominion as part of the law of that Dominion unless it is expressly declared in that Act that the Dominion has requested, and consented to, the enactment thereof.

---

8   See Jennings, 1959, generally.
9   See Dale, 1983, p 132.
10   Jennings, 1959, p 8.

C   CONVENTIONS AFFECTING LEGISLATIVE AND PARLIAMENTARY POWERS

On the macro-parliamentary level, convention governs the internal procedural operation of Parliament. There are what are known as Standing Orders of the Houses of Parliament which are codified rules; but if there is a breach in the Standing Orders, legislation arising therefrom is not rendered invalid.[11]

The conventions governing the British Parliament which are set out in Erskine May's monumental work[12] are regarded as binding on the Speaker of the elected House of Parliament.

One legislative requirement that the Head of State may either assent to a bill or withhold assent has, by convention, been taken to mean that assent will be granted and never withheld. KC Wheare[13] points out that, although the power to withhold assent is given in the respective constitutions to the King of Denmark, Norway and Sweden, it is agreed by convention that the power will never be exercised. He states that the Danish King last withheld his assent in 1865 and that, when the King of Sweden last refused assent in 1912 to a Bill, he did so on the advice of his ministers.

The same conventional principle holds good in respect of the provisions in the original Constitutions of Canada, Australia and New Zealand for the Governor General to reserve a Bill for the signification of the Queen's pleasure or which permit the Sovereign to disallow a law duly passed by the Legislature. Once again, by convention the Queen took no such action unless at the specific request of the country involved.

D   CONVENTIONS AFFECTING THE LEGISLATURE

It is also a convention that the Queen or her representative will not normally act in her own discretion to dissolve Parliament, but will only do so on the advice of the Prime Minister. KC Wheare questions whether this means that the Queen can refuse to dissolve at the request of a Prime Minister, but act on the advice of another member, if the first did not have the requisite support, while the second was able to form a new Government. The answer to this enquiry is to be found in two situations in which a Governor General found himself having to act contrary to the advice of the Prime Minister.

The first is the King/Byng disagreement in Canada. McKenzie King was Prime Minister of Canada who refused to resign and make way for Arthur Meighen, Leader of the Opposition, when the latter's Conservative Party won more seats than King's party after a general election in 1926. In 1927, he approached the Governor General (Lord Byng) for a dissolution on the eve of a vote of no confidence which he was destined to lose. The Governor General refused and called upon Meighen to form a government. Meighen's Government, however, was defeated in the House shortly thereafter and the subsequent

---

11   See *Naomi Shire Council v AG for NSW* (1980) 2 NSWLR 639.
12   Erskine May, 1982.
13   See Wheare, 1951, p 183.

election was won by King's party, mainly because he made the Governor General 'the issue'.

The second case[14] concerned the dismissal of the Australian Prime Minister – Gough Whitlam – by the Governor General, Sir John Kerr. In this case, the Senate of the Australian Parliament (an elected body) happened to have a majority of Opposition members and, in 1975, refused to pass the annual Appropriations Bill for reasons which need not detain us at this juncture. If this state of affairs continued – and the Senate was determined it should continue – salaries could not be paid and the country would grind to a halt. The Prime Minister had two courses open to him, viz, either to resign or ask the Governor General to dissolve the Senate – or even both Houses. He chose to do neither. Faced with a situation of impending anarchy, the Governor General found it imperative to dismiss the Prime Minister and to call upon the Leader of the Opposition (Malcolm Fraser) to form a Government, after having received from him an undertaking that, if appointed, he would call a general election. The Senate passed the Appropriation Bill and a double dissolution (of the House of Representatives and the Senate) ensued. In the subsequent elections, the party headed by the new Prime Minister was successful and formed the Government.

E CONVENTIONS AND THE COURTS

In this section we shall illustrate the extent to which the courts *recognise* conventions, and we shall show that a convention thus recognised can, on occasion, bring about a desirable political course of action that would otherwise not have been followed.

The courts have also been known to interpret a statute by reference to a convention. In one case, it was held that, where a delegated power is exercisable at the donee's discretion, the donee being a committee, the committee cannot sub-delegate its discretion to its chief executive.[15] When, however, a power is delegated to a minister of Government, he is at liberty to sub-delegate, since it is an incidence of responsible government that a minister does not ordinarily act in person – although he must accept responsibility for his acts.[16] Sometimes, an important convention is recognised in circumstances which run counter to the law and, where this occurs, the court will enforce the law. Thus, in *Madzimbamuto v Lardner-Burke*,[17] M was detained under Emergency Regulations promulgated by a rebel Government of Southern Rhodesia and moved the court for a declaration that her detention was illegal and that she should be released. The Southern Rhodesian rebel Government contended that the regulations were validly made.

Her Majesty's Government had, in 1961, issued a statement that it would in future be a convention that the local legislature was competent to pass all laws of an internal nature: the British Parliament, by convention, to cease to legislate for Southern Rhodesia except at its request and with its consent. Southern Rhodesia, however, remained a

---

14   The full story of this dismissal is told by the former Governor General in Kerr, 1979.

15   See *Allingham v Minister of Agriculture* [1948] 1 All ER 784.

16   See *Carltona v Commr of Works* [1943] 2 All ER 560.

17   [1969] 1 AC 645.

Colony, under the suzerainty of the Government and Parliament of the United Kingdom. In that state of affairs, the regime purported on 11 November 1965 to declare it was no longer a Crown Colony, but a sovereign independent State, and the United Kingdom promptly responded by passing the Southern Rhodesia Act 1965 which pronounced that the territory continued as part of Her Majesty's Dominions and that the Government and Parliament of the United Kingdom were still responsible for its affairs.

The Prime Minister and his colleagues, however, ignored their dismissal while the members of the Legislative Assembly took no notice of its suspension and purported to adopt a new Constitution in which the Queen was described as 'Queen of Rhodesia', represented locally by an 'Officer Administering the Government'. They confirmed the Unilateral Declaration of Independence (UDI).

The High Court (General Division) found that M was lawfully detained and, on appeal, the Appeal Court dismissed her application. The appellant then petitioned the Judicial Committee of the Privy Council which found that, although extensive legislative powers had been granted the legislature, there were important limits to those powers.

The powers of Her Majesty to legislate had not been limited, notwithstanding the fact that before the UDI, the Parliament of the United Kingdom had indeed agreed, by way of the convention, not to legislate as aforesaid on matters within the competence of the local legislature.

It was held that the UDI had made such a convention inoperative: the convention being meant to apply in a state of normality. The United Kingdom had never lost its sovereign right to legislate, despite the convention. In any event, a convention cannot override a statute. The matter was starkly set out by Lord Reid, in *Madzimbamuto*, in this way:[18]

> The learned judges refer to the statement of the United Kingdom Government in 1961, already quoted, setting out the convention that the Parliament of the United Kingdom does not legislate without the consent of the Government of Southern Rhodesia on matters within the competence of the Legislative Assembly. That was a very important convention but it had no legal effect in limiting the legal power of Parliament.

> It is often said that it would be unconstitutional for the United Kingdom Parliament to do certain things, meaning that the moral, political and other reasons against doing them are so strong that many people would regard it as highly improper if Parliament did these things. But that does not mean that it is beyond the power of Parliament to do such things.

A Canadian case, however, highlights how vital conventions can sometimes be in the constitutional scheme of things.

In *Ref re Amendment of the Constitution of Canada*,[19] the Federal Government was, in 1981, anxious for reasons mentioned below to effect the patriation of the Canadian Constitution from the United Kingdom Parliament without having to seek a majority consensus from the provinces in the following context.

The Canadian Constitution was contained in a United Kingdom statute – the British North America Act 1867 – and subsequent amending legislation, all of which could not be

---

18   [1969] 1 AC 645, pp 722–23.
19   (1981) 1 RCS 753.

altered by the Parliament in Canada except by a joint address from the two Houses of Parliament in Ottawa to the Queen, requesting the intended change. Only two of the nine Canadian provinces – Ontario and New Brunswick – were in agreement with the resolution requesting the amendments, but the then Prime Minister was minded to go direct from the Federal Parliament to the United Kingdom Parliament, since he was of the opinion that too great a delay would result from endeavouring to secure provincial consensus.[20]

Being aware of the intention of the Federal Government three of the provinces - Manitoba, Newfoundland and Quebec – launched separate challenges against the Federal Government in their respective courts in an endeavour to stop the patriation bill from being sent to London without the consent of the provinces.

The courts in Manitoba and Quebec found the patriation bill constitutional, but the Newfoundland court deemed it unconstitutional. The matter then came to the Supreme Court on a reference in which one of the questions was:

> Is it a constitutional convention that the House of Commons and Senate of Canada will not request Her Majesty the Queen to lay before the Parliament of the United Kingdom of Great Britain and Northern Ireland a measure to amend the Constitution of Canada affecting federal-provincial relationships or the powers, rights or privileges granted or secured by the Constitution of Canada to the provinces, their legislatures or governments, without first obtaining the agreement of the provinces.

The Supreme Court, by a 6:3 majority, answered this question in the affirmative, although it answered in the negative the question as to whether *in law* it was necessary to have the consent of the provinces before approaching the Queen.

In the opinion of the majority of the Supreme Court, the Federal Government would violate a constitutional *convention* requiring a 'substantial provincial consent'. But the court refused to explain what was 'substantial' – simply stating that such a determination was to be made by the politicians and not by the court.

The court left no doubt how much it thought the convention should be respected. It made this statement in its judgment:[21]

> It should be borne in mind however that, while they are not laws, some conventions may be more important than some laws. Their importance depends on that of the value or principle which they are meant to safeguard. Also they form an integral part of the constitution and of the constitutional system ... That is why it is perfectly appropriate to say that to violate a convention is to do something which is unconstitutional although it entails no direct legal consequence.

---

20 See Trudeau, 1993. In these *Memoirs*, Prime Minister Trudeau, p 300, reveals that he had already been in 'nearly continuous negotiations with many of the nine provinces since 1968'. He states: 'The more I pressed for simple patriation of our constitution the more the premiers demanded in provincial powers. And by now, I had concluded that the process of patriating our constitution from Great Britain, a process begun in 1927, would never be successful unless provincial blackmail attempts were broken. And I believed that any fair-minded observer of federal-provincial negotiations would agree that the Canadian people would never have a constitution of their own until the link between patriation and provincial powers was broken.'

21 *Ibid*, p 883.

The court's hint was not lost on Prime Minister Trudeau[22] who immediately set out to make a further effort to win the 'substantial' provincial consent. By November 1981, he had succeeded in obtaining the agreement of nine of the 10 provinces to the resolution which was eventually accepted by the Federal Senate and House of Commons and forwarded to Westminster where effect was given to it in the Canada Act assented to on 29 March 1982, on which date it came into force. The Constitution Act 1982, including the Charter of Rights and amending formula, came into force on 17 April 1982, when it was duly proclaimed by the Queen in person in a ceremony at Parliament Hill in Ottawa.

In the words of two perceptive legal scholars writing on this particular episode:[23]

> To dismiss all conventions as merely loose guidelines would now be a profound mistake.

F   CONVENTIONS AND THE JUDICIARY

The judiciary is not without its own conventions which for purposes of this work we may classify as institutional and ethical.

Institutional

Although the House of Lords, when sitting as an appellate court, normally has a panel of only Law Lords, in theory, there is nothing to prevent a peer who is not an appointed Law Lord from sitting. However, the convention has developed simply to ignore the vote of any such peer when the House delivers its judgment: *O'Connell v R* (1844) 11 CL & F 155.

Secondly, it is a convention that the Sovereign will always accept and give effect to the report of the Judicial Committee of the Privy Council when it furnishes such a report. In the *British Coal Corporation* case,[24] Lord Sankey made, in this connection, the following pronouncement:

> The Committee is regarded in the Act (of 1833) as a judicial body or court, though all it can do is to report or recommend to His Majesty in Council by whom alone the Order-in-Council which is made to give effect to the report of the Committee is made. But according to constitutional convention it is unknown and unthinkable that His Majesty in Council should not give effect to the report of the Judicial Committee who are thus in truth an appellate court of law to which by the statute of 1833 all appeals within their purview are referred.

Ethical

A judge must be economical in words and questions while hearing a case. In one of his books, *The Due Process of Law*,[25] the late Lord Denning graphically describes how Hallett J

---

22   See Trudeau, 1993, pp 316–29. In his autobiography the Prime Minister sets out graphically the political dangers involved in not proceeding as convention dictated – even though privately he did not agree with the court's decision that there was any such convention.

23   Brazier and Robillard, 1982, p 34.

24   *British Coal Corp v The King* [1935] AC 500, p 501.

25   Denning, 1980, pp 58–62.

– an English judge – found himself, in a 1957 case,[26] dominating a trial by asking more questions in total than the counsel for the plaintiff and the defendant asked in the suit. As a result, the judge had to retire – his loquacity bringing his career to a premature end – although he was actuated by the very best of motives and was a judge 'of acute perception' and 'acknowledged learning'.

A judge should not normally, after retirement, practice in the courts over which he presided.

A judge should not pass on an issue which is not before him and on which he has not had the benefit of argument from counsel.

Finally, judges should confine themselves to such pronouncements as relate to their reasons for judgment and are not, in the words of a former Chief Justice of the Supreme Court of Canada, free 'to roam public assemblies and expatiate on public issues'.[27]

G   CODIFICATION OF CONVENTIONS

Three writers have written eruditely concerning a recent pattern in Commonwealth Caribbean circles to codify well established conventions in the written texts.

Margaret Demerieux, in a useful article,[28] has outlined the attempts made in recent times to 'preserve in Caribbean constitutions several important conventions', but concludes that 'neither the distinction between law and convention, nor the rationale of conventions', has been affected by the codification.

Sir William Dale, in a scholarly work,[29] has dealt historically with the codifying idea, locating its first mention in the Constitution of Ireland in 1922, followed by the express statement in 1946 in the Constitution of Ceylon relative to the office of the Governor General, whose functions were to be exercised 'in accordance with the constitutional conventions applicable to the exercise of similar ... functions in the United Kingdom by His Majesty'. Dale sets out how the conventions have become written 'rules' affecting, *inter alia*, the office of the Governor General, the role of the Cabinet, the method of appointing the Prime Minister and the basis for dissolution. He concludes that the principal sanction against breaking the rules can be said to be the same in character as that against breaking the conventions.

---

26   *Jones v National Coal Board* [1957] 2 QB 55.

27   See comments on this aspect of judicial ethics under the *Sosa* case, below, and the *Coreen Sparks* case, below.

28   *The Codification of Constitutional Conventions in the Commonwealth Caribbean Constitutions* (1982) 31 ICLQ 263.

29   Dale, 1983, pp 140–45.

H   CONCLUDING COMMENT

Professor Albert Fiadjoe in his seminal work on public law,[30] in detailing a number of conventions sought to be enshrined in recent instruments, asks the vital question as to whether the conventions have survived the constitutional texts in the Caribbean. He concludes his exposition on this subject as follows:[31]

> We may conclude this chapter with the observation that, although some of the provisions of West Indian Constitutions reflect what may be conventions within the British constitutional system, seen in the context of the Caribbean historical experience, it is submitted that there is no need to ask the question with which we began, whether conventions of the constitution did not die the death that might be expected given the adoption of a written constitution.

Experience has shown that the categories of conventions are not closed. Further, as the constitutions in the Caribbean area undergo change and become more and more autochthonous in the 21st century, so new conventions – written and unwritten – will emerge and become respected as obligatory forms of political behaviour.

In our next chapter, we turn our attention to some leading cases.

---

30   Fiadjoe, 1999, pp 167–73. I am very much indebted to Professor Fiadjoe for his help with ideas for this chapter.
31   *Ibid*, p 173.

CHAPTER 6

LEADING BILLS OF RIGHTS CASES

INTRODUCTION

A later chapter will underscore the fact that an independent judiciary[1] is indispensable to the proper functioning of our constitutions. Certain provisions of the constitutions under which our respective countries are governed have imposed several vital functions on our courts, tending, as it were, to make them sentinels and guardians of the rights of the individual. Indeed, there can be no doubt that the fundamental rights and freedoms provisions which are common features of our constitutions, as well as of other constitutional instruments prepared by the British Commonwealth Office draftsmen for former colonial territories, starting with Nigeria, were greatly influenced by the European Convention on Human Rights.[2]

From 1962, protective provisions to guarantee the fundamental rights and freedoms of the individual have formed an integral part of the independence constitutions of former British colonies in this region. In fact, the constitutions of some colonies[3] and of the former West Indies Associated States were adorned with these novel, yet preeminently, important provisions. It was left to the judges to interpret those provisions and protect the individual's rights which, at independence, had assumed an entirely new significance.

One will better be able to appreciate the fundamental character of the functions entrusted to the courts by considering, in particular, some of the Bills of Rights provisions. All of the constitutions of the independent countries with which this work deals are declared to be 'the supreme law' of the countries to which they respectively relate;[4] and they all contain provisions prescribing the manner in which entrenched sections may be altered.[5] As a consequence of this, and in view of the protective provisions referred to above, jurisdiction has been conferred on the courts to determine questions relating to the interpretation of the constitutions;[6] to make declarations and grant relief in cases where an individual alleges a contravention of any constitutional provision (other than the protective provisions);[7] and to grant redress, by way of declarations, orders, writs and

---

1   For a comprehensive statement on the question of the independence of the judiciary, see Chapter 13.

2   Cmd 8969, 1953.

3   See, eg, the Bermuda Constitution Order 1968 SI 1968/182; the Anguillan (Constitution) Order 1976 SI 1976/50; the Anguillan Constitution Order SI 1982/334; and the Cayman Islands (Constitution) Order 1972 SI 1972/1101.

4   See Constitutions of Antigua (s 2), Bahamas (Art 2), Barbados (s 1), Dominica (s 117), Grenada (s 106), Guyana (Art 8), Jamaica (s 2), St Kitts (s 2), St Lucia (s 120), St Vincent (s 101) and Trinidad and Tobago (s 2).

5   See Constitutions of Antigua (s 47), Bahamas (Art 54), Barbados (s 49), Belize (s 69), Dominica (s 42), Grenada (s 39), Guyana (Art 66), Jamaica (s 38), St Lucia (s 41), St Vincent (s 38) and Trinidad and Tobago (s 54).

6   See Constitutions of Antigua (s 120), Belize (s 96), Dominica (s 104), Grenada (s 102), St Kitts (s 97), St Lucia (s 106), St Vincent (s 97) and Trinidad and Tobago (s 14(4)).

7   See Constitutions of Antigua (s 119), Dominica (s 103), Grenada (s 101), St Kitts (s 96), St Lucia (s 105) and St Vincent (s 96).

directions, in any case in which a person alleges that any of the protective provisions 'has been, is being or is likely to be contravened in relation to him'.[8] A right of appeal has been granted to the Court of Appeal from decisions of the High Court on any of these matters.[9]

Over the 35 years from 1965 to 2000, a formidable jurisprudence has developed in the 12 territories with which this work is concerned – viz, the Bahamas, Belize, Jamaica, Antigua and Barbuda, St Kitts and Nevis, Dominica, Barbados, St Lucia, St Vincent and the Grenadines, Grenada, Trinidad and Tobago and Guyana. The result is that any attempt to include in this book all the cases in both Bills of Rights and non-Bills of Rights issues is not a feasible proposition.

Accordingly, what the author has decided is to deal in some depth in this volume with the leading cases on nine key fundamental rights and freedoms in the order shown hereunder:

A   freedom of association;

B   equality before the law;

C   the right to personal liberty;

D   the right to life;

E   the right to protection from deprivation of property;

F   the right to retain and instruct a legal adviser;

G   protection from inhuman and degrading punishment;

H   the right to freedom of movement;

I   the right to freedom of expression.

A   FREEDOM OF ASSOCIATION

All of the constitutions to which reference has been made provided for the protection of the right of persons to be associated freely, whether it be for political, cultural or business purposes.[10] But, as the courts have ruled, this does not mean that a person can be forced to become a member of an association against his will, even though it is established by statute.[11] At the same time, freedom of association has been interpreted by Wooding CJ in *Collymore v Attorney General*, to mean 'no more than freedom to enter into consensual arrangements to promote the common-interest objects of the associating group'. The objects of the group may be 'religious or social, political or philosophical, economic or

---

8   See constitutions of Antigua (s 18), Bahamas (Art 28), Barbados (s 24), Belize (s 20), Dominica (s 16), Grenada (s 16) Guyana (Art 153), Jamaica (s 25), St Kitts (s 18), St Vincent (s 16) and Trinidad and Tobago (s 14(1)).

9   See constitutions of Antigua (s 121), Dominica (s 105), Grenada (s 103), Guyana (Art 133), St Kitts (s 98), St Lucia (s 107), St Vincent (s 98) and Trinidad and Tobago (s 108).

10   Antigua (s 13), Barbados (s 21), Belize (s 13), Dominica (s 11), Grenada (s 11), Guyana (Art 147), Jamaica (s 23), St Kitts (s 13), St Lucia (s 11), St Vincent (s 11) and Trinidad and Tobago (s 4(j)).

11   See *AG of Trinidad and Tobago v Seereeram* (1975) 27 WIR 329.

professional, educational or cultural, sporting or charitable'.[12] We shall have more to say on this point later.

In the Grenada case of *Re Hamilton and Others*[13] (unreported), the Governor General by an order[14] purportedly made under ss 34 and 35 of the Nutmeg Industry Ordinance[15] sought to dissolve the then existing Board of the Grenada Co-operative Nutmeg Association (which had been duly constituted in pursuance of the relevant provision of the Ordinance), to appoint an interim board to manage the affairs of the association and to vest the property of the association in the interim board so appointed.

The applicants sought, *inter alia*, a declaration that the order by the Governor General was *ultra vires* the Nutmeg Industry Ordinance and that it also contravened their right to protection of property and the right not to be deprived thereof without compensation. The applicants further sought declarations that the order contravened their right to protection of the law and their right to freedom of association and assembly.

Nedd J[16] ruled, distinguishing *Durayappal v Fernando*,[17] that the applicants, for reasons stated in the judgment, had *locus standi* for purposes of bringing the application and that the Governor General, in exercising his power to dissolve the board under s 34 of the ordinance, was required to comply with the rules of natural justice. His failure to communicate to the members of the board his intention to dissolve the board and the grounds on which he relied to do so, as well as his failure to afford them an opportunity to reply to any allegations which may have been made against them, contravened the rules of natural justice and rendered the order voidable at the suit of the board.[18] More importantly, the learned judge ruled that the Dissolution Order contravened the applicants' rights to freedom of association and assembly and was, accordingly, *ultra vires* the Constitution of Grenada and null and void.[19]

Citing the case of *Commissioner for Motor Transport v Antill Ranger & Co Ltd*,[20] the judge further held that the Nutmeg Board (Dissolution) Order (Validation) Act 1975[21] did not have the effect of validating the Dissolution Order 'which breached not only the Nutmeg Industry Ordinance but also the Constitution [of Grenada]'. As a consequence of his rulings above, the judge further held that, since the Dissolution Order was null and void, the purported appointment by the Governor General of the interim board was *ultra vires* and null and void. The judge therefore granted the injunction for which the applicants had prayed, restraining the members of the interim board from meddling in the affairs of the association.

---

12 (1976) 12 WIR 5, p 15. See, also, the discussion in Phillips, 1977, pp 137–39. This book will hereafter be referred to as 'the 1977 volume'.

13 *In the Matter of the Application of Bornston Matthew and Others under the Constitution of Grenada*, Suit No 403/1975, pp 1–13.

14 The Nutmeg Board (Dissolution) Order 1975 (SR & O No 15 of 1975).

15 Chapter 210 of the Revised Laws of Grenada.

16 As he then was. He was appointed Chief Justice of Grenada in April 1979.

17 [1967] 2 AC 337.

18 *Hamilton et al v Morrison et al* (1975) 1CCCBR 308/308, Grenada: Suit 403.

19 *Ibid*, p 513.

20 [1956] 3 All ER 106.

21 No 18 of 1975.

In so far as the findings of the court are concerned, it should be noted that the judge rejected the applicant's contention that the order also contravened their right under the Constitution not to be deprived of their property without compensation; and that, although the court ruled that the Governor General had violated the legal rules compendiously referred to as the rules of natural justice, the judge made no ruling in relation to the declaration sought: that the Dissolution Order constituted a contravention of the applicants' rights to protection of the law under s 8 of the Constitution. The important point which remains, however, is that the constitutional rights of the applicants to freedom of association and freedom of assembly were vindicated.

Collymore v Attorney General revisited

In the 1977 volume,[22] the case of *Collymore v AG of Trinidad and Tobago*[23] was discussed briefly and it was said to be rightly criticised in academic circles on the ground that the judges in the Court of Appeal had placed too great a reliance on the common law in determining whether freedom of association includes the right to strike. Attention was drawn to what was regarded as the 'instructive' approach adopted by *R v Nasralla*[24] by Lewis JA, who, in interpreting s 20(8) of the Constitution of Jamaica,[25] had stated that Chapter III of that Constitution 'seeks in some measure to codify those "golden" principles of freedom, generally referred to as the rule of law which forms part of the great heritage of Jamaica and are to be found both in statutes and in great judgments delivered over the centuries'.[26] In this connection, the author also proffered the following suggestion on the question of interpretation of the Constitution:

> The contents of Chapter III are not intended to alter any existing law and prohibit the Court from holding that any conflict exists between them. In order to determine what the existing law is, not only must the common law be prayed in aid but so must statute law, and the language of the constitution must be regarded as creating *new statutory rights* where the words are clear enough. See to the same effect *Re Thornhill*, a useful judgment of Georges, J, of the Trinidad High Court, in which the judge granted a declaration on the constitutional right of the applicant to consult the legal adviser of his choice and to hold communication with him in terms of section 2(ii) of the Trinidad Constitution.[27]

It is therefore somewhat reassuring to note that the approach adopted by Georges J in the *Thornhill* case, has received the unqualified approval of the Privy Council. In delivering the judgment in *Thornhill v AG*[28] on appeal from the Court of Appeal of Trinidad and Tobago, their Lordships made the following statements with regard to the trial judge's decision:

---

22 Phillips, 1977, p 138.
23 Reported at (1967) 12 WIR 5 (CA) and [1970] AC 538 (PC).
24 (1965) 9 WIR 15, pp 26–27.
25 Constitution of Jamaica, s 20, deals with 'Provisions to secure protection of law'.
26 Phillips, 1977, p 138.
27 *Ibid*, pp 138–39. The decision of Georges J, in *Thornhill v AG of Trinidad and Tobago* has since been reported; see (1974) 27 WIR 281.
28 [1981] AC 61.

Much of the judgment of Georges, J, to whose lucidity and cogency their Lordships would desire to pay respectful tribute, deals with the facts and his findings upon disputed factual issues.[29]

This judgment was delivered some twelve months before that of the Judicial Committee of the Privy Council in *de Freitas v Benny* [1976] AC 239. The Judge's analysis of sections 1, 2 and 3 of the Constitution, however, anticipates and conforms to what was said by the Judicial Committee both in that case, at pp 244–46, and in the subsequent case of *Maharaj v AG of Trinidad and Tobago (No 2)* [1979] AC 385.[30]

The judgment of the Privy Council also contains two illuminating passages which indicate the manner in which the interpretation of the fundamental rights and freedoms provisions of our constitutions should be approached:

The lack of all specificity in the descriptions of the rights and freedoms protected contained in section 1, paragraphs (a) to (k) may make it necessary sometimes to resort to an examination of the law as it was at the commencement of the constitution in order to determine what limits upon freedoms that are expressed in absolute and unlimited terms were nevertheless intended to be preserved in the interests of the people as a whole and the orderly development of the nation; for the declaration that the rights and freedoms protected by that section already existed at that date may make the existing law as it was then administered in practice a relevant aid to the ascertainment of what kind of executive or judicial act was intended to be prohibited by the wide and vague words used in those paragraphs: see *Maharaj v Attorney General of Trinidad and Tobago (No 2)* [1979] AC 385, p 395. But this external aid to construction is neither necessary nor permissible where the treatment complained of is any of the kinds specifically described in paragraphs (a) to (h) of section 2.[31]

In the context of section 1, the declaration that rights and freedoms of the kinds described in the section have existed in Trinidad and Tobago, in their Lordship's view, means that they have in fact been enjoyed by the individual citizen, whether their enjoyment by him has been de jure as a legal right or *de facto* as the result of a settled executive policy of abstention from interference or a settled practice as to the way in which an administrative or judicial discretion has been exercised. The hopes by the affirmation in the preamble to the constitution that the protection of human rights and fundamental freedoms was to be ensured would indeed be betrayed if Chapter I did not preserve to the people of Trinidad and Tobago all those human rights and fundamental freedoms that in practice they had hitherto been permitted to enjoy.[32]

In addition to the above *dicta* in *Thornhill*, the Privy Council has made other similar pronouncements which, it is submitted, would be useful guidelines to our judges in their approach to interpreting the constitutions in force in our respective jurisdictions. In this connection, the following statements from the judgment in *Minister of Home Affairs v Fisher*[33] would appear to be of compelling importance:

---

29 [1981] AC 61, p 68E.
30 *Ibid*, p 69E.
31 *Ibid*, p 70.
32 *Ibid*, p 71B.
33 [1980] AC 319.

(1) It can be seen that this instrument has certain special characteristics.

    1   It is, particularly in Chapter I, drafted in a broad and ample style which lays down principles of width and generality.

    2   Chapter I is headed 'Protection of fundamental rights and freedoms of the Individual'.

It is known that this chapter, as similar portions of other constitutional instruments drafted in the post-colonial period, starting with the Constitution of Nigeria, and including the Constitutions of most Caribbean territories, was greatly influenced by the European Convention for the Protection of Human Rights and Fundamental Freedoms (1953) (Cmd 8969). That Convention was signed and ratified by the United Kingdom and applied to dependent territories including Bermuda. It was in turn influenced by the United Nations Universal Declaration of Human Rights of 1948. These antecedents, and the form of Chapter I itself, call for a generous interpretation avoiding what has been called 'the austerity of tabulated legalism', suitable to give to individuals the full measure of the fundamental rights and freedoms referred to:[34]

(2) [A constitutional instrument should be treated as] *sui generis*, calling for principles of interpretation of its own suitable to its character – without necessary acceptance of all the presumptions that are relevant to legislation of private law;[35] and

(3) A Constitution is a legal instrument giving rise, amongst other things, to individual rights capable of enforcement in a court of law. Respect must be paid to the language which has been used and to the traditions and usages which have given meaning to that language. It is quite consistent with this, and with the recognition that rules of interpretation may apply to take as a point of departure for the process of interpretation a recognition of the character and origin of the instrument, and to be guided by the principle of giving full recognition and effect to those fundamental rights and freedoms with a statement of which the Constitution commences.[36]

At this point, it might be useful to examine the *Collymore* case briefly in the light of the recent *dicta* of the Privy Council set out above.

It will be recalled that, in the High Court of Trinidad and Tobago, Collymore and another, who were members of the Oilfield Workers' Trade Union, unsuccessfully applied for a declaration that the Industrial Stabilisation Act,[37] which had prohibited the right to strike, had infringed their freedom of association guaranteed under s 1(i) of the 1962 Constitution of that country.[38]

On appeal, the Court of Appeal, in affirming the decision of the trial judge held that:

The right of free collective bargaining and the right to strike are not included in the fundamental freedom of association recognized and declared by s 1(j) of the Constitution and are consequently not protected as such under the provisions of ss 2 and 6 of the Constitution.

---

34   [1980] AC 319, p 328F–H.
35   *Ibid*, p 329E–F.
36   *Ibid*, p 329E–F.
37   Laws of Trinidad and Tobago, No 8 of 1965.
38   The corresponding provision in the 1976 Constitution is s 4(i).

In his judgment the learned Chief Justice found that:

(1) 'the freedom of collective bargaining [had] been abridged', and

(2) 'the Act does substantially abrogate the so-called right to strike'.

He went on to state the 'nub of the issue' as being: 'Whether the freedom of collective bargaining and the so-called right to strike are, or either of them is, inherent in [in the sense of being an integral feature of] the freedom of association guaranteed by the Constitution.'[39] In the High Court, the trial judge, Corbin J, had pointed to what he described as a 'sharp distinction between the mere "*freedom to strike*" and the "*right to strike*".' The learned Chief Justice agreed with this distinction, 'but in the context of constitutionally-guaranteed rights and liberties', he preferred 'to regard the freedom, and to speak of it, as an *immunity*'.[40]

The Chief Justice then traced the development of industrial relations in Britain, commencing from the medieval guild system in that country. He referred to a long line of English authorities, starting from 1721 with *R v Cambridge Journeymen Tailors*,[41] and to the effect which certain English statutes had had on these legal authorities.

He found that, until 1933 when the local legislature enacted the Trade Unions Ordinance, the law of Trinidad and Tobago with respect to industrial disputes was the same as that which applied in England in 1875; and so it remained until 1943 when the Trade Disputes and Protection of Property Ordinance provided workers with a similar type of immunity for liability in tort which in Britain had been established by two Acts passed in 1875 and 1906. Thus, as far as the Chief Justice was concerned, the rights, freedom or 'immunities' which British workers had won as far back as 1906, and which were grudgingly extended to the workers in Trinidad and Tobago in 1943, were the rights which existed when the 1962 Independence Constitution came into force. In so approaching the matter, the Chief Justice treated the gains as having been frozen in 1943. In other words, the workers had made no advance in the intervening 19 years – which was certainly not the case.

During the course of his review which, he claimed, exposed 'the fallacy of integrating the statutory immunity with the freedom of association', the learned Chief Justice made the following further findings:

(1) the appellants' claim to a right to strike was 'in essence a claim of right to commit breaches of contract without liability to have the contract discharged for its breach';[42]

(2) 'trade unions have always regarded the power to strike as an essential weapon';[43]

(3) 'trade unions [were] no longer struggling for survival or recognition and they enjoy the wholly discriminatory privilege (no longer enjoyed by the Crown) of total immunity from liability for tort';[44] and

---

39   (1967) 12 WIR 9.
40   *Ibid*, p 10.
41   (1721) 8 Mod Rep.
42   (1967) 12 WIR 10.
43   *Ibid*, p 15.
44   *Ibid*, p 16.

(4) one of the principal objectives of a trade union, viz, collective bargaining, had been fully preserved by the Industrial Stabilisation Act.[45]

Based on his findings and his view of the applicable law, the Chief Justice held that what the Act had abridged was freedom of contract, but that this was 'not a freedom recognized, declared or guaranteed by the Constitution'.[46] Consequently, since:

> ... there is nothing in the Constitution which prohibits Parliament from restricting freedom of contract it was a policy decision for Parliament, and is not a question for the courts, whether in the interest of the country the People ... should be permitted any say on the terms of industrial agreements so as to ensure as far as practicable that, as recited in paragraph (b) of the preamble to the Constitution and repeated in s 9(2) of the Act, 'the operation of the economic system should result in the material resources of the community being so distributed as to subserve the common good'.[47]

One should not be surprised by the decision at which the Chief Justice arrived in the light of his views expressed in an earlier passage in which he had stated:[48]

> It is easy to see that at the time of the enactment of the Trade Disputes and Protection of Property Ordinance in 1943 here, the legislature might have felt the only way of giving labour an equality of bargaining power with capital was to give it special immunities which the common law did not permit.
>
> ... when under the protective cover of statutory immunities the strike weapon was so extensively used that to many it began to appear that the imbalance had tilted the other way, it is likewise easy to see that Parliament may have considered that the best means of holding the scales in equal poise was to refer to a tribunal for its impartial adjudication all disputes which the parties themselves should fail to resolve.

The other two judges of the Court of Appeal both carried out similar reviews of the relevant legal authorities and statutory enactments. Phillips JA held that:[49]

> No 'positive right' to strike exists, in the sense of a right which is legally enforceable or the infringement of which gives rise to legal sanctions. Nevertheless, whatever the nature of its juristic foundation, even a so-called 'right', however nebulous or ill-defined, assumes the character of a fundamental right or freedom if it is expressly so declared by the provisions of the Constitution. On the other hand, it is clear that the difficulty of holding that it is so declared only by implication increase in direct proportion with the extent of uncertainty of the alleged 'right'.

The opinion of Fraser JA was to a similar effect. He held that:[50]

> There is no common law right to strike and it must therefore follow that the so-called right to take part in a strike is not included in the freedom of association protected by s 2 of the Constitution.

Accordingly, they both agreed with the Chief Justice that the appeal should be dismissed.

---

45 (1967) 12 WIR 10.
46 *Ibid.*
47 *Ibid.*
48 *Ibid*, pp 15–16.
49 *Ibid*, p 32.
50 *Ibid*, p 48.

The decision of the Privy Council[51] on this point is, to say the least, most unsatisfactory. Before their Lordships, the appellants argued quite logically and soundly that:[52]

> 'Freedom of Association' must be construed in such a way that it confers rights of substance and is not merely an empty phrase. So far as trade unions are concerned, the freedom means more than the mere right of individuals to form them: it embraces the right to pursue that object which is the main *raison d'etre* of trade unions, namely, collectively bargaining on behalf of its members over wages and conditions of employment. Collective bargaining in its turn is ineffective unless backed by the right to strike as the last resort. It is this which gives reality to collective bargaining. Accordingly, to take away or curtail the right to strike is in effect to abrogate or abridge that freedom of association which the Constitution confers.

The Privy Council dismissed that logic and defined the matter in issue before them in the following terms:[53]

> The question is whether the abridgement of the rights of free collective bargaining and of freedom to strike are abridgments of the right of freedom of association.

Their Lordships had at this point already stated their view of the applicable law as follows:[54]

> It is now well recognized that by reason of the statutes cited (the Trade Union Act, 1871, the Conspiracy and Protection of Property Act, 1875 and the Trade Disputes Act, 1906) as well as by decisions such as *Crofter Hand Woven Harris Tweed Co Ltd v Veitch* [1942] AC 435 employees may lawfully withhold their labour in combination free from the restrictions and penalties which the common law formerly imposed. In this sense there is freedom to strike.

They also found that the Industrial Stabilisation Act had abridged 'the freedom to strike',[55] and the uninitiated reader of their judgment would have expected their Lordships to hold in favour of the appellants. Nevertheless, for reasons which completely escape the comprehension of the present writer, their Lordships agreed with the courts below in rejecting the appellants' argument on this point.

In holding as it did, the Privy Council stated:[56]

> It is, of course, true that the main purpose of most trade unions of employees is empowerment of wages and conditions. But these are not the only purposes which trade unionists as such pursue. They have, in addition, in many cases objects which are social, benevolent, charitable and political. The last named may be at times of paramount importance since the efforts of trade unions have more than once succeeded in securing alterations in the law to their advantage.

---

51   *Collymore and Another v AG* [1970] AC 538.
52   *Ibid*, p 546.
53   *Ibid*, p 547.
54   *Ibid*, pp 546–67.
55   *Ibid*, p 547.
56   *Ibid*.

Their Lordships lamely noted what the framers of Arts 1–5 of Convention 87 of the International Labour Organisation (ILO) considered to be comprised in 'Freedom of Association'. These articles related to undertakings by members of the ILO to give effect to:

(a) workers' and employers' right to establish and join organisations of their own choosing;

(b) the right of workers and employers' organisations, *inter alia*, to draw up their own constitutions and programmes;

(c) refraining from dissolving workers' and employers' organisations; and

(d) the right of workers' and employers' organisations to join federations and confederations, *inter alia*.

Noting that the Industrial Stabilization Act had not affected the above-mentioned rights, the Privy Council concluded:

> It therefore seems to their Lordships inaccurate to contend that the abridgment of the right to free collective bargaining and of the freedom to strike leaves the assurance of 'freedom of association' empty of worthwhile content.

Finally, on this point, their Lordships observed:

> Moreover, trade unions need more than 'freedom of association', they need to establish an organization. This involves setting up some kind of headquarters, and appointing officers to man it. Branches may also have to set up either in districts where the union has sufficient members or in particular plants or offices. Arrangements must be made for the due collection, usually weekly, of subscriptions. Recognition by the employer must be obtained as a prelude to collective bargaining. Arrangements have to be made for industrial action in the event of collective bargaining failing either wholly or partly. All this is something over and above freedom of association. It involves a union having freedom also to organize and to bargain collectively: and it is not surprising, therefore, to find this right the subject of a separate Convention (No 98) of the International Labour Organisation.

Commentary

In the first edition of this work, the writer quoted both the Trinidad and Tobago provision dealing with freedom of association and the provision contained in the 1962 Jamaica Constitution which have been followed in the case of all the other independent Caribbean States and which have been reproduced verbatim in the Canadian Charter of Rights 1982.[57] The object of quoting both sections was to emphasise that the Trinidad *Collymore* decision was based on a 'static rights' premise looking at the past rather than at the dynamic present day and future application of the protections guaranteed under the Canadian and other Caribbean Constitutions. In this connection, the author in the first edition of this volume, made this statement in comparing the Trinidad section with the corresponding section with the corresponding section in the Jamaica Constitution:

---

57   See Phillips, 1985, p 218. This book will hereafter be referred to as 'the first edition of this work'.

It is quite clear that the two sections from the Constitution of Jamaica and Trinidad and Tobago quoted above are not in the least bit similar. It is submitted that *Colllymore*'s case can be of little assistance in interpreting the provisions of our respective constitutions which guarantee freedom of assembly and association, unless the provisions are in *pari materia* with the corresponding provision of the Trinidad and Tobago Constitution with which that case dealt.

This point has been fully supported by two dissenting opinions in a case which reached the Canadian Supreme Court in 1987 in which three provincial statutes prohibited strikes and imposed compulsory arbitration. The question before the Supreme Court was whether the statutes contravened the constitutional guarantee of freedom of association provided by s 2(d) of the 1982 Charter of Rights.[58]

The majority of the Supreme Court, following the Privy Council in the *Collymore* case, held that freedom of association did not include the right to strike; but in a powerful dissenting opinion, the Chief Justice Dickson CJ, supported by Wilson J had this to say:

> While the *Collymore* case provides a relevant perspective on the meaning of freedom of association, its applicability to the Charter is undermined by the different nature of the constitutional documents. The constitution of Trinidad and Tobago is more similar in character and function to the Canadian Bill of Rights than to the Charter, accepting as it does a 'frozen rights' approach. It recognizes and declares pre-existing rights and freedoms and is not the source of new constitutional protections. It is for this reason that the courts in *Collymore* were so concerned with ascertaining whether or not the freedom to strike existed at common law prior to the introduction of statutory reform. As elaborated below, the Charter ushers in a new era in the protection of fundamental freedoms. We need not ground protection for freedom of association in pre-existing freedoms.

The dissenting judges also pointed out that:

> In the context of labour relations, the guarantee of freedom of association in s 2(d) of the Charter includes not only the freedom to form and join associations but also the freedom to bargain collectively and to strike. The role of association has always been vital as a means of protecting the essential needs and interests of working people. Throughout history, workers have associated to overcome their vulnerability as individuals to the strength of their employers, and the capacity to bargain collectively has long been recognized as one of the integral and primary functions of associations of working people. It remains vital to the capacity of individual employees to participate in ensuring equitable and humane working conditions. Under our existing system of industrial relations, the effective constitutional protection of the associational interests of employees in the collective bargaining process also requires concomitant protection of their freedom to withdraw collectively their services, subject to s 1 of the Charter. Indeed the right of workers to strike is an essential element in the principle of collective bargaining.

It is submitted that in the light of the 'new approach to constitutional interpretation' to which reference is made and for the reasons given above, the above judgments delivered in the *Collymore* case, both in the Court of Appeal of Trinidad and Tobago and in the Privy Council, should not be regarded as an authority for the proposition that 'a right to strike does not exist'; and that the highest court in the Caribbean area, when called upon to determine this issue should approach the question afresh 'with an open mind', avoiding

---

58 *Ref Re Public Service Employee Relations Act (Alta)* (1987) 1 SCR 313.

'the austerity of tabulated legalism', and should apply a generous interpretation to the relevant provision 'suitable to give to individuals the full measure of the fundamental rights and freedoms' guaranteed and protected in our new constitutions. One can only hope that when the Caribbean Court of Justice sees the light of day, it will possess sufficient judicial valour and confidence to overrule the Privy Council's judgment on this issue, but it may be that on reflection the Privy Council might be willing to qualify its previous decision in this matter in the light of the arguments adduced above.

The traditional view therefore remains that the freedom to form a trade union does not guarantee special treatment for its members, such as the right to strike or to be consulted.[59]

B EQUALITY OF THE LAW

Another common feature of all the constitutions of the independent Commonwealth Caribbean countries is the guarantee of equality before the law as a fundamental right.[60] With one exception (the Constitution of Trinidad and Tobago), this guarantee invariably takes the form of prohibition against discriminatory treatment by any person or authority. In the case of Trinidad and Tobago, however, 'the right of the individual to equality before the law and the protection of the law' and 'the right of the individual to equality of treatment from any public authority in the exercise of any functions' are two of the fundamental human rights and freedoms which are recognised and declared under the 1976 Constitution of that country.[61] The interpretation of these provisions and their applicability to other than natural persons were considered in the case of *Percival Smith and the AG v LJ Williams Ltd*.[62]

The facts of this case, which are summarised from the judgment of the Court of Appeal, delivered by Cross JA and which were not in issue, may be stated briefly. The appellant, Smith, was at all material times the chief immigration officer of Trinidad and Tobago and in this capacity he exercised certain functions in relation to persons who applied for permission to enter or to remain in that State. The respondent was a company which, in the course of its business, had on several occasions submitted such applications for Smith's approval to enable a number of persons, who represented the company's foreign principals and associates, to enter or remain in Trinidad and Tobago.

Being dissatisfied with the manner in which Smith treated these applications, when compared with the treatment accorded to other similar applicants, the company by originating summons applied to the High Court for a declaration that Smith's action had violated its right to 'equality of treatment from (a) public authority in the exercise of [his]

---

59 See Lester and Pannick, 1999, p 210.
60 Antigua (s 14(2)), Barbados (s 23(2)), Belize (ss 6 and 16(2)), Dominica (s 13(2)).
61 Constitution of Trinidad and Tobago, ss 4(b) and (d).
62 See judgment of the Court of Appeal delivered on 28 May 1982, in Civil Appeal No 19 of 1980.

functions and to equality before the law and protection of the law'. The company also sought an order for the assessment of damages for loss suffered by the company as a result of the violation of its rights. It was conceded that Smith was a 'public authority' for purposes of the relevant constitutional provisions.

At the hearing of the summons in the High Court, the trial judge, having considered the evidence and the arguments advanced, granted the declaration in the terms sought and ordered that damages be assessed by a judge in chambers. The appellants appealed to the Court of Appeal against the orders of the trial judge.

Before the Court of Appeal, counsel for the appellants informed the court that 'he did not challenge the facts found by the trial judge and made it clear that the State neither condoned nor sought to excuse the conduct of Smith which it readily conceded was discriminatory against the company'. However, he argued:

1   that the learned judge misdirected himself in finding that s 4(d) had been contravened by reason of the refusal or omission of the appellant Percival Smith in the exercise of his functions as chief immigration officer, to confer upon an applicant (such as the respondent company or persons sponsored or supported by the respondent company) a benefit unlawfully conferred upon a third party;

2   that there was no evidence upon which the learned judge could hold that the appellant, Percival Smith, in the exercise of his functions as chief immigration officer contravened the respondent company's right to equality of lawful treatment, within the meaning of s 4(d).

Since some of Smith's discriminatory acts antedated the coming into operation of the 1976 Constitution, the Court of Appeal had to consider not only s 4 of that Constitution, but also s 1 of the 1962 Constitution which the 1976 Constitution replaced. Their Lordships found that the two provisions were in identical terms. The court was, however, faced with this difficulty: whereas s 105(7) of the 1962 Constitution provided that the English Interpretation Act 1889 was to apply in interpreting the provisions of that Constitution, no such provision had been inserted in the 1976 Constitution which, accordingly, fell to be construed in the light of the Interpretation Act 1962 of Trinidad and Tobago.

Section 50(n) of that Act defined 'individual' as excluding a body corporate, while in s 34(1), the definition of 'person' includes 'corporation'. Counsel for the appellants therefore contended that the company, 'being an artificial legal entity and not a natural person, [was] not entitled to the rights declared in Chapter 1 of the 1962 and 1976 Constitutions', the headings of which both referred to 'Human Rights'. He further contended that the use of the word 'individual' in relation to the rights set out in paras (a)–(d) of ss 1 and 4 of the 1962 and 1976 Constitutions, respectively, would exclude their applicability to the company, particularly since the definition in the Interpretation Act 1962 excludes a body corporate.

In considering these arguments, the Court of Appeal first examined the following provisions of ss 1 and 2 of the 1962 Constitution which, as stated above, were found to be identical to the corresponding provisions of the 1976 Constitution:

1   It is hereby recognised and declared that in Trinidad and Tobago there have existed and shall continue to exist without discrimination by reason of race, origin, colour, religion or sex, the following human rights and fundamental freedoms, namely:

(a)   the right of the individual to life, liberty, security of the person and enjoyment of property, and the right not to be deprived thereof except by due process of law;

(b)   the right of the individual to equality before the law and the protection of the law;

(c)   the right of the individual to respect for his private and family life;

(d)   the right of the individual to equality of treatment from any public authority in the exercise of any functions;

(e)   the right to join political parties and to express political views;

(f)   the right of a parent or guardian to provide a school of his own choice for the education of his child or ward;

(g)   freedom of movement;

(h)   freedom of conscience and religious belief and observance;

(i)   freedom of thought and expression;

(j)   freedom of association and assembly; and

(k)   freedom of the press.

2   Subject to the provision of sections 3, 4 and 5 of this Constitution, no law shall abrogate, abridge or infringe or authorise the abrogation, abridgement or infringement of any of the rights and freedoms hereinbefore recognised and declared and in particular no Act of Parliament shall:

(a)   authorize or effect the arbitrary detention, imprisonment or exile of any person;

(b)   impose or authorize the imposition of cruel and unusual treatment or punishment;

(c)   deprive a person who has been arrested or detained:

(i)   of the right to be informed promptly and with sufficient particularity of the reason for his arrest or detention:

(ii)   of the right to retain and instruct without delay a legal adviser of his own choice and to hold communication with him;

(iii)   of the right to be brought promptly before an appropriate judicial authority;

(iv)   of the remedy by way of habeas corpus for the determination of the validity of his detention and for his release if detention is not lawful;

(d)   authorise a court, tribunal, commission, board or other authority to compel a person to give evidence if he is denied legal representation or protection against self-incrimination; [sic]

(e)   deprive a person of the right to a fair hearing in accordance with the principles of fundamental justice for the determination of his rights and obligations;

(f)   deprive a person charged with a criminal offence of the right to be presumed innocent until proved guilty according to law in a fair and public hearing by an independent and impartial tribunal, or of the right to reasonable bail without just cause;

(g)   deprive a person of the right to the assistance of an interpreter in any proceedings in which he is involved or in which he is a party or a witness, before a court, commission, board or other tribunal, if he does not understand or speak the language in which such proceedings are conducted; or

(h) deprive a person of the right to such procedural provisions as are necessary for the purpose of giving effect and protection to the aforesaid rights and freedoms.

From the above, it will be observed that while the rights which the company alleged had been infringed by Smith are defined in s 1(b) and (d) as 'the right of the individual', s 2, on the other hand, in particularising the laws which Parliament is prohibited from enacting, referred to the rights of persons. Until the 1976 Constitution came into operation, however, this apparent dichotomy presented no difficulty since the English Interpretation Act which, as we have shown, was applicable in construing the 1962 Constitution, defined the expression 'person' as including 'any body of persons corporate or incorporate' and did not define the word 'individual'. The court inferred from this that the words 'individual' and 'person' were synonymous and that they were both apt to include a 'body of persons corporate' such as the company was.

With respect to the second limb of the appellant's arguments (that in the Interpretation Act 1962 of Trinidad and Tobago, which was applicable in construing the 1976 Constitution, 'individual' was defined as excluding a body corporate while the definition of the term 'person' includes a corporation and that this indicated that under the 1976 Constitution the company was not intended to enjoy the rights which it alleged were infringed), the court examined the leading constitutional cases relevant to this issue. In particular, their Lordships considered and applied the *dicta* of:

(1) Lord Wilberforce in *Minister of Home Affairs v Fisher*:[63]

[T]he way to interpret a constitution on the Westminster model is to treat it not as if it were an Act of Parliament but as *sui generis* calling for principles of interpretation of its own, suitable to its character without necessary acceptance of all presumptions that are *relevant to legislation of private law* [emphasis supplied].

(2) Lord Diplock in *Ong Ah Chuan v Public Prosecutor*:[64]

As in that case, which concerned fundamental rights and freedoms of the individual ... their Lordships would give to the Constitution a generous interpretation avoiding what has been called the 'austerity of tabulated legalism' suitable to give to individuals the full measure of the fundamental liberties referred to;

and

(3) Lewis CJ, in *Camacho & Sons Ltd and Others v Collector of Customs*[65] (a decision of the Court of Appeal of the West Indies Associated States Supreme Court):

It would be a scandalous defect in the law if a company could be treated in the manner in which the company in *Camacho*'s case was treated and the law could not afford it any redress.

The Court of Appeal also gave consideration to the following passage from the decision of the Privy Council in *AG v Antigua Times Ltd*,[66] in which the board had agreed with the above-cited *dicta* of Lewis CJ, and *dicta* of Wooding CJ, in *Collymore v AG*, referred to earlier in this chapter:

---

63 [1980] AC 319, p 329.
64 [1981] AC 648, p 669.
65 (1971) 18 WIR 159.
66 (1975) 21 WIR 560.

Their Lordships agree with the opinion expressed by the Chief Justice and they have no reason to doubt that the decision in *Camacho*'s case was correct. Their Lordships also agree with the opinion of Wooding CJ in *Collymore v The Attorney-General* who said with reference to the Constitution of Trinidad and Tobago that it was intended to protect natural persons primarily but that 'some of the particular prohibitions are undoubtedly apt to protect artificial legal entities also'.

Finally, having had regard to the enacting words of s 1 of the 1962 Constitution, and on the basis of the authorities cited in the judgment, the Court of Appeal concluded that the framers of the 1976 Constitution could not have intended to, and did not, exclude corporations from the protection afforded by s 4 of the 1976 Constitution. In articulating this conclusion, the court observed that:

> To hold otherwise would be not only to admit to a 'scandalous defect in the law' which would permit Parliament by a bare majority to pass confiscatory legislation against corporate property but would also make a mockery of constitutional guarantees with respect to the right to the enjoyment of property and to equality of treatment.

Their Lordships felt fortified in their view by internal evidence drawn from the Constitution itself. Sections 4 and 5 of the 1976 Constitution were in terms identical to ss 1 and 2 of the 1962 Constitution. Moreover, s 14 of the 1976 Constitution, in manner similar to s 6 of the 1962 Constitution which it replaced, had laid down a procedure for the enforcement of the protective provisions of ss 4 and 5 of the 1976 Constitution. The Court of Appeal considered that, in these circumstances, it was inconceivable that Parliament had intended 'by the side-wind of a definition in the Interpretation Act [to] blow away the constitutional rights and freedoms which corporations had hitherto enjoyed'. In any event, the provisions of the Interpretation Act 1962[67] only extend and apply to an enactment in the absence of an intention to the contrary; and the 1976 Constitution itself had shown such a contrary intention.

Two additional, but subsidiary, arguments which were urged by counsel for the appellants were summarily dealt with by the Court of Appeal. Having regard to the persuasive opinions of the Supreme Court of Canada in *Curr v The Queen*[68] and *AG Canada v Lavell*,[69] the court did not agree with counsel's submission that the rights set out in paras 4(b) and (d) of the 1976 Constitution can only be contravened by conduct which amounts to discrimination on the grounds mentioned in that section, namely, race, origin, colour, religion or sex. Also, distinguishing *Harrikissoon v AG of Trinidad and Tobago*,[70] the Court held:

> ... the Company's application for redress under section 14 of the 1976 Constitution to be the most effective and appropriate method of seeking relief against what was clearly found to be discriminatory and unequal treatment by a public authority in the exercise of his functions.

---

67   See s 3(1).
68   (1972) 26 DLR (3d) 603.
69   (1973) 38 DLR (3d) 481.
70   [1980] AC 265.

C THE RIGHT TO PERSONAL LIBERTY

Another of the fundamental rights guaranteed under Commonwealth Caribbean constitutions is the right to personal liberty.[71] The right was in issue in two recent cases where the applicants were deprived of their personal liberty by different organs of the State.

1 The *Reynolds* case

The judgment of the Privy Council delivered in June 1979 in the case of the *AG of St Christopher/Nevis/Anguilla v Reynolds*[72] finally ended an unfortunate bit of tyranny and repression which had its origin as far back as 1967. This is the first of two cases referred to.

The respondent was detained from 11 June–10 August 1967, pursuant to an order issued by the Deputy to the Governor of St Christopher, Nevis and Anguilla[73] under reg 3(1) of the Emergency Powers Regulations 1967.[74] The regulations were made under powers conferred by s 3(1) of the Leeward Islands (Emergency Powers) Order in Council, 1959[75] which provides as follows:

> (1) The Administrator of a colony to which this Order applies may during a period of emergency in that colony, make such laws for the colony as appear to him to be necessary or expedient for securing the public safety, the defence of the Colony or the maintenance of public order or for maintaining supplies and services essential to the life of the community.

Regulation 3(1) of the Emergency Powers Regulations 1967 was in the following terms:

> Detention of persons. (1) If the Governor is satisfied that any person has recently been concerned in acts prejudicial to the public safety, order, or in the preparation or in instigation of such acts, or impeding the maintenance of supplies and services essential to the life of the community and that by reason thereof it is necessary to exercise control over him, he may make an order against that person directing that he be detained.

The detention order, which was signed by the Governor's Deputy on 10 June 1967, read as follows:[76]

---

71 Antigua (s 5), Bahamas (Art 27), Barbados (s 13), Belize (s 5), Dominica (s 3) and Grenada (s 3).

72 [1980] AC 637 (PC).

73 As that Associated State was then constituted. Anguilla is now a separate colony. The writer, who was at that time Governor, was absent from the State on business.

74 SR & O No 16 of 1967 which came into force on 30 May 1967.

75 SI 1959/2206 (UK).

76 This detention order was purportedly made under powers conferred by the Leeward Islands Emergency Powers Regulations 1967, s 3(1).

Order made under Emergency Powers Regulations 1967: Whereas I am satisfied that with respect to John Reynolds that [sic] he has recently been concerned in acts prejudicial to the public safety and to public order, and that by reason thereof it is necessary to exercise control over him: now therefore, in pursuance of the power conferred on me by regulation 3 of the Emergency Powers Regulations 1967, and all other powers thereunto enabling me, I do hereby order and direct that the said John Reynolds be detained.

Ordered by me this 10th day of June 1967.

(sgd) BF Dias,

Governor's Deputy

On 16 June 1967, the following written statement (purportedly given in compliance with s 15(1)(a) of the Constitution,[77] to which we shall refer later) was delivered to the respondent:

That you John Reynolds during the year 1967, both within and outside of the State, encouraged civil disobedience throughout the State, thereby endangering the peace, public safety and public order of the State.

Early in July of 1967, an inquiry was held by a tribunal under s 15(1)(c), (d) and (e) of the Constitution to review the cases of a number of detainees, including the respondent. At that hearing, senior Crown counsel, who appeared on behalf of the State, on being reminded by the chairman of the tribunal that he had not led any evidence against the respondent and two other detainees replied: 'I have no evidence against them. I will speak to the authorities.'[78]

The finding of the Privy Council with respect to this exchange is reflected in the following extract from the judgment:

The clear inference from those remarks was that the chairman considered that there were no grounds for detaining the plaintiff and that Crown Counsel agreed and would report accordingly to the authorities.

Incredibly, however, the respondent continued to be held in custody 'in most insanitary and humiliating conditions' until 10 August 1967, when he was released.

In January 1968, the State Legislature enacted the Indemnity Act 1968[79] which was made retroactive to 30 May 1967, the date on which a State of Emergency was declared, pursuant to s 17 of the Constitution, to have existed in the State of St Christopher, Nevis and Anguilla. Section 3 of the Act purported to preclude the institution of legal proceedings in respect of any acts done in the public interest during the State of Emergency.

---

77 The St Christopher, Nevis and Anguilla Constitution Order 1967 (SI 1967/228) which came into force on 27 February 1967.

78 [1980] AC 650.

79 No 1 of 1968 (Laws of St Christopher/Nevis and Anguilla).

In February 1968, the respondent brought an action against the Attorney General in which he claimed, *inter alia*, damages for false imprisonment and compensation under s 3(b) of the Constitution on the ground that his detention was unlawful.

In his defence, the Attorney General alleged that the respondent had been lawfully arrested and detained and that, in any case, the claims should be 'discharged and made void' under the Indemnity Act, 1968. A summons issued by the Attorney General on 28 May 1968, to have the action stayed under the Act was heard and dismissed almost five years later, viz, in April 1973. After a further delay of over three years the action finally came on for hearing before Glasgow J, towards the end of July 1976.

The trial judge in giving judgment[80] for the respondent held that, on the authority of *Charles v Phillips and Sealey*[81] and *Herbert v Phillips and Sealey*,[82] he was bound to find that the respondent's arrest and detention were unlawful. The learned trial judge also found that the Indemnity Act was in contravention of the Constitution and accordingly did not affect the respondent's claim. He accordingly awarded damages to the respondent in the amount of $5,000, which included the award of an unstated sum in respect of exemplary damages.

From this judgment of Glasgow J, the Attorney General appealed to the Court of Appeal. The respondent also cross-appealed, praying that the judgment should be varied by increasing the sum of the damages awarded by the trial judge.

The Court of Appeal, upholding the judgment in the court below, dismissed the Attorney General's appeal and allowed the respondent's cross-appeal, increasing the damages to $18,000. The Attorney General appealed to the Privy Council from both decisions of the Court of Appeal.

As stated in the judgment of the Privy Council which was read by Lord Salmon, the following three points of law and one point of mixed fact and law fell to be determined:

1   Were the Emergency Powers Regulations 1967 lawful?

2   If they were, was the detention order made against the plaintiff under those regulations lawful?

3   If the first two points or either of them is decided in favour of the plaintiff, does this claim fail because of the Indemnity Act 1968?

4   If the plaintiff's claim succeeds, ought the award of $18,000 to be reduced?[83]

With respect to the first point the Privy Council held that, for the reasons hereunder stated, the Emergency Powers Regulations 1967, were lawfully made under the enabling power contained in the Leeward Islands (Emergency Powers) Order in Council 1959.

By s 103(5) of the Constitution, the Order in Council was an existing law which continued to have effect as part of the law of St Christopher, Nevis and Anguilla until 1 September 1967. Moreover, the Order in Council had the same purpose as the provisions of s 14 of the Constitution which reads as follows:

---

80   Reported at (1977) 24 WIR 552.
81   (1967) 10 WIR 423.
82   (1967) 10 WIR 435.
83   [1980] AC 651.

Nothing contained in or done under the authority of a law enacted by the legislature shall be held to be inconsistent with or in contravention of section 3 or section 13 of this Constitution to the extent that the law authorises the taking during any period of public emergency of measures that are reasonably justifiable for dealing with the situation that exists in [the state] during that period.

However, as their Lordships pointed out, the difference between s 3 of the Order in Council and s 14 of the Constitution was that the former 'gave an authority absolute discretion, and indeed the power of a dictator, to arrest and detain any one, whilst s 14 of the Constitution allows a law to be enacted conferring power to arrest and detain only if it was reasonably justifiable to exercise such a power'. This difference meant that s 3 of the Order in Council was inconsistent or out of conformity with the Constitution.

Overruling, in part, the decisions in the *Charles* and *Herbert* cases which had held that it was impossible to construe the Order in Council to bring it into conformity with the Constitution, their Lordships, citing *dicta* from their judgment in *Minister of Home Affairs v Fisher*,[84] found no difficulty in placing the following construction on s 3 of the Order in Council in accordance with s 103(1), and in the light of s 14, of the Constitution:

The Governor of a state may, during a period of public emergency in that state make such laws for securing the public safety or defence of the state or the maintenance of public order or for maintaining supplies and services essential to the life of the community to the extent that those laws authorise the taking of measures that are reasonably justifiable for dealing with the situation that exists in the state during any such period of public emergency.

In arriving at this conclusion, the Privy Council stated that they could not accept that:[85]

The Constitution would have preserved the life of the Order in Council of 1959 for any period if the Order in Council could not be construed under section 103 of the Constitution so as to bring it into conformity with the Constitution. It is inconceivable that a law which gave absolute power to arrest and detain without reasonable justification would be tolerated by a Constitution such as the present, one of the principal purposes of which is to protect fundamental rights and freedoms.

Since, in the judgment of the Privy Council, the Leeward Islands (Emergency Powers) Order in Council 1959 could and should be construed to bring it into conformity with the Constitution, this destroyed the basis upon which the Court of Appeal had upheld the trial judge's finding that the Emergency Powers Regulations 1967 were invalid. However, in the opinion of the Board, the validity of the regulations rested on the construction of reg 3(1).

In the light of ss 3 and 14 of the Constitution, the Privy Council found that reg 3(1) could only be properly construed as follows:[86]

[I]f the Governor is satisfied upon reasonable grounds that any person has recently been concerned in acts prejudicial to the public safety or to public order and that by reason thereof it is reasonably justifiable and necessary to exercise control over him, he may make an order against that person directing that he be detained.

---

84   [1980] AC 319 – a Constitution should be construed with less rigidity and more generosity than other Acts.

85   [1980] AC 655E.

86   *Ibid*, p 656.

In arriving at that finding, the Privy Council made the following somewhat scathing observations:[87]

> Their Lordships consider that it is impossible that a regulation made on May 30, 1967, under an Order in Council which, on its true construction, conformed with the Constitution on that date, could be properly construed as conferring dictatorial powers on the Governor: and that is what the regulation would purport to do if the words 'if the Governor is satisfied' mean 'if the Governor thinks that etc'. No doubt Hitler thought that the measures – even the most atrocious measures – which he took were necessary and justifiable, but no reasonable man could think any such thing.

Their Lordships, accordingly, concluded that 'regulation 3(1) of the Emergency Powers Regulation 1967, on its true construction, does conform with the Constitution'.[88]

The second point of law to be determined by the Privy Council, as stated above, may be articulated as follows: if the Emergency Powers Regulations 1967 were lawful, was the detention order made against the respondent under those regulations lawful?

In the light of the construction which their Lordships had placed on reg 3(1), they considered that the answer to this question depended upon:

> ... whether there existed *reasonable grounds* upon which the Governor could be satisfied that the [respondent] had been concerned in acts prejudicial to public safety or to public order and that by reason thereof, it was *reasonably justifiable* and necessary to detain him[89] [emphasis supplied].

They gave careful consideration to the evidence presented throughout the course of the proceedings, including the inquiry held in July 1967, the trial before Glasgow J and in the Court of Appeal, and concluded that at no stage:

> ... was there any glimmer of a suggestion put forward by the Governor or by the Attorney General of any reason, justification or ground upon which any reasonable Governor could have been satisfied that the [respondent] had been concerned in acts prejudicial to public safety or good order. Had there been any evidence which could have shown that the [respondent's] detention was reasonably justifiable, surely it would have been called on both occasions.[90]

The Privy Council then went on to consider the statement delivered to the respondent on 16 June 1967, which, as already stated, appeared to have been given in purported compliance with the following provisions of s 15(1)(a) of the Constitution:

> When a person is detained by virtue of any such law as is referred to in section 14 of this Constitution the following provisions shall apply, that is to say:
>
> (a) he shall, as soon as reasonably practicable and in any case not more than *seven days* after the commencement of his detention, be furnished with a *statement in writing* in a language that he understands specifying in *detail* the *grounds* upon which he is detained [emphasis supplied].

---

87 [1980] AC 655E.
88 *Ibid.*
89 *Ibid*, p 660.
90 *Ibid*, pp 660–61.

With regard to the written statement, this is what their Lordships said:[91]

> As already mentioned, on the sixth day after the commencement of his detention he was served with a notice supposed to be in accordance with section 15(1) of the Constitution. It *is very short* and its barren words *bear repetition*.
>
>> That you John Reynolds during the year 1967, both within and outside of the state, encouraged civil disobedience throughout the state, thereby endangering the peace, public safety and public order of the state.
>
> It is difficult to imagine anything more vague and ambiguous or less informative than the words of this notice. It was indeed a mockery to put it forward as specifying in detail the grounds on which the plaintiff was being detained.

The Privy Council drew the irresistible inference from the statement that 'there were no grounds far less any justifiable grounds, for detaining the [respondent]'. The Board accordingly had no doubt that the detention order was invalid and, for that reason, the detention of the respondent was unlawful.

The third point of law involved consideration of the Indemnity Act, the relevant portions of which were set out in the judgment of Peterkin JA, who delivered the judgment of the Court of Appeal. Section 3 of the Act stated:

> 3(1) No action or other legal proceeding whatsoever civil or criminal shall be instituted in any court of law for or on account of or in respect of any act, matter or thing done, whether within or without the state, during the state of emergency before the passing of this Act, if done in good faith, and done or purported to be done in the execution of his duty or for the defence of the state or the public safety, or for the enforcement of discipline or otherwise in the public interest, by a person holding office under or employed in the service of the Crown in any capacity, whether naval, military, airforce or civil or by any other person acting under authority of a person so holding office or so employed; and if such proceeding has been instituted whether before or after the passing of this Act, it shall be discharged and made void;
>
> (2) For the purposes of this section, a certificate by a government department that any act, matter, or thing was done under the authority of a person so holding office or so employed as aforesaid, or was done in execution of a duty, shall be sufficient evidence of such authority or duty and of such act, matter or thing having been done thereunder, or in execution thereof, and any such act, matter or thing done by or under the authority of a person so holding office or so employed as aforesaid shall be deemed to have been done in good faith unless the contrary is proved.

Section 5 of the Act read as follows:

> All laws, Acts, Ordinances, proclamations, regulations, orders, resolutions and other legislative acts made, issued, passed or done by the House of Assembly, the Cabinet, the Governor, a Minister or any other lawful authority during the state of emergency before the passing of this Act, for the peace, order or good government of the state shall be deemed to

---

91 [1980] AC 655E, p 661.

be and always to have been valid and of full effect until repealed or superseded by such lawfully constituted legislative authority of the state, notwithstanding that any such legislative act may have been repealed, suspended or been inconsistent with the law previously in force in the state.

Their Lordships entirely agreed with the Court of Appeal, for the reasons given in the undermentioned extract from its judgment, that the Indemnity Act was unconstitutional, null and void:[92]

> The Act therefore purports not only to deem legal and constitutional the detention of the plaintiff during the state of emergency as therein defined but also prohibits his taking any action whatsoever before any court to determine the legality of his detention. It would mean in effect that the legality or otherwise of any act of arrest or detention, even if done in total disregard of the Constitution, and however, capricious, would not be justifiable. It is clear that what the Indemnity Act seeks to do is to amend section 16 of the Constitution. It seeks to take away the fundamental right of access to the High Court by the plaintiff which the Constitution ensures to him and which cannot be so easily amended, being an entrenched clause of the Constitution. In my opinion, therefore, the Indemnity Act is unconstitutional, null and void.

The final point, one of mixed fact and law, was summarily disposed of in the judgment. The Privy Council held that it could find nothing on the facts of the case which would justify interfering with the damages of $18,000 as assessed by the Court of Appeal. On behalf of the Attorney General, it was contended that exemplary damages should not have been awarded since, under s 3(6) of the Constitution, only compensation could be claimed by the respondent. However, as pointed out in the Privy Council's judgment, this argument tended to ignore the fact that s 16(1) of the Constitution made it plain that 'any one seeking redress under the Constitution may do so *without prejudice to any other action with respect to the same matter which is lawfully available*', and that, in the instant case, the respondent had claimed both damages for false imprisonment as well as compensation pursuant to s 3(6) of the Constitution.

Finally, on this question, the Attorney General argued that the Court of Appeal had erred in not quantifying the portion of damages which was awarded as 'exemplary damages'. However, their Lordships noted that the observations on this issue in *Rookes v Barnard*[93] were confined to jury trials and they were satisfied that that judgment did not impose on a trial judge sitting without a jury or on the Court of Appeal any obligation to quantify the sum awarded as exemplary damages.

The Privy Council was also asked to express its opinion as to whether the Court of Appeal was correct in considering itself bound by the earlier decisions of that Court in the *Charles* and *Herbert* cases. In upholding the right of the Court of Appeal in considering itself bound by its own decisions, the Privy Council made the following statement:[94]

> Their Lordships agree with the decision in *Young v Bristol Aeroplane Co Ltd*[95] that save for the exceptions there stated but which are irrelevant to the present case, the Court of Appeal is bound by its own decisions on points of law. So long as there is an appeal from a Court of

---

92 [1980] AC 655E, p 642.
93 [1964] AC 1129, p 1228.
94 [1980] AC 637, pp 659–60.
95 [1944] KB 718.

Appeal to their Lordships' Board or to the House of Lords, the Court of Appeal should follow its own decisions on a point of law and leave it to the final appellate tribunal to correct any error in law which may have crept into any previous decision of the Court of Appeal.

The writer is of the view that the importance of this case more than justifies the detailed manner in which it has been discussed. Not only does it finally lay to rest the contentions which had existed for over 11 years with respect to the respondent's claims, but it also clarifies, to an intensely lucid degree, the manner in which 'existing laws' and subsequent enactments of the legislature should be construed in order to bring them into conformity with the constitution. It illustrates, as well, the financial consequences which are likely to flow from acts done under the purported authority of legislation which, in reality, offends against the Constitution. This case, if properly understood, could be of immense assistance to authorities in other Caribbean territories which face problems similar to those which confronted the authorities in the State of St Christopher, Nevis and Anguilla in 1967.

Additionally, the case is important for other reasons. Certain *dicta*, to which reference has already been made, clearly emphasise the consistency of the Privy Council's approach when considering constitutional issues: '*a Constitution should be construed with less rigidity and more generosity than other Acts.*'[96]

2 The *Demerieux* case

In the case of *Demerieux v AG of Barbados*,[97] the applicant, who was a lecturer in law at the Cave Hill Campus (Barbados) of the University of the West Indies, instituted proceedings against the respondent (defendant) for redress under the relevant provisions of the Constitution[98] in respect of the contravention of her fundamental right to personal liberty.[99] The facts and circumstances which gave rise to this application are set out in the judgment of Williams J (as he then was) which was delivered on 10 February 1982.

On 4 November 1980, the applicant who, according to the judge's finding, attended the District 'A' Traffic Court 'in a dual capacity' was committed to prison for seven days by the presiding magistrate for contempt of court. On the same day, she was also ordered by the same magistrate to be committed to a mental hospital for a similar period. It is not clear whether the period of imprisonment was intended to commence at the expiration of the period of her committal to the mental hospital. It appears, however, that she was conveyed from the court to the mental hospital where she was detained in a cell until 7 November 1980.

In her application to the High Court, the applicant claimed, *inter alia*:

(a) a declaration that the order of the magistrate committing her to prison for seven days for contempt of court was unconstitutional, null, void and of no effect as contravening s 13 of the Constitution;

---

96   See fn 84 above.
97   Civil Suit No 734 of 1981 (Barbados).
98   Constitution of Barbados, s 24.
99   *Ibid*, s 13.

(b) a declaration that the further order of the magistrate committing her to the mental hospital for seven days was likewise unconstitutional, null, void and of no effect; and

(c) damages.

With respect to the magistrate's committal order for contempt of court, although the evidence presented before the learned judge at the hearing appeared to be somewhat conflicting in parts, he found that:

(1) s 122(1) of the Magistrates Jurisdiction and Procedure Act[100] prescribed 'a wide range of offences relating to the administration of justice in proceedings before Magistrates';

(2) sub-ss 122(1) and (2) of the Act 'are in addition to the provisions of any other law giving a magistrate power to deal with contempt of court';

(3) 'Section 123 [of the Act] enables a magistrate to punish contempt by fine or imprisonment';

(4) the behaviour of the applicant in court on the day in question 'would provide ample grounds for *proceeding for contempt* and there could be no complaint if the magistrate had properly proceeded *against the applicant for contempt against such a background*'; and

(5) 'the magistrate never informed the applicant of the offence with which she was charged. She was never told of the specific offence under section 122(1) or of the breach of the other law which he alleged she had committed or of the particulars thereof.'

On the above stated facts, the learned judge, citing *dicta* from the judgment of the Privy Council in *Maharaj v AG for Trinidad and Tobago*,[101] held that the magistrate's failure to inform the applicant of the specific legal provision which he alleged she had breached as well as his failure to give her particulars of the nature of her contempt had vitiated the order for committal to prison.

Turning next to the magistrate's order committing the applicant to a mental hospital, the judge considered s 55(1) of the Magistrates Jurisdiction and Procedure Act which enables a magistrate, in certain stated circumstances to adjourn a case to obtain a medical examination and report on the physical or mental condition of an accused person; and s 56 of the Act which, subject to conditions, provides for an enquiry to be held into the state of mind of a person charged with a summary offence before a magistrate. The judge found that neither section was applicable to whichever version of the conflicting evidence he accepted. The judge, *suo moto*, also examined the provisions of s 18(2) of the Mental Health Act[102] which empowers a magistrate, in certain cases, to order that an accused person, who appears to be of unsound mind, be detained in a mental hospital until an inquiry can be held into that person's state of mind. The trial judge found that on the evidence before him it was impossible to justify the applicant's detention under that subsection. The consequence of these findings was, of course, that the magistrate's order committing the applicant to a mental hospital was also unlawful.

---

100 Cap 116 of the Laws of Barbados, 1971–78.

101 [1977] 1 All ER 411, p 416.

102 Cap 46 of the Laws of Barbados.

The judge then considered the following provisions of the Constitution:

(1) s 13 which, except in certain clearly defined cases, prohibits the deprivation of a person's liberty and entitles a person to compensation for unlawful arrest or detention;

(2) s 24 which confers original jurisdiction on the High Court to grant relief to an applicant who alleges, *inter alia*, that his right to personal liberty had been contravened; and

(3) s 26(1) which saves certain existing laws from contravening any of the protective provisions of ss 12–23 of the Constitution.

In opposing the application, it was contended by counsel for the defendant that the applicant had other adequate means of redress in the form of 'proceedings by way of appeal, with an application for bail and to certiorari and habeas corpus'. However, as the learned judge pointed out 'whichever of these alternatives was pursued, the applicant would have been bound to spend some time in custody'. Moreover, 'for an alternative means of redress to have been adequate, it must be shown that the applicant would thereby have been able to recover compensation in respect of her period of detention', especially since sub-s 13(4) of the Constitution gave her the right to compensation for unlawful detention. Accordingly, the judge refused to exercise the powers conferred under the proviso to s 24(2) of the Constitution because he was satisfied that there were no other means of redress available to the applicant.

The judge also held that sub-ss 4(4) and 4(5) of the Crown Proceedings Act[103] were not inconsistent with sub-s 13(4) of the Constitution since the former excluded the Crown from liability in respect of 'private law' claims for damages, while the latter provided a claim in 'public law' for compensation on the ground of deprivation of personal liberty. The real question, however, was not whether the sub-sections of the Act were inconsistent with sub-s 13(4) but, rather, whether they were capable of excluding the Crown from liability to compensate the applicant for her detention which was clearly unlawful. For the reasons given by the judge, the answer to this question was also in the negative. He therefore held that she was entitled to compensation from the Crown.

On the question of the quantum of the compensation to be awarded to the applicant, the judge considered all the circumstances relating to her detention and ordered the payment of an award of $15,000 together with costs. He also held that she was entitled to the declarations in the terms sought.

With respect to the *Demerieux* application two final points must be made. Firstly, it is most unfortunate that the magistrate should have acted in so precipitate a manner as to cause the applicant such extreme distress, even if in a moment of weakness she appeared contemptuous of the court's proceedings. Secondly, while by comparison with the *Reynolds* case discussed above the award of $15,000 to this applicant may at first blush appear excessive as damages for four days' detention, one must bear in mind the humiliation and anxiety suffered by Miss Demerieux as a result of her 'traumatic experience'. If anything, a higher award of damages might well have been justified.

---

103 Cap 197 of the Laws of Barbados.

D   THE RIGHT TO LIFE

The right to life is indisputably the most basic and important of all the fundamental rights and freedoms of the individual protected by most of the constitutions with which this work deals. Yet, for all its importance, it is, like all of the other rights, not an absolute right but one which, by reason of practical, societal considerations is qualified. These qualifications, in a general sense, relate to the absence of intent; execution of the sentence of a court; reasonably justifiable force connected with self defence, defence of property, lawful arrest, unlawful escape, suppression of riot, insurrection or mutiny and prevention of crime. In addition, the right of life is further qualified by a lawful act of war.

The constitutional provision by which the right to life is protected usually conforms to the following general formulation, sometimes with minor variations in language:[104]

> No person shall be deprived of his life intentionally save in the execution of the sentence of a court in respect of a criminal offence under the law of [for example, Dominica] of which he has been convicted.

In Trinidad and Tobago, on the other hand, the right to life is protected in the Constitution in the following terms:[105]

> It is hereby recognized and declared that in Trinidad and Tobago there have existed and shall continue to exist without discrimination by reason of race, origin, colour, religion, or sex, the following fundamental human rights and freedoms namely:
>
> (a)   the right of the individual to life ... and the right not to be deprived thereof except by due process of law.

The very nature of the right to life, coupled with the broad sweep of the qualifications of that right, makes it all the more rare to find cases in these jurisdictions in which an individual seeks redress under the Constitution on the ground that his right to life has been, is being or is likely to be contravened. The only case to be addressed is one that arose in Trinidad and Tobago in 1978. Thereafter will follow some general comments and a reference to the death penalty.

In *Nanan v Registrar, Supreme Court of Judicature*,[106] the appellant appealed to the Court of Appeal from the decision of the trial judge, Brathwaite J, dismissing his application made by originating motion for declarations under s 14 of the Constitution that:

> (a)   his constitutional right not to be deprived of his life except by due process of law guaranteed to him by section 4(a) [of the Constitution] has been, is being or is likely to be infringed;

and:

---

104 See Antigua (s 4), Barbados (s 12), Belize (s 4), Dominica (s 2) and Grenada (s 2).
105 Constitution, (s 4(a)).
106 See judgment of Trinidad and Tobago Court of Appeal delivered in Civil Appeal No 39/1978 on 22 June 1979, (1979) 30 WIR 420.

(b) the verdict of the jury returned at his trial for murder and his consequent conviction and sentence therefor were all void and of no effect because the said verdict was not unanimous.

The facts of the case are taken from the judgment delivered by Sir Isaac Hyatali CJ, on 22 June 1979.

On 4 July 1977, the appellant was convicted at the assizes before Warner J and a jury for murder and sentenced to death. On the same day he gave notice of appeal against his conviction. Pursuant to s 16(1) of the Jury Ordinance[107] the unanimous verdict of the 12 jurors was necessary for the conviction of the appellant.

On 15 July 1977, the appellant applied by motion to Warner J to have a case stated for the consideration by the Court of Appeal of the following question:

Whether in the circumstances of the case, having regard to the facts brought to the notice of the trial judge by the affidavits and the letter from the Registrar to Counsel for the applicant, the verdict is valid.

The motion, which was supported by affidavits and statutory declarations sworn and declared by the foreman and three of the other jurors involved in the appellant's trial as well as a letter from the Registrar of the Supreme Court to the appellant's counsel, was dismissed by Warner J on 21 July 1977. He refused to state a case on the ground that the question of law involved did not arise out of the trial over which he had presided.

In essence, the documents presented to the judge at the hearing of the motion to state a case sought to show that when the foreman of the jury announced the verdict of guilty in the appellant's trial, none of the four jurors was aware that the verdict had to be unanimous; that the foreman in the presence of one of the other three jurors had, on 5 July 1977, told the registrar that he did not know the meaning of the word 'unanimous', that he thought a unanimous verdict meant a majority verdict, and that the jury was in fact divided eight to four. Because of the ground on which Warner J had dismissed the motion he was not required to, and did not, rule whether the documents were admissible.

The appellant did not appeal against this ruling by Warner J. Instead, on 23 August 1977, he filed an originating motion, supported by affidavit evidence similar to that presented before Warner J, seeking constitutional redress under s 14 of the Constitution for alleged violation of his right to life. This motion was heard on 31 January 1978, by Brathwaite J, who dismissed it on the ground that the affidavits were inadmissible to prove that the jury's verdict was not unanimous. The appellant appealed against this order to the Court of Appeal.

At the hearing of this appeal two questions fell to be determined, namely:

(1) did the High Court have jurisdiction to entertain the appellant's application for redress under ss 14(1) and (2) of the Constitution; and

(2) if the High Court had such jurisdiction, was the trial judge correct in refusing to admit the affidavits of the four jurors to prove that the verdict of guilty returned by the jury at the appellant's trial for murder was not a unanimous verdict?

---

107 Chapter 4, No 2 of the Laws of Trinidad and Tobago.

The Court of Appeal considered the above questions in the reverse order although, as the learned Chief Justice observed, if the objection to the court's jurisdiction was sustained, then there was no need to consider the second question.

In examining the content of the evidence presented by the affidavits filed in support of the motion, the Chief Justice expressed himself as having difficulty in resisting the 'conclusion that the *bona fides* of the four jurors are open to question'. However, he reminded himself, quite correctly, that in considering the second question raised by this appeal, the matter in issue was the admissibility and not the credibility of the affidavits.

Their Lordships then reviewed a long line of relevant authorities,[108] from which they distilled the following principles which were applicable to the issue raised as to the admissibility of the affidavits of the four jurors:

(1) the deliberations of a jury are completely private and confidential, a court will never receive evidence from a juror which seeks to lift the veil of secrecy which enshrouds them. This rule is based on public policy and is not only an inflexible one but fundamental to the right of trial by jury;

(2) a presumption of assent to a verdict by all the members of a jury arises when it is delivered by the foreman in their presence and hearing without protest from any of them. The corollary to that rule, of course, is that no such presumption arises when it is not so delivered and consequently this fact may be proved without renting the veil of secrecy which enshrouds the jury's deliberations;

(3) the presumption of assent to a verdict so delivered is rebuttable in a case in which it is, or can be shown, that a juror was incompetent for physical or other reasons to assent to a verdict delivered as aforesaid.

Applying the above principles to the facts of the case, the court found that:

(a) it was uncontroverted that the jury's verdict was delivered by the foreman in the presence and hearing of all the jurors without any protest from them;

(b) none of the jurors had stated in express or direct terms that he had misunderstood the question put to them by the Court Clerk; and

(c) there was no room for such a misunderstanding.

The Court of Appeal accordingly upheld the trial judge's ruling that the affidavits were inadmissible. Their Lordships also observed, *obiter*, that even if the alleged misunderstanding or misapprehension could be inferred, the affidavits of the jurors could not be received to rebut the presumption of assent.

The court then moved to consider the first question which was raised on the appeal, although not argued in the court below. In this connection, their Lordships examined the following provisions of the Constitution:

---

108 *R v Wooler* (1870) 105 ER 1280; *Raphael v The Bank of England (Governor and Co)* (1855) 139 ER 1030; *Nesbitt v Parrett* (1902) 18 TLR 510; *Elliss v Deheer* [1922] 2 KB 113; *R v Thomas* [1933] All ER 726; *Ras Behari Lal v The King Emperor* (1933) 1 TLR 1 ; *Manswell v The Queen* (1857) 8 E & B 54; *Boston v Bagshaw & Sons* (1966) 1 WLR 1136; *R v Roads* (1967) 51 Cr App R 297.

(1) The right of the individual to life, liberty, security of the person and enjoyment of property and the right not to be deprived thereof except by due process of law [s 4(a)].

(2) For the removal of doubts it is hereby declared that if any person alleges that any of the provisions of this Chapter (which includes s 4(a)) has been, is being, or is likely to be contravened in relation to him, then without prejudice to any other action with respect to the same matter which is lawfully available, that person may apply to the High Court for redress by way of originating motion [s 14(1)].

Counsel for the respondent contended, on the authority of the Privy Council's decision in *Maharaj v The AG of Trinidad and Tobago (No 2)*,[109] that:

(1) the High Court had no jurisdiction to entertain the appellant's motion;

(2) the error alleged in the motion, if established, was one of substantive law arising out of a judgment or order which was liable to be, or capable of being, set aside on appeal; and

(3) the claim for relief fell within the class of cases specified in the judgment of Lord Diplock in the *Maharaj* case (see above) and could not be entertained.

In considering the above submissions, the Court of Appeal examined the following three extracts from the judgment of Lord Diplock in the *Maharaj* case:[110]

(1) *No human right or fundamental freedom recognized by Chapter I of the Constitution is contravened by a judgment or order that is wrong and liable to be set aside on appeal for an error of fact or substantive law, even where the error has resulted in a person serving a sentence of imprisonment.* The remedy for errors of these kinds is to appeal to a higher court. When there is no higher court to appeal to then none can say there was error. The fundamental right is not to a legal system that is infallible but to one that is fair. It is only *errors in procedure that are capable of constituting infringements of the rights protected by s 1(a), and no mere irregularity in procedure is enough, even though it goes to jurisdiction;* the error must amount to a failure to observe one of the fundamental rules of natural justice. Their Lordships do not believe that this can be anything but a rare event [emphasis supplied].

(2) The claim for redress under s 6(1) for what has been done by a judge is a claim against the State for what has been done in the exercise of the judicial power of the State. This is not vicarious liability; it is liability of the State itself; it is not a liability in tort at all: *it is a liability in the public law of the State, and not of the judge himself, which has been newly created by s 6(1) and (2) of the Constitution* [emphasis supplied].

(3) It is true that instead of, or even as well as, pursuing the ordinary course of appealing directly to an appellate court, a party to legal proceedings who alleges that *a fundamental rule of natural justice* has been infringed in the course of the determination of his case, could in theory seek collateral relief in an application to the High Court under s 6(1) with a further right of appeal to the Court of Appeal under s 6(4). The High Court, however, has ample powers, both inherent and under s 6(2), to prevent its process being misused in this way; for example, it could stay proceedings under s 6(1) until an appeal against the judgment or order complained of has been disposed of [emphasis supplied].[111]

---

109 [1978] 2 All ER 670.

110 *Ibid*, pp 679–80.

111 Sections 1(a) and 6 (1), (2) and (4) cited in the above extracts refer to the 1962 Constitution of Trinidad and Tobago. The corresponding sections in the 1976 Constitution are ss 4(a), 14(1), (2) and (4) respectively.

Applying the principles of law contained in the above-noted extracts the court held that on a trial for murder, unanimity in the jury's verdict for conviction is an essential part of the right to trial by jury and not a mere matter of procedure. Their Lordships further held that the High Court had no jurisdiction to entertain the appellant's motion because:

(a) no complaint had been made in the motion of the infringement of any fundamental rule of natural justice; and

(b) the error alleged in the motion is one of substantive law which arose out of the judgment of the trial and which may be set aside on appeal.

The Court of Appeal accordingly affirmed the decision of Brathwaite J and dismissed the appellant's appeal. The Court of Appeal later dismissed the appeal against sentence ('the criminal appeal').

Nanan subsequently appealed to the Judicial Committee of the Privy Council both in respect of the substantive criminal conviction for murder and the constitutional point raised above. The appeals – which were consolidated – were duly dismissed.[112]

General comments

This right to life has its origins in Art 2 of the European Convention on Human Rights which is almost in identical terms with the prevailing corresponding articles in the various West Indian constitutions. The European Court of Human Rights (ECtHR) has characterised the right as a fundamental one while the United Nations Human Rights Committee has termed it the 'supreme' right and one 'basic to all human rights'.

Article 6 of the Convention on Civil and Political Rights (CCPR) makes corresponding provision for the right to life, at the same time dealing with the death penalty which prohibits its imposition on persons under 18 and pregnant women. It also calls for its gradual abolition.

In respect of the right to life, the United Nations Human Rights Committee, in interpreting Art 6 of the CCPR, envisages a wider range of protection than that enunciated in our existing constitutions. It states that the right is supreme: no derogation therefrom being permitted even when a state of emergency threatens the nation. It also considers that the business of the State is to avert wars and to protect the citizenry from acts of genocide – to which end the State should be alert to follow trails relative to the disappearance of individuals. At the same time it puts squarely at the State's door the responsibility for introducing measures to avert malnutrition which, in turn, would minimise infant mortality to prevent epidemics, as well as to ban nuclear activity which should be recognised as a crime against humanity.[113] The committee has also considered that under Art 4 the right to life is not subject to derogation even in a time of emergency. The ECtHR has been active in this field since its creation. Thus, it has held that complaints

---

112 (1986) 35 WIR 358.

113 But, see the Canadian case *Operation Dismantle Inc et al v the Queen* [1985] 1 SCR 441, where there was a challenge to nuclear tests. The Supreme Court refused to treat the challenge as a violation of the right to life since the arguments put forward by the anti-cruise groups amounted to nothing but speculation. There was no clear evidence that the Cabinet's decision to test cruise missiles threatened the lives of specific individuals.

of infringement of this right may be brought by a spouse or the child of a deceased person and in a proper case even by a nephew.[114]

It has also been held that it is not necessary that death should have occurred.[115]

To safeguard the right to life, the State should provide and maintain proper medical care.[116]

The question as to whether an unborn child is 'a person' has also been considered in connection with this right and this is a question one must expect will sooner or later fall to be considered in our Caribbean jurisdictions.

Under existing UK legislation, an unborn child has no existence apart from its mother and is not 'a person' under the Abortion Act 1967. However, the European Commission considers there is a case for Art 2 of the European Convention to come to the aid of an unborn child.[117]

Death penalty

As we shall have a good deal to say on what has been held to be 'inhuman and degrading' punishment in connection with the death penalty, it is considered that we should examine briefly – by way of comparison – the way the European Convention on Human Rights has dealt with that issue.

Article 2(1) makes specific provision for the death penalty, but states that it should be abolished in peace time in those jurisdictions which have adopted the sixth protocol. The protocol appears as a convention right under the United Kingdom Human Rights Act 1998 which came into force in England in October 2000.

In their seminal work on Human Rights Law and Practice, Lord Lester and David Pannick,[118] the learned authors point out that, in cases of extradition or deportation cases, there is likely (now that the United Kingdom is a party to the Sixth Protocol) to be refusal under Art 3 to expel or deport an individual from the United Kingdom if the receiving State still retains the death penalty.[119] Any independent Caribbean territory is therefore likely to be affected in the future where it wishes the United Kingdom authorities to extradite one of its citizens accused of having committed such a serious crime in the receiving State.

---

114 See *Osman v UK* (1999) 1 FLR 193, ECHR.
115 Where, as in *Osman v UK*, above, there has been a persistent threat by a mentally disturbed person, resulting in the death of one of the parties threatened, the Article may be invoked by the surviving members of the same family.
116 See ECHR App 7154/75 *Association X v UK* (1978) 14 DR 31, p 32.
117 See *Open Door Counselling and Dublin Well Woman v Ireland* (1992) 15 EHRR 244, ECHR.
118 See, generally, Lester and Pannick, 1999.
119 *Soering v United Kingdom* (1989) 11 EHRR 439, ECHR.

E THE RIGHT TO PROTECTION FROM DEPRIVATION OF PROPERTY

The right to protection from deprivation of property is guaranteed under the fundamental rights and freedoms provisions of the constitutions of all the independent Member States for the Caribbean Community (CARICOM).[120] With the exception of Trinidad and Tobago, the relevant provision in these constitutions is generally in similar terms.

Under this heading we shall review in detail a selection of cases which were decided in the courts of six of the 12 independent jurisdictions in the community. As the *dicta* from one of these cases indicate, the meaning of 'property' in the relevant constitutional provisions to which we have referred has been clarified by judicial pronouncements and, at the present time, the word is given a broad scope. Indeed, the meaning of property has been extended to include money,[121] and this might explain aspects of property which our selected cases cover.

They include applications arising out of the compulsory acquisition or taking of property by the executive under an 'existing law' or post-Constitution legislative enactment; the demolition by State authorities of a house belonging to the applicant; the effect of legislative enactment on rents due to landlords; the effect of legislation on rights under existing contractual arrangements; and the effect of fiscal measures on taxpayers. All of these acts were alleged to have, in one way or another, contravened the individual's right to property protected by the respective constitutions. However, as we shall soon see, some of the applications were successful while others were not.

1 The *Grand Anse Estates* case

In *Grand Anse Estates Ltd v Governor General of Grenada and Others* (unreported),[122] the appellant appealed to the Court of Appeal of the West Indies Associated States Supreme Court against an order made by a judge of the High Court dismissing the appellant's application for a declaration that the compulsory acquisition of 25 acres of the appellant's land by the Government of Grenada was null and void, being contrary to s 6(1) of the Constitution. That section reads as follows:

> 6(1) No property of any description shall be compulsorily taken possession of, and no interest in or right over property of any description shall be compulsorily acquired, except where provision is made by a law applicable to that taking possession or acquisition for the prompt payment of full compensation.

In the court below, the trial judge had held that the relevant provisions of the Land Acquisition Ordinance[123] under which the appellant's land had been compulsorily acquired were 'adequate and satisfied the requirements' of s 6(1) of the Constitution.

---

120 Antigua (s 9), Bahamas (Art 27), Barbados (s 16), Belize (s 17), Dominica (s 6), Grenada (s 6), Guyana (Art 142), Jamaica (s 18), St Kitts (s 8), St Lucia (s 6), St Vincent (s 6) and Trinidad and Tobago (s 4(a)).

121 *IRC v Lilleyman et al* (1964) 7 WIR 496. See, also, *Harry v Thom* (1967) 10 WIR 348.

122 See judgment delivered on 7 October 1977 in Civil Appeal No 3 of 1976.

123 Cap 153 of the 1958 edition of the Laws of Grenada.

Before the Court of Appeal, counsel for the appellant argued that the exception to the prohibition in s 6(1) of the constitution laid down three pre-conditions, namely:

(a) a law applicable at time of acquisition in existence;

(b) there must be included in that law provision for prompt payment; and

(c) the compensation must be full;

and that unless all three pre-conditions were satisfied the acquisition infringed the Constitution and was therefore null and void.

The Court of Appeal examined the relevant provisions of the Land Acquisition Ordinance which was the law applicable to the acquisition in question. Their Lordships held that the sections of that ordinance[124] relating to the payment of compensation did not contravene s 6(1) of the Constitution since, in their view the procedure established by those sections of the ordinance contemplate prompt and ready action. On the other hand, the court held that s 19(a) of the ordinance, which provides that compensation for land compulsorily acquired should be assessed on the basis of its market value at a date 12 months prior to the date of the acquisition, did not provide for 'full compensation'. Similarly, s 21 of the ordinance which limited the payment of interest on the compensation award to 5% provided less than full compensation. In the words of St Bernard JA: 'Full compensation must mean a just equivalent of the land at the time of acquisition plus any loss incurred by such acquisition plus adequate interest to the date of payment.' Accordingly, the Court of Appeal held that ss 19(a) and 21 of the ordinance contravened s 6(1) of the Constitution.

However, although those sections of the ordinance were in contravention of the constitution, this did not mean that the acquisition itself was null and void as the appellant had contended. The Land Acquisition Ordinance was an 'existing law' within the meaning attributed to that expression in para 1(5) of Sched 2 to the Grenada Constitution Order 1973;[125] and, as provided by para 1(1) of that Schedule, should be 'construed with such modifications, adaptations, qualifications and exceptions as may be necessary to bring [it] into conformity with the Constitution'. Section 19(1) of the ordinance should therefore be construed as providing for the assessment of compensation based on the market value of the land at the date of its acquisition.

In like manner, s 21 of the Ordinance should be construed to enable interest to be paid 'at a rate applicable to give the expropriated owner a just equivalent of his loss at the time of the expropriation and not a rigid and fixed rate, whatever his loss may be'.

Having so held, the Court of Appeal allowed the appeal in part and ordered that the appellant was entitled to the payment of compensation from the date on which the land in question had vested in the Crown.

The typical Caribbean constitution shows no mercy to a legislature, be it the legislature of a poor developing territory or that of a relatively better-off developing State. Nor is the constitution, or more accurately the courts – the sentinels of the constitutions – concerned with the good motives of the legislature. For them, '[a] breach of a

---

124 *Ibid*, ss 6, 7, 8, 9 and 12.
125 SI 1973/2155 (UK).

constitutional restriction is not excused by good intentions with which the legislative power has been exceeded by the particular law'.[126]

2 The case of *Yearwood v AG of St Kitts/Nevis/Anguilla*

It is in this context that *Yearwood et al v AG of St Christopher, Nevis, Anguilla and Another*[127] falls to be considered.

In an attempt to revive the rapidly declining sugar industry which was vital to the economy of St Kitts, the Government of that State enacted the Sugar Estates' Lands Acquisition Act 1975,[128] which came into force on 28 January 1975. Section 2(1) of the Act provided, in these terms:

On the appointed day the lands forming part of the estates listed in the First Schedule shall be transferred to and vested in the Crown in right of the Government of the State, free from all mortgages, charges or incumbrances.

In addition, by virtue of s 3(2) of the Act, all machinery of any kind being used on the estate lands immediately before the date of transfer and vesting was transferred and vested in the Crown.

Under s 2(5) it was further provided that:

Where by reason of inadvertence, mistake or any other circumstance or for any other cause any piece, parcel or area of land which is at present or has been under sugar cane cultivation at any time has not been included in the First Schedule, the Minister may within eighteen months of the appointed day make regulations amending the First Schedule to include the said piece, parcel or area of land and the provision of this Act shall apply to any such amendment *mutatis mutandis* from the date of the said amendment.

Compensation was provided for in ss 4(2) and 5(6) of the Act in the following terms:

4(2) The aggregate compensation to be paid for the lands transferred under the provisions of Section 2(1) shall be determined on the basis of the commercial value at the 30th day of April 1972, which a purchaser would attribute to such lands as part of a commercial undertaking for the production of sugar cane matters ancillary, incidental and related thereto and shall not exceed ten million dollars.

5(6) Compensation in respect of the transferred interest shall be paid partly in cash and partly by means of

(a) Government bonds or other securities bearing interest at the rate of 10 percent per annum and maturing on a date not later than 10 years after the appointed day; or

(b) Instalments payable out of the profits of the sugar industry so however that interest at the rate of 10 percent per annum shall be paid on all outstanding balances and that all instalments shall have been paid not later than 10 years after the appointed day. Provided that the portion of compensation to be paid in cash shall not be less than 40 percent of the compensation payable in respect of the transferred interests

---

126 *Per* Lord Diplock in *Hinds v R* [1977] AC 195, p 226.

127 Suit No 8/1975 (St Kitts/Nevis/Anguilla).

128 Laws of St Christopher, Nevis, Anguilla, No 2 of 1975.

but the Minister may pay such cash portion in four equal consecutive annual instalments and no interest shall be payable on any such instalment.

Section 6 of the Act established a procedure for negotiations with a view to arriving at a settlement where the owner of any interest in the lands transferred under the Act and the Minister were unable to agree on the amount of compensation to which the owner was entitled. Section 7 of the Act purported to confer upon the owners a right of recourse to the High Court exercisable in cases where s 6 negotiations had failed to produce a settlement. However, this 'right of recourse' was exercisable 'within one year after the end of the negotiation period'. In addition, the section also provided that a 'claim for recovery of compensation shall be proceeded with as an action under the Crown Proceedings Ordinance[129] and in accordance with the Rules of the Supreme Court'.

In an attempt to cure some of the obvious defects in the Act, the State Legislature on 30 June 1975, passed an amendment to the Act, with retrospective effect. The particulars of the amending Act are not material for purposes of this discussion.

In their statement of claim the plaintiffs claimed, *inter alia*:

(1) A declaration that the whole Act is unconstitutional, void and of no effect, and;

(2) A declaration that ss 16 and 19 of the Crown Proceedings Ordinance (Cap 22) are inconsistent with and/or not in conformity with s 16 of the Constitution and are therefore void in so far as they–

(a) preclude the court from making orders, other than declaratory orders, against the Crown; and

(b) preclude the Court from granting injunctions or making orders to give relief against the Crown–

for the protection of the fundamental rights and freedoms set out in Chapter I of the Constitution.

The evidence and arguments in this section which came on for trial before Glasgow J, on 15 July 1975, extended over 53 days. In a lengthy reserved judgment delivered on 22 June 1977, the learned trial judge, after carefully analysing the evidence in the light of the relevant legal authorities, stated that it was essential to the validity of the principal Act that it should comply with the requirements of the constitution. He found that the Act had purported to enact provisions for the compulsory acquisition of property and had prescribed the principles on which, and the manner in which, compensation therefor was to be determined and given. In his opinion, however, the principal Act failed to comply with the requirements of s 6 of the Constitution in that:

(a) it placed a limit on the amount of compensation payable for all of the lands acquired, and provided that compensation should be payable otherwise than in money. Moreover, it failed to prescribe the manner in which compensation, as contemplated by s 6 of the Constitution, was to be determined and given;

---

129 Laws of Saint Christopher, Nevis and Anguilla, Cap 22.

(b) the principles prescribed did not ensure that what was determined as payable for the property acquired was a just equivalent compensation in money for the property of which the owners were to be deprived;

(c) no provision was made in the Act for the assessment or payment of compensation in respect of the 'subsisting rights' referred to in s 3(1); and

(d) the effect of ss 5, 6 and 7 thereof was to deny or delay unreasonably the exercise of the right of direct access to the High Court for the remedies which s 6(2) of the constitution gives to every person having an interest in or right over property which was compulsorily taken possession of, or whose interest in or right over any property was compulsorily acquired.

For the foregoing reasons the judge held that the principal Act was 'unconstitutional, void and of no effect'.

With respect to the amending Act, here is how the judge expressed himself:

> If I am right in holding that the principal Act is unconstitutional, void and of no effect, I feel constrained to hold also that it is not competent to the Legislature to amend the principal Act. I am of the opinion that the power given the Legislature by section 41(4) of the constitution to make laws with retrospective effect applies only to laws validly made, and not to laws purporting to amend unconstitutional laws retrospectively. In this connexion, I respectfully agree with Wanchoo, J, who delivered the judgment of the Indian Supreme Court in *Mahendra Lal Jaini v The State of Uttar Pradesh and Others (supra)* when he said at page 929:
>
> > It is in our opinion absolutely elementary that the constitutionality of an Act must be judged on the basis of the Constitution as it was on the date the Act was passed, subject to any retrospective amendment of the Constitution.
>
> In my view, nothing but an appropriate retrospective amendment of the Constitution can make the principal Act constitutional. There has been no such amendment of the Constitution.
>
> If I am wrong in holding that the amending Act is incapable of curing the unconstitutionality of the principal Act, it is necessary to examine the principal Act as amended by the amending Act, with a view to deciding whether it is constitutional, or whether it is unconstitutional, void and of no effect as alleged on behalf of the plaintiffs.

Glasgow J, then conducted a detailed examination of the amending Act and concluded that 'both the principal Act and the principal Act as purportedly amended by the amending Act are unconstitutional, void and of no effect'. He accordingly granted the declaration which the plaintiffs had sought with respect to the Act. However, he rejected the plaintiff's claim for a declaration that ss 16 and 19 of the Crown Proceedings Ordinance were inconsistent with s 16 of the Constitution and was therefore void since, in his view, that ordinance was not affected by ss 16(2) and 103(1) of the Constitution.

3 The case of *Krakash Singh v AG of Trinidad and Tobago*

The case of *Krakash Singh v AG of Trinidad and Tobago*[130] must now be considered. In that case, the applicant sought a declaration that the demolition, by the servants or agents of

---

130 Suit No 2443/1982 (High Court).

the State, of the wooden house erected on lands tenanted to him by one Dharam Singh constituted a contravention of his right to enjoyment of his property and the right not to be deprived thereof except by due process of law. The applicant further contended that the action of the State contravened his right to respect for his private and family life and the right to equality before the law.[131]

The main submission by counsel for the applicant was that the State Lands Act[132] and the Land Acquisition Act[133] give the citizen an expectation of civilized behaviour on the part of the State and are 'settled practice'.[134] Support for this proposition was sought from *Thornhill v AG of Trinidad and Tobago*.[135] On the other hand, the main argument for the respondent was that the onus was on the applicant to show that he had a right to possession of the land, which he had failed to do by virtue of the fact that the person whom he claimed to be his landlord no longer had a right to possession: the land having been acquired by the State. A further submission by counsel for the respondent was that since the land in question belonged to the State it was merely exercising its ordinary rights as owner and consequently no constitutional remedy lies against the State.[136] In this respect, reliance was placed on the Indian case of *Dhirenda Kumar v State of West Bengal*,[137] which authority was rejected by the learned judge on the ground that the wording of the provision of the Indian Constitution concerned with rights to property is different from that in the Trinidad and Tobago Constitution, 'and also on the ground that the Constitutions themselves',[138] were different.

Having rejected the submission advanced on behalf of the respondent, Deyalsingh J, proceeded to examine the main question arising from the submissions made on behalf of the applicant, that question being whether the applicant had brought himself within the meaning of the provisions which guaranteed the individual's right to property. The judge's conclusion was in the affirmative in view of the fact that the applicant had a right to protection of his property, which was demolished otherwise than by way of due process of law. In the opinion of the judge, the State failed to follow the 'settled practice' prescribed by the State Lands Act for the removal of squatters on State lands.[139] Accordingly, on the authority of *Thornhill v AG of Trinidad and Tobago*, since the settled practice existed prior to the constitution, it was now recognised as a right thereunder which right excludes the remedy of self-help at common law.[140]

What is interesting about this decision and the decision in the *Thornhill* case is that one is left to speculate as to the extent of new rights that may have existed before the constitution that could attach to one of the new rights specified in the Bill of Rights. It is

---

131 Suit No 2443/1982 (High Court), 1.
132 Revised Laws of Trinidad and Tobago, Ch 57:01.
133 *Ibid*, Ch 58:01.
134 Suit No 2443/1982, 6.
135 [1981] AC 61.
136 Suit No 2443/1982, 7.
137 (1956) Cal Rep 437.
138 Suit No 2443/1982, 10.
139 *Ibid*, p 14.
140 WIR 498.

submitted that we must give careful thought to what is in fact 'settled practice' and ask ourselves how, for example, 'settled practice' is brought to an end.

4 The case of *Morgan v AG of Trinidad and Tobago*

In *Morgan v AG of Trinidad and Tobago*,[141] it was sought to impugn an Act of Parliament, not because land was compulsorily acquired, but because the effect of the legislation was to reduce the income of the applicant which he derived from a rental of part of his dwelling house.

In this case, the applicant, a retired pensioner, owned a house at San Juan in the Republic of Trinidad and Tobago and rented part thereof on a monthly basis. By virtue of the Rent Restriction (Dwelling Houses) Act 1981, the rental obtained by the applicant was reduced from $500 to $150 per month. Faced with this substantial reduction in the main source of his income, the applicant sought an order for a declaration that the Rent Restriction (Dwelling Houses) Act 1981 was null and void on the ground that the Act constituted an unwarranted invasion of his rights and freedoms, including the right to enjoy his property and the right not to be deprived thereof except by due process. A further ground was that the Act could not be reasonably justified in a society that has a proper respect for the rights and freedoms of the individual.

Counsel for the applicant rested his main submission on those provisions of the Constitution guaranteeing a right to property and the right not to be deprived thereof except by due process of law, equality before the law and protection of the law. This submission was made by counsel although the Act had been passed in accordance with s 13(1) of the Constitution of the Republic of Trinidad and Tobago by a three-fifths majority in each House of Parliament. Counsel further submitted that the Act was arbitrary in its effect, having reduced rents to the level obtaining in December 1978.

Section 13(1) of the Constitution, while permitting Acts of Parliament to be passed that would abrogate guaranteed rights, has an important qualification: this qualification being that an Act so passed would have effect 'unless the Act is shown not to be reasonably justifiable in a society that has a proper respect for the rights and freedoms of the individual'. As the trial judge, Des Isles J, very properly concluded: 'It is on this last provision that the whole question turns.'[142] A further submission by counsel for the applicant was that ss 3 and 4 of the Act had the effect of depriving the landlord of money which was passed on to the tenant without payment of compensation, some measure of support for this proposition (according to him) being found in the *Prakash Seereeram*[143] and the *Lilleyman*[144] cases. In both these cases, the impugned legislation was held to have violated the property rights section of the Trinidad and Tobago and British Guiana Constitutions, respectively.

The contention of counsel for the respondent was that the onus lay upon the applicant to show that the legislation *was not reasonably justifiable in the society and that the legislation*

---

141 Suit No 4304/1982 (High Court). See, also, (1987) 36 WIR 396 where the Privy Council upheld the High Court and the Court of Appeal of Trinidad and Tobago and dismissed the appeal.

142 *Ibid*, p 6.

143 (1975) 27 WIR 329.

144 (1964) 7 WIR 496.

could not be struck down unless the applicant had succeeded in discharging that duty. He had failed in that duty and since all the applicant had done was to prove that he personally had been adversely affected, the legislation could not be declared unconstitutional. For this proposition reliance was place upon the Indian case of *Mohammed Haniff Quareshi v State of Bihar.* In that case, the applicants, whose religious persuasion was Muslim, attacked the validity of certain enactments banning the slaughter of cows and other animals, SR Das CJ, in the course of delivering his judgment, made the following statement:[145]

> It is left to the Court to determine the reasonableness of the restrictions imposed by the Law. In determining that question the Court cannot proceed on a general notion of what is reasonable in the abstract. What the Court has to do is to consider whether the restrictions imposed are reasonable in the interest of the general public.

This was the gravamen of the respondent's case. Was it reasonably justifiable that the rental paid by 80,000 tenants in Trinidad and Tobago should be regulated downwards even though landlords would suffer some financial loss? In making this submission counsel for the respondent relied on the Nigerian case of *Chernaci v Chernaci*,[146] in which the court was required to rule upon certain restrictions placed on children in respect of political activity and to examine whether the restrictions were reasonably justifiable against the background of guaranteed constitutional freedoms of conscience, expression, peaceful assembly and association. It was held that the freedoms of expression, peaceful assembly and association were infringed by the legislation after an analysis of the question as to whether the restrictions were reasonably justifiable. In reaching that conclusion the Nigerian Court formulated the following guidelines:

(a) 'there is a presumption that the legislature has acted within the constitution and that the law in question is necessary and reasonably justifiable'; and

(b) the impugned restriction may be considered to be reasonably justifiable if it is necessary in the interest of public morals and public order and must not be excessive or out of proportion with its objectives.

This is what the trial judge had to say on the matter of the onus of proof[147] in this Trinidad case:

> This Court has carefully considered the submissions made on the evidence by affidavit on behalf of the applicant and the respondent as well as those made on the Law and I regret that I cannot agree with the submission of Counsel for the respondent to the effect that the plaintiff has failed to discharge the high onus. All that the plaintiff has to do in my respectful view is to show that he has been adversely affected by the roll-back of his rent and then to demonstrate from the said Act itself that a section of the society has been similarly affected. This is my view he has done.

The judge did not in any way address the very question which he indicated had to be determined, viz, whether it was reasonably justifiable that the persons affected by the legislation should be so affected. This question could only be determined by most cogent

---

145 (1958) 45 AIR 731.
146 (1960) Northern Region of Nigeria Law Reports 24.
147 (1987) 36 WIR 396.

evidence, but the judge had no such evidence on which he could hold (as he did) that the law was not so reasonably justifiable.

The Attorney General, very properly, appealed to the Court of Appeal against the finding of the trial judge.

The Court of Appeal (Kelsick CJ, Hassanali and Brathwaite JJA) had no difficulty in reversing the trial judge's finding that the Rent Restriction (Dwelling Houses) Act 1981 was not reasonably justifiable in a society that has a proper respect for the rights and freedoms of the individual.[148]

Brathwaite JA who delivered the principal judgment, after reciting at length the two principal affidavits (on which the trial judge based his judgment), made the following pronouncement on the conduct of the matter at first instance:

> It is surprising but perhaps significant that neither party to the proceedings sought leave to cross-examine the other on the contents of the affidavits. It must therefore be assumed that both sides admitted the facts deposed to in those affidavits. One would have thought that in a case where the questions involved were of such fundamental importance to the nation as a whole that a thorough investigation of the facts deposed to in the affidavits would have been undertaken by the parties or at least instigated by the judge. As it was, the judge had before him as the evidence in the motion the unchallenged sworn statement on behalf of both parties.
>
> It seems clear to me that the only question which the judge was asked to decide was whether the Act was one 'which was shown not to be reasonably justifiable in a society that has a proper respect for the rights and freedoms of the individual'. Admittedly the onus was on the respondent.

In the view of Brathwaite JA, it appeared that, at the hearing at first instance, counsel for both parties had assumed that sub-ss (a), (b) and (d) of s 4 of the Trinidad Constitution had been contravened in respect of the respondent, the applicant in the court below; but as the learned appeal court judge pointed out, the combined effect of sub-ss (1) and (2) of s 13 is that, once a Bill has been passed by the House of Representatives and the Senate, as required by these sections (and the Act so specifically declares) 'even though its provisions may violate the rights of the individual enshrined by sections 4 and 5 of the Constitution, *the Act becomes effectual and the onus to rebut the presumption of effectuality* rests on the respondent'. It was not therefore for the Attorney General to prove the constitutionality of the Act, as he endeavoured to do in the Court of Appeal by requesting permission to amend the three grounds he had originally listed as his grounds of appeal by adding a fourth, viz:

> (d) that the decision of the learned trial judge was wrong in that the Rent Restriction (Dwelling Houses) Act 1981 does not violate any fundamental rights and freedoms of the Applicant/Respondent guaranteed by the Republican Constitution of Trinidad and Tobago 1976.

All the judges of the Court of Appeal after reserving the right of disallowing this ground at the conclusion of argument thereon duly disallowed the application for that ground to

---

148 Trinidad and Tobago Civil Appeal No 11 of 1983, judgment dated 28 February 1984.

be included in the Notice of Appeal on the basis that it was an afterthought that arose subsequent to the filing of the Notice of Appeal.

It was, however, quite unnecessary for the Attorney General to add any other ground to those stated to his Notice of Appeal, as ground (c) was enough to dispose of the matter. That ground was 'that the learned judge misdirected himself and was wrong in law in his determination of the question on whom the onus of proof lies and the nature and extent of the onus to be discharged'.

It will be recalled that the trial judge had made the following statement of the onus lying on the applicant:

> All that the plaintiff has to do in my respectful view is to show that he has been adversely affected by the roll back of his rent to that of 31st December, 1978, and then to demonstrate from this said Act itself that a section of the society has been similarly affected. This in my view he has done.

In support of this statement, the judge had referred to Basu's *Commentary on the Constitution of India*, as well as two judgments of the Supreme Court of India, but, as Brathwaite JA pointed out:

> Great care must be taken before the learning set out in the judgments of the Supreme Court of India and the commentaries thereon are adopted or applied to the interpretation and construction of the Constitution of Trinidad and Tobago, and in particular with reference to the interpretation of section 13(1) of the Constitution of Trinidad and Tobago, if for no other reason than that there is no similar provision in the Constitution of India.

Brathwaite JA then quoted a further statement from the judgment of the trial judge, viz:

> I wish most respectfully to adopt these words of the learned author [Basu] and to hold that the moment the applicant showed, in support of his contention of unreasonableness, that he had been adversely affected and demonstrated from the said Act that a group of society had been similarly affected, he had discharged his onus and it is for the Court to say whether the legislation was reasonably justifiable in a society such as ours, after hearing the State who, after all, is in a much better position to justify its actions with all the information at its command, than the applicant.

In the opinion of Brathwaite JA, once again the learned trial judge fell into error in coming to the conclusions he did:

> [I]t would make a nonsense of the provisions of the subsections if they are interpreted to mean 'from the moment the applicant showed that he had been adversely affected and demonstrated from the said Act that a group of society has been similarly affected, he had discharged his onus.

Brathwaite JA further charged that the judge had misdirected himself by relying on guidelines laid down in *Chernaci v Chernaci*[149] and on *Mohammed Haniff Quareshi v State of Bihar*:[150]

> He adopted the wrong guidelines in determining the question on whom the onus of proof lay and the nature and extent of the proof to be discharged and his conclusions were coloured and directed accordingly.

---

149 (1960) Northern Region of Nigeria Law Reports 24.
150 (1958) 45 AIR 731.

On this ground alone the appeal was unanimously allowed.

All the members of the court also drew attention to the fact that there was no material whatever on which the trial judge could have arrived at the conclusion that 'the group of persons adversely affected by the Act are the landlords who can least afford to be so affected'.

In the words of the Chief Justice:

> The evidence of personal hardship suffered by the applicant falls far short of the requisite standard of proof. There is no evidence as to the extent of the numbers of landlords affected or as to their financial positions or as to the extent of the pecuniary loss suffered by them generally as a class; nor as to what was a fair and equitable rent for the premises.

> On the other hand the Attorney General had adduced evidence (which he was not obliged to do) to establish that the Act passes the justifiable test in the proviso. He advanced these propositions:

> The object of the Act is to protect 80,000 tenants by regulating the rents of their dwelling houses and avoiding unreasonable evictions.

> The loss to the applicant disclosed by the evidence on balance is far outweighed by the financial relief afforded to substantial parts of the community at a time of rising inflation and dramatic increases in rent in order to ensure that a large number of tenants and their families are satisfied with the basic needs of shelter and are not rendered homeless.

> The Act is in tune with similar enactments in other common law jurisdictions and with the Rent Restrictions Act Cap 59:50 which reproduces the Rent Registration Ordinance Ch 27 No 18, that was first enacted in 1920. Such legislation affords relief to tenants where the landlord and tenant laws due to changing conditions operate harshly on the tenants.

> The confinement of the Act to a class of tenancies where the rent falls below a prescribed figure is common form.

> The laws for the protection of tenants against landlords are a feature of progressive states.

There can be no doubt that the decision of the Court of Appeal in this case is the correct one and the members of that court deserve the highest commendation for the lucidity of their pronouncements no less than for the judicial restraint exercised in the course of overruling the learned trial judge. On this occasion, it is good that the Chief Justice could, in his judgment, remind the learned trial judge that:

(a) the legislation is in keeping with the socio-economic principles enunciated in recital (b) of the Preamble to the constitution [which refers to the fact that the people of Trinidad and Tobago respect the principles of social justice and therefore believe that the operation of the economic system should result in the material resources of the community being so distributed as to subserve the common good [and] that there should be adequate means of livelihood for all]; and

(b) the Act is the expression of the will of the substantial majority of the elected representatives of the people to which great weight must be attached.

The Privy Council in a short judgment entirely agreed with the Court of Appeal below. As stated above, the courts, in enforcing the protective provision against deprivation of property without compensation, have tended to give a somewhat liberal interpretation to the concept of property. The two cases which immediately follow provide a good illustration of the courts' approach when considering matters of this nature. In both cases, the applicants' constitutional approach was successful in persuading the courts that their rights under certain contractual arrangements had been contravened by enactments of their respective state legislatures.

5 The case of *AG of St Kitts/Nevis v Edmund Lawrence*

In *AG of the State of Saint Christopher and Nevis v Lawrence*,[151] the appellant appealed to the Court of Appeal of the West Indies Associated Supreme Court from a decision of the High Court judge, Bishop J, who had granted the respondent a declaration that the St Kitts/Nevis/Anguilla National Bank Ltd (Special Provisions) Act 1982 was unconstitutional, void and of no effect, since it contravened the fundamental right to protection from deprivation of property under s 6 of the Constitution.[152] The learned trial judge had also granted to the respondent certain ancillary and consequential relief which are not relevant for the purposes of our discussion.

The respondent's application in the court below was instituted under the provisions of s 16(1) of the Constitution which provides a procedure for enforcing the protective provisions of the Constitution.[153]

The facts of the case, which the Court of Appeal found to be not seriously in dispute, may be stated briefly. The respondent, who in 1970 had been appointed Managing Director of the St Kitts Industrial Bank Ltd, had been an employee of the bank continuously from the date of its incorporation in 1958. By the resolution of the board of directors appointing him as managing director, *it was agreed that he should hold that office until he resigned or if he ceased to be a director of the bank.* On 15 February 1971, the bank changed its name to St Kitts/Nevis/Anguilla National Bank Ltd and the respondent became its managing director and chairman of the board of directors.

On 8 March 1982, the State Legislature enacted the St Kitts/Nevis/Anguilla National Bank Ltd (Special Provisions) Act 1982 ('the Act'). The Bill for the Act was taken through all three legislative stages, received the Governor's assent and became law on the same day. On that day, too, the respondent received a letter signed by the Minister of Finance informing him that a new board of directors had been appointed in consequence of the Act and that former directors had ceased to hold office. This letter purported to remove the respondent from the office of director of the board of the bank.

On the same day, with the assistance of members of the State police force, the respondent was ejected from the bank's premises. No arrangement was made *for the payment of remuneration or compensation to the respondent and the Act itself was silent on this point.*

---

151 See Judgment of Peterkin CJ, in (1983) 31 WIR 176.

152 '6(1) No property of any description shall be compulsorily taken possession of, and no interest in or right over property of any description shall be compulsorily acquired, except by or under the provisions of a law that prescribes the principles on which and the manner in which compensation therefor is to be determined and given.'

153 '16(1) If any person alleges that any of the provisions of sections 2 to 15 (inclusive) of this Constitution has been, is being or is likely to be contravened in relation to him then, without prejudice to any other action with respect to the same matter which is lawfully available, that person may apply to the High Court for redress.'

In considering this appeal, their Lordships articulated the following well established principles:

> In determining the question of constitutionality of a statute, what the Court is concerned with is the competence of the legislature to make it and not its wisdom or motives. The Court has to examine its provisions in the light of the relevant provisions in the Constitution. The presumption is always in favour of the constitutionality of an enactment, and the burden is upon him who attacks it to show that there has been a clear transgression of the constitutional principles.

The court adopted the learned trial judge's interpretation of the impugned Act which they regarded as fair and accurate and then went on to consider two of the points argued before their Lordships. They regarded these as forming the heart of the matter to be decided.

The first question related to the *locus standi* of the respondent under s 16(1) of the Constitution: whether the respondent on the facts can allege an infringement of s 6(1) of the Constitution in relation to himself. The second question related to the property which the respondent alleged was compulsorily acquired or taken contrary to s 6(1) of the Constitution.

With respect to the second question their Lordships considered the relevant authorities[154] on this matter concluded that, although in matters of this kind earlier judgments tended to construe the word 'property' restrictively, the matter has, however, been clarified by judicial pronouncements and the word property is now given a broad scope. In our jurisdiction it has been extended to include money.

They found that s 6(1) of the Constitution applies equally to concrete as well as abstract rights of property and that management was an important incident of holding property. They accordingly adopted the learned trial judge's conclusion that the property right of which the respondent was deprived (viz, his rights under his contractual arrangements with the bank) fell within the purview of s 6(1) of the Constitution – even though that management right was an abstract one.

With regard to the other question the court held that the Act had, on 8 March 1982, purported automatically to dismiss all the directors of the bank (including the respondent) and this gave the respondent the right to bring an application seeking redress for contravention of his 'property' under the relevant constitutional provisions.

The Court of Appeal accordingly affirmed the decision of the trial judge and dismissed the appeal.

6 The *Gulf Rental* case

In the Barbados case of *Gulf Rental Ltd v Evelyn and Carvallho*,[155] a provision of the Landlord and Tenant (Registration of Tenancies) Act[156] was challenged on constitutional grounds. The Act provides a scheme for the registration of premises that are rented and

---

154 (1) *Chiranjit Lal v India* (1951) AIR, SC 41; (2) *Dwarka v Sholapur Mills* (1954) AIR, SC 119; (3) *IRC and AG (of Guyana) v Lilleyman and Others* (1964) 7 WIR 496.

155 Suit No 538/1982 (Barbados).

156 Cap 230A of the Revised Laws of Barbados.

by s 17 a surcharge is imposed on tenants at a rate to be prescribed by the Minister responsible for finance. The Act has numerous legislative devices to ensure that the scheme for the registration works and (more importantly) that the surcharge is paid and collected.[157] One such device is contained in s 14 of the Act, which provides as follows:

> Where a tenant pays rent to a landlord in respect of premises that are not registered under this Act, the tenant is entitled to a refund of the entire amount paid by him as rent during the period that the premises remain unregistered and the tenant may recover such amount as a debt in civil proceedings before a magistrate, notwithstanding that the amount sought to be recovered exceeds the normal monetary limit on the jurisdiction of the Magistrate Courts.

This case arose out of the fact that the plaintiff claimed that his premises were at all material times validly registered while the defendants' contended that the premises were not registered in respect of any period and that, by virtue of s 14 of the Act, they were entitled to set off against any amount due to the plaintiff the amount paid when the premises were not registered. Accordingly, the plaintiff instituted proceedings under s 24 of the Constitution, claiming arrears of rent due and a declaration that the premises were at all times validly registered. Further, or alternatively, the plaintiff also claimed a declaration that s 14 of the Act contravened the plaintiff's right under ss 11 and 16(1) of the Constitution of Barbados and therefore ought to be severed.[158]

Williams J (as he was) before whom the matter was heard, brought his usual erudite and learned approach to the whole issue. He began his judgment on this vital note:[159]

> The authorities are unanimous that there is a presumption in favour of the constitutionality of every statute and the onus is on the person challenging a statute to show that it is unconstitutional.

Having examined *dicta* in a number of authorities, he continued:[160]

> I propose to proceed on the following lines. Section 14 is presumed to be constitutional and the onus is on the plaintiff to show that it is not. I must approach the constitutional question with due appreciation of the importance of the matter; and I must not hold the section to be unconstitutional unless I am convinced that it does violate the Constitution.

The judge interpreted s 16(1) of the Constitution of Barbados to mean that one should not be deprived of one's property against one's will;[161] and came to the conclusion that s 14 of the Act was capable of depriving a person of his property (in this instance, money) against that person's will.

It was determined that the refund of rent required by s 14 of the Act could not be brought within the exception specified in s 16(2)(a)(i) of the Constitution whereby property could be taken in satisfaction of any 'tax, duty, rate, cess or other impost'. This, as the learned judge saw it, was because the refund did not go into the public revenue but

---

157 Cap 230A of the Revised Laws of Barbados, ss 3–8, 12, 13, 15. Also, see Suit No 538/1982, pp 10, 18.
158 Suit No 538/1982, p 7.
159 *Ibid*, p 14.
160 *Ibid*, p 16.
161 *Ibid*, p 17.

to the tenants for their private purposes and therefore lacked the public purpose element of a tax.[162]

With respect to s 16(2)(a)(ii) of the Constitution, whereby property may be taken 'under the authority of a law by way of penalty for breach of the law or forfeiture in consequence of a breach of the law', Williams J stated:

> This is the crucial question in this case the answer is not to be determined by reference to whether or not the penalty or forfeiture is for a public purpose [but] involves making a judgment on all the circumstances of the case.[163]

He then posed a further question:

> Is section 14 really and truly a provision enacted in the public interest or is it essentially a violation of the provisions of the Constitution for the protection of the property rights of the citizen?[164]

In the circumstances, Williams J determined the 'crucial question' as follows:[165]

> Parliament has power, subject to the provision of the Constitution, to make laws for the good government of Barbados. It has power to impose taxes and to legislate for the regulation and enforcement of its taxing provisions. Those powers are given to Parliament in the public interest. But at the same time Parliament's powers are circumscribed by the provisions of section 16(1) which are designed for the protection of the property of all persons. The provisions of section 14 of the Act are part of the machinery designed by the statute to force landlords to comply with its provisions. The section is presumed to be constitutional but the crucial question is whether it is so arbitrary, excessive or unreasonable as to compel to the conclusion that it does not involve the exertion of powers incidental to taxation but constitutes in substance and effect the direct execution of the forbidden power of deprivation without compensation or is the court satisfied that no reasonable member of Parliament who understood correctly the meaning of sections 11, 16 and 48(1) of the Constitution would have supposed that the provisions of section 14 of the Act were reasonably required for the implementation of the scheme of taxation laid down by the Act?

The learned judge answered the question posed in this manner:[166]

> The way in which section 14 operates, and the fact that refunds under the section are required to be made without limit as to the amount payable or the period in respect of which the refunds are to be made compels me to the view that the section is arbitrary and excessive. It is in essence confiscatory, not regulatory, and in my judgment violates the Constitution.

Accordingly, the plaintiff was granted a declaration that s 14 ought to be severed.

The author takes respectful issue with Williams J in his decision in this case to strike down s 14 of the Act, which he ruled should be severed from the rest of the Landlord and Tenant (Registration of Tenancies) Act 1977. The parliament of any country must surely be in a position to judge the necessity of making statutory provision of the kind being considered here, under which a defaulting landlord is penalised for failing to comply

---

162 Suit No 538/1982, p 18.
163 *Ibid*, pp 18–19.
164 *Ibid*, p 19.
165 *Ibid*, pp 20–21.
166 Suit No 538/1982, p 21.

with the provision to register. It was clearly not for a judge to decide that this particular section is void and of no effect on the ground that refunds are to be made to the tenant, 'without limit as to amount payable or the period in respect of which the refunds are to be made'. Indeed, as far as the period is concerned, the section states clearly that the tenant is entitled to a refund of the entire amount paid by him as rent during the period *that the premises remain unregistered* and the writer therefore finds it difficult to follow the holding of the judge on this point. It seems clear that the learned judge – whose judgments are usually very sound and with whose rulings one disagrees with great reluctance – is guilty of a conceptual lapse in this case which clearly does not involve the issue of *an acquisition of property* so much as a *regulation of contract*. Surely, it would, for example, be within the competence of Government to prescribe that any lease of property not registered shall be void and the tenant shall be entitled to receive a refund of all rents paid thereunder? Such regulation is a *matter of policy* to be determined by the *executive and the legislature*. It is *not*, with respect, one for action or a ruling by the *judiciary*.

7 *Revere Jamaica Alumina* case

The case of *Revere Jamaica Alumina Ltd v AG of Jamaica*[167] raises many issues concerning both the legislature and the executive. Following the enactment of the Bauxite (Production Levy) Act 1974, and the Mining (Amendment No 2) Act 1974, the plaintiff contended that these enactments violated an agreement between itself and the government. This agreement was for a period of 25 years and, by virtue of cls 12 and 13, the Government agreed not to impose any further taxes and royalties for the duration of the agreement.[168]

Under the Bauxite (Production Levy) Act 1974, a tax by way of a levy was imposed on all bauxite and laterite extracted or won in Jamaica after 1 January 1974. Further, by virtue of the Mining (Amendment) Act 1974, the minister was empowered to prescribe minimum amounts of minerals that must be extracted during the period prescribed.

In the circumstances, the plaintiff company sought declarations *inter alia* that the Acts in issue were *ultra vires* s 18 of the Constitution of Jamaica[169] since they deprived it of its contractual and proprietary rights under the agreement and, in addition, the tax amounted to a compulsory acquisition of an interest in or right over property within the meaning of the said s 18.

---

167 Unreported Suit No CL 1976/R004 (Jamaica).
168 *Ibid*, pp 3–4.
169 '18(1) No property of any description shall be compulsorily taken possession of and no interest in or right over property of any description shall be compulsorily acquired except by or under the provisions of a law that–
(a) prescribes the principles on which and the manner in which compensation therefor is to be determined and given; and
(b) secures to any person claiming an interest in or right over such property a right of access to a court for the purpose of –
(i) establishing such interest or right (if any);
(ii) determining the amount of such compensation (if any) to which he is entitled; and
(iii) enforcing his right to any such compensation.'

At the trial of his action, it was submitted by the Attorney General that the purported agreement was not intended to create and could not create any enforceable legal obligation as to future taxation. The Attorney General further contended that to the extent that the agreement purported to fetter future governmental action in matters affecting the welfare of the State, no contractual rights could be created in respect to such matters, as this would be contrary to public policy.[170] This latter submission was based on the doctrine of 'executive necessity' as laid down in *Rederiaktiebolaget Amphitrite v R*.[171]

One of the main issues that had to be determined, in view of the submissions of the plaintiff and respondent, was whether under s 2A of the Bauxite and Alumina Industries (Encouragement) (Amendment) Act, expanding the bauxite industry, the Minister could bind the Government as to future taxation and royalties.

On this first issue, Smith CJ was of the view that:[172]

Neither the Executive nor the Minister, acting on its behalf, can validly give such an undertaking as was given in clause 12 without express parliamentary authority. No such authority is given in section 2A or elsewhere.

In my judgment, the undertaking was invalid and, therefore, created no valid contractual right in favour of the plaintiff.

With regard to the applicability of the doctrine of executive necessity (the *Amphitrite* principle), the Chief Justice's ruling was as follows:[173]

It is clear on the authorities that the *Amphitrite* principle applies to this case as well. As I understand the authorities, the principle is not limited to the fettering of prerogative powers of the Executive, as the argument for the plaintiff seems to suggest, but extends also the statutory powers. The right to be paid royalties is a right vested in the Executive for public purposes. The power to fix the rates was delegated to the Minister, who must remain free to exercise the power from time to time as the public interest demands. He cannot, therefore, validly undertake not to exercise it. The undertaking in clause 12 in respect of royalties, therefore, conferred no enforceable right on the plaintiff.

The other main issue for determination was whether the bauxite levy was a tax, so as to be in legal alignment with one of the exceptions to s 18 of the Constitution: the relevant exception, as provided for in s 18(2)(a) being that property could be taken 'in satisfaction of any tax, rate or due'.

In this regard four grounds were advanced in support of the contention that the levy was not a tax within s 18(2)(a) of the Constitution.

The first ground was that there was no statutory limitation on the purposes for which the tax collected may be applied.[174] This ground was rejected by the Chief Justice who said that the levy was 'paid into a fund over which the House of Representatives exercises full control'.[175]

---

170 Constitution of Jamaica, ss 9–20.
171 [1921] 3 KB 500, *per* Rowlett J.
172 Suit No CL 1976/R004, pp 15–16; (1980) 31 WIR 304.
173 Suit No CL 1976/R004, 18.
174 *Ibid*, p 19. In this regard, *Mootoo v AG of Trinidad and Tobago*, below, was distinguished on the ground that there was no parliamentary control in that case.
175 Suit No CL 1976/R004, p 23.

The second ground was that the levy was not a tax but 'in pith and substance a royalty'. This contention was likewise rejected. As the Chief Justice saw it:[176]

> Once the levy fulfils the normal requirements of a tax, as I have held it does, the plaintiff's contention on this ground is bound to fail because it then becomes irrelevant whether or not the tax has characteristics of a royalty. The pith and substance principle is inapplicable in a case where, as here, the legislative power which is challenged is unrestricted.

The third ground upon which the levy was challenged was that the levy constituted an arbitrary confiscation of property since, in so far as it is based on actual production, it is part of a scheme of legislation empowering the Minister to fix minimum quantities of production, which then become a condition of the mining lease, for breach of which the Minister could revoke the mining lease, although a lease is a proprietary right within s 18(1) of the Constitution.[177] In respect of this challenge, the ruling was as follows:[178]

> It is sufficient to state that the evidence established that the minimum quantity of production prescribed for the plaintiff's plant was well within its capacity.

The fourth challenge raised against the levy was that if it was payable during any quarterly or annual period during which the producer is not in actual production, the levy is arbitrary and confiscatory and constitutes the compulsory acquisition of property without compensation, contrary to s 18(1) of the Constitution.[179] On this issue, the Chief Justice had this to say:[180]

> Once the liability is imposed on persons or companies with the means and capacity to produce, the levy cannot be said to be arbitrary and confiscatory. A company cannot validly complain if it can produce but, for reasons peculiar to that company, it does not. Where it does not produce for reasons beyond its control, the Act has given the power to the Minister, in s 6, to waive, remit or refund payment of the production levy if he is satisfied that it is just and equitable to do so.

In the final result, except for a declaration that no production levy is payable for any annual period during which there is no actual production of bauxite or laterite, the plaintiff did not obtain either damages or the declaration sought.

There is no doubt that this case has been correctly decided, but there is one minor criticism that can be levelled at the decision, viz, that the learned Chief Justice, in saying that neither the executive nor the Minister can validly give an undertaking as was given in cl 12 of the agreement without express parliamentary authority, may have given the impression that if s 2A of the Bauxite and Alumina Industry (Encouragement) (Amendment) Act, 1967, had in fact authorised the Minister to bind Parliament for 25 years then that would have been binding in law. Consequently, one is led to assume that the case could have been differently decided on that point. The constitutional reality, as the author sees it, is that under our controlled constitutions, Parliament can only bind itself as to manner and form but not as to substance. To say that no taxes or royalties

---

176 Suit No CL 1976/R004, p 26.
177 *Ibid*, p 27.
178 *Ibid*, pp 27–28.
179 *Ibid*, p 27.
180 *Ibid*, p 28.

would be increased for 25 years is a question of substance and such an undertaking must surely be invalid, whether it is given by the executive or the legislature.

Circumstances like these give us some indication as to some of the conditions precedent that are foisted upon governments of developing countries in their quest for development finance. A more recent example is s 108(1) of the Barbados Offshore Banking Act, 1979, which provides as follows:

> When in the opinion of the Minister it is in public interest to do so, the Minister may by agreement give such assurance or guarantees regarding the future taxing of a licence as it may require before commencing to do off-shore banking from within Barbados.

There is, however, a measure of control for such assurances or guarantees since by virtue of s 108(2) they are subject to an affirmative resolution of the elected house.

8 *Mootoo v AG of Trinidad and Tobago*

In *Mootoo v AG of Trinidad and Tobago*, the applicant sought to impugn the Unemployment Levy Act 1970[181] enacted by the Parliament of Trinidad and Tobago, on the ground that the tax imposed thereunder was an infringement of the right to property that was guaranteed by s 1(a) of the then existing Constitution and therefore a special Act of Parliament was required if the tax was to be *intra vires* the Constitution.[182] This argument was successfully urged in the High Court before Brathwaite J, who held that the tax was unconstitutional.

On appeal to the Court of Appeal, the trial judge's decision was set aside.[183] Corbin JA observed that the judge had fallen into error. Firstly, by a misconception of the basic issues that were to be determined and, secondly, by relying on authorities that were not relevant to the matter before him.[184] On that basis, the learned Justice of Appeal was convinced that the trial judge had cast the burden of establishing the validity of the Act on the appellant. In fact, in accordance with the presumption of constitutionality, the respondent had the onus to satisfy the court that the Act was unconstitutional.

On the whole, the Court of Appeal was satisfied that the unemployment levy fulfilled all the requirements of a tax, despite the fact that no regulations were made by the Governor General, as required by s 19 of the Act, prescribing the purposes for which the levy was to be used. As Hyatali CJ put it:[185]

> The making of regulations is not a condition precedent either to the imposition and taking of the levy (ss 5, 6, 8) or to the identification of its purpose (s 2) or to the establishment of the Unemployment Fund (s 14(2)) or to the making of advances under statutory authority from the fund (s 14(3)).

---

181 Laws of Trinidad and Tobago, No 16 of 1970.
182 Trinidad and Tobago Constitution Order 1962 SI 1962/1875.
183 *Mootoo v Attorney General of Trinidad and Tobago*, Civil Appeal No 2/1975. The High Court and Court of Appeal decisions were discussed in Phillips, 1977, pp 142–43.
184 *Ibid.*
185 Civil Appeal No 2/1975, judgment of Hyatali CJ, p 18.

Phillips JA dealt a severe blow to the argument that taxation is a deprivation of property when he said:[186]

> It is useful to contemplate the hypothetical situation of a government which has a bare majority in Parliament, and may therefore be unable to have any taxing law passed by a three-fifths majority in each House, as is required for an Act passed in accordance with s 45 of the Constitution. The absurdity of such a state of affairs leads, in my opinion, to the irresistible conclusion that the 'deprivation of property' which results from the enforcement of a taxing statute is not within the purview of that term as it is used in s 1(a) of the Constitution.

For the reasons given above, their Lordships were unanimously of the opinion that the Act did not contravene the relevant provisions of ss 1 and 2 of the Constitution. They accordingly allowed the appeal. Mootoo's appeal to the Privy Council was also dismissed.[187] Sir William Douglas, Chief Justice of Barbados, giving the judgment of the Board, declared that the public purpose element of the tax was satisfied by the words 'for the purpose of the relief of unemployment and the training of unemployed persons', even though they appeared in the definition section.[188] Concerning the power to make regulations delegated to the Governor General under s 9 of the Act, the Privy Council held that 'such a delegation is not inconsistent with the underlying structure of the Constitution'.[189]

9 The *Guyana Bata Shoe* case

In the final case, which we shall discuss in this section, *Bata Shoe Co Ltd et al v CIR and AG of Guyana*,[190] the appellants sought declarations, which were all rejected in the court of first instance, impugning the constitutionality of three legislative enactments, viz:

(1) the Income Tax No 2 (Amendment) Act 1970;[191]

(2) the Corporation Tax Act 1970;[192] and

(3) the Miscellaneous (Fiscal Enactments) (Amendment) Act 1971.[193]

However, in reviewing this case only a discussion of those aspects which raised 'constitutional issues' for the Court of Appeal's determination will be canvassed.

With regard to the Income Tax No 2 (Amendment) Act, the following amended sections which were inserted in the Income Tax Ordinance[194] were, according to the appellants, inconsistent with the Constitution:

---

186 Civil Appeal No 2/1975, p 9.
187 *Mootoo v AG of Trinidad and Tobago* (1979) 1 WIR 1334.
188 *Ibid*, p 1340.
189 *Ibid*, p 1341.
190 (1976) 24 WIR 172.
191 Laws of Guyana, No 31 of 1970.
192 *Ibid*, No 30 of 1970.
193 *Ibid*, No 25 of 1971.
194 *Ibid*, Cap 299.

> s 82 (5) No appeal shall lie to the Board unless the person aggrieved by an assessment made upon him by the Commissioner has paid to the Commissioner tax equal to two-thirds of the tax which is in dispute.

> s 98 No appeal shall lie under section 86(1)(a) to a judge by a person aggrieved by an assessment made upon him by the Commissioner or by a decision of the Board, unless that person has paid to the Commissioner the whole amount of tax which is in dispute under the assessment made upon him.

The appellants argued that:

(a) both sections violated Art 3 of the Constitution in creating a fetter on the taxpayer's right of access to the Court;

(b) they violated the doctrine of separation of powers, through the imposition by the executive and the legislature of provisions requiring the deposit of two-thirds or the full tax in dispute ('the deposit provisions') before the taxpayer could appeal to the Board of Review or to a judge, as the case may be; and

(c) citing *dicta* from *DPP v Nasralla* [1967] 2 All ER 161 (PC), the pre-independence laws relating to rights of appeal in tax cases were continued by virtue of s 5 of the Guyana Independence Order 1966 and, having been so continued, the rights conferred by them fell to be regarded as guaranteed so protected by Art 18 against the risk of being cut down by post-independence laws.

In his judgment, Crane JA disposed of the argument relating to the alleged violation of the doctrine of the separation of powers in the following manner:

> I am convinced the doctrine of separation of powers does not assist in any way in showing the appellants have any right to appeal in taxation matters. In theory, that doctrine means that all judicial powers are vested in the courts and that neither the Legislature nor Executive should encroach on the sphere of the Judiciary or interfere in any way with judicial power. But whether a right of appeal exists, concerns *jurisdiction* not *judicial power*. There is a clear distinction to be drawn between judicial power and jurisdiction. The one is concerned with decision, whereas the other with whether what has to be decided constitutes the appropriate area for the exercise of judicial power.

> The doctrine of the separation of powers merely concerns the integrity of judicial power, ie, protecting the judicial power from the encroachments of the other two organs of Government. The doctrine gives no assistance in determining whether any judicial function should be allocated to the Executive, and insofar as the right of appeal is concerned, that being a question of policy, it may or may not lie. So whether the right of appeal exists, is a matter relative to the allocation of functions between Executive and Judiciary. It does not concern the integrity of judicial power and, for this reason, the doctrine cannot assist the appellants.

With respect to the appellants' contention regarding the effect of Art 18 on existing law, the learned Justice of Appeal stated:

> The words in the passage from *Nasralla's* case 'in any matter which the chapter covers' are important in view of the fact that fundamental rights are covered in that chapter. This means to say when it is complained that a post independence enactment is in derogation of a right which an individual was accustomed to enjoy under 'existing law', in order to attach to it with justification the stigma of unconstitutionality, that enactment must be shown to be in conflict or collision with one or other of the protective provisions. In the light of our

present problem, it has to be shown an unqualified right of access to the courts in tax matters is entrenched in Art 10(8) abovementioned, and that the impugned legislation has obstructed it, or that the questioned legislation has unjustifiably obstructed freedom of movement under Art 14. So if the right existed before the coming into force of the Constitution, an alteration of the law affecting it which is not inconsistent with any entrenched provision cannot really offend the Constitution and there can be no breach thereof. As applied to the case in hand, there can be no breach of the Constitution if the deposit provisions constitute merely an alteration or a modification of pre-independence provisions conditioning the right of appeal that is not entrenched in the Constitution. There is no guarantee anywhere in the Constitution that pre-independence legislation, ie 'existing laws,' or even the Constitution itself, would escape the amending hand of Parliament.

By Art 18(1)(c), all 'existing laws' can be altered or modified by Parliament. The Constitution itself can be altered by Art 73. Altering existing laws includes making 'different provisions in lieu thereof', which is exactly what, it is thought, the deposit provisions have sought to do. It seems the true effect of Art 18(1)(c) is that it saves any *pre-independence* laws which were in fact not consistent with the Constitution at the time when the latter came into force. It also saves any *post-independence* amendments of such *pre-independence* laws, provided only that such amendments, in the form of modifications or alterations, do not increase the extent to which those *pre-independence* laws were previously not consistent with the Constitution.

I think the point to understand about Art 18(1)(c) is that it envisages the possibility of all 'existing laws' not being consistent with the supreme law on its enactment in 1966 and, for that reason, it seeks to guard against an extension of such inconsistency by providing that you may modify or alter any 'existing law' that is either consistent or inconsistent with the Constitution, but if you alter one that is inconsistent you may not do so in such a manner or to such an extent as to increase such inconsistency as there already existed.

In the light of the above statements Crane JA defined the questions to be answered on this matter as being:

(1) what is the true nature of the right which the appellants claimed to have been violated?;

(2) does the Constitution guarantee a right of appeal to the taxpayer?; and

(3) is the right of appeal really a constitutional right?

In answering these questions, the learned Justice of Appeal held that a right of appeal is a procedural right and not a vested right.[195] He also pointed out that in theory no one can have a vested right in a right to appeal which is always given by some statute, subject to certain conditions under which the individual may exercise that right. Thus, an individual can only appeal 'within the limits which the statute giving this right lays down'. By parity of reason, therefore, Art 10(8), which the appellants claimed had guaranteed the taxpayer the protection of the law, on its true construction meant that:

[W]hen the matter arises for the determination of an individual's civil rights and obligations, he is to be guaranteed a fair hearing within a reasonable time by a court or other tribunal established by law which is constituted in such a manner as to secure its independence and impartiality. Proceedings must in fact have been 'instituted' by the

---

195 See Salmond, 1966, p 461, para 128.

taxpayer for the determination of the court or other tribunal before any question of the constitutionality of guaranteed provisions can arise for argument.

The Corporation Tax Act enacted provisions which imposed a tax on the profits of companies, to be levied on their chargeable profits at the rates of 35% in respect of commercial companies and 25% in the case of other companies. In seeking to impugn the constitutional validity of that Act, counsel for the appellants advanced the following, somewhat tenuous, arguments:

(1) the Act was invalid since it purported to introduce new taxation which was not permitted and is thus *ultra vires* Art 8(1) of the Constitution;[196]

(2) the Constitution does not permit Parliament to impose new taxes, but only to make amendment to existing ones;

(3) no new tax is lawful unless compensation is paid to the taxpayer because, notwithstanding, the fact that Art 72(1) includes an implied power to tax in that it provides that Parliament shall 'make laws for the peace, order and good government of Guyana', it is subject to the Constitution, that is, to Art 8 (of the Constitution). Therefore, the Corporation Tax Act, having imposed a new tax, and there being no provision for payment of compensation, on that account it is *ultra vires* and a violation of the Constitution; and

(4) unless there is a payment of compensation, the Corporation Tax Act is *ultra vires* and void.

In support of the above arguments, counsel for the appellants relied on certain *obiter dicta* expressed by Cummings J, in *Lilleyman et al v IRC et al.*[197]

In determining the issues raised with respect to this matter, Crane JA, adopting the Attorney General's submission, drew a clear distinction between the doctrine of eminent domain, that is, the right of a government to acquire private property for public purposes, and the State's power to levy a contribution by way of taxation from all its citizens or classes of citizens to meet the expenses of the State. In the opinion of the learned Justice of Appeal, taxation necessarily excludes the obligation to make compensation to the taxpayer. The two concepts, namely 'taxation and payment of compensation are irreconcilable'. In concluding that taxation was 'incompatible with, absolutely unrelated to, and irreconcilably opposed to compensation', Crane JA further expressed himself thus:[198]

But even if it were possible to go so far as to say that a monetary tax on property can be compulsorily taken possession of, I think it would make nonsense of the article (Art 8(1))

---

196 No property of any description shall be compulsorily taken possession of and no interest in or right over property of any description shall be compulsorily acquired, except by or under the authority of a written law and where provision applying to that acquisition or taking of possession is made by a written law–

    (a) requiring the prompt payment of adequate compensation; and

    (b) giving to any person claiming such compensation a right of access, either directly or by way of appeal, for the determination of his interest in or right over the property and the amount of compensation, to the High Court.

197 (1964) LRBG 15.

198 (1976) 24 WIR 188.

under consideration to suggest that prompt and adequate compensation must become payable to the individual for so doing.

Similarly, Crane JA rejected the appellants' submission that it was incompetent and unconstitutional for Parliament to impose new taxation by legislation unless provision is made for the payment of compensation. In dismissing this argument, he stated:

> It seems to me puerile to suggest that an amendment of the Constitution is necessary before there can exist a right to impose new taxation without compensation. When the framers of the Constitution gave Parliament the power to make laws for the peace, order and good government of Guyana, that grant was clearly in the nature of an enabling power, and the maxim of the implied power immediately came into operation because of the rule of construction that whenever an Act confers a jurisdiction, it impliedly also grants the power of doing all such acts or employing such means as are essentially necessary to its execution. The maxim is: *Cui jurisdictio data est, eo quoque concessa esse videntur, sine quibus jurisdictio explicari non potuit.* It is inconceivable to think that any Government could hope to survive for long, unless it is given the power to impose new taxes or that Parliament did ever intend such a state of affairs should exist as payment of compensation following taxation. Payment of compensation which must be 'prompt' would neutralise taxation, which is clearly unnecessary because as was said by Wood, CJ, of Canada in *Hudson Bay Co v AG of Manitoba*, (1878) Temp Wood, 209:
>
> > The imposition of taxes is one of the highest acts of sovereignty. Taxes are burdens or charges imposed by the legislative power to raise money for public purposes. *The power to tax rests upon necessity, and is inherent in every sovereignty.*

For the reasons given above, the learned Justice of Appeal agreed with the trial judge that the appellants were not entitled to any of the declarations sought. Opinions affirming the judge's decision were also given by the other members of the court and, accordingly, the appeal was dismissed.

In this case, Crane JA (as he then was) made a very promising pronouncement when he declared:

> Indeed, it has been our approach over the years, whenever constitutional rights are alleged to be an issue, invariably to make it our policy to treat such cases with particular reverence and to give them priority to all others; but *fundamental rights there must* prima facie *be.*

F   THE RIGHT TO RETAIN AND INSTRUCT A LEGAL ADVISER

In the case of *Terrence Thornhill v AG of Trinidad and Tobago*[199] (to which reference has already been made), the individual's constitutional right of access to a legal adviser after an arrest was upheld. This case involved the interpretation of ss 1, 2 and 3 of the Trinidad and Tobago Constitution of 1962. Section 1 declared, in part, as follows:

> It is hereby recognised and declared that in Trinidad and Tobago there have existed and shall continue to exist ... the following human rights and fundamental freedoms namely:

---

199 [1981] AC 61.

(a) the right of the individual to life, liberty, security of the person and enjoyment of property and the right not to be deprived thereof except by due process of law;

(b) the right of the individual to equality before the law and the protection of the law ...

Section 2, in part, provided that:

... no law shall abrogate, abridge or infringe or authorise the abrogation, abridgment or infringement of any of the rights and freedoms hereinbefore recognised and declared and in particular no Act of Parliament shall

(c) deprive a person who has been arrested or detained:

(ii) of the right to retain and instruct without delay a legal adviser of his own choice and to communicate with him ...

Section 3(1) provided:

Sections 1 and 2 of this Constitution shall not apply in relation to any law that is in force in Trinidad and Tobago at the commencement of this Constitution.

In the High Court,[200] Georges J (as he then was), basing himself on his interpretation of ss 1, 2, and 3 of the Constitution of 1962, came to the conclusion that the right of access to a legal adviser after an arrest is a right which arises immediately after such arrest; it is guaranteed by the Constitution and the opportunity to exercise the right should be afforded without delay. He reasoned thus:[201]

Assuming therefore that there was no such right at common law as set out in section 2(c)(ii), I hold that the right now exists because the Constitution has proclaimed that it always existed here and that it should continue to exist. The burden is on the State to show that there was some law existing at the date of the Constitution which qualified that right and to which therefore it remains subject by virtue of section 3.

In conclusion the learned judge, having examined the relevant common law rules, declared:[202]

I am satisfied that the right to counsel was a common law right which existed before 31st August 1962, and that the Constitution merely recognised its existence and ensured its continued existence. Even if it did not exist before, the Constitution proclaimed it as existing and guaranteed its continuance.

In the Court of Appeal,[203] the Chief Justice and the two Justices of Appeal overlooked or disregarded the point that was made by Georges J in the lower court. It should be borne in mind that the Constitution of Trinidad and Tobago was (and is) the supreme law of the land.

For his part, the learned Chief Justice was satisfied that:[204]

... neither the common law nor any statute law conferred any such right at the pre-trial stage on an accused person. It follows that the law in force on 31 August, 1962, was that no

---

200 *Thornhill v AG of Trinidad and Tobago* (1974) 27 WIR 281.

201 *Ibid*, p 285. See a commentary on this decision in Phillips, 1977, p 139.

202 See *Thornhill* (1974) 27 WIR 281, p 289.

203 *AG of Trinidad and Tobago v Thornhill*, Court of Appeal No 39/1974. See (1976) 31 WIR 498.

204 *Ibid*, judgment of Hyatali CJ, pp 500–01.

one had such a right and that as such the right referred to in the Constitution must be read subject to section 3 of the Constitution.

The fallacy in this argument can be readily identified. If there was no law – common law or statute – at the commencement of the Constitution then the right referred to in the Constitution could not be subject to anything and s 3 would not apply.

Rees JA was less specific and was content simply to declare:[205]

> ... I have not been able to find any judicial pronouncement or enunciation to the effect that a person in custody at the pre-trial stage or interrogation stage had at common law a right to instruct and communicate with his legal adviser.

As noted before, the issue in this case turned on the interpretation of certain provisions of the Constitution; and whereas Georges J brought a wide and liberal interpretation to bear on the matter, the Court of Appeal approached it with a narrow construction that is more suited to an ordinary statute. It is on the basis of the wider interpretation that their Lordships in the Privy Council examined the relevant sections of the Constitution of Trinidad and Tobago of 1962. Lord Diplock, speaking for the Board, adopted in its entirety the line of reasoning of Georges J, when he said:[206]

> In the context of section 1, the declaration that rights and freedoms of the kinds described in the section have existed in Trinidad and Tobago, in their Lordships' view, means that they have in fact been enjoyed by the individual citizen, whether their enjoyment by him has been *de jure* as a legal right or *de facto* as the result of a settled executive policy of abstention from interference or a settled practice as to the way in which an administrative or judicial discretion has been exercised. The hopes raised by the affirmation in the preamble to the Constitution that the protection of human rights and fundamental freedoms was to be ensured would indeed be betrayed if Chapter 1 did not preserve to the people of Trinidad and Tobago all those human rights and fundamental freedoms that in practice they had hitherto been permitted to enjoy.

When does this right arise?

In *Thornhill*, it was held that the right to counsel (and *a fortiori* to be informed of that right) arises immediately after an arrest is made and this decision has since been re-inforced by two cases to which attention must now be drawn. In *Thompson v R*,[207] the accused made a voluntary statement before his arrest in which he admitted sexual interference with a young girl and throwing her into the sea. Since the statement was made while preliminary investigations were still ongoing and before the suspect was charged, it was held that the trial judge had rightly exercised her discretion to admit the statement. See the Canadian case of *Therens*[208] in which a breathalyser test was taken from the suspect before he was charged in circumstances where s 10(b) of the Canadian Charter of Rights requires that a person need only be informed of his right to counsel 'after detention or

---

205 *Ibid*, judgment of Rees JA, p 504 c–d.
206 *Thornhill v AG of Trinidad and Tobago* [1981] AC 61, p 71.
207 *Eversley Thompson v R* (1996) 52 WIR 203.
208 *R v Therens* (1985) 1 SCR5 613.

arrest'. Similarly, it was held in the *Whiteman* case,[209] that it is incumbent upon police officers to see that an arrested person is *informed* of his right in such a way that he understands – bearing in mind that he may be illiterate, deaf or unfamiliar with the language. It is not therefore enough that notices conveying this information are exhibited in the police station – as they usually are. A purposive reading of the Constitution admits of no other interpretation.

G   PROTECTION FROM INHUMAN AND DEGRADING PUNISHMENT

All Commonwealth constitutions[210] guarantee protection from inhuman or degrading punishment or treatment; and the very existence of these guarantees invites the many applications for constitutional redress open to the society. In this section, the main thrust will be on the punishment of hanging for murder, but it should be pointed out that lesser penalties, like corporal punishment, have not escaped attention and we deal first with one such application.

Is whipping constitutional?

In the Barbados case of *Hobbs*,[211] it was held that the whipping of a person with a cat-o'-nine-tails was both inhuman and degrading within the meaning of s 15(1) of the Constitution, and that since s 40 of the Prison Act had come into operation in 1964 (that is, before independence) and there had been no legal means in Barbados for giving effect to judicial orders for corporal punishment, whipping by a cat-o'-nine-tails would not be an act done under the authority of existing laws and could not be justified under the authority of s 15(2).

Death row cases

The first example of an application under this head is that of Stanley Abbott. Abbott was a citizen of Trinidad and Tobago.[212] Convicted of murder and sentenced to death he fought a grim and sustained battle for many months to save his life. When that battle failed he sought redress under s 14(1) of the Constitution of Trinidad and Tobago whereby he applied for a declaration that by virtue of the inordinate delay in executing the death sentence his right to life was thereby infringed. In the High Court, the Court of Appeal and the Privy Council, it was consistently held that such a delay did not infringe his right to life as alleged.

---

209 *R v Whiteman* (1991) 39 WIR 397.

210 Antigua (s 7), Barbados (s 15), Belize (s 7), Dominica (s 5), Grenada (s 5), Guyana (Art 141), Jamaica (s 17), St Kitts/Nevis (s 7), St Lucia (s 5), Trinidad and Tobago (ss 4(a) and 5(2)(b)).

211 *Victor Hobbs and David Mitchell v R* (1992) 46 WIR 42. But see a useful article by Rose Marie Antoine, 1991, pp 26–35.

212 *Abbott v AG of Trinidad and Tobago* (1979) 1 WIR 1342 (PC); see, also, *de Freitas v Benny* [1976] AC 239 (PC).

The death sentence was again challenged in *Kitson Branche v AG of Trinidad and Tobago*,[213] the issue in this case being whether it was a cruel and degrading punishment and, thus, illegal and unconstitutional.

The declaration was refused in the High Court and on appeal to the Court of Appeal that decision was affirmed. A synopsis of the whole matter was given by Kelsick JA in the following terms:

> This is another instance in which, a person convicted of murder, having exhausted without success his appeals to the Court of Appeal and to the Judicial Committee, has thereafter commenced proceedings before a High Court judge by constitutional motion, citing the Attorney General as defendant, and alleging a breach of one or more of his fundamental rights and freedoms with a view to escaping the extreme penalty.[214]

With regard to the legal technique adopted, the Justice of Appeal noted that: 'The approach in *Abbott*'s case ... and the present appeal was to acknowledge the validity of the punishment but to assail the legality of its implementation.'[215]

In the light of the binding authorities on the issue, the appeal was summarily dismissed. Sir Isaac Hyatali CJ, observing that, should the declaration sought be granted, it would be 'tantamount to the exertion by this Court of a forbidden power to declare as a nullity a valid and subsisting law of the land'.[216]

Lord Diplock, in delivering the judgment of the Privy Council in *Abbott v AG of Trinidad and Tobago*,[217] espoused certain sentiments which were to raise the hopes of many of those condemned to die, but who for divers reasons were spared the immediate execution of their sentences. The learned Law Lord had this to say:[218]

> That so long a total period should have been allowed to elapse between the passing of a death sentence and its being carried out is, in their Lordships' view, greatly to be deplored. It brings the administration of criminal justice into disrepute among law-abiding citizens. Nevertheless, their Lordships doubt whether it is realistic to suggest that from the point of view of the condemned man himself he would wish to expedite the final decision as to whether he was to die or not if he thought that there was a serious risk that the decision would be unfavourable. While there's life, there's hope.

Later he continued:[219]

> Their Lordships accepted that it is possible to imagine cases in which the time allowed by the authorities to elapse between the pronouncement of a death sentence and notification to the condemned man that it was to be carried out was so prolonged as to arouse in him a reasonable belief that his death sentence must have been commuted to a sentence of life imprisonment. In such a case, which is without precedent and, in their Lordships' view, would involve delay measured in years, rather than in months, it might be argued that the taking of the condemned man's life was not 'by due process of law'. *Riley v AG* (1982) 35 WIR 279.

---

213 Civil Appeal No 63/1977 (T & T).
214 *Ibid*, judgment of Kelsick JA, pp 1–2.
215 *Ibid*, p 13.
216 *Ibid*, judgment of Hyatali CJ, p 8.
217 (1979) 1 WIR 1342 (PC), p 1345.
218 *Ibid*, p 1345E.
219 *Ibid*, p 1348B.

But in spite of the many qualifications in the statements made by Lord Diplock, they nevertheless raised the hope of five condemned men in Jamaica. Proceedings were initiated by way of motion seeking a declaration that their execution, at that time and in the circumstances leading up to it and surrounding the issue of the death warrants, would be contrary to s 17(1) of the Constitution of Jamaica.[220] The substantial basis for the application was that the delay in carrying out their execution was caused by the *de facto* suspension of the death penalty and, consequently, they were led reasonably to hope, and/or hoped, that their execution would not be carried out. Such circumstances, it was argued, caused them mental and psychological anguish amounting to cruel and inhuman treatment within the meaning of s 17(1) of the Constitution.

The motion was heard by the full Supreme Court before Wilkie, Chambers and Carey JJ who were all in favour of the motion being dismissed, pursuant to a point made *in limine* that the court had no jurisdiction to entertain the motion.

Wilkie J 'admitted that the prospect of impending execution inevitably carries with it, as a natural concomitant, an inseparable consciousness of mental anguish and pain,'[221] this being 'part and parcel of the imposition of sentence of death'.[222]

Much reliance was placed on the fact that the death penalty was suspended between May 1977 and February 1979 during which time the issue was being debated in both Houses of Parliament. But, for Wilkie J, this was of no moment. He declared:[223]

> ... debates in the House ... cannot be interpreted as an act by an agency of the State which could be regarded as direct interference and calculated or not, add to the anguish of a person under sentence of death. To hold otherwise would be to oblige every person or every act on the part of any agency of the State to refrain from the performance of any lawful function lest by inadvertence it adds to the anguish or detracts from the peace of mind of persons awaiting execution, either directly or indirectly, and it may very well attract such proceedings as we now have.

Having determined that the motion should be dismissed, Chambers J concluded by asserting that: 'This court has no jurisdiction to interfere with the exercise of the prerogative of mercy ... so as to delay or expedite an execution.'[224] Carey J was less charitable. He sharply informed the applicants that: 'The court is an inappropriate forum for this battle.'[225]

Unmoved by the strong sentiments of the Full Supreme Court, the appellants resorted to the Court of Appeal.[226] In that court, too, the judges made equally short shrift of the case put forward for the appellants: the reasoning being similar to that of the Full Supreme Court.

With regard to the question of the delay in carrying out the sentences, the Acting President of the Court of Appeal made the categorical, but somewhat unfortunate,

---

220 (1979) 1 WIR 1342 (PC), 1348B.
221 *Ibid*, judgment of Wilkie J, p 8.
222 *Ibid*.
223 *Ibid*, p 9.
224 *Ibid*, judgment of Chambers J, p 32.
225 *Ibid*, judgment of Carey J, p 41.
226 *Riley et al v AG* (1982) 35 WIR 279.

statement that there is no law which provides a time limit within which the death sentence should be carried out.[227] He noted also that under s 90(1) of the Constitution of Jamaica the Governor General is empowered to exercise the prerogative of mercy on the advice of the Privy Council and that, when such advice is given, it is left to him to exercise his discretion as he sees fit.[228] The learned Acting President questioned whether a delay by the Governor General in the exercise of his discretion can affect the execution of the sentence of death so as to authorise a court to declare the sentence void.[229] Having examined the law and facts relating to the question, Zacca P declared thus:[230]

> ... I find no unreasonable or undue delay in any of the five cases. There has been no infringement of s 17(1) of the Constitution. It cannot be said on the evidence that such a delay as there was, when considered along with the debates in Parliament, could have led the appellants to think that their death sentences had been commuted.

Carberry JA, who gave a very enlightened judgment, traced the origins of capital punishment in Jamaica,[231] its preservation as part of the 'existing law'[232] of Jamaica by virtue of s 26(8) of the Constitution and the various constitutional tests that it has withstood in various jurisdictions.[233] He was, however, also of the view that the facts in these cases did not come within the *dictum* of Lord Diplock in *Abbott v AG of Trinidad and Tobago*[234] and, further, that as the Constitution of Jamaica then stood, execution of the appellants could not be within the provisions of s 17(1) of the Constitution.[235]

On appeal to the Privy Council, their Lordships were divided on the issue. A majority (including Lord Diplock) adopted the line of reasoning of the lower courts.[236] Lord Bridge of Harwick, speaking for the majority, said:

> ... whatever the reasons for, the length of, delay in executing a sentence of death lawfully imposed, delay can afford no ground for holding the execution to be a contravention of section 17(1). Their Lordships would have felt impelled to this conclusion by the language of s 17 alone, but they are reinforced by the consideration that their decision accords fully with the general principle stated in *DPP v Nasralla* [1967] 2 AC 238.

Rather oddly, despite the pointed *obiter dicta* of Lord Diplock in the *Abbott* case (on the matter of the length of time for carrying out of the sentence being counted in years instead of in months), he did not apply the principle then enunciated to the instant case, but was satisfied simply to concur with the opinion of the majority.

Dissenting in most forceful terms, Lord Scarman and Lord Brightman agreed with the appellants that the carrying out of the death sentences after so prolonged a delay was inhuman treatment within the meaning of s 17(1) of the Constitution of Jamaica. They conceived the majority opinion to be:

---

227 *Riley et al v AG* (1982) 35 WIR 279, judgment of Zacca P, p 2.
228 *Ibid.*
229 *Ibid,* p 3.
230 *Ibid,* p 13. A similar ruling was made by Melville JA, p 19.
231 *Riley et al v AG* (1982) 35 WIR 279, pp 21–23.
232 *Ibid,* p 3.
233 *Ibid,* pp 25–26.
234 (1979) 1 WIR 1342, see above.
235 Civil Appeal No 28/1980, p 33.
236 *Riley and Others v AG of Jamaica* [1982] 3 All ER 469, p 473.

... in error because it has adopted in the construction of the Constitution an approach more appropriate to a specific enactment concerned with private law than to a constitutional instrument declaring and protecting fundamental rights.

As far as the minority was concerned, 'an austere legalism had been preferred by the majority to the generous interpretation which in *Fisher's* case was held to be appropriate'.[237]

Thus, on the basis of the generous interpretation of s 17 of the Constitution, Lord Scarman and Lord Brightman considered that the question whether carrying out death sentences after an inordinate delay was treatment that was authorised by s 3 of the Offences Against the Person Act, saved by s 26(8) of the Constitution, must be answered in the negative. This conclusion was posited on the reasoning that:[238] The 'treatment' which has to be considered is not the death penalty in isolation. The treatment which is *prima facie* 'inhuman' under sub-s (1) is the execution of the sentence of death as the culmination of a prolonged period of respite. That species of 'treatment' falls outside the legalising effect of sub-s (2). Sub-section (2) is concerned only to legalise certain descriptions of punishment, not to legalise a 'treatment', otherwise inhuman, of which the lawful punishment forms only one ingredient. Sub-section (1) deals with 'punishment' and 'other treatment'. In the instant case, the punishment is the execution of the death sentence. Sub-section (2) is directed both to 'punishment' and to 'other treatment'. The 'other treatment', if inhuman, is not validated by sub-section (2), in our opinion, merely because lawful punishment is an ingredient of the inhuman treatment. The facts and circumstances of the appellants in this case went far beyond those in other cases. In the others there was no *de facto* suspension of the death sentence while both Houses of Parliament debated the issue. These circumstances convinced the minority that any executions thereafter 'would have been 'inhuman treatment' within the meaning of sub-s (1) of s 17 and would not have been saved from being unconstitutional and illegal by sub-s (2). The foregoing conclusion was fortified by their Lordships when it was explained that the Act of State being challenged is not the death sentence but rather the duty of the Governor General in exercising the powers conferred on him by ss 90 and 91 of the Constitution which require him in every capital case to seek the advice of the Privy Council of Jamaica so that he may be advised as to the exercise of his power to delay or commute the sentence. In this regard, their Lordships were of the view that: '[T]he exercise of this executive power is a classic illustration of an administrative situation in which the individual affected has a right to expect lawful exercise of the power but no legal remedy: that is to say, no legal remedy unless the Constitution itself provides a remedy.'

Their Lordships found support for their dissenting approach in *Abbott v AG* in which the Judicial Committee recognised that inordinate delay might mean that the taking of the condemned man's life would not be by due process of law.

---

237 *Ibid*, pp 473–80.
238 *Ibid*, p 476.

After reviewing a number of authorities concerned with cruel and inhuman punishment their Lordships concluded as follows:[239]

> It is no exaggeration, therefore, to say that the jurisprudence of the civilized world, much of which is derived from common law principles and the prohibition against cruel and unusual punishments in the English Bill of Rights, has recognized and acknowledged that prolonged delay in executing a sentence of death can make the punishment when it comes inhuman and degrading.

In the circumstances the minority were of the view that the answer to the question whether the facts surrounding these particular cases amount to cruel and inhuman punishment depends on the interpretation of s 17(1) of the Constitution. For them the interpretation depends on the criterion used in determining the meaning of 'subjection to inhuman or degrading punishment or treatment'. Their Lordships therefore interpreted the meaning and effect of s 17(1) as being:[240]

> Prolonged delay when it arises from factors outside the control of the condemned man can render a decision to carry out the sentence of death an inhuman and degrading punishment. It is, of course, for the applicant for constitutional protection to show that the delay was inordinate, arose from no act of his, and was likely to cause such acute suffering that the infliction of the death penalty would be in the circumstances which had arisen, inhuman or degrading. Such a case has been established ... by the appellants.

Pratt and Morgan v AG of Jamaica

In a vigorous dissenting opinion, Lord Steyn declared in a Bahamas case to the Privy Council in 1997[241] that 'a dissenting judgment anchored in the circumstances of today sometimes appeals to the judges of tomorrow'. He outlined how the law governing the unnecessary and avoidable prolongation of the life of a man sentenced to die by hanging continues to undergo drastic change since 1980. In 1976 and in 1979 in the *de Freitas v Benny*[242] and the *Abbott*[243] cases, respectively, it was useless complaining to the Privy Council about delays caused by resort to appellate courts. When in 1983 a case[244] involving a delay of between six and seven years in executing two condemned Jamaicans came before the Privy Council, the judges gave short shrift to the appellants in the absolute terms referred to above, adding that 'it could hardly lie in any appellant's mouth to complain', about delays brought about by appellate proceedings. In the *Riley* case, Lords Scarman and Brightman expressed dissent from the majority accusing them of preferring 'austere legalism' to the 'generous interpretation' the law requires of the Constitution. Rejecting the Jamaican Attorney General's submission that the delay was reasonable because it resulted from a prolonged political and national debate as to whether the death sentence should continue to be carried out, Lord Scarman said:[245]

---

239 *Riley and Others v AG of Jamaica* [1982] 3 All ER 469, p 479.

240 *Ibid*, p 480.

241 *Fisher v Minister of Public Safety and Immigration* (1997) 52 WIR 15. The history of the development of this branch of the law is taken substantially from Lord Steyn's judgment.

242 *de Freitas v Benny* (1975) 27 WIR 318.

243 *Abbott v AG of Trinidad and Tobago* (1979) 32 WIR 347.

244 *Riley v AG of Jamaica* (1982) 35 WIR 279.

245 See *Riley* (1982) 35 WIR 279.

> We accept that in the circumstances it was reasonable, while the debate continued, to refrain from executing the sentences. But whether it was reasonable ultimately to carry them out was another matter. We would think it clear, as their Lordships certainly recognised in *Abbott*'s case, that a time will come when the delay is such that it would be intolerable and wrong in law to carry out the sentence.

In his view the approach of the majority was 'too austere because it fails to give priority to the suffering of the victim in the interpretation of the terms "inhuman" and "degrading". They are plainly apt to describe the effect of the punishment or other treatment on him who is subjected to it'.

By the time this matter arose again – this time in the now celebrated case of *Pratt and Morgan*[246] – the position was that 23 prisoners had been awaiting execution for more than 10 years while 82 had been under sentence of death for more than five years. The Judicial Committee of the Privy Council, sitting with an exceptional panel of seven judges, saw the light. They decided to overrule their previous decision in the *Riley* case and agreed that prolonged delay in execution, amounting to five years, might be unconstitutional – thus, illustrating the soundness of Lord Steyn's *dictum* stated at the beginning of this section. In subsequent decisions,[247] the Privy Council refined this ruling, holding that the five year period was not a rigid yardstick *but a norm* from which the courts were free to depart when they considered the circumstances warranted such departure.

Fisher v Minister of Public Safety and Immigration

In the *Henfield* case,[248] the question of pre-trial delay had been raised but was not dealt with. In the later case of *Fisher v Minister of Public Safety*, to which reference is made above, Lord Steyn felt that it was time that 'prolonged and unacceptable pre-sentence delay (should) be taken into account to tilt the balance where the delay since sentence of death is two and a half years, thus falling short of the three and a half years' norm applicable on the authority of *Henfield*'. In the *Fisher* case,[249] the appellants petitioned the Privy Council to have their sentences commuted to life imprisonment having regard to the combination of a pre-trial delay as well as a post-sentence delay, but the majority dismissed the appeal. Lord Steyn, however, felt that the appeal should have been allowed. In so doing, he gave his reasons, considering the matter from a narrow and more especially from a wider perspective. His words deserve to be quoted in full:

> On a narrow view, the issue before the Privy Council may appear to be confined to the question whether mere pre-sentence delay may, as a matter of law, be taken into account in deciding whether, by reason of the lapse of time between the imposition of the death sentence and the proposed date of execution, it would be a breach of Article 17(1) of the Constitution of the Commonwealth of the Bahamas to allow an execution to proceed. But it is impossible to divorce the narrow question from related and contributory pre-sentence causes of the mental anguish of the condemned man, such as his detention in appalling conditions contrary to any civilised norm ... There is no binding authority compelling the

---

246 *Pratt and Another v AG of Jamaica* (1993) 43 WIR 30.

247 See *Guerra v Baptiste* (1995) 47 WIR 439 and *Henfield v AG of Bahamas* (1996) 49 WIR 1.

248 *Henfield v AG of the Bahamas* (1996) 49 WIR 1.

249 *Fisher v Minister of Public Safety and Immigration* (1997) 52 WIR 15.

Privy Council as a matter of precedent to decide the narrow question one way or the other. Indeed, as recently as October 1996 the Privy Council expressly left this question open for subsequent decision; *Henfield v AG* (1996) 49 WIR, p 13. Their Lordships are not called upon to decide this question on the basis of their individual views of what is desirable in the interests of the administration of justice in the Bahamas. The question must be resolved on the basis of an evaluation of the strength of the competing arguments on the proper construction of Art 17(1) of the Constitution. Their Lordships are mandated by the constitution to afford to the appellant the full measure of protection of the rights enshrined in it.

Although the noble and learned Lord of Appeal in Ordinary did not spell out what that 'full measure of protection' involved, it is reasonable to assume he was referring to the twin provisions enshrined in the Constitution of the *right to life* and the *right against degrading and inhuman punishment*. And, although he did not specifically refer to it, his arguments closely resemble the approach taken in the *State v McKwanyane*,[250] a case that was decided in 1995 by the South Africa Constitutional Court. In that case, it was held that:

> Taking into account the fact that the carrying out of the death sentence destroyed life (protected without reservation under s 9 of the Constitution); that it annihilated human dignity (protected under s 10); that its enforcement was subject to arbitrariness and inequality due to the differences in the application of the law in different parts of the country and the inability of most accused through poverty and other factors to obtain a level of legal advice and representation commensurate with the seriousness of the offence with which they were charged and the penalty with which they were threatened; that the wrongful carrying out of the death penalty through miscarriage of justice was irremediable; and notwithstanding its value as a deterrent and the fact that public opinion might still be in favour of its retention; in the context of the Constitution as purposively construed, and giving the words of s 11(2) the broader meaning to which they were entitled at this stage of the inquiry, the death penalty was indeed to be categorised as a cruel, inhuman and degrading punishment.

Commentary

As we continue to review our independence constitutions throughout the region at the beginning of the 21st century, is it too much to hope that enlightened opinion on the right to life and to human dignity would one day lead to an acceptance of the well considered approach advocated by Lord Steyn in respect of the contribution of pre-trial delay in such cases? And is it too far fetched to expect that Caribbean jurisdictions will in time wish to take a leaf out of the book of the Constitutional Court of South Africa in the matter of declaring the death penalty itself to be unconstitutional?[251] Time alone will tell.

---

250 (1995) 1 LRC 269.

251 A shot across the bows of our Caribbean Courts had already been fired in at least five cases: *Richards v AG of St Kitts and Nevis* (1992) 44 WIR 141; *Reckley v Minister of Public Safety (Bahamas)* (1995) 45 WIR 27; *Abbott* (1979) 1 WIR 1342; *Kitson Branche* Civil Appeal Trinidad and Tobago No 63/1977; as well as *Dole Chadee* (1999) 1 WIR 1709.

H   RIGHT TO FREEDOM OF MOVEMENT

The section in the Barbados Constitution on this right is substantially in the identical terms in all Caribbean Commonwealth Constitutions. The main provision is to the effect that no person shall be deprived of freedom of movement, viz, the right to move freely throughout (the particular country), the right to reside in any part of the country, the right to enter Barbados, the right to leave the country and immunity from expulsion therefrom.[252] (For some odd reason, Jamaica *is* alone in *not* providing for a right to *leave* Jamaica.)[253] There are the usual qualifications, which follow.

Nothing contained in or done under the authority of any law shall be held to be inconsistent with or in contravention of this section to the extent that the law in question makes provision for various restrictions on movement within or right to leave the country reasonably required in the interests of defence, public safety, public order, public morality or public health.[254] Whenever a person's freedom of movement is restricted (in Jamaica and in all the other jurisdictions except Belize or Trinidad) by such a law, and the person so requests at any time during the period of such restriction not earlier than six months after he last made such a request, his case shall be reviewed by an independent and impartial tribunal established by law and presided over by a person appointed by the Chief Justice from among persons entitled to practise or to be admitted to practise in the country. On any review by the tribunal, it shall make recommendations regarding the necessity or expediency of continuing the restriction, but the authority to whom the recommendation is made shall not be under any obligation to abide by such recommendation.[255] In the case of Barbados,[256] the person against whom the restriction applies within five days of the commencement of the restriction, shall be furnished with a statement in writing in a language he understands of the grounds upon which the restriction has been imposed. Not more than 14 days after the commencement of the restriction, a notification shall be published in the *Gazette* stating that the person's freedom of movement has been restricted and giving particulars of the specific law governing the restriction. The case shall then be reviewed from time to time and the person under restriction shall be afforded reasonable facilities to consult and instruct a legal adviser of his choice at his own expense.The same principles apply as to the acceptability or otherwise of the recommendations of this tribunal as applies in the other jurisdictions mentioned above.

Case law

Since the 1960s, the case law under this freedom of movement section has, peculiarly, been mainly concerned with belonger status and inter-territorial travel. We shall examine now four freedom of movement cases. What Sir William Blackstone[257] characterises as

---

252 See Barbados Constitution, s 22.

253 Jamaica Constitution, s 16(1).

254 Barbados Constitution, s 22(3).

255 Antigua (s 8), Bahamas (s 25), Belize (s 10), Dominica (s 12), Grenada (s 12), St Kitts and Nevis (s 14), St Lucia (s 12), St Vincent (s 12).

256 Barbados (s 22(4) and (5)).

257 Blackstone, 1803, Bk I, Chapter 1.II.

'the power of personal locomotion' figures only in the first two cases. In *Ramson v Barker*[258] (a case that reached the Guyana Court of Appeal), the appellant, an acquaintance and a third person were standing some distance from a point where earlier the police, acting on instructions from their headquarters, had dispersed an unlawful assembly. The appellant and his companions were discussing the police action in dispersing the crowd when a policeman in uniform (but without a number) asked what the appellant was doing by the road side. Upon the appellant replying that it was none of the policeman's business, the latter seized the appellant by the arm whereupon the appellant accused the policeman of assault and demanded his name. At that stage, another policeman came to the scene and jabbed the appellant with a stick. The appellant then found himself surrounded by about a dozen policemen, including a deputy superintendent and an inspector. The policemen ordered the appellant to move and he got into his car and drove away. The latter then wrote to the Commissioner of Police, the first respondent in the suit, and asked for the name of the policeman involved in the incident. The Commissioner did not comply but asked the appellant to submit a report so that an investigation could be held. The appellant did not accept the invitation but filed an originating motion citing both the Commissioner of Police (as first respondent) and the Attorney General and complaining that his rights to freedom of expression (Art 12), freedom of assembly and association (Art 13) and freedom of movement (Art 14) had been breached. The appellant filed an affidavit in support of his motion and the first respondent filed one in reply; but the latter affidavit relied heavily on information provided by the deputy superintendent and was largely hearsay. At the commencement of the trial before the trial judge the appellant called attention to the inconsistencies between his affidavit evidence and that of the first respondent and was allowed to call his companion C, who was present at the scene, to give oral evidence. The appellant also deposed in person and so did the inspector who was on the scene. The trial judge found that the events complained of had in fact occurred in an atmosphere that was charged with and prone to violence and at a time when a breach of the peace was likely to occur, but although such apprehension was deposed to by the first respondent there was no corroboration of the statement. However, the trial judge dismissed the appellant's motion. The appellant appealed to the Court of Appeal, where (in addition to his previous petition) he further complained of a deprivation of his right to personal liberty (Art 5 of the Constitution). It was held by the Court of Appeal that the acts of the Police did not deprive the appellant of his right to freedom of movement under Art 14(1) of the Constitution since that right did not contemplate the right to pass and repass along the highway. The court did, however, permit the appellant to raise for the first time the plea that his right to personal liberty was infringed by the seizure of his arm and ruled that such action violated his freedom from unjustifiable acts of trespass and had been committed by the executive power of the State under Art 5 in respect of which the appellant should receive compensation. The court allowed the appeal.

258 (1982) 33 WIR 183.

Smith v Commissioner of Police

In this Bahamas case[259] the facts were as follows.

Between 10.30 pm on 8 June 1984 and 1.15 am on 9 June, the police in Grand Bahamas conducted what was described as a 'police check point', in respect of which the police placed in the middle of an intersection signs reading: 'WARNING. GO SLOW. POLICE CHECK POINT AHEAD.' The police deposed to the fact that the purpose of the exercise was 'primarily to stop and search suspected vehicles supposedly conveying hidden illicit firearms, dangerous drugs and (to detect) possible traffic infractions'. The police officer in charge of Grand Bahamas stated that he had taken 'a conscious decision' that 'it was necessary for the police to spare no effort to head off the drug activity which seem [sic] to be permeating both public and private sectors'. One method of doing this was to set up what he described as a 'road block' and this had been done on 11 May 1984, resulting in nine persons being arrested: five of whom had been charged with possession of unlicensed firearms and five with the possession of dangerous drugs.

In the course of this operation, S was driving along the highway when he spotted the road block. S was accosted and the police wished to search his car. He refused permission. The police nevertheless insisted and carried out a search as a result of which S, shortly afterwards, moved the court for *inter alia* a declaration that the police had no authority or power to hinder him in the enjoyment of his right to move freely on the highway in accordance with Art 25(1) of the Constitution (freedom of movement) in the absence or reasonable cause to suspect that he had committed (or was about to commit) an offence; and a declaration that in accordance with Art 21(1) (no search of person or property without consent) the police had no power or authority to search his car without his consent in the absence or reasonable cause to suspect that he had committed an offence.

It was held, *inter alia*, that the right to pass and repass on the highway was an inseparable part of the right to freedom of movement under Art 25. It was also held that, in order to establish a breach of the right of freedom of movement under Art 25, it was not necessary to show that a person had been deprived of the right of freedom of movement, it was sufficient to show hindrance of that right – that the erection of barriers across the road under s 46 of the Road Traffic Act was *prima facie* a breach of the right to freedom of movement under Art 25, but that such a breach was justifiable as being in the interest of public order (Art 25(2)(a)(i)) which term included any measure for the prevention of disorder or crime. The court also found that the erection of barriers across the road was reasonably required in terms of Art 25(2)(a)(i), given the background of drug-dealing and the success of police raids; that the power conferred by s 46 could not be described as arbitrary; and that, in the absence of evidence to the contrary adduced by S (on whom the onus rested), the court would assume that the exercise of the power under s 46 was 'reasonably justifiable in a democratic society'. The court, however, found that to erect barriers and to stop vehicles did not incorporate a *right to search* the vehicles nor the persons of the drivers or passengers, so that the search of S's car without his consent when there was no reasonable ground on which he could have been suspected of

---

259 (1994) 50 WIR 13.

possessing dangerous drugs or firearms constituted the tort of trespass. The applicant S was awarded $100 in nominal damages and the costs of his application.

It will be observed that the view of Georges CJ as to what constitutes freedom of movement throughout (the Bahamas) conflicts with the views of George JA in the Guyana Court of Appeal in the case of *Ramson v Barker* referred to above. In the latter case, the Guyana judge took the line that Art 14 is concerned with the deprivation of the right to freedom of movement, whereas other articles on the fundamental rights section refer to a hindrance. He came to the conclusion that what occurred in the *Ramson* case was only a hindrance which 'is more in the nature of an obstruction or interference'. In his view 'the right to move freely throughout Guyana does not encompass the right of locomotion along the highway'. He expressed himself in these terms:

> The right of locomotion along the highway, ie the right to pass and repass along a highway, together with the incidental right of short stoppages, is conceptually and qualitatively of a different nature from the right to move freely about the country. *Inter alia* what Article 14(1) guarantees is the right of all citizens to go wherever they like within the country, subject to the exceptions contained in the succeeding paragraphs. It is distinct from the common law right which is vested in every individual to use the highway *eundo et redeundo*.

Georges CJ, on the other hand, was not prepared to make such a distinction in construing the section. The writer submits that freedom of movement would largely be devoid of its most obvious meaning if the Guyana Chancellor's interpretation is accepted and if the constitutions are to be interpreted in a purposive way freedom to pass and repass must surely be considered as essential ingredients of the right to move freely throughout (a particular jurisdiction). In this regard, the writer expresses respectful disagreement with Margaret Demerieux who urges a preference for the approach of George JA.[260]

The third case to be examined under this section is *Margetson v AG of Antigua*:[261] In this case, the plaintiff was born in 1928 in Montserrat (then a Presidency of the Leeward Islands). He lived in Montserrat until 1947 when he moved to Antigua (another Presidency in the said Leeward Islands) with his father who was a surgeon in Montserrat from which he was transferred to the Antigua Hospital. The appellant was appointed in 1947 as a civil servant in Antigua in which capacity he served until 1949 when he went abroad to pursue his studies – first to Jamaica and after 1952 to England. He married in England in 1956 and in 1965 sent his wife and children to Antigua to reside with his mother. He joined them in 1966 when he returned to settle permanently in Antigua. For more than a year after his return he moved freely in and out of Antigua, but on 22 December 1967, his passport was endorsed with a condition restricting his stay in Antigua up to 6 January 1968. This restriction was later extended to 5 February 1968. He was also forbidden to work without a permit. The three main questions for determination by the court were as follows:

(a) was the appellant 'a person belonging to Antigua'?;

(b) did the chief immigration officer have, on 22 December 1967, any lawful authority to impose a limit on the plaintiff's stay in Antigua having regard to the fact that the

---

260 See Demerieux, 1992, p 321.
261 See *Margetson v AG* (1968) 12 WIR 469.

appellant had been in and out of the country for years and no restrictions concerning his stay had ever been imposed on him?;

(c) did the chief immigration officer have on that said date authority to impose on him a condition that he was not to work without a work permit?

The respondents in this case relied on the submission that because the appellant did not belong to Antigua he required a permit to work therein. The judge found that the appellant did not belong to Antigua, was neither a prohibited immigrant nor a *bona fide* visitor, but a resident whose stay could not be arbitrarily limited or upon whom could be imposed a restriction that he could not work unless he were granted a work permit. His case was fully covered by s 17A(1) of the Immigration and Passport Act which reads as follows:

> Entry Permit. In pursuance of any regulation in force for the time being and subject to such special or general directions as the Administrator may see fit to give any immigration officer, a permit to enter the Colony may be issued on the authority of the Chief Immigration Officer to any person not being a prohibited immigrant. Any such permit shall be in writing and shall be subject to such conditions as may be prescribed by regulations.

The appellant was permitted on 5 February 1966 to enter Antigua: *no* conditions or restrictions on his stay having then been imposed. From that date he went out from, and returned to, Antigua without any such restrictions. At the trial, before Louisy J at first instance, counsel for the Attorney General and chief immigration officer contended that the chief immigration officer acted under the provisions of the Act in summoning the appellant and endorsing his passport with the restrictions referred to, but as the judge pointed out, such endorsement is applicable only to persons who desire to land, since the Act prescribes specifically that 'any conditions or restrictions imposed as aforesaid shall be communicated in writing to a person *about to land*'. The judge therefore rejected the contention and held that the chief immigration officer had no such authority. In this he was upheld by the Court of Appeal which also agreed with him that the appellant could not be said to 'belong' to Antigua'.

The next case to which reference should be made is the Guyana case *Re: Application by Robert Sookrajh.*[262] Here, the applicant was committed to stand trial at assizes on an indictable charge of forging certain documents relating to cinema returns and was admitted to bail before the indictment was filed. While waiting for the assizes, he wished to leave the country but was prevented from so doing, as a result of which he moved the High Court by originating motion claiming that his constitutional right of free movement had been infringed. The applicant had, at the time of his committal, already entered into a recognisance in the following terms:

(a) he was to appear before the Supreme Court at the January assizes there and then, or at anytime within 12 months from the date of the recognisance, to answer to any indictment that may be filed against him in the said court;

(b) he was not to depart the said court;

(c) he was to accept service of the indictment whenever it was ready.

---

262 (1969) 14 WIR 257.

His counsel submitted that, even if he had no right to leave Guyana, the police could not stop him. He therefore sought a declaration that the police should not be permitted to stop him without being in possession of a warrant of apprehension. The judge made short shrift of this request and dismissed the motion. The position was different when in another Guyana case a magistrate upheld a 'no case' submission in favour of a Guyanese citizen charged with arson and dismissed the charge, whereafter *the prosecution appealed*.[263]

Although the appeal had not yet been heard, the applicant tried to fly to Trinidad but was refused permission to leave the country. He applied to the High Court for a declaration that the act of preventing him from leaving was unconstitutional as it infringed his constitutional right to freedom of movement. The respondents argued that by virtue of the Summary Jurisdiction (Appeals) Act the applicant was not free to leave the jurisdiction of the court until the determination of the appeal; and that the presumption that the applicant was innocent was, in the circumstances, inapplicable.

It was held that the argument that the presumption of innocence was inapplicable was repugnant to the basic concept that everyone was presumed to be innocent until he was proved by a court of competent jurisdiction to be guilty. The decision of the magistrate acquitting the applicant was a final adjudication by him of the matter. A person who had been acquitted was free and under no obligation or restraint, until a court hearing the appeal ruled otherwise; there was no compulsion or obligation on the applicant to be present at the hearing of the appeal and he did not need permission of the court to leave the country. The constitution expressly protected fundamental rights and freedoms of the individual and those rights could not be subjected to any restraint that did not admit of legal justification. Accordingly, the act of preventing the applicant from leaving the country was unconstitutional.

I   RIGHT TO FREEDOM OF EXPRESSION

Article 10 of the European Convention on Human Rights, from which the relevant sections in Commonwealth Caribbean Constitutions owe their origin, expresses this right in positive terms as follows:

1   Everyone has the right to freedom of expression. The right shall include freedom to hold opinions and to receive and impart information and ideas without interference by public authority and regardless of frontiers. This article shall not prevent States from requiring the licensing of broadcasting, television and cinema enterprises. And after thus setting out the *rights* of citizens, the Article continues with their *responsibilities* in this way:

2   The exercise of these freedoms, since it carries with it duties and responsibilities, may be subject to such formalities, conditions, restrictions or penalties as are prescribed by law and are necessary in a democratic society, in the interest of national security, territorial integrity or public safety, for the prevention of disorder or crime, for the

---

263 *Roopnarine v Barker and Another* (1981) 30 WIR 181.

protection of health or morals, for the protection of the reputation or rights of others, for preventing the disclosure of information received in confidence, or for maintaining the authority and impartiality of the judiciary.

This is, in fact, substantially what the respective sections prescribe in the various Commonwealth Caribbean Constitutions[264] which tend to begin usually on the negative note:

Except with his own consent, a person shall not be hindered in the enjoyment of his freedom of expression;

and end with a reference to the fact that nothing contained in or done under any law shall be regarded as inconsistent with (the section) to the extent that the law in question makes provision that:

... imposes restrictions that are reasonably required–

(a) in the interest of defence, public safety, public order, public morality or public health;

(b) for the purpose of protecting the reputations, rights and freedoms of other persons, or the private lives of persons concerned in legal proceedings and proceedings before statutory tribunals, preventing the disclosure of information received in confidence, maintaining the authority and independence of Parliament and the courts, of regulating telephony, posts, broadcasting or other means of communication, public entertainment, public shows; or

(c) that imposes restrictions upon public officers that are reasonably required for the proper performance of their functions; and except so far as that provision or, as the case may be, the thing done under the authority thereof is shown not to be reasonably justifiable in a democratic society.

What amounts to hindrance?

This is a question that has arisen more than once in the Caribbean since the promulgation of our new Constitutions. Five of these cases will now be examined.

In the *Frank Hope* case,[265] the President of the Co-operative Republic of Guyana issued trade orders (made under the authority of the Trade Ordinance) the effect of which was to prohibit the importation of newsprint and printing equipment except by licence issued by the competent authority. The respondents in this case argued that the orders had the effect of hindering their freedom of expression, that is, their freedom to communicate ideas and information through the press without interference in accordance with Art 12 of the Constitution. They also averred that they had been discriminated against, since no such strictures were imposed on a rival Government newspaper. The judge at first instance quite properly struck down the impugned trade orders but his ruling was reversed by the Court of Appeal which held (rather simplistically) that, since there was no fundamental right to import newsprint or printing equipment *and since the*

---

264 Antigua (s 12), Bahamas (s 23), Barbados (s 20), Belize (s 12), Dominica (s 10), Grenada (s 10), Guyana (Art 12), Jamaica (s 22), St Kitts/Nevis (s 12), St Lucia (s 10), St Vincent (s 10), Trinidad and Tobago (s 12(i) and (k)).

265 *Frank Hope v New Guyana Co Ltd* (1979) 26 WIR 233.

impact of the restriction on the applicant was indirect, there was no such hindrance to the applicant's enjoyment of the right. In the view of the Court of Appeal, the State had the right to take action to conserve scarce foreign exchange and it was too sad if in the process the applicant was prejudiced. This was a political rationalisation supported by a compliant judiciary. It is difficult not to feel a tinge of suspicion over this 'direct impact theory' which runs counter to all principles governing the interpretation of a constitution in a generous and purposive way. The suspicion should be even greater when one examines the facts in the case of *AG of Antigua v The Antigua Times Ltd.*[266] In this case, a 1971 Act forbade the printing or publishing of a newspaper unless there was a deposit of $10,000 with the Accountant General. The relevant minister could, however, waive the payment if he was provided with a bank guarantee or an insurance policy. The stated object for requiring the payment was that it would be available to satisfy a judgment debt for damages whenever a libel action was successfully brought against the newspaper. Praiseworthy and altruistic as this gesture may be, it is submitted that its real motive was either to prevent newspapers from doing business or to warn them, if they did, that they were liable to be mulcted in damages. In other words, the real purpose behind the deposit was to hinder freedom of expression. The local courts ruled in favour of the newspapers but that ruling was overruled by the Privy Council which saw it as a measure that fell within the constitutional provision in s 10(2)(a)(ii) of the Constitution, viz:

> Nothing contained in or done under a law shall be held to contravene freedom of expression to the extent that the law in question makes provision that is reasonably required for the purpose of protecting the reputations, rights and freedoms of other persons.

In coming to their conclusion, the Privy Council applied the same 'direct impact' doctrine which the Guyana Court of Appeal had invoked in the *Frank Hope* newsprint case we have examined above.

The *Courtenay (Belize)* case[267] was one in which a member of the opposition party in that country ('the applicant') sought the permission of the television station ('the Authority') to broadcast a programme on matters of public policy, viz, the state of the economy. The chairman of the station replied to the applicant (referring to the proposed programme as 'a political broadcast') to the effect that the proposed broadcast could not be made without express approval of the Authority in accordance with reg 10 of the Broadcast and Television Regulations 1984 which in terms called for the permission of the Authority before 'any political speech or activity' could be aired. At the same time, the secretary of the Authority wrote to the applicant formally refusing permission and again characterising the broadcast as a 'party political broadcast'. The applicant instituted proceedings before the High Court claiming that his right to freedom of expression under the Constitution was being infringed and the Chief Justice (who heard the application)[268] ruled in his favour. On appeal, the Belize Court of Appeal confirmed the Chief Justice's ruling that the basis on which permission was refused was arbitrary: it could not have

---

266 In this regard, the writer is in complete accord with Professor RW James in the strictures to which he makes reference in his article entitled 'The state of human rights enforcement in the Co-operative Republic of Guyana' (1983), pp 14–35. At the same time, the writer considers that in the past decade, ie, since about 1990, there has been much judicial valour emanating from the Guyana judiciary.

267 *Courtenay v Belize Broadcasting Co Ltd* (1990) 38 WIR 79.

268 Moe CJ.

been under reg 10, since the Authority had not seen the script of the proposed broadcast, nor was the refusal expressed or shown to be authorised by any law mentioned in the limits imposed by s 12(2) of the Constitution.

The fourth case to be considered is the *Trinidad Television* case.[269] In this case Rambachan ('the applicant') moved the High Court of Trinidad and Tobago alleging, *inter alia*, breach of his right of thought and expression under the Trinidad Constitution. The averment was that the *Trinidad and Tobago Television Co Ltd* was a public authority (the station is state owned) and that it had denied him the right to reasonable airtime on the State television. In a long and exhaustive judgment, the learned judge[270] had no difficulty in finding for the applicant: the following paragraph of the picturesquely worded judgment going to the root of his findings:

> In this modern age, a free press is indispensable to the right to express political views and to freedom of thought and expression. If the free press goes, by any form of government action or censorship, then inevitably the other two related freedoms are affected and will ultimately perish. More and more, these three fundamental freedoms become the three sides of a triangle; they really form one whole and upon them hinge the liberty of the individual and the freedom of the Nation.

Lord Bridge expressed like sentiments in the fifth case we propose to consider, viz, the case of *Hector v AG of Antigua and Barbuda*.[271] This is what the learned Law Lord said:

> In a free democratic society it is almost too obvious to need stating that those who hold office in government and who are responsible for public administration must always be open to criticism. *Any attempt to fetter or stifle such criticism amounts to political censorship of the most insidious and objectionable kind* ... In the light of these considerations their Lordships cannot help viewing a statutory provision which criminalises statements likely to undermine public confidence in the conduct of public affairs with the utmost suspicion.

In this case, Leonard Hector had appealed to the Judicial Committee of the Privy Council against a decision of the OECS Court of Appeal (Robotham CJ, Bishop and Moe JJA) allowing an appeal of the Attorney General of Antigua and Barbuda, the Commissioner of Police and an additional magistrate from a decision of Matthew J who had declared s 33B of the Public Order Act 1972 (as amended) to be in part unconstitutional.

The appellant (Hector) is the editor of a newspaper published in Antigua known as *The Outlet*. He was charged in respect of an article published in his newspaper in which he made certain statements critical of the Government and the Commissioner of Police which, it was alleged, were false statements likely 'to undermine public confidence in the conduct of public affairs'. The appellant challenged the prosecution on the ground that the specific provisions of the section violated the Constitution of Antigua and Barbuda. As a first step, the criminal proceedings were stayed pending the determination of an application by the appellant to the High Court pursuant to s 18 of the Constitution. The application was heard by Matthew J who declared that the appellant's constitutional rights had been contravened by the criminal proceedings and that s 33B was

---

269 *Rambachan v Trinidad and Tobago Television Ltd*, No 1789 of 1982 (17 January 1985).
270 Deyalsingh J.
271 (1990) 37 WIR 216, p 219.

unconstitutional to the extent that it contained the words 'or to undermine public confidence in the conduct of public affairs'. The entire section (33B) reads as follows:

Notwithstanding the provisions of any other law any person who–

(a) in any public place or at any public meeting makes any false statement;or

(b) prints or distributes any false statement which is likely to cause fear or alarm in or to the public, or to disturb the public peace, *or to undermine public confidence in the conduct of public affairs,*

shall be guilty of an offence and shall be liable on summary conviction to a fine not exceeding $500.00 or to a term of imprisonment not exceeding six months [emphasis supplied].

It was in such a situation that the OECS Court of Appeal reversed the decision of Matthew J and imposed a three month term of imprisonment on the accused instead of the six month term imposed by the magistrate. It was held by the Privy Council, reversing the decision of the Court of Appeal (and *a fortiori* the magistrate) that, even given full weight to the presumption of constitutionality, the words in the section, 'or to undermine public confidence in the conduct of public affairs', offended against the constitutional provisions in relation to freedom of expression. The words were accordingly of no effect. The Privy Council accordingly quite properly quashed the ruling of the Court of Appeal and ordered costs to the appellant Hector.

The fifth case to be mentioned under this head is another Antigua case – *de Freitas v Permanent Secretary of Ministry of Agriculture*[272] where it was held by the Privy Council that a blanket restraint imposed by legislation on all civil servants from communicating to anyone any expression of view on any matter of political controversy was excessive and disproportionate. This case will be dealt with in detail in Chapter 14 below when the Public Service is being considered.

Summary

This right to freedom of expression has rightly been described as one of the foundations of a democratic society central to the entire democratic process. Under Art 10 of the European Convention on Human Rights, it has been deemed to include not only the *substance* of the ideas and information, but also the *form* in which they are expressed which embraces such forms of expression as artistic works, images, signs and dress. Only one of the Caribbean Constitutions makes a similar provision,[273] viz, Antigua, in which it is provided:

For the purposes of this section expression may be oral or written or by codes, signals, signs or symbols and includes recordings, broadcasts, (whether on radio or television), printed publications, photographs (whether still or moving), drawings, carvings and sculptures or any other means of artistic expression.

---

272 [1998] 3 WLR 675 (PC).
273 See Constitution of Antigua and Barbuda (s 12(3)).

CONCLUDING COMMENTARY

From an exposition of the cases in this chapter, it will be clear that the judiciaries in the Caribbean basin have all had a busy and productive time. In the 35 years from 1965 to 2000, the judges have developed a sound, objective and sometimes innovative corpus of human rights law. In most cases, their work is worthy of the highest praise and one can only hope that the region will continue to produce a calibre of men and women as judges who will have the independence and the impartiality to maintain that standard or even to improve upon it. To this end, it is of the utmost importance that the judges should be well paid. If not, it will not be possible to recruit the proper individuals and those who are appointed would be more likely to feel disposed to weigh their decisions against the possibility of victimisation from an executive against whom they may have to rule.

In Chapter 7, we turn to the peculiar constitutional problems faced by St Kitts and Nevis since independence.

THE AGONY OF ST KITTS, NEVIS AND ANGUILLA

It has been widely acknowledged that as long as the islands of St Kitts, Nevis and Anguilla comprised a common political and administrative unit under the name of St Kitts/Nevis/Anguilla, there was implicit in that formation a constitutional Gordian Knot. As we shall see, Nevis has tried hard ever since 1882 to cut that knot and, more recently, Anguilla successfully did just that. This chapter will show how at last Anguilla succeeded and is now, in a manner of speaking, an 'independent colony'. But a new and faster constitutional Gordian knot was tied when St Kitts and Nevis entered into a novel type of federation in September 1983 becoming at that time the last of the six Associated States in the Commonwealth Caribbean to attain independence. We shall deal firstly with Anguilla and then address the constitutional position of the independent State of St Christopher (or St Kitts) and Nevis.

A   ANGUILLA – A HISTORY OF NEGLECT: ITS EVENTUAL SECESSION AND BEYOND

Introduction

In a previous volume the author tried to convey to his readers that Anguilla had experienced centuries of arbitrary buffeting from the Colonial Office and almost total neglect from all quarters.[1] The record shows that at the time when the St Kitts Legislature reluctantly agreed to have Anguilla annexed to St Kitts, one of the conditions laid down was that the arrangement should entail no financial commitment by the larger colony and, although this particular condition has never, to the knowledge of the author, been specifically adverted to, St Kitts in fact did everything to fulfil the condition to the letter, as the following further historical details relating to Anguilla will fully demonstrate.

During most of the 19th century, when communication between the two islands was uncertain and irregular, Anguilla usually had as its representative in the Legislature a *Kittitian* with neither knowledge of, interest in, or commitment to the affairs of Anguilla; and the writer has been informed by a former Premier of the State that, as late as 1937, Anguilla was represented by an Anguillan who was resident in St Kitts and was, in fact, in charge of a sugar plantation there. He would visit Anguilla about once a year.

A short historical summary[2]

From 1825 until the end of that century the chief official of Anguilla was a stipendiary magistrate who was paid from imperial funds. He combined the functions of President of

---

1   See Phillips, 1977, Chapter IX, pp 98–106.
2   Once more I express my indebtedness to Mr Anthony Phillips, senior lecturer in history at the University of the West Indies, for having permitted to me to draw upon his work for the [contd]

the Vestry with dispenser of medicines. The then Vestry comprised the stipendiary magistrate, the rector of the Anglican church (*ex officio*) and 11 members elected by male inhabitants paying rates and taxes. The Vestry had power to impose rates and taxes; to supervise the maintenance of public roads; to regulate the salaries of public officers and generally to deal with local matters. In so far as a civil service was concerned, there was at that time a small number of public officers in the island operating by prescription. According to the Colonial Office records, the Anguillans displayed little evidence of civilisation and they continued 'to dream life away without a thought and without a care in a state of perfect happiness', in conditions of semi-barbarism.[3]

The Anguillan Court in its summary jurisdiction was presided over by the local stipendiary and a justice of the peace chosen from the total local commission, which comprised four justices of the peace. The magistrate also presided alone over a petty debt court. High Court matters were dealt with by the Chief Justice of St Kitts, who was paid an additional fee from imperial funds for this service. It should therefore come as no surprise to hear that during the 19th century there were many complaints from Anguilla concerning difficulties and delays in securing judicial remedies on the island. One interesting case was that of William Flemming, a landowner resident in England, who experienced considerable difficulty in recovering lands which were in possession of tenants as licencees. He was finally able to secure redress and to enter into possession of his lands in 1863 after a delay of three years, during which time the court had in fact not sat at all. Thereafter, a provision was made for an annual sitting of the High Court whether or not any case appeared on the list.

Life must have been dismal, too, for the stipendiaries, as is evident from two cases. In 1853, it was necessary to remove one Pickwood (who had served in this capacity in Anguilla for many years) to one of the two magisterial districts of St Kitts proper, because it was discovered that the utter solitude of the place had had a most deleterious effect upon his mental, no less than his physical, health. It was then arranged that one of the other St Kitts magistrates should be sent to Anguilla whenever emergencies arose and especially during the absence of the rector.

After Pickwood's death, it was decided that Dr Isidor Dyett, formerly in temporary charge of the Virgin Islands, should be appointed to Anguilla. Dyett's reaction was violent. He bemoaned the fact that his 32 years of faithful public service should not be considered worthy of 'some better fate, some happier lot, than that of a hopeless immolation at a place like Anguilla'.[4]

When Pickwood died in 1862 and before Dyett's appointment Benjamin Pine, Lieutenant Governor of St Kitts, had visited Anguilla to urge the candidature of Richardson, the senior JP, as stipendiary. He also then took the opportunity to make two additional proposals, viz:

(a) that an independent executive authority should be set up on the island; and

---

2   [contd] historical data in the following pages stating the position in Anguilla up to 1871, from an unpublished thesis presented to the University of London for an MA degree.

3   See CO 239/99, June 1856, No 22.

4   Phillips, 1977, p 253.

(b) that Anguilla should be separated from the St Kitts Legislature, as it had been before 1825, and its Vestry replaced by a local legislature of six to eight members, half elected and half nominated.

Pine felt that such an arrangement would meet with the approval of the people of Anguilla since they were not adequately represented in the St Kitts Legislature. He pointed out that because no Anguillan ever attended meetings of the legislature, the affairs of the island received little or no notice. The Lieutenant Governor urged that the Vestry was too large and unwieldy and that its constitution was defective. A local legislature, he felt, would do the trick. But Sir Henry Taylor in the Colonial Office poured scorn on the idea of an Anguillan Legislature. 'I should fear,' said Taylor, 'that the interest which very few Anguilla Negroes would exhibit might be much more lively than enlightened.'[5] Accordingly, Pine's proposals were ignored by both the then Governor of the Leewards (Hamilton) and his superiors in the Colonial Office. However, the Vestry was not prepared to let the matter lie and shortly afterwards it recommended that its constitution should be amended to grant the powers of a municipality jointly to the magistrate, two elected members and two nominated members, who would enact laws subject to the approval of the Lieutenant Governor of St Kitts. Although Governor Hamilton commended this proposal, the Colonial Office would have none of it.

It would appear that the first native Anguillan to enter the St Kitts legislature was EL Carter, a proprietor and cotton-grower, elected a member in April 1866. This was long overdue and the beneficial results revealed themselves immediately following his election: there arising a spate of legislation advantageous to Anguilla. Acts were passed to render the transfer of land easy and inexpensive. Legislation affecting the procedure to settle claims to land was also put on the statute book.

In 1867, an Act was passed to amend the constitution of the Vestry: thenceforth, instead of a membership of 13 there would be one of seven, viz, the stipendiary magistrate, three nominated members and three elected members.

Thus, by the time the Leeward Islands Federation of 1871 came into being, steps had already been taken gradually to integrate Anguilla into St Kitts from a legislative point of view, and relations were already significantly improved, relatively speaking. But this does not mean that conditions in Anguilla were much better than at the beginning of the 19th century. Anguilla therefore did not raise any objections to joining the Leeward Islands Federation. The islanders did not seem interested one way or the other.

On the other hand, Nevis objected violently. Sir Benjamin Pine, who in 1869 had returned as Governor of the Leewards, had a very difficult time persuading the legislature in Nevis that the union with St Kitts was desirable. Indeed, the Leeward Islands Federation had been established only after some display of force and much petitioning by Nevisians. When some years later, there was imposed an amalgamation between Nevis and St Kitts, this was even more bitterly resented by the Nevisians.

By 1873 the Anguillans had petitioned the Colonial Office requesting that the island be administered directly from Britain. It was then submitted that Anguillan trade was

---

5   Phillips, 1977, p 252.

affected and that the cost of consumer goods had increased by virtue of rule from Basseterre (the capital of St Kitts):

> The interest of Anguilla, its resources and capabilities of development are not understood ... by the [members of the] legislative body of St Christopher who are either strangers to us, ignorant of the community, careless of their wants, and therefore unequal to discharge ... the important duties of legislation for us ... this legislative dependence on St Kitts can in no sense be called a legislative union, has operated and continue[s] to operate most injuriously against us, and is mutually disliked.[6]

The position in 1882 was that St Kitts accordingly found itself with two unwilling, adopted children – neither adopted at the wish of their then mother, St Kitts.

A new era

Such was the chronic sense of grievance of the Anguillans and, even at the time that the author assumed the position of Officer administering the unitary colony of St Kitts/Nevis/Anguilla on 1 January 1966. Indeed, it can reasonably be stated that all the revolutionary happenings between 1967 and 1976 were the culmination of that pent up frustration. A full account of these happenings is documented in various other works[7] and a brief summary is given in the author's 1977 volume.[8]

A word should now be said of the UK Order in Council made in 1976 which the Anguillans regarded as having brought them 'freedom';[9] and it should here be pointed out that what follows represents the framework of the present type of colonial constitution that applies to the Cayman Islands, the Turks and Caicos Islands, Montserrat and the British Virgin Islands.[10]

As the writer pointed out in *Freedom in the Caribbean*, the Foreign and Commonwealth Office of the United Kingdom had in 1975 issued a release to the effect that a new form of administration had to be found, and a new constitution drawn up, for Anguilla under the Anguilla Act 1971. That statement ended with the words:

> HMG can see no better way forward than this arrangement which, while keeping the Associated State formally in being, will also provide for Anguilla a larger measure of autonomy in domestic affairs.[11]

The Commissioner, appointed pursuant to the 1976 Order in Council, was given such powers as were usually given to colonial governors under Instructions from the Queen.[12] He was permitted to appoint a chief secretary who would be his deputy, whenever he had occasion to be absent from Anguilla for a period of short duration. In the absence of

---

6   Phillips, 1977.
7   See, eg, a lucid account of these developments by Donald Westlake, 1973.
8   Phillips, 1977, Chapter IX, pp 98–106.
9   The Anguillan (Constitution) Order 1976 (SI 1976/50), hereafter called 'the 1976 Order'.
10 See Chapter VII of the first edition of the author's *West Indian Constitutions* (Phillips, 1985), pp 177–86.
11 Phillips, 1977, Chapter IX, p 105.
12 *Ibid*; for typical instructions, see Appendix II, p 231.

the chief secretary, the Attorney General would deputise for him, and in the absence of the Attorney General, such other suitable person as the Commissioner would appoint.[13]

The Order in Council also provided for the appointment of an Executive Council consisting of the Chief Minister, two other ministers and two *ex officio* members – the Attorney General and the Financial Secretary.[14]

The Commissioner was obliged to consult with the Executive Council whose advice he was, however, not bound to accept in any matters that in his opinion related to:[15]

(a) defence, external affairs, or internal security, including the police;

(b) appointment, suspension, termination of employment, dismissal and discipline of public servants;[16]

(c) any power conferred upon him by the constitution which he is empowered to exercise in his discretion or in pursuance of Instructions given to him by Her Majesty;

(d) any power conferred by any law other than the constitution which he is empowered or directed expressly or by necessary implication, by that or any other law, to exercise without consulting the council;

(e) any matter in which, in his judgment, the service of Her Majesty would sustain material prejudice thereby;

(f) where the matter to be decided in his judgment was too unimportant to require the advice of the council;

(g) where the urgency of the matter requires him to act before the council can be consulted.

Provided that in exercising his powers in relation to:

(i) the matters referred to in (a) above, the Commissioner was required to keep the council informed of any matters that in his judgment may involve the economic or financial interest of Anguilla; and

(ii) the matters referred to in (g) above, the Commissioner shall as soon as practicable communicate to the council the measures which he has adopted and the reasons for those measures.

There was to be a Legislative Assembly presided over by the Commissioner until such time as a Speaker was appointed; and comprising a membership of three *ex officio* members, viz, the Chief Secretary, the Financial Secretary and the Attorney General – with not less than seven elected members and two nominated members.[17]

The Order in Council also established a Public Service Commission,[18] as well as a Judicial Service Commission. The power to appoint public officers was, however, vested in the Commissioner, acting after consultation with the Public Service Commission, but in

---

13 See the 1976 Order, s 20.

14 *Ibid*, s 22.

15 *Ibid*, s 27.

16 *Ibid*, ss 64 and 65.

17 *Ibid*, s 34.

18 *Ibid*, ss 64 and 65.

so far as the Chief Secretary, Attorney General and Financial Secretary were concerned, the Commissioner would act in his own discretion. The magistrate, registrar and other officers of the High Court would be appointed by the Commissioner acting after consultation with the Judicial Service Commission.[19]

The Commissioner had a power of pardon which he would exercise in Her Majesty's name – subject to the Instructions given to him by Her Majesty under Her Sign, Manual and Signet.[20]

It was also in the Commissioner's power to constitute public offices.

The reserve powers of the Commissioner in relation to the making of laws are set out *in extenso*:[21]

(1) If the Commissioner considers that it is expedient–

   (a) in the interests of public order, public faith or good government (which expressions shall, without prejudice to their generality, include the responsibility of Anguilla as a territory within the Commonwealth and all matters pertaining to the creation or abolition of any public office or to the salary or other conditions of service of any public officer); or

   (b) in order to secure such detailed control of finances of Anguilla during such time as, by virtue of the receipt of financial assistance by Anguilla from Her Majesty's Exchequer in the United Kingdom for the purpose of balancing the annual budget or otherwise, such control rests with Her Majesty's Government ...

that any bill introduced or motion proposed in the Assembly relating to the matters referred to in subsection (1) hereof should have effect, then, if the Assembly fail to pass the bill or to carry the motion within such time and in such form as the Commissioner thinks reasonable and expedient, the Commissioner, acting in his discretion, at any time that he thinks fit, and notwithstanding any provision of this Constitution or any other law in force in Anguilla or of any rules of procedure of the Assembly declare that the Bill or motion shall have effect as if it had been passed or carried by the Assembly either in the form in which it was introduced or proposed or with such amendments as the Commissioner thinks fit which have been moved or proposed in the Assembly or any Committee thereof; and the Bill or the motion shall be deemed thereupon to have been so passed or carried, and the provisions of this Constitution, and in particular the provisions relating to assent to Bills and disallowance of laws, shall have effect accordingly:

Provided that the Commissioner shall not exercise his powers under this subsection without prior written instructions from a Secretary of State, unless in his judgment the matter is so urgent that it is necessary for him to do so before having consulted a Secretary of State.

(2) The Commissioner shall forthwith report to a Secretary of State every case in which he makes any such declaration and the reasons therefor.

(3) If any member of the Assembly objects to any declaration made under this section, he may, within fourteen days of the making thereof, submit to the Commissioner a statement in writing of his reasons for so objecting, and a copy of the statement shall (if furnished by the member) be forwarded by the Commissioner as soon as is practicable to a Secretary of State.

---

19 1976 Order, ss 66 and 67.
20 *Ibid*, s 75.
21 *Ibid*, s 55.

Concerning the power to assent, the Commissioner would assent to a Bill on Her Majesty's behalf or he may refer it for Her Majesty's assent, to be conveyed through a Secretary of State, in which case the Commissioner would signify her assent in due course by Proclamation.[22]

In this connection, the *ipsissima verba* of the Instrument might assist the reader to obtain a better understanding of the manner in which the assent to Bills is signified:

> When a Bill is presented to the Commissioner for assent he shall, subject to the provisions of this Constitution and of any Instructions addressed to him under Her Majesty's Sign, Manual, and Signet through a Secretary of State, declare that he assents to it, or that he reserves the Bill for the signification of Her Majesty's pleasure:
>
> Provided that the Commissioner shall reserve for the signification of Her Majesty's pleasure–
>
> (a) any Bill which appears to him to be in any way repugnant to, or inconsistent with, the provisions of this Constitution; and
>
> (b) any Bill which determines or regulates the privileges, immunities or powers of the Assembly or its members,
>
> unless he has been authorised by a Secretary of State to assent to it.[23]

Breach of faith

A word should now be said of the Anguilla Act[24] which brought about, as from 16 December 1980, the separation of Anguilla from the rest of the State of St Christopher, Nevis and Anguilla. It has already been pointed out that, although under the Anguilla Act of 1971 Anguilla received a new colonial style constitution in 1976, the Order in Council which made this possible[25] did not affect the integrity of the State of St Kitts/Nevis/Anguilla. Such interference would never have found favour with the then Premier of the State, Mr Bradshaw. However, when in 1979 Premier Lee Moore (who had succeeded the late Mr Bradshaw) was holding constitutional discussions in London, it was agreed that the State Government would offer no objection to the formal separation of Anguilla from the rest of the State and, at the same time, that St Kitts/Nevis would proceed to independence in 1980: this being in the nature of 'a package'.

The regime provided under the West Indies Act of 1967 for dividing an Associated State into two or more separate territories was that no order would be made to give effect to such division, unless it was made at the request and consent of the Associated State concerned.[26]

---

22 *Ibid*, s 56(2).

23 *Ibid*, s 56(2).

24 1980 C 67 UK.

25 The 1976 Order referred to above.

26 1967 C 4 (UK), s 9(1)(b). In this connection s 19(5) of the Act reads as follows: 'Any reference in this Act to the request and consent of an associated state is a reference to a request and consent signified by a resolution of the legislature of that state or, if that legislature has two Houses (by whatever name called), by a resolution of each House of that legislature.'

However, shortly after this approach was made to Premier Moore, he was replaced by a new Premier following a snap general election. The incoming People's Action Movement (PAM) Government was established by a coalition with the Nevis Reformation Party (NRP). The members of this party (as will be seen in a later section of this chapter) had, for a considerable period, been advocating the secession of Nevis from St Kitts. It would therefore clearly have been injudicious for the Premier to seek to obtain a resolution of the House agreeing to the secession of a sister island in these circumstances. Faced with this situation, Her Majesty's Government openly transgressed the terms of the statute under which the division was to take place: it purported to make the severance unilaterally and without obtaining the required 'request and consent' – Lord Trefgarne in the House of Lords justifying the action of the British Government by asserting that the move had the approval of both the Anguillans and the St Kitts Government.[27]

This is also a case in which the interest of a part of the State took precedence over the interests of the whole State. In this connection, the reader is reminded of the famous aphorism announced by the Commonwealth Office in dealing with Anguilla's affairs in 1967, viz, that it was no part of the policy of HMG that the Anguillans should continue to live under an administration they did not like.[28] In a similar way, when the matter of separation was being debated in the House of Lords, Lord Trefgarne was to put a commitment purportedly made to the Anguillans about the statutory requirement for separation in these words:[29]

> Given our commitment to the Anguillans, we cannot put off the formal separation of the island until a convenient opportunity arrives for the St Kitts Legislature to take the necessary action.

We thus have the British Parliament – which used to be termed 'the Mother of Parliaments' – passing legislation entirely to suit its own convenience and that of a people who chose to tear themselves away from a constituted State by rebellion and in open defiance of everyone.

Secession *de facto*

On 17 December 1980, a UK legislative instrument entitled the 'Anguilla (Appointed Day) Order' made what the Anguillans regarded as a great declaration, to wit:

> [T]he 19 December 1980, is appointed as the day on which Anguilla shall cease to form part of the territory of the associated state of St Christopher, Nevis and Anguilla.

Thus, the proposal which, as stated above, was first mooted by Sir Benjamin Pine *as long ago as 1862*, when he recommended that Anguilla should be separated from St Kitts as it had been before 1825, with its local legislature and independent executive authority, had in 1980, more than 118 years later, obtained the approval of the British Commonwealth Office.

---

27 See House of Lords Parliamentary Debates, Vol 996, No 19, Col 126.

28 Phillips, 1985, p 105.

29 See fn 27, above.

In 1977, the author, after looking at the 1976 Order in Council, posed the following question:

> Has Anguilla seceded? Since, stated above, it has been agreed by Her Majesty's Government that the Associated State of St Kitts /Nevis/Anguilla will formally remain in being, one can only assume that independence will be granted in due course to the entire state and not to a fraction thereof.[30]

This question has since been answered in the affirmative and the writer happened to be present to hear the formal announcement that secession had become an accomplished fact. By a curious quirk of fortune, he was, on 6 October 1981, paying his first return visit to Anguilla since retiring from the governorship of the State in 1969 and this private visit coincided with a meeting of the Anguilla Legislative Assembly in which Her Majesty's Commissioner (soon to be styled 'Governor') was reading the speech from the throne which thereafter was being debated on the same day. One item in the Commissioner's speech dealt with the island's constitution, in respect of which the Commissioner had this to say:

> History now records that on 19th December 1980 the constitutional ties with the Associated State of St Kitts/Nevis/Anguilla were finally and formally cut: happily in a spirit of good will and co-operation on all sides. On that day any remaining doubts that Anguilla was not a separate entity were finally dispelled. Equally significant, was the fact, that in a history going back to 1650, Anguilla for the first time has the right to follow its own constitution, uncomplicated by any legal or other ties. The importance and significance of this situation cannot be sufficiently emphasized for it means that Anguillans now have the opportunity to control their own political destiny. But on the other hand it also means that Anguillans will have to accept far greater responsibilities and obligations.

The Commissioner in his speech made the following proposal:

> It is the Government's hope that the necessary Order-in-Council will then be made so that the new Constitution will become effective in Anguilla as soon as possible and not later than the first anniversary of Separation Day, 19th December 1981.[31]

In August 1981, a Government delegation had visited London to ascertain what constitutional advance would be acceptable to Her Majesty's Government if a local consensus thereon could be achieved As a result, a White Paper making proposals was distributed and was available to all members so that the matter could be discussed at the meeting of 6 October 1981. The proposals, while not going as far as a request for associated statehood or internal self-government, provided for a further degree of local responsibility in the running of the island's affairs by the Government in power. (It had been made clear in London by HMG that, if any territory in future wished to attain associated statehood it would not be granted, but that HMG would be prepared to consider full independence for such an aspirant.)

---

30 Phillips, 1977, p 106.
31 In the event, the new Anguilla Constitution Order 1982 SI 1982/334 – hereafter 'the 1982 Order' – was not made at the Court at Buckingham Palace until 10 March 1982, and it came into operation on 1 April 1982, when all the amendments to the 1976 Order which have been mentioned became operative.

The Commissioner ended his discourse to the legislature with the following comforting words:

> Honourable Chief Minister, Hon Ministers of Government and other members of the Assembly, I pray that God will guide you in all your deliberations and that your endeavours will lead to social stability, social justice and national happiness.

Secession *de jure*

On 1 April 1982, therefore, an order[32] amending the main 1976 Anguilla Order introduced the following changes thereto:

(a) the Commissioner was replaced by a 'Governor';[33]

(b) the post of Chief Secretary was abolished;

(c) the jurisdiction of the West Indies Associated States Supreme Court was extended to Anguilla;

(d) provision was made for the dissolution of the Assembly when a no-confidence motion was passed in the legislature against the Government;[34]

(e) provision was made for an Acting Governor (there having been no such section in the previous order);[35]

(f) the Permanent Secretary, Finance, would replace the Financial Secretary as an *ex officio* member of the Executive Council;[36]

(g) the subject of finance would henceforth be the responsibility of a minister;

(h) the Governor would continue to be responsible for defence, external affairs, internal security (including the police) and the appointment, dismissal and retirement of public servants, but will be required to consult with the Chief Minister on matters relating to internal security (including the police) and matters relating to the public service;[37]

(i) the Governor would be empowered to appoint a member of the Executive Council to deal with matters relating to his responsibilities in the Legislative Assembly, which was being restyled 'House of Assembly'.[38]

Accordingly, the island, which in 1967 had defied everyone by rebellion and by seceding and promulgating a unilateral declaration of independence, had so fully profited from the fruits of that rebellion that it was now happily once more integrated with the rest of the Caribbean, including St Kitts itself. It has since been accepted as a separate member of the Caribbean Development Bank; it is interested in and has supported the idea of the formation of the Organisation of Eastern Caribbean States, although it has not yet formally been accepted as a member; it is already a member of the Caribbean Tourism

---

32 Anguillan Constitution Order 1982 SI 1982/334.

33 *Ibid*, s 19.

34 *Ibid*, s 25.

35 *Ibid*, s 20.

36 *Ibid*, s 23.

37 *Ibid*, s 23.

38 Proviso to s 28(4).

Association and the Caribbean Tourism Research Centre; it also participates in the arrangements of a Supreme Court in common with the members of the Organisation of Eastern Caribbean States; and it now wishes to become a full member of the Caribbean Community in its own right.

Now after all its trials and tribulations, Anguilla is proud to be a colony; to have a Governor of its own as well as its own House of Assembly and Executive Council. It may sound odd in this day and age that inhabitants of a country should regard this separate colonial status as in every way akin to independence, but that is the position in Anguilla. For relief from the shackles of St Kitts has always been, for over a century, their highest priority.

B ST KITTS/NEVIS: INDEPENDENCE IN FEDERATION

In examining the federal association into which St Christopher (St Kitts) and Nevis entered upon attaining independence, the first question which one is tempted to ask is: why was this arrangement necessary? The answer is not difficult to find. If there were no federation on terms acceptable to Nevis, the two islands would have gone their separate ways – thus, producing further political fragmentation in the Caribbean. The matter thus resolves itself into this: which is the greater evil, further subdivision or a marriage of convenience – which this federation undoubtedly is.

In *Freedom in the Caribbean*, reference was made to the long history of grievance nurtured by Nevis against St Kitts and Her Majesty's Government ever since the British Government, by imperial legislation, brought Nevis into the unitary state of St Kitts/Nevis/Anguilla in 1882. Nevis had hitherto been a separate jurisdiction with its own legislature and Lieutenant Governor. There was, at the time, considerable justification for the sense of grievance which was manifested by the people of that island. It is therefore right and proper at this stage to put the St Kitts/Nevis relationship into historical perspective. But in order to achieve this objective, the writer must perforce take his readers back to a time in the middle of the 19th century when, 'the Governor-in-Chief in and over the Leeward Islands' (hereafter referred to simply as the 'Governor') had his headquarters in Antigua after its removal toward the end of the previous century from Nevis, where it was known as Queen's House. It was in these latter surroundings that Admiral Lord Nelson and the other nabobs of the Royal Navy besported themselves in Nevis – the Admiral even finding his bride there in the person of Mrs Nesbitt.[39]

Historical background

In 1854, the Leeward Islands group was a British West Indian colony which comprised six separate administrative and political sub-units, viz, Antigua, St Christopher (St Kitts),[40] Nevis, Dominica, Montserrat and the British Virgin Islands: Antigua being at that time the seat of government of this group of islands. In the immediately preceding section of this

---

39 See fn 2, above.
40 The names 'St Christopher' and 'St Kitts' will be used interchangeably in this section, as indeed is permitted by the St Christopher and Nevis Constitution Order 1983 SI 1983/881 (UK), s 1(1), Sched 1.

chapter, we have already described the circumstances in which Anguilla became annexed to St Kitts; and, in Chapter 12, we shall give an account of the manner in which Barbuda became linked to Antigua. With respect to the islands of St Kitts and Nevis, it is worth noting that physically they are separated by a body of water, only two miles in width, called The Narrows.

The administrative structure of the sub-unit mentioned above followed a uniform pattern. The Governor of the Leeward Islands resided in Antigua, from which base he exercised a supervisory authority over all the islands referred to above. The Governments of St Kitts and Dominica were each administered by a resident Lieutenant Governor. On the other hand, the Governments of Nevis, Montserrat and the British Virgin Islands were each administered by a president: hence the expression 'the Presidency of Nevis', which was simply an administrative sub-unit of the Colony of the Leeward Islands in which the most senior bureaucrat was officially styled 'the President'. The Governor was the only political and administrative link between the Governments of the six territories, since each individual island possessed its own bicameral legislature, Executive Committee and civil service.

For the Leeward Islands, the years from 1854–71 were marked by economic stagnation and decline. However, they represented a significant period of transition in terms of the political and constitutional development of the islands. Anthony Phillips, in his well researched thesis to which reference has already been made,[41] has described in great detail the various measures which were initiated during that period, leading ultimately to the Leeward Islands Federation of 1871.

Although the idea which resulted in the Federation of the Leeward Islands in 1871 was mooted in 1868, federation *per se* was by no means a novel experience for the inhabitants of these islands, of which St Kitts was the first to be settled by English colonists. Indeed, it was from St Kitts that a number of the other islands was likewise settled, and we must bear in mind that as early as 1660 the Leeward Islands were administered by a common Governor, then stationed on the island of Barbados.

Original union of St Kitts and Nevis

As we have seen above, in 1854 the Presidency of Nevis was a separate and distinct political and administrative unit with its own institutions. However, both St Kitts and Nevis became quasi-Crown Colonies and a Commission was issued to one Captain McKenzie by the British Colonial Office, appointing him to be Lieutenant Governor of both islands. McKenzie arrived in St Kitts on 29 March 1867 and lost little time in attempting to fulfil what was clearly the real purpose of his appointment. In his very first speech to the Nevis Legislature, he raised the question of the proposed amalgamation of Nevis and St Kitts: thereafter promptly reporting to the Colonial Office that the proposal was well received by the Nevis Legislature which promised to give it serious consideration.[42] However, events were to show that the Nevisians were diametrically opposed to the merger.

---

41 See *op cit*, Phillips, fn 2.
42 *Op cit*, Phillips, fn 2, p 289.

By April 1868, less than a year after the proposals were first put forward, reports reaching the Secretary of State for the Colonies in London revealed that a spate of petitions had been presented in which the Nevisians 'prayed for' the restoration of their former constitution and the appointment of a local officer to administer the government of the former presidency, and protested vigorously against the intended merger. The main ground of opposition at the time being that St Kitts had an unusually heavy public debt and that amalgamation would, on that account, enure more to the advantage of St Kitts than to the benefit of Nevis.

Oddly enough, the amalgamation was as unpopular in St Kitts as it was in Nevis, for it was discovered that a majority of the members of the St Kitts Legislature were likely to vote against it. It was at the same time common knowledge that no one in Nevis was in favour of the proposed union and that, if the Colonial Office pressed the measure upon the Nevisians, serious disturbances were likely to ensue. Accordingly, on 18 June 1868, in an address to the Nevis Assembly, the Lieutenant Governor announced that the amalgamation proposals were being suspended pending further instructions from the Secretary of State.[43]

When, four months later, officials in London were advised that disturbances had in fact broken out in Nevis, they treated the reactions of the Nevisians with the usual scorn, concluding that the disturbances were 'disgraceful' and attributable to a 'series of errors and indiscretions on the part of the Lieutenant-Governor of a very plain and palpable character'.[44]

The fact is that, in the meantime, an attack was being levelled at Nevis from another quarter. By 1869, the proposal for a federation of the Leeward Islands had gained almost total acceptance – receiving support in all island legislatures except that of Nevis which turned out to be the last Assembly to approve – in circumstances that, in our day and age, would be considered quite unbelievable.

On the morning of 1 December 1869, the day fixed for the Federation Debate in the Nevis Assembly, the Lieutenant Governor summoned the nominated members of that body to his official residence to impress upon them that it was imperative that the measure should be carried on that day *at all costs*. It was felt that an affirmative vote was necessary, not only for the federation proposal itself, but also as an assertion of law and order in the face of threatened anarchy. The Lieutenant Governor apprehended that there could be further disturbances and, since he was of the view that the local police could not be relied on if the disturbances did take place, he arranged to land a small party of marines from a British frigate, then conveniently lying off Nevis, 'ostensibly, simply as a guard of honour', with a larger force waiting in readiness to be brought ashore if the situation warranted it.[45]

Half an hour later, after the time appointed for the commencement of the Federation Debate, the meeting of the House of Assembly was convened and proceeded at once to deal with the business of the day in the absence of the elected members of the Assembly, who had all decided to boycott the meeting. However, although at least one elected

---

43   *Op cit*, Phillips, fn 2, p 304.
44   *Op cit*, Phillips, fn 2, p 305.
45   *Op cit*, Phillips, fn 2, pp 359–60.

member appears to have been needed to constitute the required quorum, so firm was the resolve of the Lieutenant Governor to secure the approval of the measure by the Assembly at all costs that he arranged for the instantaneous appointment (and swearing in) of an additional nominated member. In his address to the House, the Lieutenant Governor outlined the benefits that would accrue to Nevis by replacing 'the narrow prejudices of a small locality' by 'high' and 'nobler feelings of pride in a nationality which [Nevisians] had helped to create and in a common country which they will help to rule'. This statement of course had no basis whatever in reality. Nevertheless, at the end of the day, the necessary resolutions were duly recorded as having been passed unanimously and it was in this extraordinary and high handed manner that in 1869 the people of Nevis were forced to signify their 'support' for the proposed Leeward Island Federation.

This was not the end of the woes of the Nevisians as far as federation was concerned. The five elected members of the legislature petitioned the Secretary of State, pointing out that they had boycotted the meeting of 1 December 1869 to emphasise their opposition to the measure; that the votes of the nominated members were insufficient to constitute a quorum; that even the swearing in of an additional nominated member could not cure that defect and accordingly the passage of the resolution was 'unconstitutional and arbitrary'.[46]

The response of the Secretary of State was predictable in the circumstances. In rejecting the petition, he pointed out that if the construction urged by the petitioners was accepted it would mean that it would never be possible to form a House of Assembly since, in the case of the first meeting of that body after a general election, none of the members could have taken the qualification oath and there would therefore be no quorum.[47]

What emerges from this response is that the officials at the Colonial Office had eventually – by a subterfuge – secured their main objective, namely, amalgamating the small islands of the Leeward Islands into a single political administrative unit. In so doing, they were not prepared to concede that the Lieutenant Governor acted unconstitutionally or arbitrarily. They were prepared to resort to any argument, no matter how irrelevant, to justify his action and sustain their position. Thus, the Nevisians may have won the battle in opposing a union with St Kitts, but they lost the war in that they were unable to avoid being incorporated into a federation in which St Kitts was also a participant.

Undaunted by the setback in the Nevis House of Assembly, the people of Nevis continued to make further representations against the federal measure and the manner in which the resolution was passed. They drew up a memorial requesting that general elections be held on the specific issue of federation. Their efforts were all to no avail, since with the passage of the resolution by the Nevis Assembly it had been made to appear that all the constituent legislatures had signified their assent to the federal union. The imperial Parliament then proceeded to ratify the decision of the island legislatures and to enact the Leeward Islands Act of 1871, creating a federal scheme which, far from being conceived by the people and receiving their spontaneous support, had been vigorously opposed by

---

46   *Op cit*, Phillips, fn 2, p 363.
47   *Op cit*, Phillips, fn 2, p 363.

the people of Nevis. Like all similarly contrived unions, this federation was doomed to failure from its inception.

The Federal Colony of the Leeward Islands, which, as we have seen, was established by the Leeward Island Act, 1871 of the United Kingdom Parliament,[48] consisted of the six territories already mentioned each with its own legislature. In 1882, however, the Legislature of the Colony of the Leeward Islands, having been authorised by ordinances passed by the respective legislatures of St Kitts and Nevis, enacted the St Christopher and Nevis Act making provision for the union of the two presidencies: s 4 of that Act providing as follows:

> The Presidencies of St. Christopher and Nevis, consisting of the islands of St Christopher, Nevis and Anguilla,[49] with their respective dependencies, shall form one Presidency, to be called the Presidency of St Christopher and Nevis.

It was by this rather involved and convoluted process that the once separate Presidency of Nevis came to be joined in an unwilling union with the Presidency of St Kitts. Both Nevis and Anguilla in this way remained as sister colonies of St Kitts – very poor relations – from 1882 until Anguilla was formally separated in 1980 and Nevis joined St Kitts in a quasi-federal union at the time of independence in 1983.

The Nevisians never ceased to protest against the union with St Kitts. In 1921, for example, the then Administrator of the Presidency wrote a dispatch to the Secretary of State for the Colonies in London urging that HMG should sanction the secession of Nevis from St Kitts. He urged in support his own convenience and the fact that the Nevisians are an independent people who should never have been tied to St Kitts. His monumental despatch received a very cold response from the then Secretary of State – Winston S Churchill (no less) – who replied, simply urging that all that was needed for welding the two colonies together was a steamer which could be purchased from the Crown Agents for £500. Churchill's response further illustrates the insensitive manner in which successive Secretaries of State for the Colonies have treated what for the Nevisians was a very real and serious grievance, viz, having to remain unwillingly bound in a union with St Kitts.

It is generally acknowledged that the federation failed on several counts. It failed to live up to the promise of greatly improved administration; it failed to produce economies in the administration of the federating islands as one composite unit; and it failed in that it did not produce any significantly greater output in terms of social development.

When one recalls that the federal scheme was avidly promoted by the British Government, acquiesced in by most of the then governments of the Leeward Islands but consistently opposed by the people of Nevis, one cannot be surprised that the union in the end proved unsuccessful. Even Dominica – one of the acquiescing entrants – was never really reconciled to remaining in this union and, following the recommendations of two Royal Commissions, was eventually separated from the Leeward Islands to become attached to the Windward Islands in 1940. The Federation itself was brought to an end by the British Parliament in 1956 at the request of its constituent units.

---

48 See the Leeward Islands Act 1882 (No 2) contained in the Laws of the Leeward Islands 1927 Revision, as Chapter 10.

49 Anguilla had by then also been linked unwillingly to St Kitts; see above.

On the dissolution of the Federation of the Leeward Islands, almost all of the federating units reverted to their former separate colonial status – all, that is, except Nevis, which continued in its unhappy union as part of the colony of St Christopher, Nevis and Anguilla. Thus, the Leeward Islands Letters Patent 1956 which provided for the administration of that group of islands, contains the following definition:

'Leeward Islands' means the Colony of Antigua, *the Colony of Saint Christopher, Nevis and Anguilla,* the Colony of Montserrat and the Colony of the Virgin Islands [emphasis supplied].

In an attempt to placate the Nevisians, various token concessions were made. One of these concessions took the form of a provision in the Instructions passed under the Royal Sign, Manual and Signet to the Governor of the Leeward Islands dated 20 June 1956, viz, that there should always be a member of the Executive Council selected from among the elected representatives of Nevis. At that time, the members of the Executive Council of St Christopher/Nevis/Anguilla comprised the following:

the Governor;

the Administrator;

two official members;

one nominated member; and

four elected members who shall be elected by the nominated and elected members of the Legislative Council of the Colony from among the elected members of that council.

Provided that whenever the number of elected members of the Executive Council of St Christopher/Nevis/Anguilla does not include a person who has been elected to the Legislative Council of the colony to represent an electoral district in the Island of Nevis, then the number of the elected members of the Executive Council shall be increased by the election thereto by the nominated and elected members of the Legislative Council of the colony of an additional member from among the elected members representing the Island of Nevis in the Legislative Council.

And so we come to the next federation into which Nevis was to find itself submerged – the West Indies Federation.

The people of Nevis did not take exception to the constitutional change brought about by the Federation of the West Indies (which was inaugurated in 1958) until Sunday, 2 April 1961, when about 4,000 persons assembled at Grove Park, Charlestown, Nevis, to take part in a demonstration which had come together to move a resolution by the people of Nevis urging that they be permitted to secede from the unitary State of St Kitts/Nevis/Anguilla.

The resolution ended with these words:

Be it therefore Resolved that this body of persons here assembled, by their resolution give to the Legislative Council Representatives for Nevis a full mandate to move at the next meeting of the Legislative Council of the Colony of St Kitts/Nevis/Anguilla that the island of Nevis secede from the Colony of St Kitts/Nevis/Anguilla, establishing the island of Nevis as a separate unit within the framework of the West Indies Federation.

The further resolution – which was to be moved at the next meeting of the Legislative Council – was also approved and was in these terms:

WHEREAS the people of the Island of Nevis in the Colony of Saint Christopher, Nevis and Anguilla having assembled at Grove Park in the town of Charlestown, in the island of Nevis, on Sunday the 2nd day of April, 1961, at 4.00 pm. DID RISE IN PROTEST against the willful and persistent indifference and neglect concerning the social, economic and political affairs of Nevis.

AND WHEREAS it is the feeling of the people of Nevis that the existing constitution of the Colony denies them the rights of free people to take active part in the government of their island,

AND WHEREAS the said people of Nevis by free, peaceful and democratic means demonstrated publicly on the day and date above-mentioned and passed the resolution, *attached hereto,* empowering their Legislative Council Representatives to move a resolution in the Legislative Council of the Colony, that the island of Nevis secede from the Colony of Saint Christopher, Nevis and Anguilla,

BE IT THEREFORE RESOLVED that this Honourable House approve of the secession of the Island of Nevis from the Colony of Saint Christopher, Nevis, and Anguilla and that the necessary constitutional exercises be immediately implemented to effect such a secession.

AND BE IT FURTHER RESOLVED that immediate steps be taken to inform the Federal Government of the wishes of the people of Nevis to have the said island considered and established as a separate unit within the framework of the West Indies Federation.

Subsequently, the Nevis representatives tried to secure representation at the London Conference in May–June 1961 when the Federal Constitution and territorial constitutions were being reviewed, but this representation was denied them.

Thus the secession movement in the West Indies, though it began *de facto* with Jamaica in 1962, had for many years previously been strongly advocated by Nevis and Anguilla as a way out of their difficulties with St Kitts. What is more, Nevis has never at any time abandoned her latent desire to secede.

On 28 March 1969, the then Governor of St Kitts/Nevis/Anguilla[50] received a communication from one of the Nevis representatives in the St Kitts/Nevis/Anguilla House of Assembly in which he enclosed a petition with a request that it be forwarded to the Foreign Secretary of Great Britain. It was dated 19 March 1969, and was signed by the Chairman of the Nevis Local Council. The petition condemned the use, or threat, of force in Anguilla, and called upon Britain to negotiate peacefully. It then went on to demand greater autonomy for the Island of Nevis 'so as to avoid the possibility of a crisis similar to that which occurred in Anguilla'. Finally, the petitioners called 'for a constitutional Conference with adequate representation in order to meet our demands'. The communication was duly forwarded to the Premier and to the British Government representative.

When one considers the firm request made in this petition in 1969, and when one reviews the constitutional history of Nevis as has been set out above, it is difficult not to feel some sympathy with the people of the island. One can also appreciate why the authorities in 1983 felt impelled to grant to Nevis at the time of independence the degree

---

50   The writer was the Governor of the State at the instant time.

of autonomy accorded it. As far back as the general elections of 1975, the NRP had, in its manifesto, stated as follows:

> The NRP will strive at all costs to gain secession for Nevis from St Kitts – a privilege enjoyed by the Island of Nevis prior to 1882.

In 1978, this firm resolve of the Nevisians to secede once again received expression. The people of Nevis on this occasion asked that Britain should confer on them the status of an Associated State. In a letter dated 5 May 1978, from the Acting Premier of the State (CA Paul Southwell) addressed to Simeon Daniel, then Chairman of the Nevis Local Council, Southwell wrote, *inter alia*, as follows:

> ... I have the honour to put forward the attached proposals for your consideration in the hope that they will successfully bridge the gap between our two parties and our two groups and bring about the unity of purpose which is not only vital to the survival of this country, but honestly expected by all right-thinking people in the State.

Southwell's proposals were for granting Nevis very little more power than it already had in so far as local government was concerned and his letter seemed to imply that Nevis was entitled to nothing more than that.

Daniel's reply was firm and resolute in the direction of secession. Here it is:

> I have read your proposals and note with regret that although in your letter you have expressed a desire to bridge the gap between our groups and to bring about unity of purpose, yet by your proposals you have openly insulted the people of Nevis.
>
> Also in the light of your Government's move for political independence for the State, my proposals and those of the other elected representatives for the island, the Nevis Reformation Party, are as follows:
>
> (a) That you recognise and take cognizance of the political aspiration and ambitions of the people of Nevis.
>
> (b) That you recognize and support the right of self-determination for the people of Nevis regardless of the size of the country.
>
> (c) That you consider the justice of the case of the people of Nevis for the right to self-determination and not seek to change their nationality against their will.
>
> (d) That you act in a statemanlike manner and request Her Majesty's Britannic Government to act under the provision of the West Indies Act 1967, Section 9, subsection 1(b), so as to divide the State of Saint Christopher, Nevis and Anguilla whereby Nevis shall become the Associated State of Nevis.

There can be no doubt, therefore, that the St Kitts Labour Party under the leadership of Bradshaw (with Southwell as Deputy Premier) was, up to 1978, steering for a head-on collision with Nevis. Bradshaw, however, died in 1978 and, a year later, unfortunately, so also did Southwell.

Notwithstanding the consistency displayed by Nevis in relation to secession, in December 1979 the then government conferred with HMG and the leadership of the NRP, at which conference it was agreed as follows:

(a) St Kitts/Nevis should proceed to independence in June 1980 as a *unitary state;* and

(b) a referendum would be held in Nevis 18 months after independence to allow the Nevisians to decide whether they wanted the arrangement to continue or whether they would prefer separation form St Kitts.

Needless to say, even after this arrangement had been reached, the NRP remained adamant that they wanted secession.

The general elections which were held in 1980 produced the following results:

St Kitts Labour Party   – 4 seats (all in St Kitts proper)

PAM   – 3 seats in St Kitts

NRP   – 2 seats in Nevis

On the basis of the outcome, a coalition Government was formed by the PAM and the NRP. The coalition was led by Dr Kennedy Simmonds of the PAM, who became Premier of the country.

As mentioned above, independence had been scheduled for June 1980, but the change of government in that year brought about a change in the timetable, since the new Government wanted time to study the issue and to formulate its own proposals. It was in these circumstances that the coalition in 1982 produced a White Paper setting out proposals for a substantial devolution of power to Nevis upon independence. The proposals set out in the White Paper were to a large extent incorporated in the independence constitution which we shall now discuss.

Federation constitution

With regard to the independence constitution of St Kitts and Nevis, the first thing to be observed is that it established what was styled 'a sovereign federal State'.[51] However, whereas in a normal federation the constituent units would each have had a Governor while there would be a Governor General of the whole Federation,[52] in this case the Federation has a Governor General while Nevis has a *deputy Governor General* appointed by the Governor General who has the power to limit the functions of his deputy and to prescribe the length of his term of office.[53] In making this appointment, the Governor General is required to act on the advice of the Premier of Nevis.[54] However, in making an appointment of a person to deputise for him whenever he has occasion to be absent from St Christopher and Nevis for a period of short duration, or is indisposed for a short period, the Governor General acts on the advice of the Prime Minister of the Federation,[55] although it is within the constitutional competence of the Governor General, acting in his own discretion, to give his deputy instructions in respect of the function he is to perform and the deputy must conform.[56]

---

51 See Schedule to the St Christopher and Nevis Constitution Order 1983 SI 1983/881), s 1, hereafter referred to simply as 'the St Kitts Constitution 1983'.

52 *Ibid*, s 21.

53 *Ibid*, s 23(2).

54 *Ibid*, s 23(6)(b).

55 *Ibid*, s 23(6)(a).

56 *Ibid*, s 23(3).

The constitution established a National Assembly of the Federation which is unicameral, but consists of 'representatives' *and* senators, as in the case of St Vincent and Dominica. One-third of the total number of senators (excluding any senator who holds the office of Attorney General) is appointed by the Governor General acting on the advice of the Leader of the Opposition while the remainder are appointed on the Prime Minister's advice.[57]

There is to be an electoral commission for the Federation of which one member will be appointed by the Governor General in his own deliberate judgment, one on the advice of the Prime Minister and the third on the advice of the Leader of the Opposition: the function of this Commission being to supervise the supervisor of elections in the performance of his duties.[58]

The Nevis administration

At this point, a word should be said about the Nevis regime and about its relations with St Kitts. The law making body of Nevis is to be styled the Nevis Island Legislature and shall consist of Her Majesty and an Assembly styled the Nevis Island Assembly.[59] The assembly comprises both elected and nominated members.[60]

The Nevis Island administration consists of:

(a) a Premier; and

(b) two other members, or not less than two or more than such greater number of members as the Nevis Island Legislature may prescribe, who shall be appointed by the Governor General. These members of the administration (which is a euphemism for 'ministers') are of course appointed by the Governor General acting on the advice of the Premier of Nevis.

The functions of the administration are to advise the Governor General in the government of the island of Nevis.[61]

The Nevis Island Legislature may make Ordinances (not 'Acts' as in the case of the Federal Parliament) for the peace, order and good government of Nevis in respect of a list of 23 subjects referred to as 'the specified matters', set out in Sched 5 of the country's constitution.[62]

The administration has *exclusive executive responsibility* with respect to the following matters:[63]

(a) airports and seaports;

(b) education;

(c) extraction and processing of minerals;

---

57 St Kitts Constitution 1983, s 30.
58 *Ibid*, s 33.
59 See the St Christopher and Nevis Constitution Order 1983 SI 1983/881, s 100.
60 *Ibid*, s 101.
61 *Ibid*, s 102.
62 *Ibid*, s 103(1).
63 *Ibid*, s 106.

(d) fisheries;

(e) health and welfare;

(f) labour;

(g) land and buildings vested in the Crown;

(h) licensing of imports into and exports out of St Christopher and Nevis.

It is to be noted that the Island Legislature may make laws containing incidental and supplementary provisions relating to matters other than the specified subjects, 'but if there is any inconsistency between those provisions and the provisions of any law enacted by Parliament, the provisions of the law enacted by Parliament shall prevail'.[64]

The Premier of Nevis shall not advise the Governor General to dissolve the Nevis Island Legislature unless he has consulted the Prime Minister.[65]

The staff of the administration shall consist of such number of public officers as may be constituted in that behalf under s 63 after consultation between the Prime Minister and the Premier.

There is an interesting provision in the constitution relating to revenue allocation, viz, the proportion to be paid to the Federal Government and to the Nevis Government will be shared by reference to the population of Nevis, on the one hand, and the population of St Kitts and Nevis as a whole, on the other hand, to be ascertained in accordance with the latest census figures; provided that the administration's share shall be subject to the following deductions:

(a) a contribution to the cost of common services provided for St Kitts and Nevis by government; and

(b) a contribution to the cost of meeting the debt charges for which the government is responsible – and such debt charges include interest, sinking fund charges, the repayment or amortisation of debt and all expenditure in connection with the raising of loans on the security of the consolidated fund and the service and redemption of the debt created thereby.

It is the Governor General who would make rules to give effect to the provisions prescribing what services are to be regarded as common services and what contributions are to be made by the Nevis Administration: but, in so doing, he must act on the advice of the Prime Minister, which advice will only be given after consultation with the Premier[66] whose concurrence is also required.

The High Court has exclusive original jurisdiction to adjudicate as between the government and administration 'in so far as the dispute involves any question (whether of law or fact) on which the existence or extent of a legal right depends'.[67]

All these clauses presuppose a high degree of amity and collaborative will as between the Government of the Federation and the Nevis administration; and it must be clear to

---

64 St Christopher and Nevis Constitution Order 1983 SI 1983/881, s 103(2).

65 *Ibid*, s 104(3).

66 *Ibid*, s 110.

67 *Ibid*, s 112.

all that the absence of such amity will most surely mean an end to the continued existence of the Government as at present constituted.

Then there is the famous secession clause which reads as follows:

> The Nevis Island Legislature may provide that the island of Nevis shall cease to be federated with the island of St Christopher and accordingly that this Constitution shall no longer have effect in the island of Nevis.[68]

This provision is followed by the regime by which such secession may be effectuated.[69]

In order to give effect to such a de-federation the necessary Bill will require a two-thirds majority of all the elected members of the Nevis Assembly and it must not be presented to the Governor General for assent, unless the following conditions are fulfilled:

(a) there must be an interval of at least 90 days between the introduction of the Bill into the assembly and the second reading thereof;

(b) after the assembly shall have passed the Bill, it must be approved on a referendum in Nevis by at least two-thirds of all votes validly cast; and

(c) full and detailed proposals for the future constitution of Nevis (whether as a separate State or a State in association with some other country) must have been laid before the National Assembly for at least six months before the holding of the referendum while those entitled to vote on the referendum must have access to those proposals at least 90 days before the holding of the referendum.

The Nevis Legislature will be competent to make arrangements for independent and impartial persons nominated by an international body to observe the conduct of such a referendum.[70]

Another unique feature of this constitution is that provision is made therein for the new 'rump' St Kitts Constitution in the event of the secession of Nevis.[71] Thus, whereas Nevis will have to concern itself with drafting its own constitution, a ready made one is forged for St Kitts.

There is one other provision in this unique constitution to which we must advert. The constitution is at pains to emphasise that the power and authority of the Governor General shall not be abridged, altered or in any way be affected by the appointment of a deputy under the relevant section and that (as mentioned above) such deputy 'shall conform to and observe all instructions that the Governor General, acting in his own deliberate judgment, may from time to time address to him'.[72]

St Kitts and Nevis has broken new ground in creating a federal structure that is *sui generis*: a Federation not between St Kitts and Nevis, but between Nevis on the one hand and St Kitts and Nevis on the other.

---

68 St Christopher and Nevis Constitution Order 1983 SI 1983/881, s 113(1).
69 *Ibid*, s 113(2)–(8).
70 *Ibid*.
71 *Ibid*, s 115 and Scheds 3.
72 *Ibid*, s 23(3).

There can be no doubt that the framers of the independence constitution displayed considerable political ingenuity; and it is not without significance that, at snap general elections held on 21 June 1984, the governing party of Dr Kennedy Simmonds (political leader of the PAM) won six of the eight seats for St Kitts in the House of Assembly while the NRP won all three Nevis seats. Thus, the coalition formed by these two parties, which took the country into independence, did, in fact, control nine seats in an 11 seat National Assembly at that time.

Call for a Nevis referendum

The breakdown in relations coincided ironically with the return to power in 1995 of the St Kitts-Nevis Labour Party – although from the author's observation the new government was most anxious to work harmoniously with the Nevis Island administration.

In the manifesto preceding the 1995 general elections, the party had indicated a desire to appoint a commission to consider constitutional reform in order to encourage 'unity among (our) people'.

Shortly after the new government came to office, it set out to regulate offshore financial services in the Federation. To this end, it introduced four Bills, viz, the Trusts Act 1996, the Companies Act 1996, Limited Partnerships Act 1996 and the Financial Services Committee Act 1996. The Federal Government's intention was to regulate these services in order to ensure that foreign organisations and other persons did not use the country as a haven for money-laundering and other illicit activities.

The Nevis Island administration contended that the real objective of the Federal Government was to place the financial and business sectors of Nevis under its control and direction. The Nevis Island administration drew attention to the fact that the specified matters in Sched 5 of the Constitution included a section entitled 'industries, trades and businesses' under which the Nevis Island Legislature alone had power to legislate and that, in any event, such finance regulating activities had always hitherto been supervised and controlled by Nevis.

The Nevis Island administration therefore reacted swiftly and angrily to the proposed legislation arguing that the Bills, if passed into law, would not only be unconstitutional, but would 'undermine the constitutional and legislative authority of the [Nevis Island administration] and result in the destruction of the economy of Nevis'.

The Premier's harshest criticism was reserved for the Financial Services Committee legislation which in his opinion was calculated to 'destroy the economic self-determination, self-sufficiency and self-respect of all Nevisians'. The rhetoric continued until 4 June 1996 when the Premier formally announced that his administration had decided that Nevis should cease to be federated with St Kitts and would invoke the modalities of s 113 of the Constitution which required, *inter alia*, the holding of a referendum.

The Premier went to the polls on 24 February 1997 urging the country to vote for secession and winning a 3:2 majority, whereafter a Separation Bill was introduced. This Bill was eventually passed on 13 October 1997 and a referendum was later set for 10 August 1998.

The Nevis Island administration did not, however, obtain the 2:3 majority of electors voting for the referendum.

In the meantime, the Caribbean Community had assumed the role of honest broker and intervened by appointing as mediator the then Chairman of the Organisation – Prime Minister Bird of Antigua – who, in turn, enlisted the support of two distinguished West Indians[73] to mediate in an effort to forestall the holding of a referendum. This team suggested the appointment of a small commission to examine all practicable bases of future relations between St Kitts and Nevis, including that of separation.

The mediation team requested of the Nevis Island administration that the second reading of the Separation Bill be deferred pending the submission of the commission's report and for a period of three months thereafter. It also asked the Federal Government to withhold promulgation of the legislation which was in dispute.

Although the Federal Government did not put the legislation into operation, the Nevis Island administration proceeded with putting the Separation Bill through all its stages in the legislature. But, as mentioned above, the referendum failed for lack of the two-thirds majority vote.

The commission which was duly appointed in December 1997 reported on 31 July 1998. Its main recommendations, as supplemented by further recommendations of a constitutional task force subsequently appointed,[74] were as follows below.

Recommendations for constitutional change

1   The monarchy should be replaced by a presidency.
2   The main powers of the Federal Presidency should embrace foreign affairs, national security, the judiciary, appointments to certain sensitive offices, appointment of independent parliamentarians; ceremonial matters.

    He would of course be assisted by two Secretaries of State to form his Cabinet.
3   The Federal President and Vice President should rotate between St Kitts and Nevis, beginning with St Kitts. The appointments to be made on this basis:

    The two island assemblies should nominate two persons from the island whose turn it is to provide for the President. One of those persons should be chosen as President in a nationwide election by secret ballot and simple majority.

    The Vice President should be elected on the same basis as the President, with the Vice Presidential nominees coming from the island other than that of the Presidential nominees.
4   A St Kitts Island administration should be established with the same powers within St Kitts as the Nevis Island administration within Nevis. Separate island Legislatures should be established on the same basis.
5   There should be a unicameral parliament.
6   The Federal Parliament should comprise equal numbers of elected members from St Kitts and from Nevis to whom will be added appointed non-voting independents.

---

73   Sir Shridath Ramphal and Sir Alister McIntyre.
74   The writer was chairman of both the Commission and the Task Force.

7 Non-voting independents representing various interests in the society other than political parties should be appointed by the Head of State after consultation.

8 The speaker of parliament should be appointed by the President, after approval by Parliament.

9 The constitutional disqualification of ministers of religion from election or appointment to Parliament should be removed.

10 An office of public defender should be established who would effectively be an ombudsman with enhanced legal powers, having the authority not only to investigate but to initiate legal action.

The public defender should report to the Federal Parliament and not to the proposed individual island legislatures but his investigative functions should apply to action at either the federal or island level.

11 The scope of s 15 of the Constitution should be extended to embrace other forms of discrimination such as gender discrimination or that against the physically challenged.

12 The declaratory elements should be re-formulated to affirm simply and positively the inalienable rights of the people of the country.

13 Each island administration should have its own cabinet to be nominated by each Premier from within or outside the legislature and be subject to confirmation by the Legislature.

14 The St Kitts and Nevis Constitution should be patriated within the framework of autochthony.

15 Conciliation machinery involving a standing committee and a CARICOM facilitating group should be enshrined in the new constitution to deal with jurisdictional disputes.

What the new Constitution Commission and the Task Force hope is that a process of public education in constitutional awareness over the next few years would continue with a view to involving the entire St Kitts and Nevis community to arrive at a final consensus as to the best form of Constitution to suit their needs. The road ahead is rough and long. And, perhaps, it would be better in the next few years to continue the dialogue begun in 1998 in the hope at eventually arriving at a mutually satisfactory constitutional destination.

Our next chapter deals with Guyana's problems.

CHAPTER 8

CONSTITUTIONAL TRAVAIL IN GUYANA

HISTORICAL INTRODUCTION

Guyana in a constitutional sense evolved typically from Dutch and British colonialism through internal self-government to independence, first under a monarchical regime and later under what has been termed 'co-operative republicanism'. But it was not plain sailing.

In so far as the colonial period is concerned, Guyana's main original representative institution was not, however, a House of Assembly patterned after the British House of Commons as was the case, for example, in Jamaica and Trinidad. In this respect, the situation differed fundamentally also from the Houses of Assembly set up elsewhere in the Caribbean. The Guyana representative institution was *sui generis* having its origin in the Dutch settlement of Essequibo, where the settlers from Holland established their first colony in the early 17th century. Later the Dutch were to settle in Demerara and Berbice as well.

In 1783, the British defeated the Dutch and took control of the settlements. However, later in that year the French recaptured the colony from the British and handed it back to the Dutch. The British were, however, once more to recapture it from the Dutch in 1796, but lost it to them in 1802, only to retake it in 1803. In 1814, Britain at the end of the Napoleonic Wars bought Guyana for £3 m and it was renamed British Guiana in 1831.

The governmental institutions were established to promote the aims and objectives of the Dutch companies engaged in trade in Essequibo: the officers of these institutions being essentially the servants of the companies. The governmental organisation traces its origin as far back as 1621 with the formation of the Chartered West India Company by the Dutch. Until 1690, the company was managed by a Commander and managers who appointed a council with a secretary; and it was this council which subsequently became a Court of Justice – thus, effectively combining judicial with administrative functions. Later the governing body became the Court of Policy and Justice and this body performed executive, legislative and judicial functions. Thus, what was a commercial body became an effective instrument of governmental policy.[1]

In 1743, another body known as a Court of Keizers of Electors had been set up with the sole object of selecting nominees from among the landed gentry for appointment to the Court of Policy. Later, when the English and French took charge of the country in 1781 and 1782 respectively, the Court of Policy was re-organised by reducing the planters' representatives thereon to three, as against five representing the company, and increasing the head tax on slaves from 2 guilders to 6 guilders. After some disagreement on these changes on the part of the planters, the Dutch Government dispatched a Commission from Holland to look into the matter. The result of the Commission's findings was the setting up of a 'Concept Plan of Redress' which the English used as a basis for a new

---

1   See section entitled 'The roots of the legal system' in Shahabuddeen, 1973, pp 1–7.

constitution after Guyana finally was ceded to them in 1814. Under this 'concept', colonists and the Company secured equal representation: a single Court of Policy of Essequibo and Demerara being then formed to comprise:

the director general of the company;

the commissioner of Essequibo;

the fiscal of Essequibo;

the fiscal of Demerara;

two private individuals from Essequibo; and

two from Demerara.

Meanwhile, the Amerindians (the original settlers in the country) had been joined by Dutch and English settlers. There had also been negro slaves brought into the colony during the late 18th century and early 19th century who, after emancipation in 1833, left the sugar estates for an independent life. It was at this point that Portuguese indentured labour was introduced. The social pattern was undergoing considerable change and the planters and commercial interests were losing their influence.

Constitutional development of 1891

The year 1891 was important in the history of constitution-making in Guyana, that being the year when the planters were finally deprived of most of their powers. Under the Political Constitution Ordinance No 1 of 1891, the membership of the Court of Policy was increased by three official Crown appointees and by three elected members; the Court of Keizers was abolished; there was a reduction in the property qualification for the elected members of the Court of Policy; the income qualification for the franchise was to be $480 per annum; and all executive powers were to be transferred from the Court of Policy to an Executive Council. The number of voters in the country increased considerably in the following years and people of African descent accounted, by 1915, for 62% of the total electorate.

There is evidence, however, that, in the first quarter of the 20th century there was racial bigotry in British Guiana at the highest official level. An example of which may be seen from a communication forwarded by the Governor to the Secretary of State for the Colonies in London in 1925. In this communication, the Governor advised that he had given firm instructions that 'no film was to be exhibited in which there is the least suggestion of intimacy between Men of Negro race and white women', being motivated by the fact that 'the white race was not to be brought to derision and disrespect'.[2]

In the early part of the 20th century, too, sugar was 'king' in British Guiana and everything seemed to revolve around the leading sugar commercial organisation in the colony, Booker Bros, McConnell & Co Ltd. The Government was completely overshadowed by the planter class, who kept the indentured Indians on the estates in much the same way as the earlier African slaves had been kept – in a state of bondage. Meanwhile, the British Government was losing its grip and in the 1920s refused to grant loans to the colony on the ground that it had no control over its finances.

---

2   Confidential Despatch, 19 March 1925, Thomson to the Secretary of State for the Colonies.

An indication of the economic plight of the colony is evident from a quotation from Cecil Clementi when, at a meeting of the Royal Colonial Institute in 1922, he is reported to have made the following statement:

> as a second reason for the failure of colonization[is] the anomalous Constitution under which the colony is governed, a constitution unique in the British Empire and a creature of pure mischance. It is open to doubt whether the abolition of the College of Keizers has not been a disadvantage. For when sugar was king, the Combined Court did at least continually pursue a policy [it was hoped] would benefit the sugar industry. But since the reforms of 1891, it is questionable whether any definite policy whatever has been consistently pursued by the Combined Court.[3]

In 1928, on the grounds that the Court of Policy and the Combined Court constituted an obstruction to political and economic progress, the British Government abolished the 1891 Constitution and replaced it by a new crown colony constitution. This was made possible by an Imperial Act – the British Guiana Act – under which the British Guiana (Constitution) Order in Council 1928 was made. The Court of Policy and the Combined Court were abolished and replaced by a Legislative Council.

Waddington Commission and suspension of the Guyana Constitution

The next 25 years were turbulent years during which there was more and more pressure from the Guyanese people to take part in their own affairs. Up to 1950, there had been little by way of party politics in British Guiana, but, in that year, the People's Progressive Party (PPP) was formed with Forbes Burnham as chairman, Dr Cheddi Jagan as political leader and Mrs Jagan as secretary of the party. (Dr Jagan, replacing Forbes Burnham – the first executive President, became President of the country in the early 1990s and died in 1997. He was succeeded by his wife, who, in an atmosphere of severe internal conflict, handed the Presidency to another member of the PPP in 1999.)

As a result of the agitation which originally followed the formation of party government, the Waddington Commission was appointed to make recommendations as to whatever changes were deemed desirable in the constitution.

The general election of 1953 was conducted on the basis of universal adult franchise which had been introduced on the recommendations of the commission. The commission had also recommended that there should be a ministerial system of government, while at the same time leaving a considerable degree of power in the hands of the Governor, who was to preside over the Executive Council and to have wide powers of veto over legislation. The Executive Council was simply an advisory body and, accordingly, the grant of ministerial portfolios was little more than a sham. There were to be three *ex officio* members of the Council, viz, the Chief Secretary, the Financial Secretary and the Attorney General. Such portfolios as defence, the law, the police, finance and external affairs could not in the view of the Colonial Office in London with confidence be assigned to elected ministers. A unicameral legislature was established comprising 18 elected, six nominated and three *ex officio* members.

---

3   This extract is cited in Harold Lutchman's monograph (1974), p 164 .

Two members of the Waddington Commission had been for abolishing nominated members and for the creation of a bicameral legislature with a (lower) House of Assembly of 24 elected members and three *ex officio* members, in addition to an upper house – a State Council – of nine members, six of whom were to be appointed by the Governor, two by the majority group holding office and one by the minority group.

It was in these circumstances that the PPP contested a general election based on a new constitution embodying the recommendations of the Waddington Commission. The PPP was successful in the elections and formed the Government. However, the new constitution was suspended after the party had been in office for only four months. Under the instrument of suspension, the entire Cabinet was removed from office and replaced by a nominated Council of Ministers. The suspension of the constitution was accompanied by the landing of British naval and others forces, part of which had travelled all the way across the Atlantic. In the course of a debate in the British House of Commons, Oliver Lyttleton, then Secretary of State for the Colonies, in justification for the landing of the troops, was to declare that: 'Her Majesty's Government is not willing for a communist state to be organised within the British Commonwealth.'[4]

FINAL STAGES TOWARDS SELF-DETERMINATION

Representative government was, however, restored in British Guiana in 1957 and, in 1961, the colony was granted a measure of internal self-government. Rough and turbulent times continued to be the order of the day throughout 1962, 1963 and 1964,[5] so much so that at the time of independence in 1966 the country was still in the grip of a state of emergency.

The 1966 Independence Constitution followed the typical Westminster pattern of constitution granted to newly independent Commonwealth countries, but it was changed in 1970 to a presidential regime where the President possessed the same ceremonial powers of the Governor General. In 1980, the Constitution was further revised to make provision for an Executive President.

In the author's 1977 work, when discussing Guyana's further approach to constitution making, reference was made to an address by the then Prime Minister, Forbes Burnham, in which he described the 1970 Constitution as:

... out of step with modern trends and our own ideas and ideologies; a Constitution which reflects for the most part the beliefs and ideologies of our former imperialist masters: a Constitution which was taken out of the drawer, so to speak, as were several others for various ex-British colonies.[6]

In his now famous Declaration of Sophia on 14 December 1974, the Prime Minister had described the patchwork of amendments made to the constitution since independence in 1966 as 'unsatisfactory, untidy and unaesthetic'.[7] At that time, the work of preparing a

---

4   See Jagan, 1966, p 129, where the statement is quoted.
5   See, eg, the action taken by the Secretary of State when the Premier of Guyana refused to resign after two other parties coalesced to form the Government. See, Phillips, 1977, p 96.
6   Phillips, 1977, p 190.
7   *Ibid*, p 189.

new constitution was already in train and the task was said to be the combined effort of the party, the public and Parliament.

Chapter II of the 1980 Constitution of Guyana[8] provides a list of 31 'Principles and Bases of the Political, Economic and Social System' drawn from the constitutions of France, Nigeria, India, Pakistan, the USSR, Cuba, China, the German Democratic Republic, Yugoslavia and the Democratic People's Republic of Korea. Many of these principles and rights were, however, intended to be declaratory of the theory of the party and Government at the time of their promulgation, rather than to be concerned with redress by the courts or other agencies.[9]

Significantly, in commenting on the rights set out in the three Arts 22, 23 and 24, Mr Burnham, by then President, made the following remarks in the House of Assembly:

> The right and duty to work, the right to leisure, the right to social care and medical care in the case of old age and disability are all declared as rights. It is not suggested for one moment, that all these rights have been fulfilled. For instance, not every Guyanese is properly housed. We are stating objectives also in this Chapter [see pamphlet, 'Forbes Burnham speaks of human rights', Guyana Information Service].

Departure from the old order

It was interesting to find at least one Caribbean territory standing on its own feet and preparing a constitution purportedly to suit its needs, although it is a matter for regret that the then minority party refused at the time of independence to take part in the deliberations of the Constituent Assembly leading up to the final preparation of the new constitution. There was evidently pragmatism in the constitution which married provisions from several countries with some of the structures from the old instrument where these were presumably deemed to be satisfactory – such structures as the Elections Commission, the Public Service Commission and the Judicial Services Commission.

IDEOLOGICAL BASIS FOR THE 1980 CONSTITUTION

There was evidently an ideological basis behind the 1980 Constitution, and we get a glimpse of this from a paper entitled 'The New Guyana constitution – philosophy and mechanics', presented by Dr Mohamed Shahabuddeen, Attorney General and Minister of Justice, to the People's National Congress (Guyana's then ruling party) held from 22–26 August 1974.

Dr Shahabuddeen, at that meeting, outlined the philosophy of the draft constitution. This in part is what he had to say on the subject:

> The existing constitution is what is known as the Westminster export type of constitution. In itself such a constitution is neither good nor bad. Whether it is good or bad depends upon its suitability for the nation which imports it. To resolve this issue it is necessary in a preliminary way to observe that Westminster constitutions are in a broader sense members

---

8   Act No 2 of 1980 assented to by the President on 20 February 1980.
9   See Wolf-Phillips, 1968, p xxv.

of the family of constitutions spawned by the intellectual matrix of the non-socialist Western world.

For the purpose of constitution making in the Third World, he said, there are two significant features of non-socialist Western style constitutions, namely:

(a) they are all capitalist oriented; and

(b) the degree of people involvement for which they provide is consequently limited.

Dr Shahabuddeen then went on to explain that Guyana had subsequently proceeded to modify the 'capitalist property right clause which was received as part of our independence constitution'. He concluded this section of his paper by explaining the reason for the Government's decision to insert a clause in the new constitution that land 'is for social use'.

In endeavouring to explain what he termed 'the degree of people involvement' under Western style constitutions, he expressed the view that their only input was at periodical elections: 'But for the rest they seem to look on from the outside.' Since 1964, Guyana had been endeavouring to make the people and their mass organisations part of the day to day decision making process of the State. It was with this objective in mind that in the draft constitution provision was made for institutionalising various 'democratic organs' which were, in fact, enshrined in the 1980 Constitution.

MAIN DEFECTS IN THE 1980 CONSTITUTION

Under the Socialist type Co-operative Constitution of 1980 (hereafter referred to as 'the original 1980 Constitution' or 'the 1980 Constitution'), 'the Supreme Organs of Democratic Power' were Parliament, the National Congress of Local Democratic Organs, the Supreme Congress of the People, the President and the Cabinet.

Parliament was enshrined in Chapter VI of which Art 51 provided that the Parliament of Guyana would consist of the President and the National Assembly. The National Assembly was composed of 65 members who were to be elected in accordance with the constitution. One of the constitutional prerequisites for election as a member of the National Assembly (see Art 53(b)) is that such person:

> ... is able to speak and, unless incapacitated by blindness or other physical cause, to read the English language with a degree of proficiency sufficiently to enable him to take an active part in the proceedings of the Assembly.[10]

The life of Parliament was for a duration of five years which could be extended for up to an additional five years any time the President 'considers that Guyana is at war'.[11] The President also had the authority 'at any time to prorogue or dissolve Parliament by proclamation'.[12] Consistent with Guyana being 'an indivisible, secular, democratic,

---

10 1980 Constitution, Art 53(b).

11 *Ibid*, Art 70(3) and (4).

12 *Ibid*, Art 70(1) and (2).

sovereign state', Parliament was given the widest law making authority[13] by Art 65 to make laws for the peace, order and good government of the country.

The President being a constituent part of Parliament is authorised to attend and address the National Assembly at any time. In addition, he may send messages to the National Assembly which 'shall be read at the first convenient sitting of the Assembly after it is received', by the Prime Minister or by any other Minister designated by the President.[14]

The President has a power of veto over legislation passed by the National Assembly. His veto may nevertheless be overridden if the Bill, on being sent back to the National Assembly, is passed by the Assembly within six months by a two-thirds majority vote,[15] for the provision of a presidential veto seems doubtful having regard to the fact that the President presides over meetings of the Cabinet[16] where presumably legislative proposals of the Government are considered and approved, and also because of the fact that the President is elected from the list of candidates which secures the majority of seats in the National Assembly.

The office of the President, at the time expressed to be one of the 'Supreme Organs' of democratic power, is established by Art 89 wherein he was designated as 'the supreme executive authority and Commander-in-Chief of the armed forces of the Republic'. Among the grounds upon which the President may be removed from office is 'if he commits any violation of this Constitution'.[17]

Under Art 182(1), it is provided:

> The holder of the office of President shall not be personally answerable to any court for the performance of the functions of his office or for any act done in the performance of those functions and no proceedings, whether criminal or civil, shall be instituted against him in his personal capacity in respect thereof either during his term of office or thereafter.

A Bill to alter Art 182 must, by virtue of Art 164, be passed by a majority of all members of the National Assembly and shall not be submitted to the President for his assent unless the Bill has been submitted in such manner as Parliament may prescribe to a vote of the electors.

The only circumstance in which the President is answerable to a court is where a tribunal is appointed by the Chancellor pursuant to a motion passed by the National Assembly for the removal of the President on account of his violation of the constitution.[18] Although the constitution allows for his removal from office by the National Assembly for proven violations of the constitution, the 'power of impeachment' could previously prove to be nugatory, having regard to the President's constitutional power conferred by Art 70(2) to dissolve the National Assembly in his discretion at any time. As set out below, an attempt has now been made by way of a constitutional provision to prevent impeachment by simply dissolving the assembly.

---

13 *Ibralebbe v R* [1964] AC 900.
14 1980 Constitution, Art 67.
15 Article 170(4) and (5).
16 Article 106(3).
17 Article 94.
18 Article 180.

The President is elected 'by the people' as prescribed in Art 177 of the constitution. Under this Article, not more than one candidate on a list of candidates for an election to the National Assembly may be designated as a presidential candidate and an elector voting at such an election in favour of a list 'shall be deemed to be also voting in favour of the Presidential candidate named in the list'. If there is only one presidential candidate the Chairman of the Elections Commission is obligated to declare that candidate President. But where there are two candidates, it is the candidate whose name appears on the list in favour of which the most votes are cast. Paragraph (3) of the same Article makes further provision for the election of a President in the circumstances where the votes cast in favour of each of the lists are equal in number, but greater than the number of votes cast in favour of any other list. In such a case:

> The Chairman of the Elections Commission[19] acting in the presence of the Chancellor and of the public, shall by lot choose one of the lists in respect of which the votes are equal in either of the circumstances aforesaid and shall declare the Presidential candidate designated in that list to be duly elected as President.[20]

Article 71(1) declared that local government was a vital aspect of socialist democracy to be organised in such a manner as 'to involve as many people as possible in the task of managing and developing the communities in which they live'. Parliament was therefore mandated to provide for the implementation of a system of local government throughout the country by establishment of organs of local democratic power as an integral part of the political organisation of the State.[21] It is from these local democratic organs that the National Congress of Local Democratic Organs (NCLDO) was elected[22] and for which Parliament was empowered to make laws respecting their establishment, membership and functions. This NCLDO is now a thing of past – being part of the socialist rhetoric which was swept away by a 2000 revision of the original 1980 Constitution.[23]

Chapter VIII provided for the establishment of the Supreme Congress of the People – a body consisting of all members of the National Assembly and all members of the NCLDO. The creation of the Supreme Congress of the People was originally clearly inspired by the existence of similar institutions under the constitutions of the socialist countries. The Supreme Congress of the People in Guyana had no legislative powers and its functions seemed to have been limited to discussing matters of public interest and making recommendations on them to the National Assembly or the Government.[24] The Congress was also intended to advise the President on all matters which he might refer to it. This organ was likewise abolished by the amendment that saw the demise of the NCLDO.[25]

---

19 Under Art 161(2), 'the Chairman of the Elections Commission shall be appointed by the President from among persons who hold or have held office as a judge of a Court having unlimited jurisdiction in civil and criminal matters or a court having jurisdiction in appeals from any such judge'.
20 Article 177(3).
21 Article 71(2).
22 Article 80(1).
23 See Act No 14 of 2000, s 4.
24 Article 83.
25 See Act No 14 of 2000, s 4.

Executive authority in Guyana is vested in the President and may be exercised by him personally or through officers subordinate to him.[26] Other executive functionaries are the Prime Minister, Vice President and the ministers, all of whom are appointed by the President.[27] In the case of the Prime Minister, he must be an elected member of the National Assembly. However, a Vice President and the ministers may be appointed from among persons who are elected members of the National Assembly or who are qualified to be elected thereto. The Prime Minister is the most senior Vice President who deputises for the President when he is out of the country.[28]

In respect of the non-elected technocrat ministers, that provision is an interesting constitutional innovation in that such ministers are, by virtue of their office, members of the National Assembly although they cannot vote therein.[29]

In so far as the Prime Minister of Guyana is concerned there is a fundamental departure from the Westminster model. Article 101(2) provides that the Prime Minister 'shall be the principal assistant of the President in the discharge of his executive functions and leader of Government business in the National Assembly'.

The Cabinet, another 'Supreme Organ of Democratic Power', is composed of the President, the Prime Minister, the Vice Presidents and ministers appointed by the President.[30] The function of the Cabinet was said to be 'to aid and advise' the President in the general direction and control of the Government of Guyana and to be collectively responsible therefor to Parliament'.[31]

It should, however, be noticed that the President is not required to act in accordance with any decision of the Cabinet. Rather he is empowered by Art 111(1) in the exercise of his functions, to act 'in accordance with his own deliberate judgment' except in the circumstance where he is required to act on the advice of any person or authority under the constitution or any other law.[32]

The Supreme Court of Judicature of Guyana consists of a Court of Appeal and a High Court with such jurisdiction and powers as are conferred by the constitution or any other law.

The judges of the Court of Appeal are the Chancellor, the Chief Justice and justices of appeal while those of the High Court are the Chief Justice and *puisne* judges.[33]

The final court in Guyana is the Court of Appeal to which appeals lie as of right from decisions of the High Court in respect of final decisions in any civil or criminal proceedings on questions as to the interpretation of the constitution and final decisions regarding the enforcement of fundamental rights and freedoms.[34] See Art 123(4) and (5)

---

26   Article 99.
27   Articles 100–03.
28   Articles 101 and 103(2).
29   Article 105.
30   Article 106(1).
31   Article 106(2).
32   Article 111(1).
33   Articles 124 and 125.
34   Article 133.

as enacted by s 11 of Act No 6 of 2001 which provide for future accession to the Caribbean Court of Justice.

The Chancellor and Chief Justice of Guyana were originally appointed by the President after consultation with the Minority Leader (now the Leader of the Opposition). On the other hand, the Appeal Court and *puisne* judges were (and still are) appointed by the President acting in accordance with the advice of the Judicial Service Commission.

The judges of the Supreme Court of Judicature enjoy security of tenure by virtue of Art 197(1) of the constitution and may, up till 2001 (when the change takes effect), remain in office until the age of 62 in the case of *puisne* judges, and until the age of 65 in the case of all the other judges.[35] Thereafter, *puisne* judges will have a retiring age of 65 and other judges 68. (See s 18 of Act No 6 of 2001.)

Need for substantial constitutional change by 2001

There can be no doubt that by 2001 the Guyana Constitution of 1980 with the inclusion of a number of Socialist type revisions had in some respects outlived its usefulness and its relevance to the changing conditions in Guyana. As has been illustrated above, the constitution introduced concepts which were not only novel but not attainable in the foreseeable future while retaining others which were traditionally sound and workable. The hybrid arrangement could not comfortably co-exist.

The question as to whether the 1980 Constitution was a creation of the people of Guyana was stridently answered by the Constitution Reform Commission ('the commission') which reported on 17 July 1999. In the opinion of the commission, the constitution 'was imposed after a controversial referendum process in 1978', which was followed by a Constituent Assembly 'which ignored representations made to it'. The report declared that 'the odium generated by the Constitution had dogged it since it was promulgated and there have been repeated calls for it to be repealed, or at a minimum, extensively amended, especially with reference to the provisions on the powers of the Presidency'.[36]

In addition to those changed conditions internally, one should bear in mind Guyana's relations in the last decade of the 20th century with the rest of the non-Socialist Commonwealth Caribbean which had become closer and more focused in terms of trade, external relations within and beyond CARICOM, commerce and legal institutions. The Guyana Government had worked harmoniously and well under President Hoyte.

His successors tried to bring to fruition the Common External Tariff among the constituent territories in CARICOM and, since 1989, Guyana was in the forefront of those jurisdictions pressing for the establishment of a Caribbean Court of Justice notwithstanding that the Guyana Court of Appeal was the final appellate tribunal from decisions of the courts in the country. It is as a result of a close working relationship with the rest of the region that Guyana was able to draw so heavily from the human resources

---

35 Article 197(2).
36 See Report of the Constitution Reform Commission to the Special Committee of the National Assembly of Guyana: presented 16 July 1999 (Georgetown, Guyana), p 26.

of the other territories when it needed CARICOM assistance in the form of mediators to settle recent internal conflicts with racial overtones. It also obtained the establishment of an audit team to re-examine the result of the general elections of 15 December 1997: the team having been suggested in the recommendations of the mediators in what has become known as 'The Herdsmanston Accord' which resulted in bringing relative peace to the country in 1998. But there is still much to be done to restore the racial harmony which previously existed.

The need for the constitutional changes was highlighted after the general elections in 1997 when severe social tensions developed in the country culminating in protest marches and racial conflicts. There was the Electoral Audit[37] which was accepted by both sides without prejudice to ongoing election petitions before the courts.[37a] It was then that the Constitution Reform Commission was set up[38] with a mandate and a broad-based membership drawn from representatives of political parties, the Labour Movement, religious organisations, the private sector, the youth and other social partners. This Commission presented its report on 17 July 1999 to the Chairman of the Special Select Committee for transmission to the National Assembly in accordance with s 6(6) of the Constitution Commission Reform Act 1999.[39]

The commission went a long way to protect the liberty of the citizen and to guard against excessive and arbitrary action of the executive. Its recommendations were largely accepted by the Parliamentary Select Committee.[40] It was this committee's recommendations which were, in turn, reflected in the constitutional revisions.

In examining the rhetoric in Chapter II of the 1980 Constitution (which deals with the principles and bases of the political, economic and social system) and in Chapter VII (dealing with local democracy), the commission found that the NCLDO and the Supreme Congress of the People are 'incompatible with the local government structure, the electoral system and the system of government being recommended for the revised Constitution, and the Supreme Congress of the People has never worked well'.[41] The Commission therefore explicitly recommended – and this was endorsed by the Select Committee – that Arts 71–78 inclusive as well as Arts 82–88 inclusive 'should be re-written to remove the references to Socialism'.[42] It was also recommended that the

---

37   See the Electoral Audit (CARICOM Agreement) Act 1998.

37a   As this book was going to press, the Guyana Supreme Court held in the Election Petition that the 1997 elections were not conducted in accordance with the law in that the provisions of the Act under which they were held were *ultra vires* Arts 59 and 159 of the Constitution and therefore null and void. (New General Elections were held on 19 March 2001.) See *Esther Perreria v Chief Election Officer et al*, Suit No 36–P of 1998. The decision in the case has already been the subject of much controversy and criticism.

38   See the Constitution Reform Commission Act 1999 (No 1 of 1999).

39   See Report of the Guyana Constitution Reform Commission to the National Assembly, 17 July 1999.

40   Rec 9.2.3.2(2) of the Commission agreed to by the Select Committee. See p 17 of the committee's report.

41   See Commission rec 9.8.3(1) and (2) and Select Committee's agreement on p 37 of its report to the National Assembly.

42   *Ibid.*

NCLDO and the Supreme Congress of the People be abolished.[43] As stated above, this abolition duly took place in 2000.[44]

In fairness to the regime which was responsible for the Supreme Congress of the People and the NCLDO, it should be pointed out that the former was an adaptation from the People's Republic of China which was intended to provide the opportunity for reporting and accounting to the people's representatives assembled in a wider forum than the National Assembly. The NCLDO was a mechanism intended to give local government bodies (re-styled local democratic organs in socialist jargon) representation in the National Assembly.

The revised constitution provides for Parliament to create a Local Government Commission. It also specifies that the Regional Development Councils (RDCs) and the National Development Council (NDC) are mandatory local government organs.[45]

Certain changes have also been made in the constitutional powers of the President. The recommendation sent to the National Assembly concerning the length of the President's tenure was that he should not be permitted to hold office for more than two consecutive terms.[46] He should be Guyanese by birth and should, immediately before election, be continuously resident in the country for at least seven years.[47] This residency requirement has justifiably met with criticism within Guyana and from Guyanese residents abroad on a non-permanent basis. These recommendations have been enshrined in the revised constitution. See s 2 of the Constitution (Amendment) (No 4) Act 2000 (Act No 17 of 2000) – hereinafter referred to as 'Act 17 of 2000'.

The Cabinet over which the President presides 'shall be collectively responsible to Parliament for the control of the Government of Guyana and must resign if the government is defeated by a majority of all members of the National Assembly on a vote of no-confidence'.[48] (See s 5 of Act 17 of 2000.)

The President who shall have ministerial responsibility for subjects and departments not assigned to ministers shall be accountable to the National Assembly for the subjects and departments so retained: assigning a minister or parliamentary secretary to be answerable to the National Assembly for such matters.[49] This has now become law in s 6 of Act 17 of 2000.

Under Art 120 of the 1980 Constitution, the President was empowered to constitute offices and to terminate them. The new Constitution provides that where such appointments involve public expenditure chargeable to the Consolidated Fund, such expenditure shall be subject to approval by the National Assembly.[50] Effect has been given to this recommendation in s 7 of Act 17 of 2000.

---

43 See Commission rec 9.8.3(3) and the Select Committee's agreement on p 38 of its report to the National Assembly.
44 See fns 23 and 25.
45 See Commission rec 9.8.3(5) and the Select Committee's agreement on p 38 of its Report to the National Assembly.
46 *Ibid*, p 30, rec 9.6.3.1(1).
47 *Ibid*, p 32, rec 9.6.3.1(2).
48 *Ibid*, p 32, rec 9.6.3.2.
49 *Ibid*, p 33, rec 9.6.3.3.
50 *Ibid*, p 33, rec 9.6.3.4.

Under Art 170(5) of the 1980 Constitution the power of the President extended to dissolving Parliament during the period of 21 days while considering whether the President should assent to a Bill or not. The commission and the Select Committee had decided (between them) that the power to dissolve Parliament in this case should be removed and that the President should be given three months within which to assent to a Bill, failing which the Bill shall be regarded as having been assented to.[51] This is reflected in s 8 of Act 17 of 2000.

The commission also critically considered Arts 179 and 180 of the 1980 Constitution relative to the removal of the President for violation of the constitution or gross misconduct as well as removal on grounds of incapacity. In the commission's view the provisions 'are over-protective' and (the) 'articles establish a mechanism designed to put the President out of reach of removal'. They accordingly recommended that, although the procedures should ensure that a substantial majority of the National Assembly be required to impeach the President on the fundings of an independent tribunal, they should not require such extremely weighted minorities as to make the prospect of impeachment unattainable.[52] The Select Committee, while agreeing with the commission's recommendation, suggested that s 180(5) of the 1980 Constitution should be amended to provide for a 2:3 majority to be required for impeachment of the President and for the deletion from the subsection of the words:

... unless he sooner dissolves Parliament.[53]

When one examines the changes made to the presidency, one is tempted to enquire whether there was in fact a serious attempt to alter his powers. His powers and privileges remain overwhelming, for example, his powers of appointing a Prime Minister, Vice President and other ministers, his right to send messages to the National Assembly, his powers unilaterally to dissolve the assembly, his complete immunity from suit in respect of the performance of the functions of his office and for any act done in the performance of those functions in respect of which no proceedings, whether criminal or civil, can be instituted against him or her during his or her term of office or thereafter. See Arts 98 and 182(1) of the constitution.

Between February 2000 and July 2001 at least six constitutional amendments were enacted. In addition, three other amendments which were passed by the National Assembly on 21 June 2001 are at the time of writing (July 2001) before the President of the country for his assent. These three[54] embracing such subjects as:

(a) the establishment of a Parliamentary Standing Committee by the National Assembly for Constitutional Reform;

(b) the establishment of parliamentary sectoral committees by the National Assembly for:

(i) natural resources;

(ii) economic services;

---

51   Commission rec 9.6.3.6, p 34.
52   See *ibid*, rec 9.6.3.7 and Select Committee's agreement at p 37 of its Report to the National Assembly.
53   See pp 34–35 of the Report of the Select Committee.
54   The three prospective enactments are Acts 6, 7 and 8 of 2001.

(iii) foreign relations; and

(iv) social services;

(c) the Preamble, coat of arms, national pledge and national anthem of Guyana; and

(d) the judiciary – appointment, retirement, misbehaviour, appointment of part time judges and of other legal personnel.

The revisions have so far covered a wide range of issues and it is a pity that the authorities did not settle for a consolidation into one document. As it stands, researchers will find it difficult to discover exactly what the constitutional position on any given subject is, unless such a researcher himself or herself brings the instrument up to date.

Still, the rulers of the country made a valiant effort to grapple with the constitutional problems with which it had been beset.

Apart from the amendments to which reference has been made above, there are two aspects upon which we wish to dwell briefly by way of conclusion:

1   The number of commissions which the revised constitution has sought to establish, viz,

   (i) the Local Government Commission;

   (ii) the Ethnic Relations Commission;

   (iii) the Human Rights Commission;

   (iv) the Women and Gender Equality Commission;

   (v) the Indigenous People's Commission; and

   (vi) the Rights of the Child Commission.

2   The attempt to solve the vexed question of 'consultation' when the President is expected to consult some other person in carrying out of his functions.

The interpretation of the term is now set out in an addition of a new definition to Art 232 whereby 'consultation' or 'meaningful consultation' means that the person or entity responsible for consulting will identify the person to be consulted and specify *in writing* the subject of the consultation, giving a date for the decision.

The person consulting must then ensure that the person consulted is given a reasonable opportunity to express his views on the matter.

Finally, the person consulting must prepare a record of the consultation and circulate the decision to each of the persons consulted.[55]

It is expected that this definition will contribute towards the solution of a matter which has caused much controversy throughout the Caribbean since independence. Consultation has always tended to be perfunctory in the extreme.

---

55   See Act No 17 of 2000, s 12.

CONCLUDING SUMMARY

Guyana may have wisely revised its constitution to keep pace with the changing times, but does that mean that its troubles are over? Far from it. Although blessed with abundant natural wealth, it has in recent years suffered from a colossal brain drain – not to mention the violence that has consistently flared up again and again in the streets. The commissions and other institutions the revised constitution has spawned require individuals of character to man them. The public service and the judiciary require high calibre technocrats to enable these services to achieve any measure of economic development.

Above all, a good infrastructural base, good incentives and peace, both within the country's borders and with her neighbours, are all a *sine qua non* if foreign entrepreneurs are to be attracted to invest in the country.

Let us hope that all these requirements can be achieved so that the country and its people can move on.

Despite the efforts and the declared intention of the new dispensation to eschew all references to socialism in the revised constitution, s 1 still declares that:

Guyana is an indivisible, secular, democratic sovereign state in the course of transition from capitalism to socialism.

And there has been no attempt to amend this fundamental statement.

Nor has there been any attempt, as far as one can see, to alter the principle laid down in s 18, viz:

Land is for social use and must go to the tiller.

Unless steps are taken to involve the populace in altering such basic principles, the constitution is telling a lie about itself and the leaders of the country must now choose which ideology they truly wish to embrace.

CHAPTER 9

VICISSITUDES IN TRINIDAD AND TOBAGO

HISTORICAL INTRODUCTION

Trinidad

In his foreword to a book published on the occasion of the independence of Trinidad and Tobago in 1962, the late Dr Eric Williams – an outstanding historian in his own right – gave a lucid account of the constitutional history of both islands.[1] In respect of Trinidad, he made mention of the means by which the Spaniards decimated the Amerindians, the original settlers of the island;[2] of the problems of labour which the island encountered after the emancipation of slaves in 1833;[3] of the island being a model slave colony;[4] of the influence of the metropolitan powers – Spain and France – on the colony up to the time that the awakening dawned for independence;[5] of the vicissitudes that befell those who were bold enough, between 1921 and 1956, to urge that the island should be granted self-government, notably Andrew Cipriani;[6] and of the last stages of the journey to independence, via the 1956 general elections which was won by his party (the People's National Movement (PNM)) and the federal experiment (which lasted from 1958–62).[7] Of Tobago, Dr Williams also had a great deal to say, both of its chequered history and of the neglect the island had suffered throughout its colonial past. He also reviewed at great length how the union between Trinidad and Tobago eventually came about in 1898.[8]

In the course of his exposition, Dr Williams outlined the very many Royal Commissions of Enquiry that had been 'sent out' from London to investigate various aspects of the colony's affairs in the 19th and 20th centuries.[9] To this formidable list must

---

1   Williams, 1961.
2   *Ibid*, Chapters 1, 2, 3.
3   *Ibid*, Chapter 8.
4   *Ibid*, Chapter 7.
5   *Ibid*, Chapter 5.
6   *Ibid*, Chapter 15.
7   *Ibid*, Chapter 16.
8   *Ibid*, Chapters 10, 11.
9   *Ibid*, see Dr Williams' references to the following Royal Commissions:
    (a) Commission on the Administration of Civil and Criminal Justice, p 74;
    (b) the West Indian Royal Commission of 1897, pp 113–14, 149–50, 157, 161–63, 165–66, 228, 251;
    (c) the Royal Franchise Commission of 1888, pp 115–16, 170, 173, 193–94, 218;
    (d) the Royal Commission of Public Revenues of 1882, pp 136–38, 252;
    (e) the Water Riots Commission of 1903, pp 182–86;
    (f) the Hosea Riots Commission of 1884, pp 188–96;
    (g) the Major Wood Commission of 1921, pp 217–20, 251–54;
    (h) the Sugar Commission of 1929, pp 227–30;
    (i) the Trinidad Disturbances Commission of 1937, pp 220–34; and
    (j) the Closer Union Commission of 1932, p 252.

be added those commissions which visited the area in connection with the federal exercise of 1958–62.[10] It is however very fair to say that those many commissions did not have significant effect in ridding the country of the colonial yoke, and it is the advent of the PNM – led by Dr Eric Williams and a number of other dedicated Trinidad and Tobago nationals – that cast new light on constitutional reform in the country when it took office in 1956.

In *Freedom in the Caribbean,* the author has set out in some detail the part played by the PNM in bringing Trinidad and Tobago from colonial status to internal self-government and, finally, in 1962 to independence shortly after the collapse of the Federal Government of the West Indies.[11] In that work, too, the author referred to the political upheavals that set in towards the late 1960s, culminating in the Black Power Revolution of 1970 when the Government of Trinidad and Tobago came within an ace of being overthrown.[12] As a result of these disturbances, the newly independent State set up a high powered Commission under the chairmanship of a distinguished local jurist, Sir Hugh Wooding, the object of which was to review the existing Constitution to meet the changing and turbulent times the country was then experiencing. Subsequent to the submission of the report,[13] there was promulgated the 1976 Republican Constitution,[14] the main features of which may be summarised in the following two paragraphs.

A republican form of government replaced the previous monarchical regime. Under the new arrangements the President became the Head of State[15] while the Prime Minister remained Head of Government and Chairman of the Cabinet,[16] but with certain reduced powers.

Provision is also made under the Constitution for the following innovations:

(i)   the President is to be appointed by an Electoral College consisting of all members of the House of Assembly and the Senate assembled together;[17]

(ii) the post of Ombudsman is created;[18]

(iii) the post of Director of Public Prosecutions is also created;[19]

(iv) provision is made for an Integrity Commission;[20]

(v) even though the country adopted a republican status, appeals to the Judicial Committee of the Privy Council are retained;[21]

(vi) for the first time in the history of the country the President in his capacity as Head of State could make such appointments as the Chairman and members of the Electoral

---

10 See Phillips, 1977, pp 28, 30, 33.
11 *Ibid,* pp 15–16. See, also, Selwyn, 1972.
12 *Ibid,* p 191.
13 *Ibid.* See a summary of these recommendations, pp 617–29, App VI of Phillips 1985.
14 *Ibid.* See the text of this constitution, pp 649–730, App XIV.
15 The Schedule to the Constitution of the Republic of Trinidad and Tobago Act 1976 (No 4 of 1976), s 74.
16 *Ibid,* s 75.
17 *Ibid,* ss 28 and 29.
18 *Ibid,* s 91(1).
19 *Ibid,* s 90.
20 *Ibid,* s 138.
21 *Ibid,* s 109.

and Boundaries Commission (s 71), the ombudsman (s 91(2)), the Chief Justice (s 102) and Acting Chief Justice (s 103), the three appointed members of the Judicial and Legal Service Commission (s 110(3)), the Auditor General (s 117), the members of the Public Service Commission (s 122(2)), the members of the Police Service Commission (s 122(2)) and the members of the Teaching Service Commission (s 140(1)).

Thus, as the writer has pointed out elsewhere,[22] the Trinidad Constitution is the first in the Commonwealth Caribbean deliberately to distance itself from the Westminster model in shifting certain key functions from the shoulders of the Prime Minister to those of the Head of State.

RECOMMENDATIONS FOR MORE POST-REPUBLICAN CONSTITUTIONAL REVIEW

It was because the President exercised one of his undoubted powers under the Constitution shortly before demitting office in 1987 that the newly installed government, headed by ANR Robinson as Prime Minister, saw fit to establish a further Constitutional Commission to review the Republican Instrument promulgated in 1976. What the President did was to make one appointment to the Public Service Commission in December 1986, and one each to the Police Service and the Judicial and Legal Service Commissions on 14 March 1987 before he left office on 18 March 1987.

For some unknown reason, the incoming government was unhappy about one or other of these appointments and decided to initiate legislative action to amend the Constitution to provide (unbelievably) for the expiry of appointments made in respect of the three specific commissions and of independent senators upon the retirement from office of the President who made them during his tenure.

To that end, the necessary Bill was drafted and circulated for comment. When the Bill was published, there was a mixed reaction, but it would appear that many members of the public favoured a review of the entire Constitution in lieu of the *ad hoc* piecemeal amendment contemplated. It was in response to this sentiment of public opinion that a Review Commission was appointed to review all aspects of the Constitution which, in any event, had been in operation for more than 10 years. The Commission was chaired by Sir Isaac Hyatali, a former Chief Justice of Trinidad and Tobago.[23]

The Commission made a number of far reaching recommendations, a summary of which we must now record under various heads.

1 Fundamental rights

These should continue to be expressed in positive terms – without too complicated qualifications.

The Supreme Court should allocate one or two courts to deal specifically with constitutional motions and leave of the court should be obtained before a motion is filed

---

22 Phillips, 1977.
23 The Commission will henceforth be referred to as 'the Hyatali Commission'.

so as to avoid abuse of the judicial process.[24] (It would be a pity if this recommendation were to be accepted as the expense involved in obtaining such leave will inhibit access to the courts.)

2 Citizenship

Citizens of the Commonwealth Caribbean should no longer be required to renounce their citizenship as a condition precedent to the grant of citizenship by Trinidad and Tobago and such persons who surrendered their citizenship should be permitted to re-apply without losing their Trinidad and Tobago citizenship.[25]

3 The President

The Prime Minister should consult with the Leader of the Opposition within not more than 90 days nor less than 60 days of the end of the term of the outgoing President as to their joint nomination for the new President.

There should be a permanent Vice President of the republic who will be the President of the Senate, and who will be appointed by the same regime as is provided for the President of the country.[26]

If at any time the Vice President is unable to perform his functions, they will be performed by the speaker of the House of Representatives.

4 Parliament

Parliament should continue to be a bicameral institution. The first past the post system should continue to apply to elections to the House of Representatives.

The office of President of the Senate, as a separate post, should be abolished – since this office will be filled by the Vice President of the Republic. The office of Vice President of the Senate should likewise be abolished.

The Senate should increase in membership from 31–36, to be made up as follows:

(1) 20 members to be appointed on the advice of the Prime Minister;

(2) 12 on the advice of parties not supporting the Government party – the 12 to be distributed in proportion to the votes cast at a general election; and

(3) four selected by the President in his own judgment, chosen from various social and economic groups.

The speaker of the House of Representatives should be chosen from outside Parliament.[27]

---

24 Hyatali Commission, Chapter 3, paras 94–122, pp 19–24.
25 *Ibid*, Chapter 4, paras 123–28, pp 24–25.
26 *Ibid*, Chapter 5, paras 129–43, pp 25–27.
27 *Ibid*, Chapter 6, paras 144–79, pp 27–34.

5 The executive

(a) One Cabinet Minister should be assigned as Minister for Tobago Affairs.

(b) A Deputy Prime Minister should be constitutionally recognised.

(c) Provision should be made in the Constitution for a Legal Adviser to the President, the post to be financed from the public purse.

(d) The Prime Minister's right of veto should be removed in respect of the Director of Public Prosecutions (DPP), the Solicitor General (SG), the Chief Parliamentary Counsel (CPC), the Chief State Solicitor and Registrar-General.[28]

6 Judicature

The Judicial and Legal Service Commission should, before making appointments to the High Court and the Court of Appeal, consult the Law Association.

Judges should be rehired after reaching the retirement age of 65. (There is of course a danger that the independence of the judiciary might be compromised, unless the rehiring is in the sole gift of the Judicial and Legal Service Commission.)

The Commission made a recommendation that appeals to the Privy Council should cease and that until a Caribbean Court of Justice is installed, there should be a Supreme Court of Trinidad and Tobago which will be the final court for the country: the present Court of Appeal to continue to operate in the usual way, vested with the same jurisdiction as is conferred on it by the Constitution.[29]

There is, however, by the year 2001 considerable discussion on the establishment of the Caribbean Court of Appeal, but no one can predict at this stage with certainty if and when that court will materialise.[30]

7 The Public Accounts Committee and the Public Accounts (Enterprises) Committee

The Commission made recommendations for streamlining the operation of these two committees, both of which became creatures of the Constitution for the first time when the Republican Constitution came into being in 1976.[31]

It was also recommended that:

(a) the Chairman of the Public Accounts (Enterprises) Committee should continue to be one of the senators appointed by the President on the advice of the Leader of the Opposition;[32] and

(b) s 119(6) of the Constitution should be amended to enable–

---

28 Hyatali Commission, Chapter 8, paras 224(a) DPP, (b) SG and CPC, (c) Chief State Solicitor and Registrar General.

29 *Ibid*, Chapter 11, paras 240–83, pp 45–54.

30 See Chapter 13 below on the Caribbean Judiciary.

31 Hyatali Commission, Chapter 12, para 298, p 57.

32 *Ibid*, Chapter 12, para 302(f), p 57.

(i) the House of Representatives to decide on the numbers of members to comprise the Committee, and

(ii) each House to appoint an equal number of its members to the Committee.[33]

8 The ombudsman

The Commission recommended that:

(a) the ombudsman should be given his or her own budget with power to administer it with necessary accountability;[34]

(b) whenever he or she requests it, the ombudsman should be given by the head of the department involved reasons for a decision giving rise to a complaint;[35]

(c) provision should be made in the Constitution not only that the ombudsman's report will be laid in the House of Representatives, but that it will be debated there;[36] and

(d) ministers should give high priority to addressing faults in administration brought to their attention by the ombudsman.[37]

9 Auditor General

The retiring age of this officer should be changed from 60 years to 65 years.

The Commission also recommended that the Auditor General should be given his own annual fiscal vote with control over it, subject to the necessary accountability.

It is also proposed that when the Auditor General has occasion to appoint auditors to relieve the pressure on his or her staff, such auditors should work under his or her direction and control.

The Auditor General should be required and not merely empowered to perform audits on State enterprises since s 116(2) of the Constitution stipulates that such accounts 'shall be audited' and reported on by him/her.

Although the Constitution requires that he/she should be given staff adequate for the due performance of the duties of the office, the Commission did not recommend that the Auditor General be given the power to *hire* such staff, although he/she should be permitted to make an input into their appointment.[38]

10 Service commissions

The Hyatali Commission made some useful recommendations in respect of the various service commissions, viz:

---

33 *Ibid*, Chapter 12, para 302(g), p 57.
34 *Ibid*, Chapter 10, para 239(a), p 44.
35 *Ibid*, Chapter 10, para 239(b), p 44.
36 *Ibid*, Chapter 10, para 239(c), p 44.
37 *Ibid*, Chapter 10, para 239(d), p 44.
38 *Ibid*, Chapter 12, paras 285–97.

(a) that there should be a *Permanent Disciplinary Tribunal* which would concentrate on disciplinary issues, relieving the other commissions of this exercise and speeding up the whole process: the tribunal to consist of a legally qualified chairman with not less than four nor more than eight members. The chairman would be appointed on the advice of the Judicial and Legal Service Commission while the other members would be appointed by the President after consultation with the Prime Minister and the Leader of the Opposition;[39]

(b) *the Public Service Appeal Board* should be reconstituted to provide for a chairman and deputy chairman – both to be appointed on the advice of the Judicial and Legal Service Commission – while the other five members should include three retired public officers;[40]

(c) there should be included in the Constitution a *Statutory Authorities Service Commission*, subject to the same appointment and dismissal regime as the other commissions;[41]

(d) there should also be enshrined in the Constitution an amalgamated *Public Service and Statutory Authorities Appeal Board*;[42]

(e) the *Public Service Commission* should have its membership increased to include a *chairman*, a *deputy Chairman*, and not less than seven nor more than nine members. It will then be able to sit in two panels – one chaired by the chairman and the other by the deputy chairman;[43]

(f) the *Police Service Commission* should also have its membership enlarged to not less than four nor more than six members apart from the Chairman.[44] A number of police promotions boards should be established by statute and the boards should simply inform the Commission of appointments made. Generally, more delegation should be practised both in promotions and in disciplinary matters;[45]

(g) the *Teaching Service Commission* should be expanded in size to include a chairman and not less than six nor more than eight other members, at least three of whom should possess qualifications and experience in education.[46]

11 The Salaries Review Commission

The Commission recommended that s 141(1) of the Constitution be amended to compel a review of salaries and other conditions of service of all offices for which this Commission is constitutionally responsible at fixed intervals of not less than two nor more than five years.[47] The Commission is to have a chairman and not less than six other members (instead of four) among whom should be a management expert, a public administration expert, an economist and an attorney at law.[48]

---

39 *Ibid*, Chapter 13, para 335(a), p 63.
40 *Ibid*, Chapter 13, para 335(b), p 63.
41 *Ibid*, Chapter 13, para 335(c), p 63.
42 *Ibid*, Chapter 13, para 335(d), p 63.
43 *Ibid*, Chapter 13, para 335(e), p 63.
44 *Ibid*, Chapter 13, para 335(f),(i), p 63.
45 *Ibid*, Chapter 13, para 335(f)(ii), (iii), (iv), (v) and (vi), p 64.
46 *Ibid*, Chapter 13, para 335(g), p 63.
47 *Ibid*, Chapter 15, para 376(a), p 70.
48 *Ibid*, Chapter 15, para 376(b), p 70.

12 Integrity Commission

The Hyatali Commission recommended that either:

the Integrity Commission should be abolished; or (if it is to continue);

(a) there should be inserted in the relevant Act a provision 'to vest in the Commission a duty to promote and secure integrity in public life and all necessary enabling powers to discharge it effectively';

(b) the Act should include provisions to empower the Commission to subpoena persons to testify before them; to require the production of documents; to pass on to the Director of Public Prosecutions any material in their possession which in their view might support a prosecution; and to report to the House of Representatives through the speaker on any member of the House or any minister or parliamentary secretary who has been the subject of an investigation; and

(c) the jurisdiction of the Commission should be expanded to include within its purview chairmen, executive directors and/or chief executive officers of State enterprises and statutory corporations as well as mayors, chairmen of local government bodies, chief technical officers and officers of similar rank.[49]

TERMINATION OF APPOINTMENTS MADE IN THE DISCRETION OF AN OUTGOING PRESIDENT

As has been mentioned above, it was this matter that triggered the appointment of the Hyatali Commission in 1987 in the first place. The Commission, in the course of its deliberations, gave lengthy and anxious consideration to the proposal and, with becoming wisdom and reason, rejected it. The writer can do no better than quote the words of the Commission:

419. The fact of the matter is that the power to make these appointments is not given to a President because he has any control over, responsibility for, or even connection with, those whom he appoints. He does not have an 'administration' in the same way, for example, as a Prime Minister does. The power of appointments is vested in the President because he can be trusted to exercise that power conscientiously, impartially and in the best interest of the country, free from any political influence or extraneous constraints. And not because he makes such appointments do the appointees become, as it were, the 'President's Men' beholden to him and with obligations to carry out his wishes and directions. Indeed, it would be intolerable in our democracy, if that were so.

420. For these reasons we are of the opinion that it would be irrational to make the tenure of office of the persons appointed to the important offices under reference depend on the expiration of a President's tenure of office or his premature demission from office and that the question posed should be answered in the negative.

421. We accordingly recommend as follows:

---

49   *Ibid*, Chapter 14, para 361, p 68.

No person appointed to an office by the President in his sole discretion or in his discretion after consultation with the Prime Minister and the Leader of the Opposition should automatically cease to hold office or be required to vacate his office at the same time as the President leaves office.[50]

TOBAGO

In order to understand the constitutional position of this island, we must turn to history. In his aforementioned work,[51] Dr Williams gives an account of the tribulations through which Tobago passed: living, as he put it, 'in a state of betweenity, buffetted from pillar to post, changing national flags and political allegiance'.[52] The island lived between France, England, Holland and Courland in the 18th century. For a time it 'went it alone' under the suzerainty of Britain. Then Britain amalgamated Tobago with Barbados, Grenada, St Vincent and St Lucia. When Barbados withdrew from this union, Britain proceeded to form a new association of Tobago, St Vincent, St Lucia and Dominica. According to Dr Williams, Tobago suffered from 'betweenity' – both 'metropolitan' and 'colonial' – and finally decided to settle for Trinidadian betweenity.

It was in such circumstances that, in 1889, Tobago was to become annexed to Trinidad as a dependency. In his book, Dr Williams sets out in great detail the following steps taken to reach this end.[53]

After HMG had caused a notice to be published in the *Gazette* and in the newspapers of both colonies intimating its desire to have Tobago annexed to or made part of the Colony of Trinidad, the planters of Tobago expressed a preference for Tobago to be annexed to Trinidad as a dependency having a separate Treasury with a subordinate legislature. They would have a Customs Union, a uniform code of laws and a single Governor and Chief Justice for both islands, along with a Financial Board to advise the Governor on all matters dealing with internal taxation and expenditure for Tobago.

The Trinidad Legislature also agreed to the merger. The Governor, who presided, was able to assure the Legislative Council that since the British Government was dismantling 'the establishment' in Tobago, the question of financial subsidy to their smaller neighbour would not arise, and his forecast of the extra cost to Trinidad was £50 per year. He added that Trinidad would be committed to sharing no other functionary with Tobago (and certainly to creating no new offices for Tobago) except the Governor and the Chief Justice. All this was in 1887. The Trinidad Legislature duly passed their resolution along the lines mentioned, as a result of which a type of confederation was formed. However, when the Royal Commission of 1897 visited Tobago, its members recommended the complete amalgamation of Trinidad and Tobago and the abolition of a separate account of revenue and expenditure: 'Tobago would then become a ward, or district, of Trinidad and the two islands would have a common exchequer.' The resultant legislation by the British

---

50   *Ibid*, Chapter 18, paras 415–21, pp 78 and 79.
51   Williams, 1961, p 139.
52   *Ibid*, p 123.
53   *Ibid*, Chapter 11, 'The Union of Trinidad and Tobago', pp 140–51.

Government was an Order in Council of April 1898, under which the Order of 6 April 1889, was revoked. The new order contained the following provision:

> On or after the date of the coming into force of this Order, the Island of Tobago shall be a Ward of the Colony of Trinidad and Tobago.

It would appear that what was in fact created was a *de facto* type of colonial union in which Tobago was to have no local institutions and would henceforth be subject to the laws and institutions of the Colony of *Trinidad and Tobago*. Support for this thesis is given by the further clauses of the Order in Council:[54]

> All future Ordinances enacted by the Legislature of the Colony shall extend to Tobago: Provided that the Legislature of the Colony may at any time by Ordinance provide for the special regulation of all or any of the matters and things dealt with in the several Acts, Ordinances and Regulations of Tobago enumerated in the Schedule hereto, and of any other and further matters and things in respect of which it may be deemed necessary to enact special and local Ordinances or Regulations applicable to Tobago as distinguished from the rest of the Colony.

> The Acts, Ordinances, and Regulations of Tobago enumerated in the Schedule hereto shall, until repealed or amended by the Legislature of the Colony, continue locally in force in Tobago, but such Acts, Ordinances and Regulations shall in every case be construed as amended by and read together with this Order; and in particular whenever in such Acts, Ordinances and Regulations any duty is imposed or power conferred upon any specified officer or person, such duty or power shall be performed or exercised by such person or persons as the Governor may from time to time by Proclamation appoint for the purpose.

Thus, Tobago became amalgamated with Trinidad to suit the financial and administrative convenience of the British Government following the decline of sugar in the Caribbean, in very much the same way (and more or less at the same time) as the Turks and Caicos as well as the Cayman Islands were annexed to Jamaica; Barbuda was joined to Antigua; and both Anguilla and Nevis were attached to St Kitts. This was a time when, in an effort to effect economies, the British Government was amalgamating Caribbean territories throughout the area – as witness also the amalgamation of Barbados in 1833 with Grenada, St Vincent, Tobago and (in 1835) St Lucia.[55] Later, when Barbados seceded from this group, the British Government decided to unite Tobago with Grenada, St Vincent and St Lucia. As Eric Williams was to exclaim in a speech in 1957, quoting what Julian Amery said in a biography of Joseph Chamberlain: 'In the gradual evolution of events the West Indies, once our most treasured possessions, had become in 1895, the Empire's darkest slum.'

In a speech made to the Trinidad Legislature in 1957, the Premier Dr Williams, was scathing in his criticism of past governments for their neglect of the island of Tobago. In the course of the address he made these pronouncements:

(a) For close to 60 years the Government of Trinidad, up to the present one, has had the opportunity of emphasising its neglect and underlining the betrayal of the trust imposed on it by the Act of Union.

---

54 *Ibid*, p 150.
55 See Phillips, 1977, pp 7–9.

(b) In the past four years, Mr Deputy Speaker, up to 1956 that long period of neglect, that betrayal of trust, has been exemplified by the addition of a mere nine miles of road to the main road system of Tobago.

(c) The betrayal of trust, the years of neglect are exemplified in the most ghastly fashion by the broken-down bridge at Parlatuvier lying in the water for eight years without any action taken on it.

TOBAGO MOVES FOR INTERNAL SELF-GOVERNMENT

That was at a time when the PNM had the support of the voters from Tobago and, accordingly, had two members of Parliament from Tobago in the House. By 1976, the party (which was still in power) had lost the confidence of those voters and on 14 January 1977, one of the former supporters of the PNM (who had by now broken away to form his own party), moved a resolution in the House of Representatives requesting internal self-government for Tobago. The representative was ANR Robinson (later President of the Republic). The resolution was an appeal to the Government to honour the very trust of which the Premier (by 1976 the Prime Minister) had so eloquently spoken 20 years before. It is not without significance, for example, that the bridge to which he had referred in 1956 – see (c) above – had not been repaired.

As a result of the motion moved by Robinson, the House of Representatives, at its sitting on 4 February 1977, unanimously passed the following resolution:

BE IT RESOLVED:

That this Honourable House is of the opinion that all proper and necessary steps should be taken to accord to the people of Tobago internal self-government in 1977 in such measure as will not be contradictory to the constitutional reality of the independent unitary state of Trinidad and Tobago, such proper and necessary steps to take into account:

(a) the views of the majority of people of Trinidad and Tobago;

(b) the cultural, financial and economic realities and potential of Trinidad and Tobago; and

(c) the impact of any such change on other parts of Trinidad and Tobago.[56]

It must here be emphasised that in his speech to the House in June 1957, Dr Williams himself had made the point that Tobago was not just another county council:

I hope, I do not go too far in suggesting that Tobago, as an island detached from Trinidad, cannot simply be put on the same footing as the County Council of Caroni, of Victoria, or of some other part or district in Trinidad.[57]

At this point, it is important (if one is to understand the latest movements of the central government) to detail the powerful submissions of the leading spokesman for Tobago in 1977, ANR Robinson, to whom reference has already been made. His submissions were put on both a political and an economic basis but we will deal here only with the political aspects. Here are his arguments.

---

56   Excerpt from *Hansard*, Trinidad House of Representatives, 4 February 1977.
57   *Ibid*, Friday, 7 June 1957, p 1927.

In condemning the 1898 colonial union, Dr Williams in his address to Parliament had, in 1957, put it very succinctly when he said: 'Tobago exchanged the neglect of United Kingdom imperialism for the neglect of Trinidad imperialism.'

The appointment in colonial days of a Warden (later a Commissioner) for Tobago never really helped, as all their instructions had to come from a Governor stationed in Trinidad who was in any event looking after the affairs of the colony.

When Trinidad and Tobago became independent in 1962, the PNM had already won the two seats allocated to Tobago in 1956, and again in 1961; and over the six year period, the PNM had tried two different administrative techniques in an effort to give special attention to the problems of that island. At first, a separate Ministry for Tobago Affairs was created with a Minister and a Permanent Secretary, both of whom resided in Tobago. The resident minister was later replaced by a non-resident Minister for Tobago Affairs.

However, when in the 1976 elections the PNM lost the two seats in Tobago, the Ministry of Tobago Affairs was discontinued and Tobago reverted to the neglect of which Dr Williams had so bitterly complained. Meanwhile, the two representatives of the Tobago electorate could not do much for their people, since the PNM ministers would give them little or no co-operation. Thus, any development in Tobago came to depend upon whether or not the Tobagonians voted for the government in power. Robinson's plea was for a structure that did not depend only upon the party in power. Furthermore, Tobago was not represented in the Senate during the 1976–81 Parliament, nor was it so represented in the 1981–86 Parliament. Thus, although the Tobago party has two representatives in the House of Representatives, there is no one in the Senate to speak on its behalf. Thus, spoke the champion of Tobago's cause.

The Trinidad Government in this respect may well wish to take a leaf out of the book of Antigua where, as mentioned in Chapter 12 below, Barbuda (half the size of Tobago) is permitted, under the existing Constitution, to have a Barbudan in the Senate appointed on the advice of the Prime Minister as well as the member of the Lower House appointed by the people of Barbuda. No amendment can be made to the Barbuda Local Government Act without the agreement and consent of the Barbuda Council, which is the equivalent of the Tobago House of Assembly.

A measure of support for this approach came in a recommendation from the Wooding Commission when it reported to the Governor General in 1974. The Commission pointed out that Tobago was different from Trinidad, not only in a historical sense, but in the fact that the Tobagonian is entirely different in temperament.[58] The Commission stated that at one time a small group had advocated secession from Trinidad but that, before the Commission, Tobagonians seemed to have modified their stand in that all they were then asking was that provision should be made in the new Constitution for a referendum at some future time to determine whether or not Tobago wished to remain part of the union. The Commission rejected this demand on the ground that further fragmentation in the area should be avoided at all costs.[59] Rather, the commissioners made recommendations aimed at strengthening the material unity of Trinidad and Tobago.

---

58 Report of the Constitution Commission, presented to the Governor General on 22 January 1974, s 326, p 80.
59 *Ibid*, ss 327 and 328, pp 80–81.

One of these recommendations was that Tobago should have as the local head of their administration a commissioner who should be vested with power to make important executive decisions and to take action in Tobago without constant reference to Trinidad.[60]

The Commission did not agree that Tobago should have its own mini-Parliament with power to pass laws and that it should have representatives in the National Parliament[61] – in other words, that there should be a federal or quasi-federal solution to the problem. The solution was seen to lie in the establishment of a Regional Council which:

> ... would carry out those duties and functions now performed by the Tobago County Council and such other duties as may be prescribed by county councils. As an advisory body, the Council would advise the Minister charged with the responsibility for Tobago Affairs on, and make recommendations in connection with, development plans for implementation of programmes in Tobago.[62]

This regional council was to be specially referred to in the new Constitution.[63]

This writer considers, with respect, that the Commission's recommendations did not go to the root of the acute problems of Tobago, as he will illustrate later in this section.

To return to the resolution of 4 February 1977. The member for Tobago must have been surprised to find that the PNM Government made no attempt to reject or amend this motion. Indeed, it would have been difficult for them to take any such action, in the face of the statements by the Prime Minister to which we have already alluded.

What happened thereafter was that a Joint Select Committee of both Houses was appointed to examine the Tobago resolution along with another motion concerning local government in general. After views had been asked from the public, the Committee submitted their findings which could be summarised as follows:

(a) the people of Tobago should be permitted the utmost participation through their representative institutions in the policy and implementation process;

(b) the geographical position of Tobago warrants special treatment. There must be co-ordination of the work of the various ministries in Trinidad if efficiency and a high level of service to the people of Tobago are to be achieved. It was agreed that the isolation in Tobago of the various departments from their head offices in Port of Spain resulted in uncertainty, misunderstanding and delay. Whatever structure evolved, the object should be (a) the effective co-ordination of the various services of the Central Government located in Tobago and the promotion and liaison with the elected body in Tobago; (b) the institution and maintenance of consultation with that local body, especially with respect to budgetary proposals for Tobago's development programme as well as the operation of the state owned enterprises which serve Tobago, principally sea and air communications; and

(c) the formulation of policy and its implementation by the people of Tobago through the democratic process.

---

60 Report of the Constitution Commission, s 329, p 81.

61 *Ibid*, s 331, pp 81–82.

62 *Ibid*, s 334, p 82.

63 *Ibid*, s 336, p 82.

In the course of moving his resolution in Parliament, Robinson had stated that he was not requesting secession; and it would appear from a document produced by his party, the Democratic Action Congress – which the author has seen – that what he in fact wanted was a federation. It is submitted that this could have been accommodated within the structure without secession taking place.

The model set out in the document provided for:

1   an assembly of not more than 15 members elected on the basis of universal adult suffrage –

   (a) representing the seven parishes of the island;

   (b) including the island's elected representatives in the national Parliament;

   (c) together with senators resident in Tobago;

2   the assembly to elect a chairman and deputy chairman from among its members. The chairman to make appointments on behalf of the President of the Republic;

3   the function of the assembly to be to make laws for the good government of the island of Tobago, subject to prescribed limits and procedures;

4   direction and control of day to day internal affairs to rest with a council appointed from among assembly members;

5   the leader of the majority party in the assembly to select and head the council;

6   the chairman to appoint the council on behalf of the President of the republic;

7   a system of committees to be established to render expert advice to members of the council in respect of matters for which they are responsible. Committee members will be selected on the basis of their expertise and experience and will be appointed by the chairman of the assembly;

8   the concept of revenue sharing developed in both federal and unitary systems, for example, the USA, Nigeria, Canada, France, Antigua, to be applied to the financing of internal services. Acceptance to be sought for the general principle that revenue generated by production, consumption and exploitation of resources in the island, whether through the local or national tax system, to be to the use of the island;

9   the public business of the island to be executed by a service comprising direct employees, employees on contract, and employees on transfer or secondment from the public service of the republic;

10 community and parish councils having prescribed powers over special matters affecting day to day life in the community to be established. Parish councils to be elected by members of the community councils.

Government moves

By 1980 all indications were that the Government was serious about granting Tobago 'internal self-government' within a unitary framework – somewhat of a contradiction in terms. A bill was drafted and circulated to the general public with the comments of the Attorney General and this bill was to be the basis of instructions given to Mr Lionel Seemungul QC, who was mandated to finalise the necessary legislation for the establishment of an elected body in the island to be known as the Tobago Island Council.

The draftsman in due course duly completed his task and Government passed what came to be known as the Tobago House of Assembly Act 1980 (Act No 37 of 1980), the long title of which was:

> An Act to establish the Tobago House of Assembly for the purpose of making better provision for the administration of the Island of Tobago and for matters connected therewith.

In the first edition of this work, published in 1985, the author wrote as follows:[64]

> Would it not have been more sensible to have a Federal Parliament of Trinidad and Tobago and two law-making Houses of Assembly, one for Trinidad and one for Tobago, with a Senate comprising a proportionate number of members from both Trinidad and Tobago? The writer has already seen signs of severe tension between Trinidad and Tobago over the operation of the present Act and it is his view that the tension will intensify.

One sign of tension evident in 1985 was the suit brought by the Tobago House of Assembly relative to the assembly's responsibility (as against the central government's) for establishing health facilities including psychiatric clinics. But in a number of other respects the Act proved well nigh unworkable.[65]

Then there was the resolution passed in the House of Assembly in late 1983 in which reference was made to the fact that 'repeated constitutional mandates given to its duly elected representatives by the electorate of Tobago within the unitary state of Trinidad and Tobago have met with lack of sympathy, indifference and arrogance from the Government of Trinidad'.

At the end of that resolution there was a thinly veiled threat of secession.

By 1987 the situation had deteriorated. It was in such a context that the Hyatali Report could make this statement:[66]

> 386. In our view a good deal of the strained relationship could be relieved by promoting a greater sensitivity to the legislative needs of Tobago. This highly desirable goal could be achieved by allowing the Assembly to prepare draft legislation in respect of Tobago on the clear understanding that it would have to be approved and enacted by Parliament to become effective. Such draft legislation should be confined to the Concurrent List and should be presented to Cabinet and to Parliament by the Minister with responsibility for Tobago. Before any such legislation is presented to Cabinet and to Parliament that draft resolution must be approved by resolution of the Tobago House of Assembly.

The Hyatali Commission recommended that the assembly be allowed to prepare draft legislation in respect of Tobago on the clear understanding that it would have to be approved and enacted by Parliament to become effective.[67]

This recommendation was accepted by Government as a result of which a constitutional amendment was effected,[68] bringing into being – as part of the

---

64 See Phillips, 1985.
65 See *ibid*, for comments as to the difficulties of operating ss 17(2), 21(3), 23(3), 42 and 59.
66 The Hyatali Report, para 386, p 72.
67 *Ibid*, para 36, p172.
68 See the Constitution (Amendment) Act 1996 (Act No 39 of 1996).

Constitution – the Tobago House of Assembly and enshrining such offices as its presiding officer, the Chief Secretary, and other secretaries as well as such organs as the Executive Council of the Assembly and the Tobago House of Assembly Fund.

The recommendation also resulted in the passing of the 1996 Act which was clearly a step in the right direction, giving (as it does) a considerable measure of self-government to Tobago.

Even though he has, on reflection, now altered his views as to a federal solution, the writer is still unable to understand why the assembly cannot pass its own laws. Clearly, before such laws are passed, it will be necessary for the Tobago House of Assembly to clear their contents with the Cabinet but this should present no problem especially as the Act prescribes for regular consultation between the Prime Minister and the Chief Secretary.[69]

One can only express the hope that a period of more harmonious relations has now dawned between Trinidad and its sister island.

CONCLUDING COMMENTS

Since independence in 1962, Trinidad and Tobago has thus shown commendable enterprise and originality in trying to forge an autochthonous form of constitutionalism, while at the same time preserving worthwhile aspects of the Westminster model. It was good to see the Government implement some of the Wooding Commission recommendations including the proposal for a Republic. It is also encouraging to observe that some recommendations of the Hyatali Report – including the all important Tobago relationship aspect – have also been implemented.

Constitutional hiccups since 1976

The constitutional problems which have been shown to affect other newly independent Caribbean mini-States have not passed Trinidad and Tobago by – as we shall see in these concluding words.

In 1986, there was a change of government from the 30 year rule of the PNM to the advent of the National Alliance for Reconstruction (NAR). By 1990, however, the new Government had become somewhat unpopular as a result of a reduction of the price of oil and a general downturn in the economy. One group that considered it had a special grievance in the country was the Jamaat al Muslimeen – a sect of Afro-Trinidadian Muslims who had had a running dispute with the Port of Spain City Council and the Government from 1969–90 over a plot of State land at No 1 Mucurapo on which the group had constructed a mosque and some other structures without the necessary planning permission. (The group was said to be allied to H Rap Browne of the United States Black Panther Movement and Abu Bakr, its leader, was a paid missionary sent to spread Islamic gospel in the Caribbean.) By July 1990, there was fear among the Jamaat

---

69   See Tobago House of Assembly Act 1996, s 31.

that the State was contemplating the demolition of the Mucurapo buildings for lack of compliance with the necessary regulations.

It was in these circumstances that on 27 July 1990 the group seized and held hostage at gunpoint at the Red House – seat of the country's Parliament – the then Prime Minister (ANR Robinson), six other Cabinet ministers and several non-ministerial parliamentarians, as well as some executives of the Government television station. The rebellion ended with the surrender of the rebels on 1 August 1990 after much anxiety and some loss of life. However, while the rebellion lasted the Acting President of the Republic had signed an amnesty to the perpetrators (under s 87(1) of the Constitution) couched in the following terms:

> I as required by the document headed 'Major Points of Agreement' hereby grant an amnesty to all those involved in acts of insurrection commencing on Friday July 27th 1990 ending with the safe return of all Members of Parliament held captive.

> This amnesty is granted for the purpose of avoiding physical injury to the Members of Parliament referred to above and is therefore subject to the complete fulfilment of the obligation safely to return them.

When the mediator who had been appointed returned to the Red House with this pardon on 29 July 1996, the situation eased somewhat and the leader of the Muslimeen declared that 'the hostage status' was at an end. The Prime Minister was released the next day while the other hostages were set free two days later on 1 August 1990 when the Muslimeen surrendered.

Subsequent to their surrender, Abu Bakr and his followers – numbering altogether 114 – were arrested and detained, being on 10 August 1990 charged with treason, murder, assault and other offences which the State alleged had been committed while the insurgents were jointly involved in acts of insurrection. Not surprisingly, they moved the High Court claiming that their detention and prosecution contravened their constitutional rights under the pardon and for a writ of habeas corpus. These motions were summarily rejected by the High Court and that decision was affirmed by the Court of Appeal. The grounds of rejection were that an accused in a criminal matter is provided by s 32 of the Criminal Procedure Act with an opportunity to plead a matter of law and fact. In other words, it was the opinion of both courts that the plea of pardon could only be made upon their arraignment. Before such an arraignment the accused had no right to challenge the conduct of the State in respect of any offence for which they might be charged and which might be fully covered by the pardon. And since the section quoted was 'an existing law' it could not be contended that the section contravened the terms of the Constitution.

The Muslimeen appealed to the Privy Council[70] which reversed the decision of the courts of Trinidad and Tobago. In giving judgment for the Muslimeen, the Privy Council – speaking through Lord Ackner – declared that the court had no discretion to refuse the application for the release of the 114 accused. This is how he set out the rationale of the Board's decision:

---

70   See the judgment of the Privy Council, *per* Lord Ackner (1991) 40 WIR 416. The facts and judgment are at pp 412–24.

The basis of the appellants' application for the writ was a simple one. They had established a *prima facie* case that they were beneficiaries of a valid pardon pursuant to section 87(1) of the Constitution in respect of the charges laid against them for which they had been committed to prison. At no stage in the proceedings either in the court below or in the Court of Appeal, had there been any attack upon the validity of the pardon. The decisions in the court below proceeded upon the assumption that the pardon was a valid one. In the circumstances they were entitled as of right to the immediate determination as to lawfulness of their imprisonment. It was submitted on their behalf that the existence of a right under section 32 of he Criminal Procedure Act, exercisable some years hence, to raise the existence of the pardon as a plea in bar when arraigned on the indictment, was totally irrelevant. The existence of an alternative but wholly unsatisfactory remedy did not disentitle them to the writ, which is a writ of right, granted *ex debito justitiae*.

In the further opinion of their Lordships of the Privy Council:

No civilized system of law should tolerate the years of delay contemplated by the courts below.

This was of course in reference to the fact that for the purpose of the committal proceedings and the subsequent trials, the Muslimeen accused had been divided into five 'batches' to be proceeded against separately. At the time of the judgment of the board, viz 1992, such proceedings against the first set were still in progress and were unlikely to be completed until mid-1993. The actual trial was unlikely to begin until 1994. Committal proceedings against the other four batches had not commenced two years after the events for which they are charged. It is on this account that Lord Ackner came to the conclusion that:

If the appellants are only able to assert their pardon by way of a 'plea in bar' at their eventual trial, as the Court of Appeal has held in both judgments, it follows that they are likely to remain in custody for many years on charges relating to offences for which, for the purposes of these appeals only, it must be assumed they have been validly pardoned.

The tragedy of the Muslimeen attempted 'takeover' is that it can recur. Indeed, when one studies the attitude and statement of Abu Bakar (their Imam), one realises that he regards himself as somewhat of a Messiah. Speaking in an address to the Trinidad people shortly after news of the coup broke, he attributed his success in the operation to the will of Allah. He gave Allah full credit for the overthrow of the lawful Government and for holding its Prime Minister and other ministers in a shameful state of detention – bound hand and foot. He (Abu Bakr) did not possess any power – he declared: 'Only the Almighty Allah did.'

He must have been even more encouraged when the High Court and the Court of Appeal later declared that the pardon granted was valid. The matter was again taken (this time by the Attorney General) to the Privy Council which declared that the pardon was invalid.[71]

The board did not however come to that decision on the main ground argued by the Attorney General, viz, that the pardon was granted under duress. The board concluded that the judges in the courts below were wrong in treating the pardon as valid: they considered that the Muslimeen wished, as it were, 'to have their cake and (to) eat it'.

---

71   See *AG v Phillip* (1994) 45 WIR 456.

In the words of the Board:

Having received the pardon, they sought to achieve their objectives which were reflected in the 'Major Points of Agreement'. Although the period of negotiation may have been protracted by the tactics perfectly properly adopted by Col Theodore to bring the insurrection to a peaceful conclusion until the end of the second stage of the insurrection the Muslimeen were still intent on achieving their broader objectives. They were certainly not surrendering or treating the insurrection as at an end. In doing so they were not complying with the condition to which the pardon was subject and, as a result, even on the most charitable interpretation, the pardon was no longer capable of being brought into effect by complying with the condition to which it was subject.[72]

The result therefore of the decision of the Board is that the pardon was and is invalid. That means that it was not unlawful to initiate a prosecution of the Muslimeen in relation to the events arising out of the insurrection and to arrest them for the purposes of that prosecution. However, in those proceedings the Muslimeen could well have been in a position to raise a plea in bar on the basis of abuse of process. The Board does not venture an opinion as to whether the plea would have succeeded; it would have been a decision for the court before whom the trial was to take place. However the order of habeas corpus having been made, the Board is able to assist the Attorney-General and the Director of Public Prosecutions, as they requested, by saying that after the order of habeas corpus was made it could be an abuse of process to seek once more to prosecute the Muslimeen for the serious offences committed in the course of the insurrection.[73]

Thus, the Muslimeen – no doubt with the powerful aid of Almighty Allah – was able to thrive and live to fight another day, despite the atrocities they had committed.

Judicial upheaval

The second major problem faced by this jurisdiction was a 1999 blazing row between the Chief Justice and the Attorney General. It culminated in the appointment of a Commission of Inquiry with terms of reference set out in a later chapter,[74] after the Right Honourable Mr Justice Telford Georges had visited Trinidad to try to settle the difference between the judiciary and the executive – where an uneasy truce still exists at the time of writing (January 2001).

Head of State contretemps

The fact that the President of the Republic wields certain limited (but important) executive powers under the Constitution is likely to be misinterpreted by certain holders of the office. This in turn can only generate troublesome constitutional problems in the years ahead. A clear example of such a problem is set out in the following paragraphs.

Under the 1976 Constitution, the Senate consists of 31 members, of whom 16 are appointed by the President on the advice of the Prime Minister, six on the advice of the

---

72   *AG v Phillip* (1994) 45 WIR 456, pp 474(g)–(i).
73   *Ibid*, pp 475(j) and 476 (a)–(b).
74   See Chapter 13, below.

Leader of the Opposition, while the President appoints nine in his discretion to represent various interests in the community.[75]

There are seven grounds of disqualification for senators, viz:[76]

If an appointee –

(a) becomes a citizen of a country other than Trinidad and Tobago;

(b) is a member of the House of Representatives;

(c) is an undischarged bankrupt;

(d) is mentally incompetent under the country's mental health laws;

(e) is under sentence of death or serving a sentence of imprisonment exceeding 12 months;

(f) is disqualified from membership in the House of Representatives; and

(g) is not qualified to be registered as an elector under Trinidad and Tobago law.

After the general elections which took place on 11 December 2000, the Prime Minister duly submitted the names for 16 persons for appointment as senators, seven of whom had been unsuccessful at the general elections: the intention being to appoint some of them to ministerial office. Despite not being disqualified under any of the heads set out above, the President refused to accept the nomination of the seven who were therefore not sworn in as senators. The reason given by the President was that their appointment would be an insult to the electorate of the country and that it was his duty to protect the Constitution against the Prime Minister who was taking the country down the road to dictatorship.

It need hardly be stated that in taking the step he did, the President was, by quiet decree, purporting to amend the Constitution by adding a further disqualification to those mentioned above – even though it is clear he had no power so to do. If the framers of the Constitution were minded to provide for such a stricture, they could quite easily have inserted such a provision as is to be found in the St Kitts and Nevis Constitution in the following terms:[77]

> A person shall not be qualified to be appointed as a Senator who has at any time since Parliament was last dissolved stood as a candidate for election as a Representative without being so elected.

Much pressure was brought upon the President to give way. A joint opinion was submitted to the President signed by four most eminent Caribbean jurists, viz, two former Presidents;[78] a highly respected former Chief Justice of three Commonwealth jurisdictions (Tanzania, Zimbabwe and the Bahamas) who is also a Privy Councillor;[79] and a private practitioner of the highest quality.[80] The opinion urged the President not to pursue his approach and the four lawyers spoke to him for more than three hours – to no

---

75 See 1976 Constitution of Trinidad and Tobago, s 40(1) and (2).

76 *Ibid*, s 42(1).

77 See St Kitts and Nevis Constitution Order 1983 SI 1983/881, s 24(4).

78 Sir Ellis Clarke and Mr Noor Hassanali.

79 Mr Justice Telford Georges.

80 Mr Tajmool Hosein QC.

avail. CARICOM offered its help – likewise without success. After a delay of 55 days, the President at last saw the light and performed his constitutional duty.

Some lawyers tried to justify the President's action on the basis that he was exercising a convention which had been in force since independence in 1962. The short answer to that argument is that where such a convention conflicts with the law of the land (in this case the Constitution itself) the law takes precedence. The writer has in a previous chapter[81] discussed this aspect at some length and there is no need for repetition here.

Situations like this illustrate in a forceful manner how a Head of State who tries to advise himself can become immersed in a constitutional morass from which it may become impossible to extricate himself. In the process he can only succeed in dividing the country he is appointed to unite.

There is certainly urgent need for the country to consider further constitutional change (as recommended by both the Wooding and Hyatali Commissions).

Grenada's unique constitutional recent past must be examined in the next chapter.

---

81 See Chapter 5, above.

CHAPTER 10

GRENADA – GRENADA'S REVOLUTION AND BEYOND

CONSTITUTIONAL HISTORY UP TO 1979

In our 1977 study,[1] the chequered constitutional history of Grenada since 1945 was outlined. In this chapter, a short summary of the developments in that island from about 1962 leading up to the tragic events of October 1983 will be attempted. The constitutional implications of these developments will also be examined.

It will be remembered that 1962 was the year of the dissolution of the Federal Government of the West Indies, when both Jamaica and Trinidad and Tobago proceeded to independence on their own. General elections had been held in Trinidad and Tobago in December 1961 and after the elections the political leader, speaking at a convention of the party, called the Federation 'a disgraceful episode' and unequivocally rejected a suggestion that his country should enter into a new federation with the Eastern Caribbean territories (including Grenada) since by that time Jamaica had expressed its desire to 'go it alone' to independence. The Trinidad People National Movement's resolution on the issue of federation did, however, leave the door open for a new association whereby the smaller territories would be permitted to join Trinidad on a unitary statehood basis.

Grenada expressed a desire to join the unitary state of Trinidad and Tobago and when a new Government came to power in Grenada in 1962, the scheme was that in one year the modalities for Grenada's absorption would be completed. In the event, the merger did not materialise mainly because the new Grenada Government seemed to have lost its enthusiasm for the proposal.[2] Thus, we find the same economic historian Dr Williams, advocating, in 1962 – albeit for a very sound reason – the very same type of merger which he had earlier condemned as characteristic of the British Government in the 19th century.

The next attempt at some type of association between Grenada and other territories was made in 1972 when representatives of Dominica, Grenada, Guyana, St Kitts/Nevis/Anguilla, St Lucia and St Vincent met in Guyana on 8 November 1971. The representatives issued a statement expressing the very sound view that the only salvation for their people lay in the creation of a federal State and the setting up of a Preparatory Commission which was to be established within the Commonwealth Caribbean Secretariat under a budget to be separately provided by the participating territories.[3]

Needless to say, this further effort came to naught as well, mainly because there was no wherewithal for the budget. Even if there was a genuine will to federate (which the author seriously questions), the result would have been the same.

---

1   See Phillips, 1977, pp 18–20 and 95. See also a full account of Grenada's constitutional history by Patrick Emanuel (1978).

2   *Ibid*, pp 70, 71.

3   *Ibid*, pp 206, 207.

Instead of joining a federation, Grenada was busy considering becoming an independent State, for two years later the usual Independence Conference was held in London, resulting in the Grenada Constitution Order 1973,[4] by which the country became an independent State within the Commonwealth. However, before independence was attained there was serious civil unrest stemming mainly from the fact that by this time the Premier, Eric Gairy, was encountering fierce opposition from the New Jewel Movement (NJM),[5] a left-leaning party that had come into being in 1973 and was rapidly mobilising the 'broad masses of the people'.

By 1973, the position of the Premier was becoming desperate and he set out to suppress the NJM at all costs, using the conventional resources of the police, but relying even more on the unconventional resources of a group of ex-convicts known as 'the Mongoose Gang'.

Although in 1973 the total strength of the parliamentary Opposition Party, the Grenada National Party (GNP), was only two members, the NJM, though lacking seats in the House of Representatives, had constituted an unofficial opposition and continued to hold frequent meetings on a countrywide basis in the course of which it was organising the workers into 'cadres', giving ideological training to the youth, and developing its own trade union movement support.

Three developments took place towards the end of 1973 and at the beginning of 1974 which must be specifically mentioned here:

1   the arrest and brutal ill-treatment of six members of the NJM by the organised (and disorganised) police personnel of the Government on 18 November 1973;

2   the announcement by the Government that independence was fixed for February 1974; and

3   demonstrations and marches by all sections of the community protesting against the repression and corruption being practised by the Government.

It was the combined effect of the above mentioned developments that led Premier Gairy to agree to the appointment of a high powered Commission of Enquiry to make diligent enquiries into and report upon all the facts relating to the matters set out hereunder, viz:

(1) all the circumstances leading up to the arrest and charging of six persons on Sunday, 18 November 1973;

(2) the alleged brutality by the police and the alleged denial of prompt medical and legal assistance to the arrested persons;

(3) the refusal by the magistrate to grant bail;

(4) the administration of justice in the State;

(5) to make specific recommendations upon:

(a) breaches of the Constitution as disclosed before the Commission,

and

(b) any evidence of a general breakdown of law and order within the State.

---

4   SI 1973/2155.
5   The NJM resulted from a merger of two political organisations, viz, Movement for Assemblies of the People (MAP) and the Jewel, an acronym for Joint Endeavour for Welfare, Education and Liberation.

The Commission, which deliberated and examined a long string of witnesses for several months, submitted its report to the Governor General on 27 February 1975.

The Commission came to the conclusion that the demonstrations, which commenced in early January 1974 and continued until towards the end of that month, were organised by two local trade unions led by Eric Pierre to protest the fact that certain undertakings given by the Premier had not been honoured. It found that persons other than trade union members (for example, people from the committee of 22)[6] participated in the demonstrations which they saw as an ideal opportunity for airing grievances of one kind or another. However, the Commission was at pains to point out that although the demonstrations were large and popular they were nevertheless peaceful and orderly.[7]

It then went on to refer to a particularly repressive piece of legislation passed by Parliament on 3 January 1974, calculated to prevent shopkeepers from closing their shops in protest against the Government.[8]

The Commission formed the view that the Premier believed the demonstrations were aimed at trying to delay the independence of Grenada (which had already been granted by imperial legislation) and that 'his commitment to lead Grenada to independence was an objective so desirable that the possibility of delay by recurring demonstrations was not to be countenanced'.[9]

The Commission made the following other findings of fact:

(a) there was a stone-throwing incident in the town of Gouyave when Mr Gairy's party endeavoured to hold a meeting there and this incident, coupled with the daily demonstrations taking place, led the Premier to recall the 'police aides' who were people of known bad character, but who were at the beck and call of the Premier: Mr Gairy being well aware of the excesses of brutality for which they were notorious;

(b) that the Premier had, under pressure, faithfully promised to disband the police aides (known locally as 'the Mongoose Gang');

(c) that Mr Gairy nevertheless recalled these thugs on the evening of 20 January – having heard there was to be a massive demonstration on the following day;

(d) that Mr Gairy personally recruited 300 of these men and on 21 January 1974, despatched them to the scene of the demonstration on the Carenage at Otway House, St George's, the headquarters of the trade unions. In doing so, he himself admitted that he said to them, 'Go to the Esplanade to Georgi's for lunch', knowing full well that, because they were leaderless and they were wont to look after his interests, they would attack the demonstrators, which they did with stones and other missiles;

(e) that the attack by the police aides against the demonstrators brought a response from the crowd who fired molotov cocktails at the aides, and that this was the cause of the riot;

---

6   This committee comprised representatives from 22 professional, religious and social groups.

7   *Report of the Commission of Enquiry*, para 188, submitted to the Governor General on 27 February 1975. The Chairman of this Commission was Sir Herbert Duffus.

8   *Ibid*, para 188.

9   *Ibid*, para 189.

(f) that instead of trying to restore calm, the official police took the side of the police aides and opened fire on the demonstrators, killing Rupert Bishop, the father of the leader of the NJM.[10]

The Commission summed up the reasons for the riot as follows:[11]

(i) gross negligence on Mr Gairy's part; and

(ii) a deliberate violent confrontation by the police aides with the demonstrators.

The Commission also found[12] that there was a complete breakdown of discipline in the police force where the senior officers felt insecure and were reluctant to assume individual responsibility for decisions relating to the dreaded police aides. The Commission very severely criticised the conduct of the police in respect of an inquest into the death of Rupert Bishop, who had died between 1 pm and 2 pm on 21 Monday January 1974. Although an autopsy had been performed by Dr Brathwaite at 4.15 pm the same day, and the post-mortem report was written on 22 January 1974 (the next day), the doctor's report was not requested by the police until 9 May 1974 – the day before he was asked to appear before the Commission. The Commission described the behaviour of the police as:

> ... an appalling indifference among members of the Police Force about the investigation of criminal conduct by a large number of persons, including physical injuries to Garfield Brathwaite by gun fire for which a policeman was responsible and also the death of Rupert Bishop by violence.[13]

In Commonwealth jurisdictions where constitutional conventions are observed, the Prime Minister and his entire Cabinet – in the face of such a scandal – would have promptly resigned, but Gairy was prepared to carry on to the bitter end.

In December 1976, there was yet another general election when Gairy was again the victor, although the Alliance (which comprised the NJM, the GNP and the United Political Party (UPP)) won a total of six seats – against nine seats won by Gairy's Grenada United Labour Party (GULP). On this occasion, in spite of suspected widespread electoral malpractices committed by the ruling party, the combined opposition won 48% of the votes to Gairy's 52%. The evidence from all sides is that, recognising the true import of this electoral result, the Prime Minister became even more repressive and heavy-handed than previously.

The repression and heavy-handedness of Gairy, which during the post-1976 election period appeared to be calculated to terrorise and subdue the mounting opposition to his government, manifested themselves in some of the grossest abuses and violations of human rights of the people of Grenada. It is this period that the late Prime Minister of Grenada, Maurice Bishop, referred to as 'the long dark nights of terror'. During 1977 and 1978, there were numerous recorded incidents[14] of persons disappearing in mysterious circumstances, of persons being assaulted, shot and wounded or killed by the police, of

---

10 *See Report of the Commission of Enquiry*, paras 188–92.

11 *Ibid*, para 201(5).

12 *Ibid*, para 201(7) and (8).

13 *Ibid*, para 200.

14 See (1) Hughes, 1977.

persons being beaten, brutalised and subjected to torture, inhuman and degrading treatment while in police custody, of persons being arbitrarily arrested and detained by the police, and of the general denial of the rights and freedoms of thought, expression, assembly and association. Gairy appeared to have been totally oblivious or ignorant of the fact that these unpunished atrocities violated not only the laudable affirmations of fundamental rights and freedoms set out in Chapter I of the Constitution of Grenada but also the Universal Declaration of Human Rights and the American Convention on Human Rights.[15]

THE PEOPLE'S REVOLUTIONARY GOVERNMENT SEIZES CONTROL

It was in these circumstances that at 4 am on the morning of 13 March 1979 the NJM led by Maurice Bishop seized power at a time when Gairy was visiting the United States and declared that constitutional Government 'had been interrupted as a consequence of the violations and abuses of democracy committed by the administration of Eric Matthew Gairy under the guise of constitutionality'.[16]

One of the first acts of the new regime was the suspension of the Constitution of Grenada.[17] In addition, it established a People's Revolutionary Government (the PRG)[18] and ordained that the Queen would remain Head of State, with her representative, the Governor General, continuing in office.[19] However, executive power was no longer to be vested in Her Majesty – and locally in her Governor General – but in the PRG. Likewise, legislative power was no longer to be vested in the Parliament of Grenada consisting of Her Majesty, a Senate and a House of Representatives, but in the PRG.[20]

A Supreme Court of Grenada was established (consisting of a High Court and a Court of Appeal)[21] while appeals to the Privy Council were abolished later in 1979;[22] the existing laws of Grenada were to continue in force 'save as hereinafter provided or herein or hereafter amended or repealed';[23] a People's Revolutionary Army (PRA) was formally established which 'shall have the powers of arrest and search as are vested in the members of the Royal Grenada Police Force'.[24] Civil servants' pensions rights as provided under the Grenada Termination of Association Order 1973 were preserved.[25]

In so far as future promulgation of laws was concerned, the laws would be called 'People's Laws' and would 'become effective upon oral declaration and/or publication

---

15 Signed at the Inter-American Specialised Conference on Human Rights, San Jose, Costa Rica, 22 November 1969.
16 Declaration of the Grenada Revolution on 13 March 1979. See Grenada People's Laws 1979, 13 March to 31 December 1979.
17 People's Law (hereafter (PL)) No 1.
18 PL No 2.
19 PL No 3.
20 PL No 2.
21 PL No 4.
22 PL No 84.
23 PL No 5.
24 PL No 7.
25 PL No 9.

on Radio Free Grenada by the Prime Minister or in the official *Gazette* under the hand of the Prime Minister'.[26]

The regime then proceeded by means of one of its Proclamations to appoint first a Prime Minister[27] and then the members of the PRG – which turned out to be a list of 23 persons.[28] The very next Proclamation[29] was entitled 'Appointment of Ministers' and under this enactment the Prime Minister proceeded to name the ministers and secretaries responsible for the various departments of government. There then followed a further edict[30] in which the regime purported to restore the following sections of the 1974 Constitution (dealing with the subjects mentioned seriatim opposite each section):

s 68:   appointment and functions of the secretary to the Cabinet;

s 70:   appointment of Attorney General and circumstances when Director of Public Prosecutions may be appointed;

s 71:   appointment and duties of Director of Public Prosecutions;

s 83:   appointment and removal of Public Service Commission;

s 84:   appointment of public officers;

s 85:   power of Prime Minister over appointment of secretary to the Cabinet, permanent secretaries and heads of department;

s 86:   conditions of service of Director of Public Prosecutions;

s 87:   conditions of service of director of audit;

s 88:   appointment of magistrates, registrars and legal officers;

s 89:   appointment of police force;

s 90:   appointment and removal of Public Service Board of Appeal;

s 91:   procedure for appeals in disciplinary cases;

s 92:   pensions;

s 93:   power to withhold pensions in certain events;

s 94:   conditions dealing with the grant of citizenship to

s 95:   persons born in Grenada; persons who became citizens;

s 96:   of Grenada by registration after independence day;

s 97:   7 February 1974; persons born outside Grenada on or

s 98:   after 7 February 1974; and persons who become

s 99:   citizens by virtue of marriage to a Grenadian.

s 111(8): regime dealing with removal and dismissal of Public

(9);(10): officers not to apply to Director of Audit.

---

26   PL No 10.
27   PL No 11.
28   PL No 12.
29   PL No 13.
30   PL No 15.

That same PL[31] abolished the Judicial and Legal Services Commission and gave the Public Service Commission power to appoint all judicial and legal personnel. It also made provision that the existing laws and the foregoing provisions shall as from 13 March 1979 be construed with such modifications, adaptations, qualifications and exceptions as may be necessary to bring them into conformity with the laws and proclamations of the PRG.

MILITARY COUP OF OCTOBER 1983

By mid-1983 after the PRG had governed Grenada for more than four years, it became obvious that, from the inception, Prime Minister Bishop had encountered severe internal ideological dissensions within the central committee of the party. These dissensions were to culminate in the arrest of the Prime Minister on 12 October 1983, the resignation of the deputy prime minister, and the surfacing of a severe rift and total confusion among the membership of the central committee. It was clear that one section of the committee supported the Prime Minister and another section the deputy prime minister (who had resigned from the central committee one year previously, but who also had the bulk of the army as well as Radio Free Grenada behind him). On 19 October 1983, seven days after he was put under house arrest, the Prime Minister was released by a large number of his supporters and taken in triumph through the streets of St George's. At first he was thought to be heading for the Market Square where he would address the crowd, but instead, he went to Fort Rupert, formerly the headquarters of the PRA, for reasons that are still shrouded in mystery. While he was planning his strategy for addressing his supporters with three of his other ministers and two trade unionists, and for re-asserting his authority as Prime Minister, he and his ministers along with the two trade unionists were brutally executed by the Army. Many innocent persons (including children) were also gunned down. Shortly thereafter, General Austin (head of the PRA) declared himself chairman of a Revolutionary Military Council (RMC) of 16 and proclaimed a 24 hour a day curfew for four days in an obvious attempt to dispose secretly of Bishop's body and those of his colleagues.

MILITARY INVASION

On Tuesday, 25 October 1983, six days after the RMC was established in Grenada, heavily armed contingents of United States Rangers and Marines, supported by personnel from the Jamaican and Barbados armed forces, invaded Grenada and engaged the local and Cuban workers on that island in armed combat which ended on 31 October 1983.

Several reasons have been advanced in an attempt to justify the invasion of Grenada, which was condemned by a resolution of the United Nations General Assembly by a vote of 108:9 with 27 abstentions. According to one report, it appears that Sir Paul Scoon, the Governor General of Grenada, faced with the total breakdown of law and order following the violent overthrow of the PRG and the brutal slaying of Prime Minister Bishop and his ministers, issued an 'invitation' to the Organisation of Eastern Caribbean States (OECS)[32]

---

31   *Ibid*.
32   The OECS was established by a treaty signed on 18 June 1981.

along with the Governments of the United States of America, Jamaica and Barbados to come to the assistance of the people of Grenada. It is not quite clear just when and through what medium the 'invitation' was issued. However, on 25 October 1983, the very day of the invasion of Grenada, the Central Secretariat of the OECS published the following 'Statement on the Grenada Situation':

The Member Governments of the Organisation of Eastern Caribbean States met at Bridgetown, Barbados, on Friday, 21st October 1983 to consider and evaluate the situation in Grenada arising out of the overthrow of Prime Minister Maurice Bishop and the subsequent killing of the Prime Minister together with some of his Cabinet colleagues and a number of other citizens.

The Member States were deeply concerned that this situation would continue to worsen, that there would be further loss of life, personal injury and a general deterioration of public order as the military group in control attempted to secure its position.

Member Governments considered that the subsequent imposition of a draconial [sic] 96-hour curfew by the military group in control was intended to allow them to further suppress the population of Grenada which had shown by numerous demonstrations their hostility to this group.

Member Governments are also greatly concerned that the extensive military build up in Grenada over the last few years had created a situation of disproportionate military strength between Grenada and other OECS countries. *This military might in the hands of the present group posed a serious threat to the security of the OECS countries and other neighbouring States. Member Governments considered it of the utmost urgency that immediate steps should be taken to remove this threat.*

Under the Provisions of Article 8 of the Treaty establishing the OECS, concerning Defence and Security in the sub-region, *Member Governments of the Organisation therefore decided to take appropriate action.*

Bearing in mind the relative lack of military resources in the possession of the other OECS countries, *the Member Governments have sought assistance for this purpose from friendly countries within the region and subsequently from outside.*

Three Governments have responded to the OECS Member Governments' request to form a multi-national force for the purpose of undertaking a pre-emptive defensive strike in order to remove this dangerous threat to the peace and security of their sub-region and to establish a situation of normality in Grenada. These governments are Barbados, Jamaica and the United States of America. Barbados and Jamaica are members of Caricom and Barbados is linked to some of the OECS Member Governments in a Sub-regional Securing [sic] Agreement.

It is the intention of the Member Governments of the OECS, that *once the threat has been removed they will invite the Governor-General of Grenada to assume executive authority of the country* under the provisions of the Grenada Constitution of 1973 and to *appoint a broad-based interim government to administer the country pending the holding of General Elections.*

It has been agreed that while these arrangements are being put in place, the presence of former Prime Minister Eric Gairy and others who might further complicate the situation, would therefore not be welcomed in Grenada.

It is further intended that arrangements should be made to establish effective police and peace keeping forces in order to restore and maintain law and order in the country.

After normalcy has been restored, non-Caribbean forces will be invited to withdraw from Grenada.

Member Governments of the Organisation of Eastern Caribbean Sates wish to solicit the diplomatic support of all friendly countries for this initiative.

[Emphasis supplied.]

In the view of the writer this statement is remarkable in many respects. Not only does it set out quite unequivocably the 'security concerns' which ultimately resulted in the invasion of Grenada, but it also anticipated with prophetic accuracy some of the measures which would be taken by the Governor General of Grenada in the aftermath of the military intervention.[33] Incredibly, also, the statement makes no mention of any 'invitation' having been issued by the Governor General to the OECS and other governments to come to the assistance of the people of Grenada. One may therefore legitimately question whether any such invitation had indeed been issued at the time the statement was made.

The 'Statement on the Grenada Situation' reproduced above shows that the Member Governments of the OECS decided to take appropriate action under Art 8 of the Treaty in order to remove the serious threat to the security of the OECS countries and other neighbouring States posed by the military might of the RMC. It is necessary therefore to direct our attention to a consideration of the OECS, in general, and Art 8 of the treaty in particular, in an effort to determine if, and to what extent, the action of those governments was permitted or justified under Art 8 or any other provision of the treaty.

The recent history of sub-regional integration and functional co-operation in the Eastern Caribbean dates back to November 1966 when the West Indies Associated States Council of Ministers (WISA) was established. This coincided with the grant of associated statehood by Britain to six of her former colonies.[34] This inter-governmental grouping comprised the former colonies of Antigua, Dominica, Grenada, St Kitts/Nevis/Anguilla, St Lucia and St Vincent and the colony of Montserrat and was based on a loose administrative arrangement for joint action 'to administer certain common services and to perform such other functions as may be agreed upon from time to time'.

By May 1979, a majority of those territories had either become independent or were rapidly moving towards the attainment of independence.[35] The Council of Ministers, being apparently satisfied with the relationship in which they had participated for the past 13 years, agreed that it should be deepened through the establishment of an organisation possessing an international legal personality. Accordingly, the Council adopted a resolution retaining and formalising the arrangements for joint action among Member States and accepting in principle a draft treaty establishing the Organisation of Eastern Caribbean States. This treaty (the Treaty of Basseterre) which was signed on 18 June 1981 by representatives of the governments of Antigua, Dominica, Grenada, Montserrat, St Kitts/Nevis, St Lucia and St Vincent and the Grenadines came into operation on 4 July 1981.

Article 3 of the Treaty sets out in considerable detail the purposes and functions for which the organisation was established. However, for the purpose of the present enquiry,

---

33 See pp 190–92, below.
34 See Phillips, 1977, pp 84–116.
35 By 1984, all the territories except Montserrat had attained independence.

we need only concern ourselves with two of them, namely those contained in sub-paras 1(b) and 2(q) which are, respectively, in the following terms:

1(b) to promote unity and solidarity among the Member States and to defend their sovereignty, territorial integrity and independence;

and

2   to co-ordinate, harmonise and pursue joint policies particularly in the fields of:

(q) Mutual Defence and Security.

To accomplish the functions entrusted to the organisation under the treaty, Art 5 established a number of institutions, including the Authority of Heads of Government of the organisation (the supreme policy-making institution of the OECS) and the Defence and Security Committee. This committee comprises 'Ministers responsible for Defence and Security or other Ministers or Plenipotentiaries designated by Heads of Government of the Member States'.[36]

The importance which the framers of the treaty appear to have placed on decisions of the authority is reflected in para 5 of Art 6 which reads as follows:

The Authority shall have power to make decisions on all matters within its competence. *All such decisions shall require the affirmative vote of all Member States present and voting at the meeting of the Authority at which such decisions were taken provided that such decisions shall have no force and effect until ratified by those Member States, if any, which were not present at that meeting or until such Member States have notified the Authority of their decision to abstain.* Such decisions by the Authority shall be binding on all Member States and on all institutions of the Organisation and effect shall be given to any such decisions provided that it is within the sovereign competence of Member States to implement them.

[Emphasis supplied.]

The intention of this provision seems to be to ensure that a Member State is not adversely affected by a decision whether or not it is present at the meeting of the authority at which the decision is taken, since ratification by absent Member States is required for such decisions to be effective.

Much has been made of the fact that the OECS decision to send in a multi-national force into Grenada was illegal because the Government of Grenada did not participate in the decision and that the treaty provides for the affirmative vote to all members present and voting and for ratification of the decision by Member States not represented at the meeting. Grenada was, of course, not present (no government being then in existence). These arguments however appear to fall far short of the mark since they seem to ignore the reality of the situation with which the authority was then dealing. According to the OECS 'Statement on the Grenada Situation' (above), Member Governments were greatly concerned about the 'disproportionate military strength between Grenada and other OECS countries'.

They considered that the military might of the RMC posed a serious threat to the security of the OECS countries and other neighbouring States and that it was of the utmost urgency that immediate steps should be taken to remove this threat. They

---

36   Treaty establishing the OECS, Art 8, para 1.

accordingly decided to take appropriate action under Art 8 of the Treaty. Assuming the sincerity of the OECS concerns, would it have made any difference whether or not there was a government in existence in Grenada? Would it have made any difference whether the government was headed by Prime Minister Maurice Bishop or General Hudson Austin? Does anyone believe that the other OECS countries would have invited the Government of Grenada to send a representative to a meeting of the authority at which the sole question to be discussed was whether or not a hostile military force should be sent to Grenada? Does anyone think that if such a decision had been taken in the absence of a Grenadian representative it would have been logical to expect that those who had so decided would await ratification by the Government of Grenada before the decision was put into effect? In the writer's view, what matters is whether that decision was consistent with the terms of the treaty and what are the likely consequences, in constitutional terms, of such a decision in the case of other Caribbean countries. For there can be little doubt that the decision has set an extremely dangerous precedent for the region.

The OECS Member Governments, in deciding to remove the perceived military threat posed by Grenada, purported to act under Art 8 of the Treaty. We should therefore examine that Article to see to what extent, if any, such action was provided for, or permitted. In doing so, it should be borne in mind that the situation in Grenada on 21 October 1983, regardless of the 'draconian measures' instituted by the RMC, can only be described as a purely internal matter – an internal power struggle by local forces, albeit with potential civil war consequences; and that prior to 25 October 1983, there was no action, taken or anticipated, which could by any stretch of the imagination be objectively categorised as external aggression.

The relevant provisions of Art 8 of the Treaty (viz, paras 3 and 4) are as follows:

3   The Defence and Security Committee shall be responsible to the Authority. It shall take appropriate action on any matters referred to it by the Authority and shall have the power to make recommendations to the Authority. It shall advise the Authority on matters relating to external defence and on arrangements for collective security against external aggression, including mercenary aggression, with or without the support of internal or national elements.

4   The Defence and Security Committee shall have responsibility for coordinating the efforts of Member States for collective defence and the preservation of peace and security against external aggression and for the development of close ties among the Member States of the Organisation in matters of external defence and security, including measures to combat the activities of mercenaries, operating with or without the support of internal or national elements, in the exercise of the inherent right of individual or collective self-defence recognised by Article 51 of the Charter of the United Nations.

When one examines these provisions, it becomes obvious that the competence of the Defence and Security Committee of the OECS is limited to:

(a) matters relating to *external defence*;

(b) arrangements for collective security against *external aggression*, including *mercenary aggression* whether or not supported by internal or national elements;

(c) collective defence and the preservation of peace and security against *external aggression*; and

(d) matters of *external defence and security* including measures to combat the activities of mercenaries, operating with or without the support of internal or national elements.

Unless the action taken against Grenada can be classified under one or more of the above heads (and it clearly cannot), the OECS Heads of Government could not have relied on Art 8 to justify the decision taken on 21 October 1983, with respect to the Grenada situation. It has been reliably reported that in their original form, paras 3 and 4 of Art 8 were not restricted to matters of external defence and aggression and that the existing limitations were, ironically, introduced by the Government of Grenada and unanimously adopted by the other OECS governments before the final draft of the treaty was settled.

Apart from Art 8, can any other provision of the treaty be relied upon to justify the OECS sponsored 'pre-emptive defensive strike' against Grenada? The answer must be in the negative. As already stated, one of the major purposes of the organisation is the promotion of unity and solidarity among the Member States and the defence of their collective and individual sovereignty, territorial integrity and independence. The OECS action could hardly have been intended to further any of these objectives. On the contrary, it was clearly subversive of unity and solidarity with Grenada and an unjustifiable act of aggression against the sovereignty, territorial integrity and independence of that country.

Attention is drawn to a poignant assessment of the situation by Dr Mohammed Shahabuddeen, a former Vice President and Attorney General of the Co-operative Republic of Guyana, in the National Assembly on 28 October 1983 while the intervention was still ongoing. This is what he had to say:

> So then, Cde Speaker, we are left with this. There being not a scintilla of evidence to justify the action on the basis of self-defence, whether anticipatory or not, or any other of the pleaded grounds, the action constitutes an armed intervention in another state. And that is clearly illegal for, as has been recently said by the distinguished President of France, the only way that a country's armed forces can enter the territory of another with which it is not lawfully at war is by way of invitation. It is a wry reflection that the only invitation of which there was any credible evidence before the invasion was an invitation by those only recently emancipated from the political tutelage of a relatively modest metropolitan power for the restoration of colonialism and the return of imperialism at the astronomically elevated level of super-power domination.

THE GOVERNOR GENERAL TAKES CONTROL

At this point the Governor General took control, issuing on 31 October 1983 Proclamation No 1 which was an order in which he announced his intention to assume executive authority over the country either personally or after consultation with an Advisory Council which would shortly be appointed.

On that same day, he issued Proclamation No 2 ordering all Grenadian diplomatic officers 'to close their respective Embassies, High Commissions and Missions immediately and return to Grenada at the first available opportunity and to report to (him) on their return'. This order was extended to non-diplomatic staff abroad who were Grenadian nationals.

On 4 November 1983, Proclamation No 3 was issued. Under this Proclamation, the following PL 'ceased to be operative and lapsed on October 19th 1983':

(i) the law that brought the PRG into being (PL2);

(ii) the law that derogated from the full authority of Her Majesty's representative (the Governor General) to the extent that it attempted to effect such derogation (PL3);

(iii) the law that prescribed how, under the PRG, new laws were to be promulgated (PL 10);

(iv) the law setting out the new composition of the Cabinet (PL 16); and

(v) the law purporting to assign new duties to the Governor General (PL 18).

This Proclamation declared that a number of provisions in the 1974 Constitution were 'once more in force', to wit: Chapter I, Chapter II (ss 69–74 inclusive), and Chapter VII. It declared a state of emergency for purposes of Chapter I of the Constitution.

The opportunity was taken to revoke the following People's Laws:

(a) the law dealing with the PRA;

(b) the law creating a Preventive Detention Tribunal; and

(c) the law relating to the grant of pardons.

Proclamation No 4 became effective on 11 November 1983 and was to be read as one with Proclamation No 3. By this Proclamation, the following sections of the 1974 Constitution were revived: ss 68, 70, 71, 82, 83–100, 111(8), (9) and (10); ss 86, 87 and 93 were amended by deleting from them certain subsections, viz, sub-ss 86(10), 87(10) and 93(4) respectively.

This Proclamation also revoked the law which dealt with the appointments of the Attorney General, Director of Public Prosecutions and members of the Public Service – provided they were appointed between 1973 and 1983 (PL 15) as well as the law amending the Newspaper Ordinance: Cap 197-PL 81.

Proclamation No 5 was the most important of all decrees issued by the Governor General. It was passed on 17 November 1983, bringing the Advisory Council into being. This body would advise the Governor General on the making of ordinances. Curiously, it would have no powers to advise him in changing the Constitution or to legislate in relation thereto, that function being only for the Governor General who, by Art 7 thereof, was charged *by order* with restoring sections of the original Constitution 'subject to such modifications (if any) as may be specified in the order'. The Governor General was also by this Proclamation empowered to amend or revoke any such order 'by further order (of the Governor General)'.

Article 26 of this Proclamation expressly authorized the Governor General to amend or revoke the Constitution 'acting in his own deliberate judgment'.

It was with such authority that, on 9 November 1984, the Governor General made what was described as the Constitution of Grenada Order 1984. By this order, all sections of the 1974 Constitution still then suspended were restored, with the exception of those relating to the judiciary.

If the writer has expressed some apprehension over the procedure followed to reintroduce sections of the Constitutions and to restore a modicum of legal normality, this must not in any way be regarded as a personal attack on the *bona fides* of the Governor General. Indeed, it is providential that under the PRG he was permitted to remain the Queen's representative, as Head of State; for if there had been a vacuum at the top, the mind boggles at the State of anarchy, bloodshed and confusion that would have ensued after the RMC seized power on 19 October 1983. There would almost certainly have been such a fierce and bloody civil war that the country may well have gone over the slippery slope with little hope of ever being retrieved. On this account the Governor General deserves the commendation of the entire nation. The safety and integrity of the State having been his paramount consideration. His legal advisers were perhaps overzealous about the extent of the powers they asked him to take (which he accepted in good faith).

This is therefore a case in which, when one looks at the records in the years to come, one may well find the answer to the question: could the Governor General have achieved legal continuity without doing so much violence to the Constitution and other statutory enactments? The attempt will not, however, be made to answer this question in this volume in the absence of the necessary empirical evidence.

RELEVANCE OF DEFENCE OF STATE NECESSITY

In terms of the Grenada Constitution, the action taken by the late Maurice Bishop in March 1979 and those taken by the Governor General of Grenada on and after 31 October 1983 in relation to the administration of Grenada amounted to usurpations of power in both cases. In the former case, Bishop and his colleagues illegally seized State power, established the PRG and proceeded to exercise both executive and legislative power in the name of the people of Grenada for a period of four and a half years. In the case of the Governor General, while executive authority could legitimately be exercised by him under s 57 of the Constitution, the unannounced assumption and exercise by him of legislative authority were *prima facie* contrary to the relevant constitutional provisions. The acts of both usurpers can only be justified if it can be shown that the measures respectively taken by them were dictated by the necessity to save the State from chaos and disintegration and were in the best interest of the State and its inhabitants. In other words, their acts could be justifiable on the basis of the doctrine of State necessity.[37]

The doctrine of State necessity is based on the application of three well known maxims, namely: *that which is otherwise unlawful, necessity makes lawful; the safety of the people is the supreme law; and the safety of the State is the supreme law.* These maxims, which have been generally relied on to justify the acquisition of private property by the executive for the defence of the State in times of war, have also been accepted as being applicable to other instances of national emergency which threaten the security of the State[38] and that is what the Governor General purported to do. His actions were vindicated when the matter was subsequently brought to court after a constitutional regime was restored, as we shall see in the immediately following paragraphs.

---

37 See view expressed on this doctrine in an article by Leslie Wolf-Phillips entitled 'Constitutional Legitimacy: A Study of Doctrine of Necessity': published in Third World Quarterly, October 1979, Vol 1, No 4, pp 97–133. See also Monograph 6 published by Third World Quarterly Foundation, New Zealand house, 80 Haymarket, London (hereafter referred to as 'Monograph 6').

38 FW Maitland, *Constitutional History of England* (CUP, 1959 ed) pp 283–86.

THE COURTS HAVE THEIR SAY

The High Court

When order was restored, Andy Mitchell and 18 others were duly charged with the murder of the former coup leader (and former Prime Minister) Maurice Bishop and others. The accused were awaiting trial before the High Court for Grenada and they applied thereto under s 101 of the 1974 Constitution, seeking a declaration that the court was not competent to hear the charges, having itself been unconstitutionally appointed. Their contention was that:

(a) they were by the Constitution guaranteed a fair trial by a tribunal established by law;

(b) the court established by the Courts Order of 1967 was the only constitutionally established Supreme Court of Grenada;

(c) the court which PL No 4 purported to appoint was unconstitutional; and

(d) the Governor General had assumed legislative powers when he issued Proclamation No 3 purporting to validate PL No 4.

The Chief Justice would have none of this. He dismissed the application on the following grounds:

(a) when the PRG temporarily suspended the Constitution with the declared intention to draft and introduce a new Constitution, as well as to preserve certain sections of the 1974 Constitution, a first step had in fact been taken to replace the pre-revolutionary grundnorm with another regime;

(b) a further step was taken with the revocation of the 1967 order and a new courts system;

(c) that although the PRG had seized power by unconstitutional means the application of the doctrine of State necessity validated its acts, having regard to the acceptance by the people of Grenada of the acts, and the urgent need therefor as well as the absence of any alternative means of achieving its aims;

(d) the court was satisfied that the effectiveness of the rule of the PRG over a period of four years validated and/or legitimated the legislative enactments of the regime;

(e) where a government was thus firmly established as legitimate, its legitimacy would relate back to cover legislation passed by the regime from the inception of its control (see the Seychelles case of *Controller of Customs v Ramjikal* (1981) CLB 1249. See, also, *AG v Mustafa Ibrahim* (1964) CLR 195);[39]

(f) the West Indies Associated Supreme Court withdrew from Grenada after the PRG seized power. It left a vacuum which had to be filled and the vacuum was filled by PL No 14 which adopted with slight variations the judicial system previously in existence. In this way PL Nos 4 and 14 could be regarded as creating their own judicial grundnorm in succession to the previous courts regime;

---

39   This case has been exhaustively analysed in Phillips, 1985, pp 40–42.

(g) since throughout the revolutionary period, the Queen remained Head of State, the court was unable to entertain the contention of the applicants that the acts of Her Majesty's representative were constitutionally improper. It is the proper function of Her Majesty's representative in such circumstances to take every step to save the country – thus threatened – from extinction and to preserve the society and the community from anarchy;

(h) the Governor General's Proclamations were accordingly a legitimate exercise of his legislative powers in the peculiar circumstances of the case. See *Special Reference No 1 of 1955* (1955) FCR 439.[40]

The Court of Appeal

Against the High Court's decision the accused appealed to the Grenada Court of Appeal (Haynes P, Peterkin and Liverpool JJA) who gave separate judgments described by Lord Diplock when the matter reached the Privy Council as having dealt 'extensively and eruditely with the constitutional validity of the exercise'. The Court of Appeal in June 1985 dismissed the appeal, declaring both PL Nos 4 and 14 to be effectual and valid. Haynes P and Peterkin JA made no comment on PL No 84 – dealing with termination of appeals to the Privy Council – holding that it was irrelevant to the issue before the court.

It should be noticed that, although the challenge to the local system of courts failed, the Court of Appeal, by a majority, held that the system's validity was only transient, being founded on the doctrine of state necessity, so that its continued existence beyond the period of that necessity would not be legitimate. In the words of Haynes P:

> The legality is temporary only until either effective steps shall have been taken to resume the State's participation in the pre-revolution Supreme Court or constitutional legislation shall have been passed in compliance with section 39 of the Constitution to establish another Supreme Court in its place. [See p 72 of his mimeographed judgment.]

Peterkin JA expressed his stricture thus:

> [I]n my view one thing is certain, namely, that the present Court cannot be given indefinite recognition for the future [p 8 of his mimeographed judgment].

As far as Liverpool JA was concerned, the court system established by the PRG was permanent and legitimate.

The Privy Council

An unsuccessful attempt was thereafter made to have the matter further adjudicated at the level of the Judicial Committee of the Privy Council.

---

40 This case was also analysed in Phillips, 1985, pp 42–48.

In rejecting it for want of jurisdiction Lord Diplock stated that the appellants had sought declarations that the High Court as then comprised was unconstitutional and not competent to try them for murder and conspiracy to murder and that PL No 84 of 1979 purporting to abolish appeals to Her Majesty in Council was inconsistent with the independence Constitution of 1973 and void.

His Lordship, after reviewing the relevant legislation, concluded as follows:

> The words of People's Law No 84 were absolute and unambiguous. In effect they purported to repeal the whole of section 104 of the Independence Constitution and had since been confirmed and validated by an Act of the legitimate Parliament of Grenada passed by a procedure by which section 104 might validly be repealed or amended. The repeal had therefore altered the Constitution of Grenada since February 21st 1985 and deprived their Lordships of any jurisdiction to entertain the petition.

A Commission of Inquiry was subsequently appointed by the Government of Grenada[41] to enquire into the 1974 Constitution and to make recommendations for any amendments, reforms and changes as might be necessary and desirable for promoting the peace, order and good government of the country.

One of the recommendations of the Commission was that, for the purpose of promoting the continued unity of the Eastern Caribbean Supreme Court system on Grenada rejoining the system (which was recommended), the Constitution should be re-amended to restore appeals to the Privy Council. By virtue of two local enactments, arrangements were in 1991 made to restore appeals from the new Grenada Court of Appeal to the Privy Council.[42] Thus, the position in Grenada court-wise had come full circle. Justice and democracy were duly restored. The country was thereafter to sail in calmer judicial waters.

CONCLUDING SUMMARY

What lessons has the region learnt from the problems that followed the Grenada revolution of 1979? It is discovered that a government cannot continue with impunity indefinitely to be repressive and that it is essential to involve all sections of the community in the business of public administration. The Caribbean learned the hard way that replacing a constituted government with thugs at the barrel of a gun does not solve a country's woes and that when law and order break down to the point of anarchy, novel measures must be adopted to protect the citizens.

It is here that convention gives way to civil or State necessity. A Governor General who had hitherto been a constitutional monarch who reigned, suddenly becomes a ruling sovereign applying the letter of the law that the executive authority of the country is vested in Her Majesty whose accredited representative he or she is. *Salus populi suprema*

---

41 The writer was appointed as chairman of this commission which submitted its report to the Governor General on 5 November 1985.

42 See the Constitutional Judicature (Restoration) Act 1991 (No 19 of 1991) and the Constitutional Judicature (Restoration) (Amendment) Act 1991 (No 37 of 1991), s 9.

lex becomes the basis on which order must be restored, since constitutional government abhors a vacuum.

The judges in the famous case of *AG (of Cyprus) v Mustafa Ibrahim* when faced with a similar situation had this to say:

> The Court is faced with the question whether the legal doctrine of necessity should or should not be read in the provisions of the written Constitution of the Republic of Cyprus. Our unanimous view, and unhesitating answer to this question, is in the affirmative.

It was in this same vein that the doctrine was also read into the Grenada Constitution: the first time such a device was used in this area. Let us hope it will be the last.

The next chapter addresses similar extra-legal constitutional problems which developed in Dominica and St Lucia and discusses a mini-rebellion in St Vincent. It also tells the story of an inchoate mini-federation of the Windward Islands and of an even later attempt to introduce arrangements likely to foster freedom of movement with restrictions on travel documents as well as on an economic union in the sub-region, to be referred to as the Eastern Caribbean Union of Independent States.

CHAPTER 11

DOMINICA, ST VINCENT, ST LUCIA
AND A NEW FEDERAL ATTEMPT

In this chapter, we shall consider developments of constitutional significance which have taken place in Dominica, St Lucia and St Vincent since the 1960s. In each of these territories, which became independent between 1978 and 1979, there was civil commotion of one kind or another shortly after independence. In Dominica, the civil unrest was much more serious and sustained than in the other two territories; and, in addition, external elements played a much larger role than in either of the other two. In St Lucia, the political difficulties stemmed mainly from a leadership struggle within the governing party, whereas in St Vincent the civil disorder took the form of a short-lived 'mini-rebellion' which occurred in one of its dependencies. We shall now examine in turn the problems which each territory experienced.

The final section of this chapter alludes to a little-known attempt towards the end of the 20th century to establish a federal union comprising these three territories and Grenada. It unfortunately came to naught for reasons which will appear.

DOMINICA

As far back as 1976, the Government of Dominica requested Britain to terminate the status of associated statehood which had existed between the two countries since 1967. The Premier, Patrick John, had first made public his intention to proceed to independence at a convention of his party, the Dominica Labour Party (DLP), which was held in the village of Salisbury in August 1976. This statement became known thereafter as the 'Declaration of Salisbury'.

At that time the opposition Dominica Freedom Party (DFP) was of the view that the provision of s 10(1) of the West Indies Act 1976[1] should be invoked, by virtue of which a referendum was required to determine whether the country should terminate its then current political status. If two-thirds of the people voting in the referendum decided in favour of terminating the association it would automatically have come to an end and the State would thereupon proceed to independence. This view was rejected by the DLP Government which asked Her Majesty's Government to terminate the association under s 10(2) of the Act, as Grenada had done in 1974 when it became independent, and as all the former associated States have since done. Under that sub-section, Her Majesty was empowered by Order in Council to terminate the association and to grant independence to that State at the request of the State Government, signified by a resolution passed by its legislature.

Following the promulgation of the Declaration of Salisbury, a Green Paper was published by the Dominica Government. Thereafter, both parties held a series of public meetings to explain the issues to the people and to prepare them for independence.

---

1   1967 C4 (UK).

In May 1977, a constitutional conference was held in London at which fundamental differences between the Government and the Opposition became evident. The main points of contention between the two parties were:

(a) whether Dominica should have a republican system of government with an elected Executive President. This was the proposal put forward by the DFP, while the Government wished to retain the Queen as the Head of State of Dominica, being represented locally by a Governor General; and

(b) whether there should be a unicameral or bicameral legislature and the basis on which persons would be appointed to that body.

On the question of the type of constitution (republican or monarchical), the DFP had proposed that the country, upon attaining independence, should become a republic with an executive President as Head of State. The President should be elected and should himself preside over the national assembly. He should also have the power to delay for one month, or until the next sitting of the House of Assembly, any Bill which affected special interests which did not have the opportunity of making their views known. The House of Assembly should, by a 75% vote of its members, have the power to annul any decision of the President. With regard to elections to the proposed legislature, the DFP wished to have a mixture of the two electoral systems, viz, first-past-the-post and proportional representation: the suggestion being that 13 members should be elected to the 21 member House by the first system and the remaining eight members should be elected on the basis of proportional representation.[2]

At the conference it was not possible to reconcile these differences. However, the conference chairman decided that, having regard to size of the Government majority in the House of Assembly, he would proceed on the Government's proposals which were slightly modified as follows:

(a) the Queen would remain Head of State and be represented by a Governor General;

(b) parliament would be a unicameral body comprising 21 elected and nine nominated members – and the electoral regime would be first-past-the-post.

The chairman, however, left the door open on these two issues, suggesting that the Opposition should continue to canvass their point of view in Dominica in an effort to persuade the House of Assembly when the matters came on for debate.[3]

It was further decided that at the end of the conference a paper would be prepared by the Foreign and Commonwealth Office setting out the areas of agreement reached on the terms of the Constitution. At the same time, the Foreign and Commonwealth Office would prepare a draft constitution in collaboration with the Attorney General of Dominica for submission to Parliament.[4] The British Government, however, wished to be satisfied that the move to independence commended itself to the majority of Dominicans. The conference had anticipated that a further process of consultation between Her Majesty's Government and the Dominica Government might become necessary if the

---

2   See *Report of the Dominica Constitutional Conference*, 1977, Annex C, p 2.

3   *Ibid*, para 9, p 4 and para 28, p 8.

4   *Ibid*, para 27, p 8.

local parties became deadlocked.[5] As a result of these differences, the target date set by the Government (November 1977) for the attainment of independence was altered to early 1978.

Later in 1977, the British Government proposed, with the concurrence of the Dominica Government, that RN Posnett (as he then was), an official experienced in constitutional affairs, should visit Dominica in May 1978 to discuss with the parties concerned the outstanding points of disagreement and to test the state of public opinion on the question of independence. The *Posnett Report*, which was published in July 1978,[6] recommended that the matter be finalised on the basis that further agreement between parties was unlikely.[7]

In the process of consultation the Government had accepted the proposal for a republican-type constitution. However, it still had not agreed to the position of the President as Head of State, which had been originally proposed by the DFP. The Government's proposals with respect to the office of President were as follows. Under the constitution the President would be a ceremonial figure and would be advised on all matters of policy by a Cabinet of ministers. He would be elected by the House of Assembly and would hold office for a term of five years: provided that, where the Prime Minister and Leader of the Opposition had agreed on a nominee to the office of President, they would submit his nomination in writing to the Speaker, who would declare that candidate to have been duly elected without putting the matter to a vote.[8] With respect to the regime for holding elections of members to the House, the system of first-past-the-post would continue. In addition, there would be a unicameral legislature comprising the President and a House of Assembly.[9]

It was also agreed that the House of Assembly would consist of nine senators and such number of *representatives* as may be recommended by an Electoral and Boundaries Commission to be established by the Constitution. Five of the senators would be appointed by the President on the advice of the Prime Minister while the other four would be appointed on the advice of the Leader of the Opposition. These decisions were duly incorporated into the constitution, which came into force on 3 November 1978 when the country became independent as the Commonwealth of Dominica.

Six months after the attainment of independence in Dominica, the Prime Minister, Patrick John, ran into serious trouble with his Cabinet and with Parliament. On 29 May 1979, when he tried to rush two very controversial Bills through Parliament, a peaceful demonstration estimated at between 15,000 and 20,000 persons gathered outside Parliament to voice their opposition to these two measures. One of these Bills (to amend the Industrial Relations Act) had as its main object the prohibition of strikes, especially by civil servants and essential services workers while the other (to amend the Libel and Slander Act) was clearly designed to restrict the publication of criticism against the Government. It should be mentioned that the latter measure was being passed at a time

---

5   *Ibid*, para 29, pp 8–9.
6   *Dominica Termination of Association*, 1978.
7   *Ibid*, para 48, p 15.
8   See Commonwealth of Dominica Constitution Order 1978 SI 1978/1027, Sched 1, hereinafter referred to simply as the Dominica Constitution, ss 18 and 19.
9   *Ibid*, ss 29, 30 and 57.

when the Government seemed to have been engaged in serious negotiations with South Africa relative to the creation of an industrial free zone in Dominica.

The demonstration against these legislative measures was broken up by heavy-handed security men whose draconian behaviour resulted in the death of one person and in the wounding of several others. This incident turned out to be 'the last straw that broke the camel's back'; as a consequence a general strike was immediately called by all the trade unions, which brought commercial and other activity in the capital city, Roseau, to a virtual standstill. The Prime Minister's response to this state of affairs was simply that the DFP was endeavouring to stage a coup against him, but that he would not yield in any way to pressure.

The next blow to the Government was the resignation of Oliver Seraphin, the Minister of Agriculture, who confirmed the rumour about John's South African connections and negotiations. This revelation in turn prevented John from obtaining any military or other support from his Caribbean neighbours in his effort to maintain himself in office. Indeed, when the news of his dealing with South Africa reached Trinidad and Tobago that Government summarily rejected an application for financial aid which had been previously made by the Government of Dominica.

The Dominican Prime Minister then endeavoured to appease local discontent by withdrawing the two Bills referred to above and dismissing the then Attorney General. At the same time, he announced that he would appoint a Commission of Enquiry into the events of 29 May 1979 and would agree to UN supervision over the next general elections.

Meanwhile, a Committee of National Salvation (CNS) which had been formed on the day of the shootings had been meeting daily to consider other means of forcing the Prime Minister to resign. This Committee comprised all the major factions opposed to John, including the DFP, the Chamber of Commerce, the trade unions, the farmers and the Civil Service Association. In the midst of this pressure, the President of the country hurriedly left Dominica without taking the steps prescribed in the constitution for appointing an Acting President. The relevant provision reads as follows:[10]

(1) Whenever the holder of the office of President is unable to perform the functions of his office by reason of his absence from Dominica, by reason of illness or by reason that he is suspended from the exercise of those functions under section 25(3) of this Constitution, those functions shall be performed–

    (a) by such person as may with his consent have been designated in that behalf by the holder of the office of President, acting after consultation with the Prime Minister and Leader of the Opposition, by writing under his hand; or

    (b) if there is no person so designated or if the person so designated is unable to act, by such person as may have been elected in that behalf by the House in accordance with the like procedures as are prescribed by section 19 of the Constitution for the election of the President.

(2) A person shall not be qualified to act as President unless he is qualified to be elected as, and to hold the office of, President:

---

10   Dominica Constitution, s 28.

Provided that the Speaker or the Deputy Speaker may act as President, in which case he shall cease to perform the functions of his office during any period during which he or she is so acting.

(3) A person acting as President under this section shall cease to act when he or she is notified-

    (a) that another person has been designated or elected to act; or

    (b) that the holder of the office of President is about to resume the performance of the functions of his or her office.

Another event which further complicated the situation was that the Speaker of the House had tendered his resignation at about the same time the President had left the country.

But despite the President's failure to designate an Acting President, and notwithstanding the fact that Parliament could not meet to make such an appointment, the Prime Minister in desperation purported to designate *suo moto* a former Governor to act as President in the hope that this appointee would do his bidding by dissolving the House of Assembly and setting a date for new elections. Unfortunately, the crowds set fire to the Acting President's car and stoned his house. When he failed to obtain protection from the police (who were also incidentally on strike), he instantly resigned. As a result of these events, Dominica was without a Head of State for a period of 23 days. During that period, the angry Roseau crowds had taken to looting commercial places and had burnt to the ground the registry of the Supreme Court. There was total chaos in the country. All work had ground to a halt, and there was a total breakdown of law and order. The situation was further exacerbated by the fact that the CNS had vowed that this state of affairs would continue until Patrick John resigned from the office of Prime Minister.

In these circumstances the CNS, *de facto*, took over the reins of government and set out the following 11 specific points for immediate action:

1   that the elected members of Parliament other than the Ministers of Government and ministers of State form a Parliamentary caucus, and that this Parliamentary caucus should elect a Prime Minister to head an Interim Government in consultation with the CNS;

2   that the present nine (9) Senators immediately resign and that nine (9) Senators be appointed on the advice of the CNS;

3   that the President resigns and that a new President be appointed in consultation with the CNS;

4   that the Interim Government set up machinery for the holding of free and fair elections on a list compiled on the basis of island-wide enumeration and that supervision be provided by a neutral body for both enumeration and election;

5   that the Dominica Broadcasting Service be democratised immediately;

6   that the Interim Government mount a public enquiry into the events of 29 May 1979;

7   that in the interest of national solidarity and unity the CNS recommends that the Hon Oliver J Seraphin be elected as Prime Minister in the Interim Government;

8   that the Interim Government carry out a full and thorough enquiry into all contracts with South Africa and other such dubious financial dealing;

9   that the Interim Government examines the question of compensation for striking workers and farmers;

10 that the Interim Government set up a Constitution Commission to review the present Constitution and to make recommendations for amendments;

11 that the Prime Minister, Ministers of Government and Ministers of State resign from Cabinet and from the House of Assembly.[11]

Since Seraphin had been named as Prime Minister, the CNS had daily discussions with him for several days on the persons who were to be appointed as ministers and senators. At the end of these discussions, the strike was temporarily called off and a degree of calm was restored. This procedure was akin to a people's forum (or a Senate hearing), since all the candidates concerned were screened and their suitability duly passed upon by a crowd of people who daily attended the Goodwill Parish Hall in Roseau to discharge this form of civic responsibility. To quote the expressive words of an eye-witness who has written on this peculiar situation: 'It was in effect people's democracy in action.'

After every effort to secure John's resignation had failed, the CNS came to the conclusion that Parliament would have to be reconvened in order that a vote of no-confidence could be passed against the Government, after which an Acting President would have to be installed to make the appointment of the new 'ministers'. At this point, in endeavouring to illustrate the predicament of the CNS, the writer can do no better than give a summary of what Dr Nicholas Liverpool had to say on this question:

> There were six elected members and four senators in Dominica at that particular time who were opposed to the Government. These persons, together with Mr Seraphin and another of his colleagues, would have been able to satisfy the constitutional requirement that before a matter can be validly determined by the House of Assembly at least twelve of its members must take part in the voting on that matter.

> Such a meeting would have been quite competent to appoint the Acting President, but could not pass a no-confidence motion against the Government which was required to be supported by a majority of all the elected members of the House.[12] Mr Seraphin therefore needed to ensure that the necessary majority of elected members attended the particular sitting of the House due to be held on 19th June 1979, if the motion was to be successful.

The composition of Parliament on that fateful day in Dominica's history was as follows:

Government bench: no member present;

Opposition Bench: 13 elected members plus 4 Senators.

At that meeting, the Leader of the Opposition, having withdrawn her motion for a vote of no confidence in the Government, requested of the Speaker that 'all elected members should state whether they had withdrawn their support for the present Prime Minister and whether they supported a caucus of Government to appoint a government for the interim period before the holding of the next general elections in accordance with provisions of the Dominica Constitution'.[13] All 13 elected members then present

---

11 In this account of what happened in Dominica the writer has drawn heavily from an admirable article by Dr NJO Liverpool (1978) from which the facts mentioned above are taken.

12 See Constitution of Dominica, s 46(1), Proviso.

13 Liverpool, 1978, p 12.

expressed their intention to withdraw their support for the Prime Minister and to support an Interim Government. The meeting was then adjourned until Thursday, 21 June 1979, during which time the issue would be canvassed over the local radio station.

On 21 June the following resolution was duly passed in the House of Assembly:

WHEREAS the Committee for National Salvation has proposed the formation of an Interim Government headed by the Honourable Oliver Seraphin;

AND WHEREAS at the request of the Committee for National Salvation a meeting of Parliamentary Representatives approved the recommendation of the Committee for National Salvation that the said Oliver Seraphin be chosen to head the Interim Government;

BE IT NOW RESOLVED THAT this House recommends the appointment of Honourable Oliver Seraphin as Prime Minister of the Interim Government pending the results of a General Election in accordance with the provisions of the Dominica Constitution.[14]

The Speaker advised the House of the joint nomination of Jenner Armour as Acting President and that Armour had agreed in writing to serve in that office as required by the Constitution.[15] The House then adjourned. Thereafter, the Acting President proceeded to appoint the Prime Minister and six other ministers, three of whom were senators. Six additional senators were also appointed to complete the composition of the House of Assembly.

Following the formation of the Interim Government, the strike was called off. The new Prime Minister declared that his immediate objectives would be to try to repair the shattered economy of the country while arranging the necessary electoral processes in preparation for general elections. He also promised a full investigation into the conduct of both John and his Attorney General.

But this was not yet the end of Seraphin's woes for, in October 1979, he found it necessary to dismiss one of his key ministers, Atherton Martin, on alleged ideological grounds. Seraphin also found himself at loggerheads with the Committee for National Salvation whose functions he considered to have been 'spent'. In addition, the dismissal of Martin was severely criticised by three of the other ministers, who were themselves shortly afterwards dismissed by Seraphin because they had questioned the length of time he was taking before calling general elections.

By December 1979 political pressure was being exerted against Seraphin by members of the Catholic Church, the trade unions, the business community and the civil service to force his resignation from the office of Prime Minister. While this drama was being acted out, the President, Frederick Degazon, tendered his resignation from abroad, to be followed very shortly thereafter by that of the Acting President, who wished to contest a seat in the forthcoming general elections. At this point, a candidate for the post of President was found acceptable to all parties so that he was duly elected by the Speaker's declaration.

Such was the travail that befell Dominica within seven months of the country becoming independent.

---

14 *Ibid.*
15 See Dominica Constitution, s 28.

In the general elections which were held on 21 July 1980, the candidates of the DFP were successful in 17 of the 21 polling districts. Two of the seats were won by the Dominica Democratic Labour Party (DDLP) while the remaining two seats were won by independent candidates. Significantly, both John and Seraphin failed to gain re-election to the House of Assembly. As a consequence of its electoral victory, the DFP (described as 'liberal, democratic and anti-communist') formed the new Government; and its leader, Eugenia Charles, a distinguished lawyer and businesswoman, became the new Prime Minister of Dominica. The 1980 elections thus brought a temporary respite to the disturbances. But as we shall soon see, Dominica's political problems were far from over.

Almost from its inauguration, the Government led by Miss Charles was plagued with internal civil commotion. In December 1980, barely six months after it had come to power, it became necessary for the authorities to disarm the Dominica Defence Force when it was discovered that weapons from the force's armoury were being traded in exchange for marijuana from the 'Dreads' (the name by which the Rastafarian cult in Dominica was called). Later, the Government found it necessary to transfer all weapons in the defence force armoury to the central police station where a strict inventory would be kept, it having become evident that most of the members of the defence force had been recruited by former Prime Minister Patrick John on the basis of their personal and political loyalty to him. On this account, a number of officers had been given compulsory leave of absence by the new administration. There were, however, a number of members of the Force who were loyal to the Government, for there were demonstrations in the defence force demanding the resignation of the army commander (Major Newton), at the same time as John was praising him and stating publicly that the army was being disarmed in preparation for the conversion of the country into a 'one party state'.

In February 1981, the Dreads kidnapped a prominent planter in retaliation for the killing of two of their colleagues by the police in the course of a 'shoot-out' in the southwest of the country. After setting fire to the home of the kidnapped man, they released his wife with a note, evidently extracted from him, setting out the conditions of his release. These conditions included the release of two Dreads who were being held under sentence of death; an enquiry into the conduct of the anti-drug squad; and an end to 'police brutality'. Miss Charles immediately declared a state of emergency and, in her speech promulgating the state of emergency, she replied that she would not be prepared to accede to the Dreads' request until they had released the kidnapped planter unharmed and had surrendered their weapons. The planter was subsequently found murdered.

On 7 March 1981, the Prime Minister announced that she had received information of a plot to overthrow her Government during the carnival celebrations which were due to take place a week later, that is, in mid-March. As a result the commander, the deputy commander and three other officers of the defence force were arrested. It transpired that Captain Reid (one of the arrested officers) had originally been detained after the Martinique authorities had advised the Dominica Government that he and another defence force officer had been endeavouring to purchase drums of acid in Martinique, and after a letter he had written to Major Newton (his superior officer), containing details of the planned coup, had been intercepted by the police.

In the meantime, in the United States, the FBI discovered that there was a definite involvement of certain Ku Klux Klan activists in the said coup. Two of them were subsequently sentenced to prison for violating the US Neutrality Act and for conspiracy. Seven others pleaded guilty to violation of the Neutrality Act by mounting an armed expedition against a friendly nation: five being sentenced to three years imprisonment and two juveniles being sent to young offenders' institutions. A Texas businessman and an electrical contractor from Mississippi were also indicted for similar offences, as was a Tennessee lawyer who, on 21 June 1981 committed suicide. The Texas businessman and the electrical contractor were subsequently acquitted by a federal court in New Orleans.

The evidence in the US courts revealed that the ringleader of the planned coup had originally contemplated a mercenary invasion of Grenada in April 1979 (that is, one month after Maurice Bishop had taken control of that island), but had subsequently switched his attention to Dominica. It is reported that the alleged ringleader had received a total of US$75,000 from unnamed co-conspirators and had actually commenced recruiting mercenaries for the job from among members of several right-wing organisations. There was also evidence that the US conspirators had held a meeting with former Prime Minister John, Major Newton (the defence force commander) and Captain Reid in a Dread stronghold to finalise plans for the coup. In the course of this meeting Perdue had been accorded the rank of captain in the Dominica Defence Force.

According to the report, the object of the coup was to have Patrick John restored as Prime Minister of Dominica for which the alleged ringleader would receive US$150,000 from Dominica Government funds. In addition, he would be given Dominican citizenship and be appointed a Cabinet minister. The amazing thing is that even after John and his cohorts had been arrested in Dominica, their American counterparts still continued planning the coup from their US base and, but for the timely discovery by undercover agents of the US Bureau of Alcohol, Tobacco and Firearms, who were able to arrest the mercenaries on 27 March 1981 on the eve of their departure for Dominica, there could well have occurred a takeover of the island by criminal adventurers from the United States.

Some Canadian citizens were also involved in the preparation of the proposed coup. A Canadian citizen, who had apparently been sent to Dominica in advance on behalf of the Grand Wizard of the Ku Klux Klan of Canada, was arrested in Dominica, convicted and sentenced to three years' imprisonment. Another Canadian citizen and a British national were deported from Dominica in May and September 1981, respectively, after going to that island for the avowed purpose of freeing the Canadian who had been sent as an advance guard.

In 1981, a state of emergency was again declared when, on 19 December, there was a concerted attack on the police headquarters and the prison, resulting in the murder of a police officer and injury to several others (including the commissioner of police) at the police station. Ironically, one of the attackers killed at the prison was identified as an officer who had previously been acquitted (for lack of evidence) of taking part in the attempted coup earlier in the year.

The alleged objective of the December 1981 attack was to release Patrick John and his fellow defendants from prison prior to the hearing of their case, which was due to come on for trial the following month. The December 1981 state of emergency which lasted until March 1982 provided for censorship of the press, a curfew, and the grant to the police of wide powers of arrest. Among those arrested were three French citizens who were said to be involved in the smuggling of arms into Dominica from the adjacent French island of Martinique, where the authorities actively co-operated with the security forces of the Government of Dominica.

Meanwhile, there was further dissension and disintegration on the political front as well. Michael Douglas, elected to the House of Representatives in 1980, was one of the two DDLP members who left that party, the leader of which was Oliver Seraphin. As noted above, Seraphin had failed to retain his seat at the 1980 general elections, and as a result he had come under heavy fire from Douglas to surrender to him the leadership of the party. This Member of the House then combined with his brother, 'Rosie' Douglas, to form a new party called the United Dominica Labour Party. (Rosie Douglas subsequently became Prime Minister in early 2000, but died suddenly after being eight months in office.)

The events related above appear to illustrate, in a somewhat painful manner, the problems which can arise in operating a Westminster-type constitution, promulgated by the easy means of securing the passage of an Order in Council by Her Majesty, rather than by employing the alternative, but politically more sound, procedure of obtaining the concurrence of the people of the country through a national referendum. The former method, it is submitted, produces a constitution which is supported by the political party with the majority of members in the legislature and gives only token recognition to the wishes of the minority party. The latter arrangement might, at least, ensure that the people are afforded the opportunity of participating in the process of formulating a constitution by which their lives and livelihood will be regulated.

The foregoing events also further emphasise the need for the recognition and observance of those vital conventions without which the basic structure of our constitutions cannot function effectively and smoothly. Patrick John's posturings in June of 1979 in an effort to secure the appointment of his nominee as Acting President in order to ensure the dissolution of the House of Assembly would, clearly, have been impossible in a country which recognises and observes the constitutional conventions which operate when a Prime Minister has lost both the moral and political authority to govern. However, as has been stated elsewhere, the conventions will take time to develop roots in our jurisdictions.

Review of the Dominica Constitution

On 10 September 1997, after the Republican Constitution had been in operation for nearly 19 years, the Cabinet of Dominica appointed a Review Commission to consider, examine and inquire into the constitution. The commission was chaired by the Right Honourable P Telford Georges, a distinguished legal luminary who was born in Dominica and who served as Chief Justice and Justice of Appeal in several jurisdictions, but was then living in Barbados in retirement.

The Commission reported in February 1999 and its main recommendations are set out below:

1   The existing structure of the Westminster model should be retained in which executive power remains vested in a non-executive President but is largely exercised on the advice of the Prime Minister.

2   A person qualified to serve as President should be appointed as deputy president who would act as president whenever the President is unable to perform his functions until his resumption or until a vacancy occurs.

3   Parliament should continue to be unicameral but the number of elected members should be reduced from 21 to 15 and they would be elected on the present first-past-the-post system.

There should however be an additional seven members of the House of Assembly who would be elected by a list system of proportional representation, each party submitting a list setting out the names of its nominees in the order in which they are to be elected in proportion to the votes cast. Such 'list' members will be styled senators. No party will be entitled to any such seat unless it obtains at least 10% of the valid votes cast.

4   A Constituency Boundaries Commission should be established which will submit its report to the speaker as follows:

(a) whenever a census of the population is held;

(b) whenever Parliament alters the law dealing with the number of constituencies into which Dominica is divided; and

(c) on the expiry of eight years after the Boundaries Commission has last reviewed the boundaries of constituencies in accordance with the provisions of the Constitution.

In the delineation of boundaries the rules to be applied should be amended by adding a rule that the electorate in any constituency shall not be more than 110% or less than 90% of the total electorate of Dominica divided by the number of constituencies in the Island.

5   Under the existing Constitution, section 59(6) provides that the President shall remove the Prime Minister from office if a resolution of no-confidence in the government is passed by the House and the Prime Minister does not within three days either resign from his office or advise the President to dissolve Parliament. It is recommended that in such a situation the President should not be compelled to act on the advice of the Prime Minister and dissolve the House but should act in his or her deliberate judgment, assessing whether there is another member who can command the support of a majority of the members and who is willing to accept the Prime Minister's position.

6   The Commission recommends that the term 'Leader of the Opposition' should be changed to 'Leader of a Minority Party'; and where there are two or more such parties, each should be so styled.

7   The Commission declined to suggest a change in the Constitution to empower an incoming political administration to appoint officers at the highest level of the Civil Service except through the prevailing Public Service Commission mechanism.

8   It was recommended that the post of Attorney General should be filled by a qualified person who has been elected in a constituency or as a Senator who can be a member of Cabinet by reason of being a Minister and not by reason of being Attorney General.

9   The Commission recommends the deletion of the proviso to section 72(6) of the Constitution under which the Director of Public Prosecutions should only exercise his powers to discontinue criminal proceedings 'in accordance with such general or special directions (if any) as the Attorney General may give him'.

10 The recommendation concerning the Public Service Commission is that this body should be appointed by the President in his or her deliberate judgment, after consultation.

11 In so far as the Police Service Commission is concerned, the President should also appoint the members in his or her deliberate judgment after consulting the Prime Minister, Leader of the Minority parties, Officials of the appropriate representative body and such other persons as the President may deem fit to consult.

12 The Commission urges the appointment of the Parliamentary Commissioner with support staff, as provided under Chapter IX of the Constitution.

13 The Commission recommends that provision should be made by an Act of Parliament confirming the right of a person who has been arrested to consult with reasonable promptness after arrest an attorney of his of her choice. In the case of a minor, the right of access should be to a parent or guardian.

14 The recommendation is made for the enactment of legislation to enable a judge to pay the taxed costs of an unsuccessful litigant in a case where the judge is of the view that the issue raised in the challenge was one of substance.

15 As regards amendment of the Constitution, the Commission recommends that a referendum should only be held in respect of Chapter I – Protection of Fundamental Rights and Freedoms. Bills for the amendment of any other sections of the Constitution should not be regarded as being passed unless they are supported by the votes of not less than three-quarters of all the elected members of the House. There should also be an interval of not less than ninety days between the introduction of the Bill in the House and the beginning of the proceedings on the second reading, during which period the House should go into Committee and invite the public to submit written memoranda or attend in person before the Committee to express their views on the proposed amendment.[16]

ST VINCENT AND THE GRENADINES

As stated in the author's 1977 work, St Vincent was until 1959 administered as one of the four Windward Islands, the other territories of the that group being Dominica, Grenada, and St Lucia. A single Governor, who then resided in Grenada, was responsible to the Colonial Office for the administration of this group of territories as one unit. The day to day running of the affairs of each of these colonies was, however, under the direct charge of a resident administrator who was answerable to the Governor for the due discharge of his official functions. St Vincent was also a constituent unit of the West Indies Federation which was inaugurated in 1958 and dissolved in 1962 in circumstances also fully described in the 1977 volume.[17]

When the attempt to form 'The Little Eight' proved abortive in the mid-1960s, St Vincent began negotiations with the metropolitan power (Britain) with a view to becoming an associated State; but because of local differences, it only attained associated

---

16 See *Report of the Commonwealth of Dominica Constitution Review Commission*, presented by the Commissioners, February 1999, App A I–V.

17 See Phillips, 1977, Chapter VI, pp 53–73.

statehood in 1979, although five other British colonies in the Caribbean had assumed that status since 1967.[18]

In 1972, an event occurred in St Vincent which made a mockery of the two-party system. In that year an election took place for a new 13 member House of Assembly. The results were: six seats to the People's Progressive Party (hereafter called PPP) led by ET Joshua; six seats to the St Vincent Labour Party (hereafter called SVLP) led by RM Cato; and one seat to an independent candidate.

The independent seat was secured by James Mitchell (later Sir James), a former minister of the SVLP. But, on this occasion, he elected to align himself with the PPP on one condition, viz, that in consideration of such an alignment he would become the Premier.[19] This condition was accepted and the political leader of the PPP was then appointed deputy premier in the new Government. Two years later, that is, in 1974, Joshua and his wife, who was then a parliamentary secretary, disagreed with the Premier on certain matters of policy, and co-sponsored a successful motion of no confidence in the Government. In the result, the legislature was dissolved and general elections were held in December 1974. This time, the PPP and the SVLP entered into a 'unity agreement' for the purpose of contesting the elections – as a result of which the SVLP won 10 of the 13 seats and the PPP won two. The leader of the SVLP, Cato, accordingly became the new Premier.

One of the terms and conditions of the so called 'unity government' under which the SVLP and the PPP contested the 1974 general elections appears to have required that the leader of the latter would have been assigned responsibility for the administration of a department of government: for Joshua was appointed by the Premier to be Minister of Trade in the new Government. It also seems that the joint SVLP/PPP election strategy was directed to minimising the effect in the legislature of James Mitchell who was then the only other member of that body and whose political position was independent of both political parties. Mrs Joshua, the wife of the leader of the PPP and a member of that party, was originally also a member of the new Government. This meant that Mitchell, the only member in opposition to the Government, would logically be appointed to be the Leader of the Opposition. However, in what at the time appeared to be an odd move, Mrs Joshua declared that she no longer supported the government and, thus, became the other member of the legislature on the opposition benches.

While one can but speculate on the motives for such a strange move, the subsequent actions of the Government made it clear beyond conjecture what the objectives were. In 1975, the Government procured the passage of a Bill in the legislature for an Act to amend the provisions of the Constitution of St Vincent relating to the Leader of the Opposition. The amendment which inserted the following provisos to the relevant section marks, in the writer's view, the high water mark of *ad hominem* legislation in that country:

> Provided that, if there are two or more such Elected Members who do not support the Government but none of them commands the support of the other or others, the Governor may, *acting in his own deliberate judgment*, appoint any one of them as Leader of the Opposition.

18 *Ibid*, Chapter VII; see Liverpool, 1978, p 81.
19 Mitchell's new party – the National Democratic Party (NDP) – won a sweeping victory in general elections held in July 1984 when he was duly appointed Prime Minister.

Provided further that in the exercise of his judgment the Governor *shall be guided by* the seniority based on length of service of the Elected Member and/or by the number of votes polled by the Member at the General Election[20] [emphasis supplied].

In the event, therefore, Mrs Joshua was appointed to be the Leader of the Opposition. Although she had no greater support in the legislature than Mitchell (they were both opposed to the Government and to each other), Mrs Joshua appears to have gained the nod over him by virtue of the second proviso referred to above. It was well known that Mrs Joshua had been a member of the legislature for many years before Mitchell had entered electoral politics, and that she always won her seat at the general elections by a massive majority, equalled by few other local parliamentarians.

The cases must indeed be rare in which legislation confers a discretion on a person to act 'in his own deliberate judgment' and at the same time prescribes legislative guidelines which on the then existing facts ensure that that discretion can only be exercised in a particular manner. What the provisos, shorn of all their legalisms, in fact meant was that where there are two elected members of the legislature, neither of whom is qualified to be appointed to be the Leader of the Opposition, then the Governor *shall* select as leader the one who has had a longer period of service as an elected member and/or the one who polled the greater number of votes at the general elections at which he/she was returned as a member of the legislature. The amendment also created the patent contradiction of the leader of the PPP (Joshua) supporting, and indeed being a minister of, the Government while his wife, the only other member of that party in the legislature, was appointed as the Leader of the Opposition.

One is bound to bemoan the tendency which has been manifested in certain of the smaller territories of the Commonwealth Caribbean to regard the constitution as being an instrument designed to assist the respective governments in the attainment of party political objectives. The two St Vincent events related above clearly constitute yet another classic illustration of that tendency.

Certain events which occurred in St Vincent in 1978 had the effect of further obscuring the position of the Leader of the Opposition in the legislature. In the months immediately preceding the visit of the Premier to London, in mid-April 1978, to discuss the proposals for a new constitution with the British Commonwealth Office, serious disagreements arose between Premier Cato and ET Joshua, the Minister of Trade, with respect to the timing of independence. These disagreements led to Joshua's dismissal from the Government and he, accordingly, joined his wife and Mitchell on the opposition benches. At that stage, by some extraordinary piece of logic, Mrs Joshua was retained as the Leader of the Opposition, even though her husband was the political leader of the party (PPP) of which they were both members and he was infinitely more articulate and generally more qualified to serve in that capacity than his wife who could hardly read or write.

In early 1978, Premier Cato announced that he intended to commence negotiations with the British Government with a view to attaining independence for St Vincent under s 10(2) of the West Indies Act. We have referred above to the disagreements which arose between Cato and Joshua with respect to the timing of independence for that country and that these disagreements had led ultimately to the latter assuming a position in

---

20 See the St Vincent Constitution (Amendment) Act 1975 (No 5 of 1975).

opposition to the Government. In support of his Government's decision to lead the country into independence, the Premier put forward a case that his party (the SVLP) had won a majority of 68.52% of the votes cast at the 1974 general elections, thereby receiving a clear mandate from the electorate. On this issue Joshua (for the Opposition) countered that there had in fact been a reduction of 22% in the overall number of voters who were eligible to vote at the elections and that this was the result of the instructions he had given to the members of his party in the various constituencies where his party did not field candidates – that they should not vote if they found they could not conscientiously support the 'unity agreement' to which reference is made above.

Despite the arguments of the Opposition, which at first accepted the invitation to attend the constitutional conference and later refused to do so, the conference took place in London from 18–21 September 1978, under the chairmanship of Ted Rowlands, a UK Minister of State. This conference reached agreement on the draft constitution, in which were included proposals submitted to the Government by a group called the National Independence Committee, as well as by other local groups. The draft was to be published in St Vincent for further discussion before being finally presented to the House of Assembly for debate.

It was not until 8 February 1979, that the proposals for the draft constitution were brought to the House, where they were passed by 10 votes in favour to none against. The PPP and Mitchell's New Democratic Party (NDP) had refused to take part in the proceedings at either the committee stage during the reading of the Bill or the final voting.

There was further posturing by the PPP and NDP who then petitioned the British Secretary of State, requesting him to consider further representations in respect of the draft constitution. In a spirit of compromise, the Commonwealth Office requested the Premier to accept some of the proposals made by the opposition political parties in order that a full consensus could be achieved. Accordingly, Premier Cato decided to accept three amendments put forward by them, so that on 5 July 1979, in the British House of Commons, Rowlands could say: 'I think that the patient process to achieve the maximum possible consensus around the Constitution has been carried out.'

Independence

St Vincent and the Grenadines (as the State is now known) became independent on 27 October 1979. Subject to minor variations, the Independence Constitution of that country is similar to those of Grenada, St Lucia and Dominica which, by that time, had all attained independence. It will be sufficient to illustrate these minor variations by reference to the following examples. The constitutions of both Grenada and St Lucia establish bicameral parliaments consisting in each of a Senate and a House of Representatives (or assembly).[21]

In the discussion above with respect to the Constitution of Dominica, it has already been pointed out that while the legislature of that country is unicameral, the constitution has oddly made provision for the appointment to the House of Assembly of a number of

---

21   See Constitutions of Grenada (s 23) and St Lucia (s 23) (SI 1978/1901).

senators.[22] A similar provision appears in the Constitution of St Vincent.[23] In addition, the constitutions of Dominica and St Vincent both disqualify ministers of religion from sitting in the respective legislatures, either as elected members or as appointed senators.[24] In general terms, the corresponding provisions of the Constitution of St Lucia are to like effect.[25] On the other hand, a person who is a minister of religion is not disqualified under the Constitution of Grenada from being a member of the House of Representatives or of the Senate.[26]

The name of the country

At the constitutional conference in London, it had been agreed that the country should upon independence be officially styled and be known as 'St Vincent and the Grenadines'. This has been reflected in the constitution.[27] The Government, in taking this decision, must have decided that this would be the best means of showing the Grenadine Islands, which are 'dependencies' of St Vincent, that they were at least being officially recognised as an integral part of the country. Whether this gesture will have the desired effect, time alone will tell; but barely six weeks after the country had become independent and two days after the general elections that followed, there occurred a mini-rebellion in one of these very dependencies – Union Island – in the following circumstances.

The Union Island uprising of 7 December 1979

On the morning of 7 December 1979, information reached the Minister for National Security of St Vincent and the Grenadines that there had been an uprising on Union Island, one of the St Vincent Grenadines, 40 miles south of the mainland. A group of armed men were said to have effectively taken over the island. Details appeared to have been as follows: the police station was attacked and dynamited and the airport blocked off.

According to the Minister for National Security, the Government of St Vincent was not yet properly constituted, as these events took place only two days after the general elections. Although the electoral proceedings had not yet been completed, the results of the polls which were then at hand were sufficient to indicate that the SVLP had already been successful in the majority of polling divisions and would, thus, form the Government.

Ministers were hurriedly sworn in by the Governor General and the following emergency action was immediately taken by the Minister of National Security:

(1) a state of emergency was declared and a dusk to dawn curfew imposed;

---

22 Dominica Constitution, ss 29 and 30.
23 St Vincent Constitution, ss 23 and 24 (SI 1979/916).
24 Dominica Constitution, s 32(1)(b) and St Vincent Constitution, s 26(1)(b).
25 St Lucia Constitution, ss 24(1)(c), 26(1)(b) and 32(1)(b).
26 Grenada Constitution, ss 26 and 31.
27 See Preamble to St Vincent Constitution.

(2) military assistance was requested from, and given by, the Government of Barbados; and

(3) the local police force was put on full alert.

In the face of these preparations the uprising was quelled with minimal loss of life or injury to persons.

There were at the time of the rebellion many theories as to its origin. According to one such theory it was made to appear that some arms in the possession of the rebels came from Carriacou, a ward to Grenada. This may have led some people to speak of a 'Grenadian connection'. However, the subsequent extradition of the rebel leader from Grenada, where he had sought refuge, would seem to have scotched all such rumours. What seems clear is that the rebels were reacting to what they perceived to be gross neglect on the part of the central government. Apparently it was fairly widely known on Union Island that the group of men who later featured in the uprising were arming themselves. Whether there was inadequate intelligence on the part of the members of the police force stationed on Union Island, or whether the urgency of the situation was not fully appreciated by the central police force, it is difficult to say. Suffice it to state that the central government was caught off guard and it is anyone's guess what would have been the outcome if one group of, say, 20 well armed men had attacked the police stations at Kingstown (the capital), Bequia, Canouan and Union Island simultaneously – and if help from outside was at the same time not forthcoming.

It is interesting to note that the mini-rebellion in Union Island was put down by the Government of St Vincent and the Grenadines with the active support of policemen and army personnel sent for that purpose by the Government of Barbados. Quite understandably, there was little or no international comment about the Barbados action in this regard. It was quite clearly of a far different character from the violation in 1983 of the sovereignty and territorial integrity of Grenada which occurred when the armed forces of the United States of America, Jamaica, Barbados and Member States of the Organisation of Eastern Caribbean States (OECS) invaded Grenada. This matter has been fully discussed in Chapter 10, above.

We must now look at the constitutional and other related developments in St Lucia as they took shape before and after independence in 1979.

ST LUCIA

St Lucia was also one of the territories which, under the umbrella of the then federal government, was given a measure of internal self-government in 1959, having been a constituent member of the federal establishment while it lasted from 1958–62. Grenada, St Vincent, Dominica, Antigua and St Kitts were in a similar position.

At the time of the introduction of the ministerial system in St Lucia in 1956, the ministers were chosen from the St Lucia Labour Party (SLP), headed by George Charles, to form the Government. Charles became Chief Minister on 1 January 1960, at the time of the introduction of a new constitution for all the territories in the Windward and Leeward Islands. However, in 1961, certain differences arose between the older and younger members of the SLP. Several of the younger members left the party when they found that the differences could not be resolved. In any case, problems continued to plague the party, so much so that the Government collapsed in 1964 (before it could run its full course). The collapse had occurred after two members of the House resigned, thus robbing the Government of its majority. At the ensuing general elections in that year John Compton became Chief Minister and continued in that position as the political leader of a new party called the United Workers' Party (UWP), the members of which were drawn from the National Labour Movement (NLM) and the People's Progressive Party (PPP).

In 1967, with the advent of associated statehood, John Compton (later Sir John) became Premier of St Lucia and the Legislative Council became the House of Assembly. Although provision was made in the constitution for a Senate, this provision remained dormant, as the senators were in fact nominated members of the House of Assembly. As occurred after associated statehood in all the territories upon which the status was conferred, the administrator at that time became the Governor, each country being then *de facto* independent in all its internal affairs but dependent upon Britain for the maintenance of its defence and the conduct of its external affairs.[28]

There were, at one stage, strong feelings in the area that the Associated States should endeavour to seek independence as a group. When, however Eric Gairy, the Premier of Grenada, moved in 1973 for separate independence, the other territories also decided to negotiate individually with Britain to seek independence on a unilateral basis.

At the 1974 general elections, the UWP was again returned to power and, in 1975, the party decided to move to independence alone. The negotiations were very protracted because of the fragmented nature of the opposition political parties, which Her Majesty's Government quite properly insisted must be involved in the independence talks. Consequently, it was not until February 1979 that St Lucia became an independent country within the Commonwealth, with John Compton as its first Prime Minister. He had then served as Head of Government of that country for more than 15 years and St Lucia was regarded as being one of the most politically stable of the Eastern Caribbean States.

However, at the general elections held in July 1979, Compton's party was heavily defeated when a resuscitated SLP was voted into power: the SLP winning 12 seats and the UWP taking five. Allan Louisy, the SLP leader, thus became the Prime Minister of St Lucia.

The political stability which St Lucia had enjoyed for the previous 15 years was severely shattered by events which took place shortly after the July 1979 elections.

Within months of the inauguration of the new administration a blazing row developed over this leadership issue which unfortunately received considerable publicity, not only in St Lucia, but throughout the Caribbean. In an interview[29] given early in 1980, the Prime Minister sought to assure the people of St Lucia that the matter had been finally resolved through the good offices of the Inter-Christian Council and the Civil Service Association. Notwithstanding that assurance, there followed in the ensuing months many

---

28 See Phillips, 1977, Chapter VII, pp 79–93, for a full exposition of the history and operation of associated statehood.

29 See the *West Indies Chronicle*, December 1980/January 1981 issue.

overt acts manifesting the disagreement between the Prime Minister and his deputy: one of these acts being the cancellation of Odlum's designation as 'deputy prime minister' and the removal from his portfolio of the Departments of Industry and Information. (The post of deputy prime minister is not an office established or recognised by the constitution.)

By 1981, Odlum and three other ministers who supported him came out in open revolt against Prime Minister Louisy; and when the Government presented the annual budget, they voted with the five members of the opposition party to defeat it. But even prior to that defeat, the Prime Minister had had the humiliating experience of witnessing Odlum and his supporters walk out of Parliament as soon as the Acting Governor General had entered the chamber to deliver the speech from the throne. In this way, they protested the appointment of Boswell Williams as Acting Governor General of the country.

As a result of the defeat of the Government on so vital an issue as the national budget, Prime Minister Louisy, acting constitutionally and to some extent astutely, opted to resign from office rather than advise the Governor General to dissolve Parliament. In so doing, he at least ensured that the SLP Government remained in power. Of course his resignation also meant that the offices of all ministers became vacant.[30] In any event, even if Louisy had advised in favour of a dissolution the Governor General could constitutionally have refused to dissolve Parliament if, acting in his own deliberate judgment, he considered that the Government could have been carried on without a dissolution and that it would not have been in the interests of the country to dissolve Parliament.[31]

Following discussions within the party to select a candidate for appointment to the office of Prime Minister, Winston Cenac, the former Attorney General (who by then had also resigned) and Peter Josie, the Minister of Agriculture, emerged as front runners. In the end, the mantle of leadership fell upon Cenac – more by default than by design; and despite massive protests from all sections of the community, the Acting Governor General exercised his discretion and called upon him to form the Government.[32]

When Cenac took office in April 1981 the SLP held nine seats, the UWP five, and the Odlum faction of the SLP – which subsequently became known as the Progressive Labour Party (PLP) – held three seats. The first attack against the new administration was a call for a vote of no-confidence, which it barely survived. It is significant that the motion was moved by Compton and seconded by Michael Pilgrim, the deputy chairman of the PLP, in terms that the Government had brought the country to 'a state of impending bankruptcy'. Although that motion failed, a further opportunity to bring down the Government came shortly thereafter when it sought to amend the relevant law[33] to

---

30 See St Lucia Constitution, s 60(9)(b).

31 *Ibid*, s 55(4), proviso (a).

32 In making this appointment, the Governor General acted under s 60(2) of the constitution: '... wherever the Governor-General has occasion to appoint a Prime Minister he shall appoint a member of the House who appears to him likely to command the support of the majority of the members of the House.'

33 St Lucia Constitution, s 32(1), provides as follows: 'A person shall not be qualified to be elected as a member of the House if he ... (f) subject to such exceptions and limitations as may be prescribed by Parliament, has an interest in any Government Contract.'

exempt the elected members of Parliament from the disqualification section thereof, after it was disclosed that a member of the governing party had been the notary in a government transaction. It was allegedly to legalise this irregularity and to introduce legislation having the effect of relieving ministers from having promptly to bring to account funds remaining from advances received in respect of overseas visits, that Government had, on 11 January 1982, introduced a Bill in Parliament to amend the existing legislation on this matter.

This move served to heighten the fears of the people of St Lucia concerning the *bona fides* of the Government. As a consequence, public servants and members of the Chamber of Commerce, the churches and the Small Businessmen's Association took to the streets in a spate of massive demonstrations to urge the resignation of the Government. The resulting political pressure was too much for the administration and accordingly the SLP Government led by Cenac resigned in January 1982.

Once again, as occurred in the case of Dominica,[34] necessity demanded that some means be found to run the country after Cenac was forced to resign as Prime Minister and until a general election could be held. It was in these circumstances that an extra-legal expedient had to be designed so that the government of the country could continue, for even if a dissolution had been requested and obtained, the then Prime Minister would have been expected to continue to head a caretaker government until the results of the election were made known; and neither Cenac nor the various organisations which had pressed for the resignation of the Cabinet wished to accede to such a holding arrangement.

The three parties – the SLP, the UWP, the PLP – and the outgoing Prime Minister chose, as the compromise candidate for the interim prime ministership, Michael Pilgrim (the deputy leader of the PLP) who was sworn in on 17 January 1982. Once more, too, the Governor General endorsed the choice by recourse to his constitutional discretion to choose such a member of the House as he considered likely to command the support of the majority of all the elected members. The Government was described as a government of 'national unity' and this description was borne out by the fact that Louisy – the Prime Minister from 1979–81 – held the portfolio of Attorney General. In addition, John Compton, the former Prime Minister of long standing, and George Odlum, the former deputy prime minister, were designated 'advisers' to the Government – on finance, and foreign affairs respectively.[35]

Finally, the events to which reference was made above – in this chapter as well as those to which we adverted in Chapter 10 above – regarding Grenada – present an object lesson in the extra-constitutional transfer of governmental authority. They vividly show the extent to which the populace and revolutionaries will ultimately go in order to redress what they perceive as gross wrongdoing on the part of the political directorate.

---

34 See above, pp 200–03.

35 The writer interviewed the Rt Hon Mr Compton (as he then was) Prime Minister of St Lucia, on 17 April 1984, when the Prime Minister revealed that, although he was at the time appointed as an Adviser on Finance during the interim administration, he was never in fact consulted during Michael Pilgrim's tenure of office as Prime Minister.

A FURTHER INCHOATE ATTEMPT AT
SUB-REGIONAL POLITICAL UNION

An analysis of recent constitutional developments in the territories which make up the OECS would not be complete without some reference to the initiative launched in May 1987 to create a single State out of the separate nation States which constitute that organisation. In a speech in Tortola, Mr James Mitchell (now Sir James), at that time Prime Minister of St Vincent and the Grenadines, proposed a referendum in the territories of the OECS on whether or not there should be political union. Confident that the answer would be 'Yes', he proposed that a constitution should be designed and that there should be another referendum to endorse that constitution after it had been endorsed by the Parliaments of each of the territories.

The proposal and the procedures which should be adopted to secure its realisation were discussed from time to time among the Heads of Government of the OECS. Quite early on, Antigua and Barbuda made clear that it was not interested in pursuing closer union. The Windward Islands – Dominica, Grenada, St Lucia, and St Vincent and the Grenadines – did, however, remain a core group seriously committed to the achievement of closer union.

In August 1990, the Heads of Government of these countries met on Palm Island. They agreed as follows:

> It would now be appropriate to establish a Regional Constituent Assembly involving Parliamentarians, political parties and special interest groups to discuss and make recommendations on the necessity for political union and on appropriate institutional arrangements for bringing it into effect.

> That the proposed Constituent Assembly should be constituted of 40 persons (being 10 persons from each of the Windward Islands). The persons in the Assembly should be selected from the Parliament (Government and Opposition), political parties (being five in number), and the other five from the private sector, the trade unions, the church, youth groups and the farming community.

The Regional Constituent Assembly was set up by an inter-governmental agreement signed in St Vincent and the Grenadines on 26 November 1990. It was to undertake the following functions:

(a) To examine and advise on the necessity for Windward Islands political union with specific reference to the economic and social viability of union, the economic costs of union and the external relations and administrative implications of union.

(b) To examine and advise on the possible forms of union, that is whether the proposed union should be a state which is either federal or unitary or of some other form.

(c) To examine and advise on the structure of government and elements of a constitution which would be most appropriate to the union, including the administrative and electoral mechanisms.

A deadline of 31 March 1991 was fixed as the date on which the Regional Constituent Assembly was to present its reports to the Government. These reports were to be debated in the Parliaments of the four countries as a White Paper. Thereafter, referenda were to be held in the four countries. If proposals for closer union were approved in the Parliaments, a constitutional conference of parliamentarians would be convened to draft a constitution based on such recommendations of the Regional Constituent Assembly as had been adopted.

The Regional Constituent Assembly (chaired by Mr Justice Telford Georges) held four sessions. The first was in St Vincent and the Grenadines from 14–18 January 1991; the second in St Lucia from 22–28 April 1991; the third in Dominica from 1–6 September 1991; and the fourth in Grenada from 20–25 January 1992.

The Regional Constituent Assembly had the benefit of the advice of a number of technical consultants in the areas of law, political science and economic affairs. The discussions were animated, wide ranging and well informed.

At the first meeting it was agreed that the existing co-operation among the States had created more favourable conditions for economic and social development in each State. There was every reason to conclude that with deepening and strengthening, the situation would be further improved. Political union was necessary if that deepening and strengthening was to be realised.

All were agreed that a larger unified State would help in the preservation of fundamental rights and freedoms because it would ensure greater stability arising from mutual support.

Significantly, delegates from the governing parties in the four States favoured the creation of a unitary State with the component countries becoming in effect local government bodies. This was not acceptable. The consensus favoured what could be described as a 'federal' arrangement with a strong centre and with provisions for units to transfer powers of legislation and functions of administration to the centre. Breaking with tradition, the delegates overwhelmingly favoured a United States style executive presidency.

The Regional Constituent Assembly in due course submitted to the Governments a report on their conclusions which included what was, in effect, instructions which could constitute the basis for the preparation of a draft constitution.

This document was laid on the table in each of the four Parliaments and was in the course of time debated and approved as a parliamentary document. There the process ended.

There is no obvious explanation for the abandonment of this initiative. It was unique in that it was launched in the region by the parties holding the reins of government. It received tangible support from opposition parties in St Vincent and the Grenadines and Grenada. At the earliest stages, it involved participation by the representatives of important segments of the society – the trade unions, the churches, the youth, the women and the business community. In the end, there was a reluctance to take the final step of challenging the forces of insularity and surrendering some measure of sovereignty.

REVIVED INTEREST IN FURTHER UNION

Shortly after Dr Ralph Gonsalves became Prime Minister of St Vincent and the Grenadines, following a crushing defeat of the NDP at the polls in March 2001, he attended his inaugural meeting of CARICOM in Nassau, Bahamas. At this gathering, he announced his intention to revive the idea of political union, if possible beginning with the Windward Islands of St Vincent, Grenada, St Lucia and Dominica. Later that month, the Prime Minister repeated his plan at a meeting of the Heads of the OECS Authority in Roseau, Dominica, at which the Heads of Government agreed to work towards a 1 January 2002 deadline for introducing free movement of OECS nationals among the Member States – the details to be pursued under the supervision of Dr Ralph Gonsalves and Dr Kenny Anthony, Prime Minister of St Lucia (as a task force). The Heads expect freedom of movement to involve removal of restrictions on work and residency permits, now required for OECS nationals wishing to move from one territory to another.

The Task Force has been requested to examine the feasibility of issuing a 'common passport' for OECS nationals under an entity to be known as the Eastern Caribbean Union of Independent States (ECUIS) with the holder's country of birth inscribed below. A common identification card is to be issued for inter-regional travel. The Caribbean Union is to be modelled on the European Union with an executive drawn from the leaders of the States and a regional Parliament involving both Government and Opposition members. Are we beginning to see the thin edge of the wedge towards a further political union? The development is a welcome and encouraging sign.

Developments in Antigua and Barbuda, Barbados, Jamaica and Belize will be addressed in the next chapter.

CHAPTER 12

ANTIGUA AND BARBUDA, BARBADOS, JAMAICA AND BELIZE

ANTIGUA AND BARBUDA

Introduction

In the author's 1977 volume,[1] he referred to the status of associated statehood that had been granted to Antigua, in common with the other five territories of St Vincent, St Lucia, Dominica, Grenada and St Kitts/Nevis/Anguilla. In dealing with the future of Antigua, it was stated that in 1974, George Walter, Premier of the country (then under a government of the Progressive Labour Movement (PLM)) had made it clear that the 1976 elections would be fought 'on an independence ticket'.[2] The 1976 elections were, in the event, won by the Antigua Labour Party (ALP) headed by Vere C Bird (later Sir Vere), a veteran and distinguished politician, whose party had at first taken the line that, although it favoured independence, there should be a referendum to determine the wishes of the people in the matter. Walter's intention to take Antigua to early independence had, of course, been understandable since, although Antigua was the first territory to be created an associated State, by 1974 Grenada, which obtained that status after Antigua, had already become an independent country within the Commonwealth.

In 1978, the ALP Government declared that Antigua was ready to take its place as an independent state in the international community. The Government justified its *volte face* on the independence issue by the argument that between 1974 and 1978 the economic foundation for independence had been well and truly laid.

The Government, however, did the decent constitutional thing of calling early elections to secure from the people a mandate to proceed to independence. This mandate was generously given, for in the general elections held in 1980, the ALP won 13 of the 17 seats in the House of Assembly. Shortly afterwards the Government requested Her Majesty's Government to convene a conference in London as a preliminary to terminating the status of association between HMG and Antigua under s 10(2) of the West Indies Act. Invitations were duly issued to the PLM, the Barbudan Member of Parliament and the Chairman of the Barbuda Council to attend.

In the meantime, the Antigua Government had prepared a draft independence constitution which was debated and approved in the House of Assembly with some amendments. The PLM had prepared its own draft commentary on the Antigua draft. When the news reached Barbuda, there was violent reaction by the Barbudans to the idea of being integrated with Antigua in independence; and it was this reaction which delayed the conference until December 1980. Incidentally, in March 1981, at the Barbuda local elections all the seats had been won by the Barbuda People's Movement which had

---

1   Phillips, 1977, Chapter VIII, pp 78–93.
2   *Ibid*, p 93.

vigorously campaigned for secession. But we must return to the London conference of December 1980.

At this conference the PLM (the Opposition party) made the following proposals for amending the Government's draft:

(a) they questioned the time by which a person arrested should be told of the grounds of his arrest;

(b) they wished to see inserted in the document:

    (i) the right to legal representation and its extension to government legal aid;

    (ii) the right to bail;

    (iii) the time limit within which an accused person should be brought before a court;

    (iv) the circumstances in which a person unlawfully arrested or detained should be in a position to obtain compensation and from whom;

    (v) the time within which compensation should be paid for property compulsorily acquired;

    (vi) a right to strike, to bargain collectively and to collect union dues;

    (vii) provision for a unicameral instead of a bicameral legislature;

    (viii) provision for a system of proportional representation for the Senate and for reducing the size thereof;

    (ix) a clause permitting a minister of religion to become a member of either House;

    (x) an age reduction from 21 to 18 for qualification for membership of either House;

(c) they questioned why a member of the House of Representatives should have to vacate his seat if he sought to cross the floor of the House;

(d) they asked that, in appointing the chairman of the Constituency Boundaries Commission the Governor General should seek the concurrence of both the Prime Minister and the Leader of the Opposition; and they raised other issues relating to the security of tenure of this Commission;

(e) they requested that mandatory provisions should be included in the Constitution for a Leader of the Opposition, regardless of whether or not there was an Opposition presence in the House – in which case the minority leader in the Senate should become Leader of the Opposition; and

(f) they argued that the members of the Public Service Commission should be appointed with the concurrence of both the Prime Minister and the Leader of the Opposition.

As far as the *Barbudan delegation* was concerned, this is how the conference chairman summed up in a nutshell their general position:

> The Barbudan delegation stated that they could not agree to any constitutional arrangements which did not provide a separate future for Barbuda; that any other constitutional arrangements would have to be referred by them to the people of Barbuda; *and that their participation in the discussions was for the purpose of seeing whether constitutional safeguards for Barbuda could be agreed which they could lay before the people of Barbuda* [emphasis supplied].[3]

---

3   See the Report of the Antigua Constitutional Conference, December 1980, para 43.

The reply from the Antigua Government delegation was that because Barbuda had been an integral part of the State since 1860, the Government could not permit it to have a separate existence at this stage, but that every effort would be made to give a greater say to the Barbuda Council in the conduct of their local affairs and that the Government would abolish the office of the Minister for Barbuda Affairs in the Central Government if it was satisfied that alternative arrangements could be made after independence for proper liaison between itself and the Barbuda Council.

At this point, the matter of the original merger of Antigua and Barbuda should be put in proper historical perspective. The following résumé sets out how Barbuda came to be regarded as a part of Antigua.

Merger of Barbuda with Antigua

When one examines the record carefully one finds that what has been said about the 'arbitrary buffeting' in the case of Anguilla[4] applies equally to Barbuda. The 19th century was a time when the Colonial Office was engaged in a process of regional consolidation for its own administrative convenience. In the Leeward Islands, there were Anguilla, Barbuda, Crab Island, Passage Island and Sombrero, in respect of which they needed to find large islands to which to attach them – the linking of the first two being the most important.[5]

Barbuda had first been granted to Christopher Codrington as far back as 1685 under Letters Patent. There was an original 99 year grant which had been renewed in 1805 for a further term of 50 years, and when the grant came up for renewal in 1854, HMG expressed their desire to resume occupation of the island. They were, however, prepared to permit Codrington to enter a rental agreement with the Government of Antigua of which Barbuda would become a dependency – though not in reality an integral part. It was then suggested by one Colonial Office official that the wisest course would be to make a Mr Nugent, Codrington's agent, Lieutenant Governor of Barbuda and to grant him power to make laws subject to confirmation by the Governor of Antigua. This was clearly impractical, however, as Mr Nugent was at the time the Speaker of the Antigua House of Assembly. In any event, the then Colonial Secretary considered it absurd that Barbuda with a population of less than 1,000 should have a Lieutenant Governor of its own.

At this time Barbuda was used by Codrington mainly as a place to run deer and feral stock, as well as to provide wood, charcoal, lime and ground provisions for Codrington's Antigua plantations. It has also been claimed in some quarters that the island was used by Codrington as a stock farm for breeding slaves, but this claim has been seriously doubted.[6] An additional source of income to the Codringtron family was the salvage arising from the many wrecks caused by the treacherous reefs surrounding the island.

Codrington's renewed lease therefore brought into question the future status of Barbuda, and on an approach being made to Governor Higginson of Antigua, it was agreed that Antigua would be prepared to have its laws extended to Barbuda. Codrington would then have a gratuitous tenancy for a period of 50 years, in

---

4   See the opening two paragraphs under 'Anguilla', Chapter 7, above.
5   See Confidential Despatch, 19 March 1925, Thomson to the Secretary of State for the Colonies.
6   See Lowenthal and Clarke, 1977, pp 510–35.

consideration for which he would meet the expenses of a resident clergyman who would be sufficiently versatile to be a Justice of the Peace and to perform minor medical operations.[7]

While examining the matter of merger it was discovered that in the original grant of 1684 Barbuda had been described as 'one of the Caribbean Islands and always deemed an appendant member of the island of Antigua'. It was also discovered that for some peculiar reason the Great Seal furnished on the consolidation of the Leeward Islands Governments in 1833 was 'the Great Seal of Antigua and Barbuda'.

It was at this stage that the Colonial Office despatched to Antigua as a guide a copy of the St Kitts Act of 1825 under which Anguilla was annexed to St Kitts.[8] As a result, the Governor sent a message to the Antigua Legislature recommending that Barbuda should merge with Antigua. The outcome was a legislative declaration of incorporation under which provision was made for a right of representation by Barbuda in the Legislature of Antigua.

The annexation of Barbuda was, however, to lead to complications which in turn brought about the surrender of the lease by Codrington. And so, in the words of Anthony Phillips: 'The last vestige of the 17th century proprietary system was then ended and the anomaly of a community without public institutions or laws was recitified.'[9]

It was perhaps no doubt in recognition of so bizarre a union that the Government of Antigua showed a marked inclination to grant special concessions to the Barbudan delegation throughout the conference.

However, before we consider the firm proposals put forward by the Barbudan delegation it is worth examining the contents of an impassioned plea from the Barbuda representative at the conference to let his people go. He began by pointing out that his delegation had come, sent by his people, to obtain separation from the administrative control of Antigua, to which the people had been joined against their will by Her Majesty's Government by an Order in Council of 1 August 1860:

> History also shows that at no other time were the wishes of the people of Barbuda sought to approve of this relationship of master and servant imposed upon them by a well meaning but imperial nation, acting in accordance with principles and policies of that era.

He went on to emphasise that neither at the time of associated statehood in 1967 nor at the instant time of impending independence were their views sought as to whether they wished 'to continue (our) enslavement' and he averred with evident sincerity that it was the wish of the Antiguans 'to keep us in a state of servitude for ever'. After praying in aid several sections of the United Nations Charter in support of the Barbudan claim for separate autonomy he made the following pronouncement:

> We have submitted several documents on this subject to various bodies including Her Majesty's Government, Your Excellency's officials and the United Nations, commencing with a statement to the Committee of 24 of the United Nations in 1968, by the then Barbuda representative, culminating in a list of grievances against the Antigua Government,

---

7   See CO 7/116 January 1861 No 2.
8   This matter has been fully canvassed in Chapter 7, above.
9   See unpublished dissertation referred to in Chapter 7, fn 2.

submitted to the Right Honourable Secretary of State for Foreign and Commonwealth Affairs, approximately one month prior to this Conference.

These documents, spreading over a period of more than 12 years, tabulated generally and specifically incidents of:

(a) human rights violations;

(b) exploitation of Barbuda and its people by the Antigua Government;

(c) obvious attempts by the Antigua Government to deprive Barbudans of their customary rights to the lands of their island acquired by them and their ancestors from time immemorial;

(d) discriminatory treatment against Barbudans;

(e) refusal by the Antigua Government to recognise the inherent dignity and the equal and inalienable rights of the people of Barbuda. To put it in local dialect, 'Dem tink dem betta dan we';

(f) systematic efforts on the part of the Antigua Government to prevent orderly economic, social, cultural and political development of Barbuda and its people; and clear evidence of their attempts to deceive Barbudans and the world, by stating and writing one thing while doing the opposite; and

(g) the inability of Antigua, a financially bankrupt State, to take care of, or develop Barbuda, or even to deal effectively with its own economic, financial and developmental problems.

He continued:

> We are tired of hearing statements from Ministers of the Antigua Government, to the effect that the 'territorial integrity' of Antigua must not be violated. By these words, they seek to justify and emphasise their rights to oppress the people of Barbuda and place their own desire to rob the people of their natural wealth and resources, contrary to the principles enunciated in the United Nations Charter, on a respectable footing.

> As far as we are aware the words 'territorial integrity' are used with reference to nations, that is, peoples and territories who have already taken over full control of their internal and external affairs, and not with respect to dependencies of metropolitian governments as Antigua and Barbuda undoubtedly are.

He then went on with these significant words:

> As we see it, the people and territory of Barbuda are under the overall administrative control of the United Kingdom. Her Majesty's Government at some earlier era delegated this authority to the Government of Antigua, who are nothing more than an agent of Her Majesty's Government. That agent has abused its trust in every way imaginable and we the people of Barbuda are today asking Her Majesty's Government to *dismiss that unjust steward* and deal with the people of Barbuda in a manner in conformity with the principles of the United Nations.

Barbudan delegation's proposals to the conference

We now turn to the actual proposals made by the Barbudan delegation at the independence conference, the gravamen of which was as follows:

1   Barbuda should have the status of an independent state in association with an independent Antigua, the Government and Parliament of which should be vested with powers to look after the defence, external affairs, and citizenship affairs of Barbuda.

These arrangements should be protected by entrenched provisions in the proposed Antigua/Barbuda constitution. The Government of Antigua will, however, be required to consult Barbuda when dealing with the latter's defence and external affairs:

2   The Barbuda Council should be upgraded to a House of Assembly which will have power to make laws for all matters specified in the 1904 and 1976 Ordinances, as well as for education, transport and communications matters: this power to be exclusive. The Assembly would also be empowered to approach external authorities with a view to securing aid for Barbuda.

3   The new Constitution should confirm and enact the customary land law regime of Barbuda. All disposition of land in Barbuda to persons not resident or domiciled there must be confirmed by the Barbuda Assembly as well as by the majority of the electorate in Barbuda.

4   Although police stationed in Barbuda would be members of the Antigua Police Force they would, while in Barbuda, be under the command of the Barbuda House of Assembly: the Assembly alone to have the power to decide when additional police personnel should be sent to the island; the normal strength to be one Sergeant and two Police Constables or such other strength as the Barbuda Police Commissioner might agree.

5   The Antigua Public Service Commission would send to Barbuda such public servants as the Assembly would from time to time request, but the said personnel must first be approved by the Assembly to which they would be exclusively responsible.

6   The Assembly should have the power of raising, collecting and spending taxes in Barbuda and utilising such taxes as it considers fit. The Assembly should also have the exclusive right to establish a Philatelic Bureau on the island and to use the funds accruing therefrom for public use locally.

7   The Assembly should be entitled to receive all customs and other duties levied on goods coming into Barbuda at its port of entry. The Assembly should keep proper books of account and should be subject to public account in the normal way.

8   A Common Services Commission to be set up to determine the exact cost of all services rendered by the Antigua Government to Barbuda; the Commission to comprise two representatives from Antigua; two from Barbuda; and a chairman provided by the Commonwealth Secretariat.

9   A proportion of the capital funds made available by HMG on independence to be allocated to Barbuda, the quantum to be decided by HMG itself.

10   A consolidated 1904 Ordinance and Local Government Act 1976 to be annexed to the Constitution, and to be entrenched so that both the legislative and executive powers of the Assembly could not be altered without the approval of two-thirds of the Assembly and two-thirds of the electorate of Barbuda.

11   The operation of the Constitution to be reviewed by the Commonwealth Secretariat after an initial two years and every three years thereafter. If the Secretariat reports that the constitutional arrangements between the two states are not working satisfactorily, it

would be open to either Antigua or Barbuda to secede within six months of the publication of the Report: such a decision to secede to be reached only by referendum.

12 There should be 'a common system of Courts' for the two states. There should be a final right of appeal to the Privy Council – to be entrenched.

What the Barbudans were demanding was anything other than being in a unitary relationship with Antigua. The writer has been informed by one of the key participants at the independence conference that the Barbudans would settle for a federation; for being given a separate colonial status as a dependent territory of Great Britain; or for becoming an independent country. It was a type of Anguillan ultimatum all over again, but with the added proposal for separate independence for a miniscule population of 1,200, of whom there are only about 500 adults.

As has been stated above, in rejecting these proposals the Antigua delegation and the UK representatives were speaking the same language.

It is, however, clear from the record that the Antigua Government did not summarily dismiss the proposals but gave careful consideration to them over a 12 day period. However, in the end wide gaps remained and it was largely because of these divergencies that neither the PLM delegation nor the Barbudan delegation felt able to sign the conference report which was nevertheless accepted on all sides as an accurate record of the positions of the respective parties. As has become usual in such circumstances, despite the fact that the conference report was signed by only the Antigua and British delegations, the Commonwealth Secretary decided that there was no alternative but that the country should proceed to independence under the new name of Antigua and Barbuda on 1 November 1981.

Antigua Government attempts to placate Barbuda

It is an earnest of the concern shown by the Antigua Government for the representations made to the conference by the Barbudans that the Government saw fit to agree in the end to the insertion of a clause[10] in the new constitution under which a severe fetter would be placed on Government's power to amend the Barbuda Local Government Act of 1976. More will be said on this question later.

At this point it would be instructive to examine how the Houses of Parliament at Westminster dealt with the legislation creating Antigua an independent State. What transpired in both the House of Commons and the House of Lords in July 1981 during the course of the debates on the termination of the association between Great Britain and Antigua[11] is worthy of detailed analysis, if only to show the extent of the lobby developed by the Barbudans in the British Parliament.

The debate was opened by the Under-Secretary of State for Foreign and Commonwealth Affairs (Richard Luce).[12] After explaining that the order was being made

---

10 Antigua and Barbuda Constitution Order 1981 SI 1981/1106, s 123, Sched I (hereinafter referred to as 'Antigua and Barbuda Constitution').

11 See *Hansard* on the House of Commons Debate on the Antigua (Termination of Association) Order 1981 (pp 514–31).

12 *Ibid*, pp 514–18.

pursuant to s 10(2) of the West Indies Act, which prescribes that any such order should be laid in draft before Parliament for approval by resolution of each House, he proceeded to reveal that the order would come into operation on 1 November 1981 when Antigua would become a fully independent sovereign State – to be known as Antigua and Barbuda – and that the Antigua Government had announced its intention to apply for membership in the Commonwealth.

He then reviewed the history of Antigua. The island had been discovered by Christopher Columbus and named Antigua during his second voyage to the Caribbean in 1493. Where the French and Spanish failed to create settlements in Antigua, the British had succeeded in 1632. Sir Thomas Warner had first introduced tobacco and settlers had brought sugar by the end of the 17th century. The island was finally ceded to Britain by the Treaty of Breda of 1667. Horatio Nelson was based in Antigua when the British Naval Dockyard in that island was the centre of naval activity in the West Indies: 'The territory has thus played an important role in upholding Royal Naval traditions in the area' – whatever that may mean.

Mr Luce then referred to the West Indies Act 1967 which introduced the concept of associated statehood under which six small Caribbean territories were permitted to look after their internal affairs while their external affairs and defence became matters for metropolitian attention. This Act provided for termination of the association in two ways, viz:

(a) under s 10(1), the State's legislature could enact a law for the termination, provided that two-thirds of the elected members approve and a national referendum also support the bill; or

(b) under s 10(2), the association status could be terminated by the British Government by Order in Council at the request of the State.

It was the latter method that had so far been used to terminate the status and to move to independence in the cases of Grenada, Dominica, St Lucia, St Vincent and which Antigua proposed to adopt. The policy of the Conservative Government was the same as that of former Labour Governments, viz, that whenever s 10(2) was prayed in aid, the necessary order would be moved so long as two requirements were satisfied, viz:

(i) that it was proved to the satisfaction of Her Majesty's Government that the majority of the inhabitants of the country wanted independence; and

(ii) that there were provided in the independence constitutions the necessary fundamental rights and freedoms.

The Under-Secretary revealed that since in the 1976 Antigua general elections the ALP had not won on an independence mandate, when they announced in 1978 that they had changed their mind, the Secretary of State had visited the territory to advise them they should demonstrate that independence was what the people wanted; that, accordingly, they had set about drafting a constitution and holding elections in 1980 at which independence was the main issue raised by all three parties which had taken part in the elections; that the ALP (which in 1980 formed the Government) had secured an overwhelming victory when it secured 13 of the total of 17 seats in the legislature.

There had been a mandate in the Antigua House of Representatives on the draft constitution and, on 12 August 1980, a resolution was approved therein requesting that a constitutional conference be convened in London to consider the termination of the status of association. At this point the Secretary of State had invited the Government, the Opposition 'as well as the independent member of Barbuda and, exceptionally, the chairman of the Barbuda Council, to London'.[13] It was in these circumstances and under these auspices that the Antigua Constitutional Conference took place between 4 and 16 December 1980.

Mr Luce made reference to the result of the Lancaster House Conference and expressed the British Government's satisfaction that the revised draft constitution which emerged following the exhaustive discussion 'will provide the independent State of Antigua and Barbuda with a framework for stable democratic government affording proper protection for fundamental human rights and freedoms'.[14] He also pointed out that the constitution had, after the London conference, been fully debated in the Antigua Parliament in April and May 1981, having been approved by 13 votes for and none against, but with the three Opposition members and one Barbuda member absent.

The Under-Secretary then turned his attention to Barbuda after having said a few words on the British proposed aid package after independence. The gravamen of his statement on Barbuda was that every effort had been made by the Antigua Government to meet the demands of the Barbudans: the British Government having joined hands with the Government of Antigua in the effort, but to no avail.

Although nearly half the plenary sessions at the independence conference had been spent in considering the grievances of the Barbudan representatives, they remained dissatisfied, as a result of which they declined to sign the conference report. He outlined the following steps which had been taken by the Antigua Government, supported by Her Majesty's Government, to meet the Barbudans' demands:

(i) the Government of Antigua had in May 1981 made certain amendments to the Barbuda Local Government Act granting exclusive administrative powers to the Barbuda Council in the areas of agriculture, medical services and public utilities;[15]

(ii) a British financial expert had been dispatched to the territory at the request of the Government of Antigua and his recommendations as to the manner in which the financial arrangements between Antigua and the Barbuda Council might accommodate the revised responsibilities were reflected in the new Act referred to in (i) above;

(iii) the Antigua Government had made a commitment to grant to Barbuda an annual revenue of at least EC$300,000 from stamps bearing Barbuda's name and to establish two ports of entry in Barbuda;

(iv) Barbuda's special position had been fully safeguarded by the entrenchment arrangements to which reference has already been made and which will be fully set out later.

The Under-Secretary's statement was followed by several speeches in the House of Commons. It is, however, significant that the question of Antiguan independence was hardly mentioned by any of the other speakers who all spent their time urging that

13 *Op cit, Hansard,* fn 11, p 515.
14 *Op cit, Hansard,* fn 11, p 515.
15 See the Barbuda Local Government (Amendment) Act 1976 (No 3 of 1981).

Barbuda should either to granted independence or colonial status. One wonders whether their concern for Barbuda was genuine or whether it was largely a response to well timed lobbying by high powered lobbyists.

Mr Giles Radice felt strongly that Barbuda should be accorded a separate status. The feelings of the inhabitants of the island should be given some weight. They are a hard-working, peaceful people who are prepared to use constitutional methods to achieve their aims but one should not take advantage of their peacefulness. It is this trait that should entitle them to a fair hearing. The Barbudans very deeply distrust the Antiguans, who should not have control of their destiny after independence since the Barbudans feel the Antiguans will simply exploit their island. The Barbudans were afraid that the Antiguans would send them Antiguan policemen well known to be biased against Barbudans. The Barbudans also feared their lands would be 'bought up and exploited by Antiguans'.[16]

Mr Bowen Wells, while conceding that 'this is a great occasion for both Britain and Antigua', went on to question the entire arrangement, by which the mini-States of Grenada, St Vincent, St Lucia and Dominica were granted independence. He also castigated Her Majesty's Government for infringing the terms of the West Indies Act by not obtaining the advice and consent of the Government of St Kitts/Nevis/Anguilla in severing Anguilla from the rest of the associated State at the time. In his view: 'That example will return to haunt the House and Antigua.' This member of Parliament ended on the note that he hoped that when all these mini-States were independent they would once again enter a Caribbean federal union.[17]

Mr Enoch Powell, the next speaker, was not equally hopeful. He restricted his comments to a rather cynical lambasting of Her Majesty's Government for having initially joined Antigua with Barbuda and for having granted sovereignty to these mini-States:

> The State of Antigua and Barbuda comprehends those two territories because the imperial Power so decided about 130 years ago. There is nothing else which joins together in holy matrimony Antigua and Barbuda. How, then, do we proceed when the moment comes for independence? One is even permitted to use a word forbidden to ourselves, the United Kingdom, in this context – 'sovereignty'. [As if soliloquising, he mused:] What are we to do? It is said that one cannot create a midget State and that it would be an absurdity to recognise the separate identity of Barbuda. But we are in the midst of absurdities. We are creating independence on a scale and endowing sovereignty in circumstances foreign to the natural meaning of those concepts.[18]

In his contribution, Mr Russell Johnston affirmed that 'the affection people have for islands is unique, not to be treated lightly'; and he found the attitude of the British Government difficult to comprehend: 'It seems to be the same, whether we are talking about Gibraltar, the Falkland Islands, or bits and pieces here and there: the view of the Foreign Office, is that it is all a bit of a nuisance.' According to him, when the Minister of State said he hoped the Barbudans would respond positively what he in fact meant was: 'I hope they agree with what we are doing, but we do not care terribly if they do not.' 'It is,' he continued, 'as bald, bleak and straightforward as that.' In his view, 1,200 to 1,500 people may not be able to exist as an independent entity, but that was no reason for trying

---

16 See *op cit, Hansard*, fn 11, pp 518–19.

17 *Op cit, Hansard*, fn 11, pp 520–22.

18 *Op cit, Hansard*, fn 11, pp 522–25.

to force them into a unity they do not want. He then enumerated the following eight points:

1   the majority of Barbudans reject the merger. The Barbudan Member of Parliament and the nine members of the Barbuda Council are all against it;

2   the People's Liberation Movement – the former Government of the State – oppose it;

3   the 1,200 people of Barbuda have always in their 200 year history supported themselves on fishing and agriculture and they do not want to be dictated to by neighbouring Antigua;

4   the Barbudans have lost faith in Antiguans, since the latter have not lived up to the provisions enshrined in the 1976 Local Government legislation;

5   the Barbudans have not been given funds voted for them since 1 June 1980;

6   the UK has no interest in compelling Barbuda to become part of Antigua;

7   the Antiguans do not need Barbuda for anything except to satisfy their pride;

8   lastly, there is no reason why HMG should not do for Barbuda what they had done in similar circumstances for Anguilla. Although the State Government had objected in 1971, by 1981 it had accepted that secession was inevitable and reasonable.[19]

Mr DN Campbell-Savours at this point intervened to express his deep concern for the plight of the Barbudans and to state that the House should put on record its thanks to Mr David Lowenthal and Mr Colin Clarke for the data they had provided to certain members of the House and the way they had helped to shape UK public opinion on the matter. He asked:

> Are the Government seeking to divest themselves of total responsibility, as against the responsibility that would apply were we to retain our links with Barbuda, because they were fearful of the minute public expenditure implications of retaining that link?[20]

In his winding-up reply, Mr Luce stressed the importance of the constitutional safeguards that had been provided for Barbuda: describing the safeguards as 'unprecedented in our experience'. He hoped he reflected 'the view of the majority in the House in wishing all those people well'.[21]

In Lord Thurso's view:

> ... the Antiguan Government had not allowed local government to work under the Barbuda Local Government Act 1976 – so how can the Barbudans expect anything better after the passing of this Order? ... What guarantees would ensure that local government powers would be respected and local government costs defrayed after independence in November 1981?[22]

In the House of Lords some days after, it was Lord Hooson's view that Parliament was not performing its duty as trustee 'by putting 1,500 people in a distant island into an alliance which they do not want ... without any of the doubts and the questions they have raised being satisfactorily answered'.[23]

---

19   *Op cit, Hansard*, fn 11, pp 523–25.
20   *Op cit, Hansard*, fn 11, pp 525–27.
21   *Op cit, Hansard*, fn 11, pp 528–30.
22   *Hansard*, HL, 14 July 1981, p 1173.
23   *Ibid*, p 1177.

For Lord Pitt the grant of a separate status for Barbuda had serious implications for the destabilisation of the area and should in no wise be countenanced.[24]

It was in these circumstances that Barbuda became an unwilling partner in the independent State of Antigua and Barbuda which was born on 1 November 1981.

Fetter upon the sovereignty of Antigua

The section of the constitution which prevents the Parliament of Antigua and Barbuda from amending the Barbuda Local Government Act 1976 without the approval of the Barbuda Council deserves to be quoted *in extenso*:[25]

1   There shall be a Council for Barbuda which shall be the principal organ of local government in that island.

2   The Council shall have such membership and functions as Parliament may prescribe.

3   Parliament may alter any of the provisions of the Barbuda Local Government Act, 1976, specified in schedule 2 to this Constitution (which provisions are in this section referred to as 'the said provisions') in the manner specified in the following provisions of this section and *in no other manner whatsoever* [emphasis supplied].

4   A bill to alter any of the said provisions shall not be regarded as being passed by the House unless after its final reading in that House the bill is referred to the Barbuda Council by the Clerk of the House and the Barbuda Council gives its consent to the bill by resolution of the Council, notice of which shall forthwith be given by the Council to the Clerk of the House.

5   An amendment made by the Senate to such a bill as is referred to in subsection (4) of this section which bill has been passed by the House and consented to by the Barbuda Council shall not be regarded as being agreed to by the House for the purpose of section 55 of the Constitution unless the Barbuda Council signifies to the Clerk of the House the consent by resolution of the Barbuda Council to that amendment.

6   For the purpose of section 55(4) of this constitution, an amendment of a bill to alter any of the said provisions shall not be suggested to the Senate by the House unless the Barbuda Council signifies to the Clerk of the House the consent by resolution of the Barbuda Council for the House so to suggest the amendment.

7   (a) A bill to alter any of the said provisions shall not be submitted to the Governor-General for his assent unless it is accompanied by a certificate under the hand of the Speaker (or, if the Speaker is for any reason unable to exercise the functions of his office, the Deputy Speaker) that the provisions of subsection (4), (5) or (6), as the case may be, of this section have been complied with.

(b) The certificate of the Speaker or, as the case may be, the Deputy Speaker, under this subsection shall be conclusive that the provisions of subsection (4), (5), or (6), as the case may be, of this section have been complied with and shall not be enquired into in any court of law.

---

24   *Op cit, Hansard*, fn 22, pp 1178–80.
25   Antigua Constitution, s 123.

What is even more extraordinary is that s 123 (just quoted) cannot itself be amended unless the following conditions are fulfilled, viz, a bill to alter it shall not be submitted to the Governor General for his assent unless:

(a) there has been an interval of not less than ninety days between the introduction of the bill in the House and beginning of the proceedings in the House on the second reading of the bill in that House;

(b) after it has been passed by both Houses of Parliament or, in the case of a bill to which section 55 of this Constitution applies, after its rejection by the Senate for the second time; and

(c) the bill has been approved on a referendum, held in accordance with such provisions as may be made in that behalf by Parliament, by not less than two-thirds of all the votes validly cast on that referendum.

Thus, the provision dealing with the regime for amendment of the Barbuda Local Government Act of 1976 has, by the provisions of the 1981 Antigua and Barbuda Constitution, become deeply entrenched.

Great credit is also due to the Barbudans that, in the years which have elapsed since 1981, the Barbudan representatives in both Houses of Parliament have taken part fully in the deliberations of these bodies and tried to settle their differences with the central government peacefully.

LAND IN BARBUDA

In the earlier part of this section reference was made to an address to the Lancaster House Conference by the Barbudan delegate to the Conference in which he stated he had produced to the Antigua Government, the British Colonial Secretary and the Foreign and Commonwealth Office documents which illustrated 'the obvious attempts by the Antigua Government to deprive Barbudans of their customary rights to the lands of their island acquired by them and their ancestors from time immemorial'.

This pronouncement confirms the fact that many Barbudans claim ownership of all the land in Barbuda because their forbears have lived and toiled the soil there ever since Codrington first received his grant from the English King in the 17th century. They claim all the land in the island as having devolved to them in a form of common tenancy; and it is that claim that has always bedevilled the relationship between the central government and the Barbudan community. But if the whole country is to develop as a unitary State it is imperative that the people of Barbuda – both now and in the future – should come to terms with the true legal position in so far as the ownership of land is concerned. Continued misunderstanding of this issue accounts in large measure for the bitterness and sense of grievance with which successive generations of Barbudans approach collaboration with the central government. It is for this reason that we now outline the statutory position and refer to some recent case law on the subject.

The provisions relevant to land in Barbuda are set out in ss 4–9 of the Barbuda Act, Cap 42 of the Laws of Antigua and Barbuda (hereafter referred to as 'the Act').

Section 2 of the Act repeals all ordinances of the State of Antigua, together with all rules, regulations, bylaws and other instruments made thereunder in so far as those provisions are repugnant to the provisions of the Act or to any bylaws or other instruments made thereunder.

Section 4 of the Act declares all lands in Barbuda to be vested in the Governor General on behalf of the Crown and are to be dealt with in accordance with the provisions of the ordinance.

Section 5(1) makes all inhabitants of Barbuda tenants of the Crown, holding land only under the provisions of the Act or any bylaw made by the council in that behalf.

Section 5(2) states: 'Nothing in this section shall be construed as precluding the grant by the Crown of any interest in or over any piece or parcel of land within Barbuda.'

Section 5(3) prescribes that:

Notwithstanding the provisions of any other law, no person shall acquire the ownership of any piece or parcel of Crown land within Barbuda by prescription.

Sub-sections (4), (5), (6), (7) and (8) of s 5 provide for redress in the High Court by way of compensation within a reasonable time if an inhabitant of Barbuda can show any material loss arising from a grant by the Crown in respect of the use he has been making of a piece of land held by virtue of s 5(1).

In contrast to the wide powers contained in s 5(2) where the Crown is able to convey any interest in land to anyone whether or not an inhabitant of Barbuda, limited powers are conferred on the Barbudan Council.

Section 6 of the Act confers powers on the council to allot, distribute and divide all land within the village (that is, of Codrington) amongst villagers subject to conditions contained in sub-paras (a)–(d). The enabling powers in ss 6, 7, 8 and 9 can be exercised only with the approval of Cabinet.

Cases on Barbuda land

Since independence several cases have been determined in the courts between the Barbuda Council and the central government concerning the grant of interests in Barbuda land. The cases are indicative of the degree of confrontation and acrimony which is the hallmark of the relationship between the two sides. They also bespeak the misconception which persists on this vexed question of land tenure. Despite submissions from legal representatives of the council to the contrary, the courts have consistently held that land in Barbuda is vested in the Crown which is competent to dispose of it, as provided in the Barbuda Act, while recognising that many Barbudans have traditionally been in undisputed possession of their allotments in the village of Codrington for more than two centuries. Four such cases will be considered.

In a case filed in the High Court in 1988 but not decided until 1994,[26] the issue before the court was whether the Barbuda Council was empowered by law to control the mining of sand in Barbuda and, if so, whether it was solely entitled to the revenue from the said sand-mining as well as to any other dues and taxes incidental thereto.

---

26 *Barbuda Council and AG* (Suit No 456 of 1988, High Court of Antigua and Barbuda).

Redhead J (as he then was) gave an extensive review of the powers of the council before and after independence. He also considered whether the council had the power to enact bylaws to change the system of allotment or distribution of land for villagers under s 13 of the Barbuda Act and came to the conclusion that it did not. At the same time, he ruled that the power under s 18(2)(a) 'to administer agriculture and forestry' did *not* give the council, as counsel had suggested, *control* over the land in Barbuda. But the council did have the power under the Act to collect dues arising from the sand-mining.

The second case to be examined is one which involved the lease of a parcel of land by a company for the purpose of erecting an hotel. The original question before the court was whether the council could unilaterally grant such a lease (as it had purported to do in 1996 by way of a resolution that did not specify the site of the project). The council had earmarked Spanish Point as a conservation area, but it was held that the council by itself had no such power since the power to set apart lands for public purposes (for example, to establish conservation areas and national parks) could only be lawfully exercised with the sanction and approval of Cabinet. It was also held that the council could not in any case grant a lease or concur in the grant of a lease of land which it did not own. That power vests in the Crown alone and is unfettered.[27]

Subsequently, on 27 November 1997 a lease was granted *by the Crown* to Unicorn Development Limited to develop the same area of 34.72 acres of land at Spanish Point for the erection of the hotel. The Barbuda Council then sought a declaration from the court[28] that the granting of the lease was unlawful. The court found that the area at Spanish Point had been set aside by the council for provision ground and that the council had not given its permission to changing the character of the land.

O'Meally J in that case found that the area within which Spanish Point is located was set apart as provision grounds well before 1915; that to alter the character of lands set apart as provision grounds, or as grazing land, requires the consent of the Barbuda Council which was not given. Nor was the consent of the council given to the granting of the lease.[29]

The case which should since 1989 have brought closure to the doubts as to the position of Barbudans in relation to land in Barbuda is *TH Frank and AG of Antigua and Barbuda* which went to the High Court and then to the Court of Appeal where it was dismissed.

At first instance, the judge (Mitchell J) gave a reasoned and erudite judgment (124 pages) in which he reviewed not only the history of the land problem in Barbuda, but a consideration of applicable case and statute law.

The court was asked to make a declaration:

(a) that on the island of Barbuda there was a system of land tenure under which all Barbudans are allotted plots for houses in or near Codrington Village which they occupy as of right and which on their deaths pass to their closest relatives;

27 *Unicorn Development Ltd and Barbuda Council* (Suit No 68 of 1998, High Court of Justice: Antigua and Barbuda), *per* Georges J.

28 See *Barbuda Council and AG* and *Unicorn Development Ltd* (Suit No 412 of 1998, High Court of Justice: Antigua and Barbuda).

29 Suit No 259 of 1985 (High Court of Justice, Antigua and Barbuda) judgment given on 22 November 1989 (appeal dismissed in Civil Appeal No 1 of 1990).

(b) that all Barbudans enjoy rights in common to graze animals and work provision grounds throughout the Island, save in those parts set apart for public use;

(c) that land can only be developed or granted to non-Barbudans with the consent of the people of Barbuda traditionally signified by a village meeting;

(d) that these customs and rights bind the Crown;

(e) that the Crown cannot lawfully grant Barbudan land for development or other purposes to any person in violation of the said customs and rights of the inhabitants of Barbuda; and

(f) that the section is invalid which gives the Crown the power to grant any interest in land in Barbuda to any person whether or not that person is an inhabitant of Barbuda – that section being s 2 of the Barbuda Ordinance (Amendment) Act 1982.

The applicant/plaintiff was a senator for Barbuda at the time of the initiation of the suit who later became the Member of the House of Representatives for Barbuda.

The trial judge was faced with a preliminary objection to dismiss the suit on the basis of *locus standi*, but was prepared to hear the arguments and to rule on the matter after so doing. In the event, the exercise turned out to be an educative one which should have given the Barbudans cause for pause.

The trial judge found, *inter alia*, as follows:

1 The lands vested in the Crown were not held in trust for any other person or group of persons.

2 It was the intention of the legislature in 1901 to create Barbuda inhabitants tenants at will who were tenants of the Crown – and that is still the position.

3 The tenants of the Crown in Barbuda were not tenants in common of a legal estate or a legal title in the land.

4 Section 15 of the 1901 Barbuda Ordinance swept away any previously loose or supposedly customary practice with regard to the occupation of areas of land in Barbuda, imposed the exclusive use of land apportioned for the erection and maintaining of houses for residence, the imposition of the obligation to pay when none existed before and stipulated a procedure for ejectment of the tenant in the event of non-payment of rent.

5 Section 19 of the 1904 ordinance concerning provision grounds restrains the indiscriminate use of land all over the island for provision cultivation and confers power on the council to set aside particular portions of land as provision grounds. No collective farm was created.

6 It is not correct to postulate that the inhabitant tenants of the land in Barbuda have rights in the land which they are exercising individually over what belonged to them collectively.

7 The construction to be placed on the provisions of the 1901 and 1904 ordinances (as amended) suggest that the inhabitants of Barbuda did not at any stage have *rights to the land* at all. The lands belonged to the Crown absolutely, but was originally granted to lessees. Later, after 1904 the Crown permitted the inhabitants to have a tenancy at will.

8   The lessees could not, between 1628 and 1898, as private persons have passed an interest in the land to the then inhabitants of Barbuda, who were living on the island without any status or recognised rights. Those lessees had no lawful authority to pass any such interest to the inhabitants.

9   The inhabitants did not before 1901 exercise customary rights. What they exercised were certain licences or practices. In this connection, the judge quoted what Lord Chancellor Hatherley had to say in the case of *Warrick v Queen's College*, 6 Ch 726:

> Where you find an undoubted exercise of a right (of long-continued duration) you must, if you can, find a legal origin for it. If you entirely fail in that, however long the apparent right may have been, you cannot establish it.

In this connection, the judge made this further statement:

> Even though there is the assertion of the exercise of a practice as stated over a long period, I find there is no legal origin for the exercise of those practices by the inhabitants of Barbuda.

10 Assuming, but not admitting, that the 1901 Ordinance did not sweep away, abolish or extinguish any practices or customary rights, if they existed: if however that Ordinance embraced and confirmed any or all the rights which previously existed by conceived custom or practice, the effect was what those rights became henceforward statutory rights and lower rights by custom or practice were merged into and extinguished by the higher statutory rights derived from the Ordinances.

11 On the matter of customary rights, this finally is what the judge had to say:

> If the 1901 Ordinance embraced and confirmed the practices of the inhabitants which existed before, and if those practices existed as custom, the said 1901 Ordinance was repealed by the provisions of section 3 of the 1904 Ordinance and replaced by the 1904 Ordinance.

> The result of that repeal of the 1901 statute dealing with the practices or customs of the inhabitants of Barbuda did not revive any right to any old practices or any customs as they stood before the repealed statute was passed.

12 The applicant Hilbourne Frank had no prescriptive right to any land in Barbuda against the Crown nor did the evidence in the case support any such finding in favour of anyone else in Barbuda.

13 The inhabitants of Barbuda have no customary enforceable rights against the Crown.

14 Such rights as the inhabitants of Barbuda then had were exercised by virtue of and in accordance with the legislative enactments since 1901.

15 Hilbourne Frank could not claim as an inhabitant of Barbuda, that he was suing on behalf of himself and the other inhabitants of Barbuda. After an examination of all the facts, the judge reached the conclusion that Frank did not have *locus standi* in the action.

16 All the declarations sought in the action were refused.

One finds it difficult not to wonder why, over a 16 year period since 1985, the Barbuda Council was in High Court litigation nine times as plaintiff and twice as defendant. This state of affairs underscores the soundness of the recommendation for an arbitral body, made by the Commonwealth Review Team, which in 2000 considered the relations between the central government and the council and to which further reference will be made later in this section.

The council

The powers of the Barbuda Council are very extensive indeed. It holds elections and there is a Supervisor of Elections 'who shall have charge of, and exercise general supervision over, the conduct of elections'.[30] The council is also empowered to make bylaws on a very wide variety of subjects,[31] including: the regulation of the supply and distribution of water; the prevention of waste and pollution of such water; the regulation of the supply and distribution of electricity and the imposition and collection of water rates and electricity rates. Such bylaws are not, however, to be repugnant with the laws of the State of Antigua.[32]

The council is also empowered to collect taxes and dues for *its own use* in respect of transactions carried out in the island, and such taxes include export duty;[33] excise;[34] trade licences;[35] tobacco duty;[36] tonnage duty;[37] tobacco control;[38] weights and measures;[39] licensing of intoxicating liquor;[40] hotels tax;[41] embarkation tax;[42] and vehicles and road traffic taxes.[43]

The Commonwealth Team 2000

In July 2000, a two person independent review team was appointed by the Commonwealth Secretary General in London to review the operation of the arrangements between the Antigua and Barbuda Government and the local council on Barbuda. This review had been agreed at the Antigua constitutional conference held at Lancaster House, London, in December 1980. The team consisted of Professor Dennis Benn of the University of the West Indies and Pierre Bienvenu, a leading Canadian lawyer.

The team reported in November 2000 when the Commonwealth Secretary General journeyed to Antigua to present the report.[44]

The team recommended that for the future there should be a mediating structure to discuss issues and reconcile differences and suggested such a purpose would be served by establishing a joint consultative committee to serve as a mediating medium within the existing constitutional and statutory arrangements.

---

30 See Pt IV of the Barbuda Local Government Act 1976 (Cap 44 of the Laws of Antigua and Barbuda).
31 *Ibid*, s 19.
32 *Ibid*, s 19(5).
33 The Export Ordinance (Cap 265).
34 The Excise Ordinance (Cap 136).
35 The Trade Licences Ordinance (Cap 273).
36 The Tobacco Duty Ordinance (Cap 271).
37 The Tonnage Duty Ordinance (Cap 272).
38 The Tobacco Control Ordinance (Cap 332).
39 The Weights and Measures Act (Cap 335).
40 The Licensing (Intoxicating Liquors) Act (Cap 268).
41 The Hotel Tax Ordinance 1962 (No 14 of 1962), as amended.
42 The Embarkation Tax Ordinance 1966 (No 3 of 1966), as amended.
43 The Vehicles and Road Traffic Ordinance (Cap 283).
44 See *Report of the Commonwealth Review Team,* to review the operation of the arrangements between the Government of Antigua and Barbuda and the Barbuda Local Council (Commonwealth Secretariat, Marlborough House, Pall Mall, London, SW1Y 5HX, UK, October 2000).

The committee would have an equal number of members from the central government and the Barbuda Council. The chairman would be a high-ranking official from the Prime Minister's Office with the chairman of the Barbuda Council or someone from the Council nominated by him being ice chair. The committee had already begun to hold meetings by July 2001. Initially, there would be monthly meetings and thereafter meetings would be held as the committee considers necessary. The main business of the committee would be to formulate a development plan for Barbuda in respect of the next 5–10 years – a plan which would involve the private sector no less than the Government and one in which both the central government and the Barbudans have a say. The committee would also serve as a mechanism for the resolution of sensitive issues about which there has been disagreement and when the committee cannot reach agreement it should be at liberty to refer the matter to an independent external mediator – such a decision being reached by a simple majority.

The team identified strengthening of human resources in the council as being a pre-requisite to the proper functioning of the council in several ways, including the preparation of budgets and expressed the wish that assistance should be forthcoming for capacity building from such organisations like the United Nations Development Programme and the Commonwealth Fund for Technical Co-operation.

It was also recommended in the team's report that:

> it would be useful that a neutral external agency, such as the Commonwealth Secretariat or another suitable international organisation, monitor progress in the implementation of the new arrangements and even offer, in the process, advice which could further improve their operation.

Constitution Review Commission

In the meantime, the Government of Antigua and Barbuda had, in December 1999, appointed a Constitution Review Commission (the commission) one of the terms of reference of which was to:

> ... review the administrative and constitutional arrangements between Antigua and Barbuda and to establish machinery to enhance these arrangements for the future to ensure the peaceful and orderly development of the state as a whole.

The commission, with the writer as its chairman, was to examine, consider and enquire into the Constitution of Antigua and Barbuda and other laws and matters generally and, after due examination, to furnish such recommendations as are considered necessary and desirable for promoting good government. Apart from being asked to examine the Barbuda situation the commission was to have special regard to:

(i) ensuring that parliamentary and multi-party democracy continues to enjoy constitutional protection;

(ii) establishing mechanisms to ensure that government, political parties, the media, the non-governmental organisations uphold and promote democracy and exercise responsibility and accountability in this regard;

(iii) strengthening the accountability of parliamentary representatives to their respective constituents;

(iv) strengthening the capacity of the public service to deliver efficient and responsive support in the administration and implementation of government programmes;

(v) strengthening the fundamental and basic rights, liberties and freedoms of the individual, and ensuring that there is no discrimination in the national life of the State;

(vi) strengthening government machinery for transparency and accountability in the management of public funds; and

(vii) evaluating the benefits, if any, for changing from a monarchical to a republican system of government and making recommendations in respect of any changes in the executive form of government that result from such an evaluation.

It was also asked to make recommendations on how the present constitution can be patriated and to examine the desirability of retaining or abolishing the Senate.

In the period during which the commission carried out its work, it visited the Island of Barbuda to hear representations from its council and people. For the same purpose, it traversed the length and breadth of the Island of Antigua. It interviewed NGOs and heads of government departments and commissions. It heard from both the Prime Minister and the Leader of the Opposition. From those contacts and its interaction with the media, the commission was left in no doubt that a strong awareness was being developed of how a constitution could become out of date, if not irrelevant, and why it should be amended 21 years after independence. The commission's report will be submitted to the Governor General towards the end of February 2002 and, when considered with the report of the Commonwealth Review Team already referred to, one can only hope that its recommendations will go some way towards producing a revised constitution that will have the effect of strengthening democracy in the State and fostering future peace and prosperity.

The commission has been urged to recommend as follows:

1 There should be a non-executive presidential form of government with a President as Head of State, sharing powers of a limited nature with the Prime Minister who would continue as the executive Head of Government.

2 The existing service commissions should continue as at present but a Teaching Service Commission should be added.

3 The electoral laws should be revised: the existing legislation having outlived its usefulness.

4   As far as Barbuda is concerned, there should be enshrined in a revised constitution a joint consultative committee on the lines recommended by the Commonwealth Review Team in 2000.

5   If the public service is to perform efficiently and effectively, government should pay more attention to standards of qualification of new entrants to the service (and to the number of such entrants) who are classified as non-established. At the same time, the commission appreciated the need in the developing State of Antigua and Barbuda of recruiting professional and technical advisers who are non-established employees.

6   The second chamber of Parliament (the Senate) should be retained but its members should be elected on a basis of proportional representation.

7   Local Government bodies should be enshrined in a revised constitution in order that more members of the community could share in the business of government.

8   A team of experts should urgently be put to work to assist in bringing up to date the annual public accounts of the country (which have not been submitted to the director of audit since 1992) so that there can be conformity with the terms of s 97(2)(b) of the constitution.

9   Government should embark on a sustained educational programme (involving all sections of the community with the help of the NGOs, the UWI, the UNDP, the OAS and international institutions), with a view to educating the public on a long-term basis about the contents and objectives of a constitution. Thereafter, a constituent assembly should be set up to finalise a draft revised instrument and to promulgate it as the patriated constitution.

10   The provisions for fundamental rights and freedoms should be reworded to express them in terms intelligible to the layman. They should be expressed in positive rather than negative terms and not restricted to civil and political rights; disadvantaged members of the society who, because of lack of resources are unable to access the courts, should be given legal aid for the purpose. A new charter of rights along the lines of the Jamaica Charter should become part of the revised document.

BARBADOS

The Cox and Forde Commissions

As far as this territory is concerned, there are two major points of constitutional importance to which attention must be drawn between 1966 and 2001, viz, the Barbados *Reports of the Constitution Review Commissions* of 1979 and 1998, the terms of reference of which were, *inter alia*, to report in writing, making such recommendations and providing for consideration such amendments, reforms and changes in the constitution and related laws and administrative procedures as are, in the opinion of the commissioners, necessary and desirable for promoting the peace, order and good government of Barbados.

We first turn our attention to some of the recommendations of the Constitution Commission of 1979 (hereafter referred to as the Cox Commission).

Here then are some of the more important findings of the Cox Commission:

1   *The Constitution should be repatriated.*[45] In this connection we have already made reference to such a constitution promulgated by Belize at the time of its independence in 1981.

2   The monarchical system should be retained[46] and any *change in the form of government to a republican system should first be referred to the electorate at a general election.*[47]

3   (a)   Provision *should be made for freedom to vote and to form political parties*[48] *as one way of ensuring constitutional protection to multi-party parliamentary democracy.*

     (b)   There should be an independent *Boundaries and Electoral Commission.*[49]

     (c)   There should be a provision that members of either House of Parliament should not engage in contracts with the Government unless such contracts are duly disclosed to the House in respect of which the contracting party is a member and the House expressly approves the involvement of the member in the contractual arrangement.

4   The following new provisions should be entrenched under section 49(2) of the Constitution:

     (a)   the right to vote of every citizen of 18 or over;

     (b)   the right to the formation of political parties;

     (c)   the division of Barbados into constituencies;

     (d)   the appointment and functions of the Boundaries and Electoral Commission;

     (e)   the restriction on the extension of the life of Parliament;

     (f)   provision for the appointment of the Public Accounts Committee; and

     (g)   the method of amending the Constitution.

5   *The functions of the Senate should be expanded to cover Money Bills.*[50]

6   *Provision should be made in the Constitution for a Deputy Prime Minister and an Attorney General.*[51]

7   *The Prime Minister should be permitted to resign without ceasing to be a Member of the Assembly.*[52]

8   The appointment of judges should be effected (as was the case between 1966 and 1974) by the Judicial and Legal Service Commission instead of on the advice of the Prime Minister after consultation with the Leader of the Opposition.[53]

---

45   *Report of the Commission Appointed to Review the Constitution and to Consider a System of National Honours and a National Table of Precedence*, para 3, under the chairmanship of Sir Mencea Cox.

46   *Ibid*, para 43.

47   *Ibid*, para 44.

48   *Ibid*, para 69(ii).

49   *Ibid*, para 69(iii).

50   *Ibid*, para 89.

51   *Ibid*, para 92.

52   *Ibid*, para 93.

53   *Ibid*, para 104.

9   The Constitution should be amended to provide:

   (a) that laws existing before independence should not automatically prevail over the fundamental rights clauses of the Constitution;[54]

   (b) that the age in respect of deprivation of property under section 16(2) of the Constitution should be reduced from 21 years to 18 years;[55] and

   (c) that the High Court should have jurisdiction to redress a fundamental breach of the Constitution even where adequate means of redress are or have been available to persons aggrieved under any other law. See Proviso to section 24(2) of the Constitution.[56]

Altogether the Cox Commission in 1979 made 64 recommendations, only three of which were implemented by 1998, and the Forde Commission reporting in 1999 were clearly embarrassed by this inaction and put its thoughts on the matter as follows:

   Much of what was said in that Report is still pertinent and applicable today ... We do not speculate on the reasons for, nor do we pass judgment on, the failure to date to implement any more than three of their sixty-four recommendations.[57]

The Forde Commission then proceeded to add another 20 recommendations, some of which repeated what had been advocated in 1979.

   The 1998 commission dealt with the following matters:

   The Preamble should be re-written.[58]

   The section naming the Constitution as the supreme law should be retained.[59]

   The responsibilities of the citizen to uphold the rule of law should be spelt out.[60]

   As regards citizenship, children born in Barbados should be deemed citizens at birth only where at least one parent is a citizen of Barbados, a permanent resident, an immigrant of Barbados or a person registered under the Immigration Act of 1996.[61]

   A child under the age of 18, neither of whose parents is a citizen, who is adopted by a citizen of Barbados shall, upon application, be registered as a citizen of Barbados.[62]

   Dual and multiple citizenship should be retained.

   Persons who are prohibited immigrants should not be permitted to obtain citizenship by marriage.[63]

   The Constitution should be amended to allow the non-national spouses of Barbadian-born persons to be equally treated, subject to matters of policy regarding marriage of

---

54   *Op cit*, Cox Commission, fn 45, paras 19–21(a).
55   *Op cit*, Cox Commission, fn 45, para 21(b).
56   *Op cit*, Cox Commission, fn 45, paras 17 and 21(c).
57   See the *Report of the Forde Commission*, para 1.
58   *Ibid*, Chapter 3.7.
59   *Ibid*, Chapter 4.6.
60   *Ibid*, Chapter 5.9.
61   *Ibid*, 6.14.
62   *Ibid*, 6.16.
63   *Ibid*.

convenience.[64] [This matter of preventing persons who engage in sham marriages from qualifying for citizenship has also been dealt with by the Commission.][65]

Protection of fundamental rights

The commission repeated the now familiar cry for simplification of the language of the constitution, 'in order to make its meaning clear to non-specialists'.[66] The rights should also be expressed in positive rather than negative terms.[67]

It considered that *gender* should be included in the definition of 'discriminatory'.[68]

It repeated the recommendation of the 1979 Cox Commission that the constitution should enshrine the right of every citizen to vote and form a political party. (See para 69II of the *Cox Commission Report*.)[69]

It came to the conclusion that 'the apparatus for the vindication of those rights remains largely remote and theoretical for many ordinary people', and suggested adoption of a proposal by the Trinidad and Tobago 1974 Wooding Commission that the High Court should be empowered to order that the costs of an unsuccessful claimant in proceedings for the enforcement of a right protected by the constitution should be borne by the State where:

(a) the point of law raised in the proceedings is one of public importance; and

(b) it was reasonable to institute proceedings given the particular circumstances of the case.[70]

Existing law clause

Section 26 of the constitution provides for the saving of existing written law by excluding from the purview of the human rights provisions any law that was enacted before 30 November 1966 (the date of Barbados independence), 'and has continued to be part of the law of Barbados at all times since that day'. The Forde Commission endorsed the view of the Cox Commission that this law protects pre-independence laws from challenge on constitutional grounds and agreed that the section has the effect of eroding the supremacy of the constitution and should be deleted.[71] This is a matter on which Caribbean scholars have dealt for some time. (See the erudite writing of Dr Francis Alexis on this subject.)[72]

---

64 *Op cit*, Forde Commission, fn 57, 6.26.
65 *Op cit*, Forde Commission, fn 57, 6.35.
66 *Op cit*, Forde Commission, fn 57, 7.2.
67 *Op cit*, Forde Commission, fn 57, 7.3.
68 *Op cit*, Forde Commission, fn 57, 7.12.
69 *Op cit*, Forde Commission, fn 57, 7.18–21.
70 *Op cit*, Forde Commission, fn 57, 7.22–28.
71 *Op cit*, Forde Commission, fn 57, 7.40.
72 See Francis Alexis' erudite article (Alexis, 1976).

Head of State

The commission recommended that Barbados should become a 'parliamentary republic' the Head of State of which should be a President, who would replace the Queen of England. Executive power would continue to be exercised by a Cabinet, with the Head of Government being the Prime Minister.[73]

The President would be a citizen of Barbados by birth or descent, not less than 40 years of age, who has been resident in Barbados for a period of at least five years prior to election.[74]

He should hold office for a fixed term of seven years.[75] His election should be by an electoral college comprising the Senate and the House of Assembly: 10 senators, the Speaker and 14 other members of the House of Assembly forming a quorum.[76]

In other respects, the regime for this election and removal will be identical to the regime currently in place in Trinidad and Tobago as well as in Dominica. This is set out in Chapters 9 and 11 above, respectively.

Parliament

The main change recommended under this head concerns the *composition* of the Senate, though it is recommended that its number remains the same.

The recommendations are as follows.

(a) Where there is a Leader of the Opposition –

  (i) *12* senators to be appointed on the Prime Minister's advice;

  (ii) *four* on the advice of the Leader of the Opposition;

  (iii) if there are members of a political party who do not support the Prime Minister or the Leader of the Opposition; *two* senators to be appointed acting on the advice of that political party or parties (where there is more than one such party);

  (iv) if there is no such party as described in (iii), *two* Senators appointed in the President's own discretion after consultation with the leader of any political party supported by the votes of at least 10% of all those who voted in the election, as well as such other persons as the President would wish to consult;[77]

  (v) *three* senators to be appointed by the President in his discretion after consultation with such persons as he considers should be consulted.

(b) Where there is no Leader of the Opposition –

  (i) *12* Senators to be appointed on the advice of the Prime Minister;

73   *Op cit*, Forde Commission, fn 57, 8.1–11.
74   *Op cit*, Forde Commission, fn 57, 8.12.
75   *Op cit*, Forde Commission, fn 57, 8.14.
76   *Op cit*, Forde Commission, fn 57, 8.19.
77   *Op cit*, Forde Commission, fn 57, 9.4.1.

(ii) *six* by the President after consultation 'with the leader of any party receiving at least ten percent of the votes in the election and such other persons as the President may wish to consult';

(iii) *three* senators by the President in his own discretion, 'after consultation with such interests as he wishes to consult'.[78]

It was also recommended that the constitution be amended to permit the Senate to debate money resolutions before expenditure on such resolutions are authorised.[79] (This is a repetition of a recommendation previously made by the Cox Commission, para 89.)

The only other substantive recommendations relating to Parliament made by the Forde Commission concerns parliamentary committees which, in the submission of the commission, should be given adequate financial resources and appropriate staff, 'so that they may better be able to ensure government accountability and to provide opportunities for concerned and interested persons to make representations to Parliament through its committees on issues that affect the community'.[80] (Exactly how this expanded committee system would operate, and in respect of what subjects, has not been made clear by the Commission.)

Ministers going from House to House

The commission recommended that a minister who is a member of one House of Parliament should have the right to attend the sitting of the other House and take part in any debate or other proceeding of that House relating to a matter for which the minister has been assigned responsibility under the constitution.[81] Such an arrangement is already in existence and works most satisfactorily in Antigua and Barbuda. (See the Antigua and Barbuda Constitution.)[82]

The judicature

It was recommended that senior judicial personnel should be appointed as follows:

The *Chief Justice* should be appointed by the President on the joint nomination of the Prime Minister and the Leader of the Opposition after they have consulted the Judicial and Legal Service Commission.[83]

Other judges are to be appointed by the President on the recommendation of the Judicial and Legal Service Commission after the Commission has consulted the Prime Minister and the Leader of the Opposition.[84]

---

78 *Op cit*, Forde Commission, fn 57, 9.4.2.
79 *Op cit*, Forde Commission, fn 57, 9.6.
80 *Op cit*, Forde Commission, fn 57, 9.14.
81 *Op cit*, Forde Commission, fn 57, 10.21.
82 Antigua and Barbuda Constitution Order 1981 (SI 1981/1106), s 37.
83 *Op cit*, Forde Commission, fn 57, 11.10.1.
84 *Op cit*, Forde Commission, fn 57, 10.11.2.

The Chief Justice and other judges should have a retirement age of 72,[85] but the Head of State, after consulting with the Prime Minister and the Leader of the Opposition, may authorise the Chief Justice to continue in office until he is 75.[86]

Removal of judges

In view of the proposed new constitutional arrangements whereby Barbados would become a republic, the regime for removing members of the senior judiciary would naturally need to be altered. The new recommendation is as follows:

> Advice that the question of removing a Judge from office for inability to discharge the functions of his office or for misbehaviour should in future be tendered to the Head of State by the Judicial and Legal Service Commission *after consultation with the Prime Minister and the Chief Justice.* Advice relative to the removal of the Chief Justice should be tendered to the Head of State by the Judicial and Legal Service Commission after consultation with the Prime Minister and the Leader of the Opposition.[87]

The commission also recommended that the Head of State should then refer the matter to a tribunal after consultation with the Prime Minister, the Leader of the Opposition, the Judicial and Legal Service Commission and – except where the Chief Justice himself is the subject of investigation – the Chief Justice.

> The tribunal will hear and determine whether, for any of the stated reasons, the judge ought to be removed and will so advise the Head of State who will be required to act on that advice.[88]

The magistracy

The commission considered the constitutional position of the magistrates and recommended that the magistracy should be recognised in the constitution as part of the judicial system of the country:[89] the whole question to form the subject of an urgent and detailed study by the Government.[90]

Integrity Commission

The Forde Commission recommended the creation in the constitution of an Integrity Commission to receive declarations, assets, liabilities and income of Members of Parliament, with powers to investigate any declaration.[91] The Barbados political directorate may wish to consider the doubtful views of the Trinidad Hyatali Commission on the value of this institution in halting corruption (see Chapter 9, above).

---

85   *Op cit*, Forde Commission, fn 57, 11.16
86   *Op cit*, Forde Commission, fn 57, 11.17.
87   *Op cit*, Forde Commission, fn 57, 11.27.
88   *Op cit*, Forde Commission, fn 57, 11.28.
89   *Op cit*, Forde Commission, fn 57, 11.33.
90   *Op cit*, Forde Commission, fn 57, 11.34.
91   *Op cit*, Forde Commission, fn 57, Chapter 15, para 11, p 101.

The Privy Council

The Forde Commission recommended the abolition of the Barbados Privy Council and in its place the enshrinement, in the revised constitution, of a Presidential Council in which members would have a seven year term instead of a 15 year term. The existing maximum age of 75 years for service on this body should be removed.[92] It would continue to deal with the exercise of the prerogative of mercy and could cease to hear appeals in disciplinary matters from public officers who would have the right to opt to have their disciplinary matters heard either by the Presidential Council or the new Public Service Appeal Board.[93]

Service commissions

The commission recommended:

(a) the establishment of a Protective Services Commission[94] with responsibility for the appointment, removal, organisation and discipline of the police, fire and prison services (under the existing arrangement the police service is served by the Police Service Commission while the fire and prison officers come within the purview of the Public Service Commission); and

(b) the establishment of a Teaching Service Commission.[95]

The appointment of chairmen and members of the above commissions, which should all have separately staffed secretariats, is to be made by the Head of State after consultation with the Prime Minister and Leader of the Opposition and such other persons as the Head of State may consider desirable.

Public Service Appeal Board

The Forde Commission took a leaf out of the book of the Trinidad 1990 *Hyatali Commission Report* in recommending that this board should have:

(i)   a Chairman who should be a retired judge who is a citizen of Barbados, and

(ii) two other members, one of whom should be a retired public officer.[96]

Public Service Boards of Appeal have, however, been enshrined in the constitutions of the Organisation of Eastern Caribbean States territories since 1967 to hear appeals in disciplinary matters from the Public Service Commission as well as the Police Service Commission.

Summary

Such are the recommendations made by the Forde Commission in 1999.

---

92   *Op cit*, Forde Commission, fn 57, Chapter 15, para 15, p 103.
93   *Op cit*, Forde Commission, fn 57, Chapter 12, para 12.45, p 24.
94   *Op cit*, Forde Commission, fn 57, Chapter 15, para 18(c), p 104.
95   *Op cit*, Forde Commission, fn 57, Chapter 15, para 18(b), p 104.
96   *Op cit*, Forde Commission, fn 57, Chapter 12, paras 12.44–49, p 74.

One recommendation, viz, the change in the Head of State, has at the time of writing (January 2001) already attracted much attention: a resolution having been passed in the House of Assembly for the holding of a referendum to test the feeling of the electorate on the issue.

One can only express the hope that the other recommendations will not suffer the fate of those of the Cox Commission – remaining dormant in the files of the powers that be, as so often happens to reports of Caribbean commissions. One thing is certain, the televised sessions and the radio coverage of the Commission's deliberations over a two year period could not fail to acquaint the Barbados people as to how the country was being governed and to give them an insight into the deficiencies of the present constitution. But even after the report was submitted, there is still much work to be done in that regard and the education process must begin in the schools and be carried on by all sections of the community on a sustained basis.

JAMAICA

Introduction

Jamaica has had a long and colourful constitutional history which has been documented in many well researched volumes.[97] In this work, it will suffice if we point out that the island has been subjected to typical colonial domination since 1655 when it was conquered and colonised under Cromwell's 'Great Western Design' by Puritan and Jewish emigrants. Thereafter, we find a situation in all the islands in which the assemblies became the mouthpiece of the white and creole communities, who tended to obstruct any legislative or other measure that was not in their interests. Their attitude was that the assembly was a Jamaica House of Commons and should be treated as such.[98]

It had been widely felt that, after the surrender of the old representative system, which took place in 1865 following the famous Morant Bay Riots, Jamaica was no longer in the hands of the planter class since by then the emancipated slaves were, as a group, beginning to make their powers felt. Trevor Munroe questions this assumption. His view is that the gubernatorial autocracy which was a feature of the new order (pure Crown colony rule) 'did not seriously interrupt the traditional patterns of power in the plantation society'. Although there was more identity at this stage with the new social order brought about by emancipation, the Governor tended to be guided in his actions by the social clique of which he was inevitably an integral part.[99] The writer respectfully agrees with Dr Munroe.

Even Sir Sydney Olivier, a well known Fabian Socialist and a sympathetic Governor who understood the negroes and their aspirations, could say as late as 1936 in his memoirs that the Crown colony system was working well and that Jamaica was not yet

---

97 See particularly Barnett, 1977; Munroe, 1972; and Lewis, 1968; as well as Eaton, 1975; and Nettleford, 1971.
98 See Whitson, 1929, p 159.
99 Munroe, 1972, pp 11, 12.

ready for responsible government.[100] But such a statement contrasted sharply with a view held nearly 100 years previously, in 1849, by Earl Grey, then Secretary of State, that Jamaica should have been given the same measure of responsible government as Canada – a view which was of course summarily rejected by the local white oligarchy at the time.

Constitutional development since 1944

In all the Caribbean islands throughout the 19th century there was a great gulf fixed between the legislature and the executive; and it was pressure from the local council after emancipation that led to the establishment of an Executive Committee of the Privy Council in Barbados and Jamaica. This committee was to be a link between the Governor and the assembly and it would have the power of proposing Money Bills in the name of the Crown and of advising the Governor generally in the preparation of estimates. In this particular change, Jamaica led the way, followed by Barbados, Tobago, St Kitts, St Vincent, Nevis and Antigua. However, the Committee was to fail in all the islands except Barbados and Jamaica. When, in 1944, Jamaica received a measure of internal self-government, this Executive Committee was to become the Cabinet, but it is of some interest that both these territories have reserved a Privy Council, the functions of which are to exercise the prerogative of mercy and to review disciplinary cases for civil servants.

Jamaica's lead in upgrading its constitution was to be followed by Trinidad (1956), Barbados (1959), and the Windward and Leeward Islands (1959). Between 1962 (when Jamaica and Trinidad became independent) and 1984, the area was to witness the independence of nine other territories in the Caribbean.[101] This period of 22 years must therefore be regarded as the most active period constitutionally since Columbus discovered these islands more than 500 years ago.

Jamaica has so far not had an eventful or turbulent post-independence constitutional history. In the first 10 years of its independence, the country continued to follow the even tenor of its way.

In 1972, the Government in power was one which espoused the doctrine of 'democratic socialism' or (as some of its adherents would describe it) 'scientific socialism'. Consistent with this ideology, the Government was moving in the direction of republicanism and a constitutional committee was working on the review of the constitution. Also, consistent with its political beliefs, the Government distanced itself from such trappings as British honours and, even though the regime remained monarchical in form, the Governor General was not – as is usual where the Head of State is the Queen, represented locally by a Governor General – permitted to receive from Her Majesty the honour of Knight Grand Cross of the Most Distinguished Order of St Michael and St George (GCMG) during the period that Michael Manley, Prime Minister, and his Government (the People's National Party) remained in office from 1972–80. Nor did Manley himself become a member of Her Majesty's Privy Council. Shortly after Edward Seaga, political leader of the Jamaica Labour Party (JLP), became Prime Minister after

---

100 Lewis, 1968, p 109.
101 Barbados 1966; Guyana 1966; Bahamas 1973; Grenada 1974; Dominica 1978; St Lucia and St Vincent 1979; Antigua 1981; St Kitts/Nevis 1983.

leading his party to victory in 1980, both honours referred to above were conferred on the Governor General and the Prime Minister, respectively.

Under the Manley regime, too, Jamaica aligned itself closely with Cuba, which is its closest neighbour to the north, and with the Soviet Union, with which it entered into trade agreements while at the same time being an active member of the Caribbean Community, CARICOM.

Thus both on the political and economic fronts, the leaders in the Caribbean, over the period under review, came to terms with what became known in the area as 'ideological pluralism'. Guyana, Grenada and Jamaica, up to 1980, followed a socialist, eastern bloc pattern of development while the other territories pursued a capitalist western line. We have already considered how prevailing ideological thinking affected the Grenada 1974 Independence Constitution between 1979 and 1983, as well as the making of the new Guyana Socialist Constitution of 1980.

In Jamaica, on the other hand, the JLP consistently attacked the leftist leadings of the People's National Party (PNP) and attributed the grave economic situation in the country to the fact that no new capital investment was coming to the country while, at the same time, there was a flight of capital by those who had previously invested in Jamaica. There is no doubt whatever that there was a dramatic flight of *talent* and the author was able to see at first hand in the course of his frequent visits to Jamaica on business what a considerable brain-drain developed in the country between 1974 and 1980. Doctors, lawyers, architects, engineers and accountants left Jamaica in droves to settle mainly in the United States and Canada. (Incidentally, Guyana has since 1970 experienced a similar brain-drain.)

Whether the economic situation in Jamaica is, as so many allege, inextricably tied to the former Marxist persuasion of the PNP is, however, questionable since three years after the JLP took office the economy of the country continued in serious trouble. As one taxi driver said with an air of resignation to the author: 'Under the People's National Party Government there was money in our pockets, but nothing in the shops for the money to buy. Now under the Jamaica Labour Party Government there is much merchandise in the shops, but no money with which to purchase it.'

The apologists for the Seaga regime, however, insist that the economic calamity later experienced was the direct result of the mismanagement inherited from the previous PNP rule.

With the abolition of Communism, there has been a return from the socialist direction in which it had been headed to a pro-western capitalist system.[102]

Despite a sense of gloom over the plight of the Jamaican people, all changes of government since independence in 1962 were happily achieved via the ballot box, although sometimes accompanied by some degree of violence. It is also a commentary on that people's peace-loving nature that the 1983 development discussed below unfolded against a backdrop of decreased violence.

---

102 In the volume entitled *Jamaica's Michael Manley ... Messiah ... Muddler ... or Marionette,* under the *nom de plume* Christopher Arawak, the author of the volume poses the question: 'Has this disastrous experiment with "Democratic Socialism" wrecked Jamaica's economy beyond repair?'

Constitutional impasse in Jamaica in 1983

The outstanding issue of post-independence constitutional significance in this country between 1977 and 2002 relates to the political impasse under which the PNP boycotted the general elections called in 1983 by the Government – the JLP – in the circumstances set out below.

The Westminster system of parliamentary politics contemplates both a Government in power and an Opposition. These two opposing forces play according to the procedural rules of the game inside and outside of Parliament. Indeed, the Jamaica Constitution has prescribed a number of situations in which the Opposition, outside Parliament, has to be consulted if the machinery is to be seen to be running smoothly.

Let us therefore look at the position and status of the Opposition under the Jamaica Constitution, as well as its functions.

First of all, the Leader of the Opposition is appointed by the Governor General by instrument under the Broad Seal and this functionary is the member of the House of Representatives who, in the Governor General's judgment:

> ... is best able to command the support of those members who do not support the Government or if there is no such person, the member of the House who commands the support of the largest single group of such members who are prepared to support one leader.[103]

The following appointments can be made only by the Governor General on the recommendation of the Prime Minister *after he has consulted with the Leader of the Opposition:*

(a) the appointment of the Chief Justice – s 98(1) of the constitution;

(b) the appointment of the President of the Court of Appeal – s 104(1);

(c) the three appointed members of the Judicial and Legal Services Commission – s 111(3);

(d) the members of the Public Services Commission – s 124(1); and

(e) the members of the Police Services Commission – s 129(2).

Even when it is desired to extend the length of service of the Director of Public Prosecutions beyond the normal retiring age, the extension may be effected by the Governor General only on the recommendation of the Prime Minister after he has consulted the Leader of the Opposition (s 96(1)(b) of the Constitution).

The constitution then goes on to prescribe that:

> During any period in which there is a vacancy in the office of Leader of the Opposition by reason of the fact that no person is both qualified in accordance with the Constitution for, or unwilling to accept, appointment to that office, the Governor General shall act in accordance with the advice of the Prime Minister in any matter in respect of which it is provided in this Constitution either:
>
> (a) that the Governor General shall act on the advice of the Leader of the Opposition; or

---

103 See the Jamaica (Constitution) Order in Council 1962, Sched 2 (hereafter referred to simply as the 'Jamaica 1962 Constitution'), s 80.

(b) that the Governor General shall act on the recommendation of the Prime Minister after he has consulted with the Leader of the Opposition.[104]

Thus it is envisaged in the constitution that a situation might conceivably arise when there is no Leader of the Opposition and, as the law stands at present, it is possible for the country to operate without an Opposition. As a matter of practical politics, however, the long term effects on the country would be disastrous if the Government were at any time to use the permanent absence of the Opposition over a prolonged period as an opportunity to effectuate legislative measures which were themselves unpopular to a large section of the populace. In making this statement, the author does not propose in this work to attempt to apportion blame to either the Government or the Opposition, even if he were in possession of the facts. It is, however, common knowledge that the Government resigned and asked for a dissolution when a member of the Opposition accused the Prime Minister of misleading Parliament by stating that Jamaica had passed an International Monetary Fund test when, in fact, it had failed the test. The Prime Minister duly obliged, on the ground that the point was well taken and resignation was the proper course to follow in the circumstances.

Caribbean politicians are not usually as ready to give up political office as the Jamaican leader demonstrated in this case, and it is difficult to avoid the conclusion that the Opposition played into the Government's hands and gave them a golden opportunity which they would not otherwise have had. The Opposition promptly raised a hue and cry, claiming that the resignation demanded was intended to be that of the Minister of Finance. But, in this case, the Minister of Finance happened to be the Prime Minister.

The Opposition, of course, accused the Government of a breach of faith since (it was alleged) the Government had promised that there would be no further general election until the electoral register had been revised and brought up to date and that this event had not yet taken place. The Prime Minister's retort was that the call for resignations superseded any such promise (which in any event he refused to concede had been given as a precondition to the holding of elections as suggested by the Opposition).

The Opposition then decided to boycott the general elections and the result of this regrettable parliamentary contretemps was that the JLP held all the seats in a 60 seat House of Representatives with a normal term spanning 1983–88.

The Leader of the Opposition, however, stated that although the Prime Minister would have the Parliament, he would have 'the people'. Also, in early 1984, there were statements appearing in the national press of an 'Opposition in Exile'. Meantime, the Opposition took to holding a monthly ex-Parliament forum at the Sports Stadium in Kingston at which matters of moment being discussed in Parliament were raised: all participants being given an opportunity to express their views thereon.

In the words of Professor Rex Nettleford, a political analyst:

It is all these things which rob power, or those who have it, of moral authority which in the final analysis is what matters. It is easy to win an election, in such circumstances, and yet lose the country.[105]

---

104 *Ibid*, s 81.

105 See article entitled, 'Nettleford warns of winning election and losing country' (1983) *Trinidad Guardian*, 6 December, p 17.

The Prime Minister of the country, while regretting the decision of the Opposition not to contest the elections, expressed the view that the PNP pushed the Government 'into a position where they had to go to the people'.

It was nevertheless obvious that the Prime Minister felt some sense of unease with a situation which resulted in a one party House – even though it may not have been of his own creation. He therefore proposed that there should be a novel form of public participation in parliamentary debates during the life of the House. He, also, claimed to have selected eight of the 21 senators from persons in no way affiliated to his JLP:[106] these being the senators who in the ordinary course of events would have been nominated by the Leader of the Opposition after a general election.

There can be no doubt that the former of these two measures is novel, if not unprecedented, but it was an indication of the desire of the Government in power to pay attention to non-party voices in the running of the country's affairs, which voices might well have been dissentient.

It was interesting to hear what Prime Minister Seaga had to say about the absence of the Opposition when he was sworn in:[107]

> Their absence from the House has aroused fears that debates will be one-sided. This would indeed be the case and such fears would be justified if we took no steps to compensate for this absence of a formal Opposition in the House.

> But in keeping with what is our expressed and over-riding intention to encourage opportunities for the expression of opposing views, it is not our intention that the House of Representatives should be a forum of debate with views from one side only.

> Accordingly, I propose to establish a procedure using a little-known and less used provision in the Standing Orders which regulate debate in Parliament which enables any person or group having an interest in a matter under debate to make a presentation to Parliament by appearing at the Bar of the House. Open invitations will be given to any participant wishing to participate in debates on legislation to do so. In practice, when the House resolves itself into Committee as it must do in the passage of any Bill, the public will be invited to comment at this stage.

> If the matter under consideration is complex a Select Committee of the House or of the House and Senate will be set up to allow further detailed examination of the measure under debate and participating groups will have the further opportunity to engage in this examination until a product is ready for final approval of Parliament.

> In plain language, the whole wide range of talent which this country produces representing the whole wide range of interests which this country has, will be the panel from which capable and expert opposition will be drawn to engage in debate and frame legislation.

> Like the proposed new Senate this will without doubt produce a Parliament of more vigorous high-level debate in the House of Representatives.

> Parliament without an elected Opposition is far from dead. It is far more likely to come alive in a dynamic manner attracting greater interest in debate and being truly a forum for the widest cross-section of views than ever before.

---

106 (1983) *Jamaica Daily Gleaner*, 30 November.
107 (1983) *Jamaica Daily Gleaner*, 21 December: ss C C1 and C5.

> And I have no doubt that appearing before the Bar of the Jamaican Parliament will prove more interesting, rewarding, useful and purposeful than any appearance at the bar of the Pegasus Parliament.
>
> Again, making bold use of this little used procedure to openly admit public comments from the Bar of the House will generate a dynamic tradition, begun in our 21st Year of Independence which I believe will never be erased from future parliamentary life for it will give a voice of greater strength to the people, a direct channel to communicate with Parliament which public interest groups will never wish to surrender or have retracted or down-graded by any Parliament of the future.

Thus, while there was no formal opposition in the House of Representatives, members of the general public representing specific interests were able to appear and speak during the committee stages of a Bill at the Bar of the House. At the same time, the *Senate* had the advantage of hearing an independent and almost certainly non-party approach to many matters canvassed in that body. Altogether it was in the writer's opinion a most commendable effort to show to the world that the Government was ready to 'hear the other side', to entertain criticism and not to exercise a rule of tyrants. It was interesting, too, to see statements from individual non-party senators,[108] statements in which the legislators expressed laudable views of the way they intended, through this medium, to assist in the deliberations of Parliament.

One thing emerged from all this, viz, that the Prime Minister of Jamaica, despite the absence of the Opposition, made every effort to ensure that Parliament functioned as intended. At the same time, the Opposition elected also to play its part 'in exile'.

Their forum meetings in the Stadium likewise, it is hoped, went a long way toward involving the populace in the business of government.

This could therefore be a case where, in the ultimate analysis, out of political evil came much constitutional good.

Constitutional reform proposals

It was no doubt on account of situations such as those described in the immediately preceding pages that a process of constitutional review began in Jamaica in 1991 with the formation of a Joint Select Committee on Constitutional and Electoral Reform, charged with recommending 'the precise form and content of constitutional amendments both with regard to an Electoral Commission and other aspects of reform'.

After a series of meetings and after considering a proposal from the Leader of the Opposition for the establishment of a Constituent Assembly to frame a new constitution the Joint Select Committee recommended that Parliament should establish a Constitution Commission to examine proposals from 'the public as well as to initiate discussions on points raised by its own membership'.

The Commission was duly appointed under the chairmanship of Mr Justice James Kerr – a distinguished legal luminary – whereupon Parliament in February 1992 suspended the work of the Joint Select Committee. The Commission in turn convened 36

---

108 See two statements from Mr Keith Worrell and Mr Errol Miller published in the 2 January 1984 and the 5 January 1984 issues of the *Daily Gleaner* respectively.

meetings, hosted 13 consultations which were held in each of the parishes. It received 129 submissions from individuals and organisations. (The commission will be referred to hereafter as 'the Kerr Commission'.)

Meanwhile, in September 1993, the Senate had approved the appointment of a select committee and on 5 October 1993 the House of Representatives had taken a similar step. Both committees were charged jointly to recommend to the legislature the precise form and content of a revised constitution and they began work on 27 October 1993 when they selected Senator David Coore QC, a renowned jurist who was President of the Senate, as their chairman. The Joint Select Committee was to be re-appointed with the same membership following a prorogation of Parliament in April 1994. It duly considered the voluminous recommendations of the Kerr Commission and eventually submitted its report to Parliament in May 1995.[109]

Although the Jamaican Constitution has not up to the time of writing (January 2002) been revised on the basis of the Select Committee's recommendations, the research and well considered proposals it has published have been avidly studied in the other territories of the Caribbean area – and especially in those jurisdictions which have, like Jamaica, been engaged in reviewing their own constitutions.

We must now address some of the more pertinent recommendations made and consider how they have influenced other constitution making.

Head of State

The Select Committee's recommendation was for a President as Head of State of Jamaica *vice* the Queen. Such a Head of State is to be selected 'by a national process symbolizing the unity and identity of the Jamaica nation'.

Since 1995, there has developed overwhelming support for a similar change of Head of State by the majority of persons who appeared, for instance, before the St Kitts and Nevis Constitutional Review Commission, not only in St Kitts and Nevis but in several cities in Great Britain, Canada and the United States and those who appeared before the Barbados Constitution Commission. The position seems to be developing in the same direction in Antigua and Barbuda where a Constitutional Review Commission was appointed in December 1999,[110] one of the terms of reference of which is:

> ... evaluating the benefits, if any, for changing from a monarchical to a republican system of government and making recommendations in respect of any changes in the executive form of government that result from such an evaluation.

The Jamaica recommendation is that the President will operate under a Westminster system of parliamentary democracy in which he will accept the advice of the Cabinet through the Prime Minister or a minister designated by Cabinet. The President will, however, make appointments in his own discretion to certain sensitive posts after consultation with the Prime Minister and the Leader of the Opposition. The posts in question would include the Chief Justice, the President of the Court of Appeal, the

---

109 See *Final Report of the Joint Select Committee* (1995), hereafter called 'the Select Committee' or 'Joint Select Committee'.

110 The author was appointed Chairman.

appointed members of the Judicial Service Commission, the chairman and members of the Police Service Commission, the public defender, the contractor general and the independent members of the Electoral Commission.

Such presidential appointments, however, are to be confirmed by Parliament, although the Select Committee did not determine the exact process of parliamentary confirmation – a matter to be left to Parliament when the issue is finally debated.

Impeachment

Jamaica alone of Caribbean countries has decided to adopt a system of impeachment to make senior public functionaries accountable for corruption, misappropriation of funds, consistent neglect in their duties, abuse of power.[111] The Joint Select Committee suggested that those subject to impeachment should include the Head of State; parliamentarians; ministers of Government; contractor general; chief electoral officer; chairmen; chief executive officers and heads of department carrying out public duties as officers of bodies established wholly or partially out of public funds; chairmen of disciplinary bodies established by the constitution or by statute; and ambassadors, high commissioners and other such principal diplomatic officers.[112] The resignation or dismissal of an officer should not automatically bring impeachment proceedings to an end.[113]

Procedure

When a complaint is made that a person subject to impeachment has committed an impeachable offence, the President of the Senate or the Speaker of the House of Representatives will lay the complaint before the Joint Select Committee on Impeachment (a body that is appointed within 30 days of the first meeting of Parliament following a general election). The complaint may be laid by any three parliamentarians of their own motion; any three parliamentarians pursuant to a petition to Parliament supported by the authenticated signatures of 1,000 electors or by the auditor general, contractor general, Director of Public Prosecutions, the director of elections, the Integrity Commission, the public defender or any commission of enquiry.[114]

The Joint Select Committee on Impeachment has a membership of seven members comprising two members from the House of Representatives appointed on the Prime Minister's advice and two on the advice of the Leader of the Opposition; one from the Senate appointed by the Prime Minister and one by the Leader of the Opposition; with the President of the Senate as chairman.[115]

---

111 Select Committee, para 79.
112 *Ibid*, para 80(1)–(4).
113 *Ibid*, para 81.
114 *Ibid*, para 83.
115 *Ibid*, para 85.

Conduct of proceedings

It is the duty of the Joint Select Committee on Impeachment simply to discover whether a *prima facie* case against the defendant is established and at least five members are required to make such a decision. If the reply is in the negative, the proceedings are closed. If, however, it is in the affirmative, the committee proceeds to draw up Articles of Impeachment containing a Statement and Particulars of the alleged offence which is placed before Parliament for transmission to the Impeachment Tribunal[116] which is made up of five non-parliamentarians, viz, one appointed by the Prime Minister, one by the Leader of the Opposition, and three persons appointed by the Head of State after consulting with the nominees of the Prime Minister and Leader of the Opposition. The appointment of the three is made within 15 days of the appointment of the first two and it is from the three that the chairperson is selected by the five members.[117]

The decision to impeach must be taken by at least three of the five member panel. The sanctions are censure, removal from office or disqualification from holding public office for a specified time or indefinitely.[118]

The person against whom impeachment proceedings are brought must be given every opportunity to defend himself:

> ... he must be permitted to retain counsel of his choice. Although the tribunal will regulate its own procedure the rules of evidence to be applied are those applicable in a criminal court, viz, proof beyond reasonable doubt.[119]

The hearings of both the Joint Select Committee on Impeachment and of the Impeachment Tribunal will be open to the public and the impeachment process will be subject to judicial review.[120] It remains to be seen whether the other jurisdictions in the Caribbean area will turn their faces against these impeachment arrangements or whether they will adopt them as a safeguard against lack of accountability evident in some quarters in public life. The Jamaican authorities are to be applauded for their industry in trying to maintain integrity and transparency in public life and it is hoped that the measure will find favour with Parliament when the revised constitution in being finalised.

Parliament

It has been recommended that the existing bicameral system should be retained. So, too, should the electoral first-past-the-post system.

Whereas the number of senators provided in the 1962 Constitution was 21, it was recommended that the number should now be increased to 36 to facilitate representation by wider interests than is permissible under present arrangements. However, the Prime

---

116 *Ibid*, para 86.
117 *Ibid*, para 87.
118 *Ibid*, para 89.
119 *Ibid*, para 90.
120 *Ibid*, para 91.

Minister's nominees should always be less than two-thirds of the total membership of the House.[121]

The Select Committee has also recommended the creation of special Parliamentary Committees for such purposes as impeachment, the confirmation of senior appointments and consideration of foreign affairs issues.

Fundamental rights and freedoms

The Kerr Commission and Select Committee have also led the way in strongly urging that the rights and freedoms should in future be stated positively and in much simpler form than exist at present. They have suggested that the rights should be set out in a charter that will constitute a guarantee that the State preserve and protect the rights stated therein.[122]

The St Kitts and Nevis Constitution Review Commission[123] and the corresponding Forde Commission in Barbados[124] have drawn heavily on the Jamaica recommendation, not only in this respect, but in regard to the creation of parliamentary committees.

Citizen's Protection Bureau

In considering how to ensure that citizens whose rights are infringed secure proper redress, the Jamaica Joint Select Committee realised that many such persons lack the means of financing proper legal representation. It was also realised that the ombudsman was effective only in dealing with complaints arising from administrative action and that the office was powerless to enforce recommendations made.

To meet those concerns, the Select Committee recommended the establishment of a Parliamentary Commission to be known as the Citizen's Protection Bureau, the Head of which would be the public defender.[125]

This bureau, which has now been established, has two functions:

(a) it replaces the ombudsman, but in addition to the powers previously exercised by that officer the public defender can compel compliance with its decisions and in a proper case can even make recommendations for disciplinary action; and

(b) it ensures that complaints alleging infringement of citizens' rights are provided with ready access to professional advice and, where necessary, legal representation.[126]

Already St Kitts and Nevis is considering the inclusion in their new constitution of a public defender: the Phillips Commission having recommended, accordingly, after studying the Jamaica proposals.[127]

---

121 See Select Committee, p 10.

122 *Ibid*, p 10, para 16.

123 See *Phillips Commission Report* (St Kitts/Nevis), Vol III, Chapter 7, paras 1–3 and Appendix.

124 See *Forde Commission Report* (Barbados), Chapter 12, para 5, pp 96–97.

125 See Select Committee, s 71.

126 See Public Defender (Interim) Act, 16 April 2000, ss 13, 14 and 15.

127 See *Phillips Commission Report*, Vols III and IV, Chapter 7, para 17, pp 9–10.

Privy Council

The Select Committee recommended that the Privy Council of Jamaica should be abolished and replaced by a President's Council. Barbados, too, has evidently seen the wisdom of such a change and the Forde Commission has suggested the Barbados Privy Council should be styled 'the Presidential Council'.

The Jamaica President's Council will continue to exercise the prerogative of mercy.[128]

Service commissions

The Joint Select Committee recommended that the size of the membership of the Judicial Service Commission, the Public Service Commission and the Police Service Commission be increased. The Judicial Service Commission should move from six to nine members and three members would be members of the non-legal or non- judicial public service.[129]

The Public Service Commission's nine members will be – *two* selected from a panel of five nominated by the Civil Service Association, *one* from a panel of three nominated by the Permanent Secretaries Board; *six* members appointed by the Head of State either:

(i)   acting on the advice of the Prime Minister after he has consulted the Leader of the Opposition (this being the *Majority* opinion)or

(ii) after consultation with the Prime Minister and the Leader of the Opposition (this being the opinion of the Minority).[130]

The Police Service Commission is to be appointed by the Head of State after consultation with the Prime Minister and the Leader of the Opposition; the appointments to be subject to parliamentary confirmation. The recommendation is for an increase in the membership from five to seven. The Joint Select Committee felt that these additional two members should be appointed at the discretion of the Head of State, while the Kerr Commission felt they should be selected from professional, philanthropic, religious and other organisations.[131]

The contractor general

The Select Committee accepted the Kerr Commission's recommendation that this office be enshrined in the constitution, having regard to the status, function and purpose for which the office was created.[132]

---

128 Select Committee, paras 126–29.
129 *Op cit*, Forde Commission, fn 57, paras 130–31.
130 *Op cit*, Forde Commission, fn 57, paras 133–34.
131 *Op cit*, Forde Commission, fn 57, para 135.
132 *Op cit*, Forde Commission, fn 57, para 136.

The Electoral Commission

An Electoral Commission with its director, the chief executive officer, should be enshrined in the revised constitution, paying due regard to its central role in the effective functioning of the democracy.[133] The constitutional provisions should reflect the independence and impartiality in so far as the appointment and tenure of its members are concerned.[134]

Concluding comments

The work of constitutional reform in Jamaica, as is the case in other Caribbean territories, is an ongoing process. Although the matter had been under active debate since 1991, no constitutional amendments had been undertaken up to 2002 to implement the recommendations discussed above – although interim legislation has been enacted bringing into operation the office of public defender which is to be enshrined in the constitution when it is eventually revised. But the debate has helped to educate not only Jamaicans, but citizens in the other Caribbean countries, on the desirability of constitutional change.

This section is being completed in December 2001 and the time cannot be far distant when the proposals from the Joint Select Committee of Parliament (reflecting the many well considered views of the Kerr Commission) will become law in a new or revitalised Jamaica Constitution.

BELIZE

Patriation of the Belize Constitution

As regards Belize, this country became independent in August 1981 and the most interesting aspect of the Independence Constitution is that it was an Act of the Belize Parliament that brought the Belize Constitution into being, albeit simultaneously supported by a UK Order in Council.

Monarchical regime

It is in other respects a traditional monarchical type of instrument very much like the constitutions of Jamaica, Barbados and the Bahamas, but with the undermentioned variations, some of which are quite substantial.

---

133 Select Committee, paras 139–40.
134 *Ibid*, para 141.

Deputy prime minister

Specific provision is made in the constitution itself for a deputy prime minister, 'to whom the Prime Minister may from time to time depute such of his functions as he may specify'.[135]

Local Privy Council

Belize has a local Privy Council comprising not less than six persons and this body is designated the Belize Advisory Council.[136] In many ways it resembles the Jamaica Privy Council, even in so far as the appointment of a senior member is concerned. As in Jamaica and Barbados, the Governor General is the chairman of the council, or, in his absence, the senior member.[137] The Advisory Council of Belize performs the identical functions as the corresponding bodies in Jamaica and Barbados in respect of the prerogative of mercy, but in Belize it is also the authority responsible for executing enquiries into the removal of Supreme Court as well as Court of Appeal and High Court Judges. It is, too, the body that advises the Governor General in respect of the removal from office (for inability to perform his office or for misbehaviour) of the Director of Public Prosecutions.

Parliament

The legislature in Belize is said to consist of 'the National Assembly, comprising two Houses, viz, the House of Representatives and a Senate'.[138]

In Jamaica,[139] Barbados[140] and the Bahamas,[141] Parliament consists of Her Majesty, a Senate and a House of Assembly or a House of Representatives (as the case may be).

Public Service Commission

Whereas the other territories dealt with in this chapter have both a Public Service Commission and a Judicial and Legal Services Commission, Belize has provision only for a Public Services Commission.[142] This body consists of a chairman and 12 other members – including the following *ex officio* members: the Chief Justice; a judge nominated by the Chief Justice; the permanent secretary to the Minister of Defence; the commandant to the Belize Defence Force; and the commissioner of police. The 12 member Public Services Commission (other than the chairman) sits in divisions as follows:

(a) four are responsible for public service matters, other than those relating to the judicial and legal service and the police;

---

135 Belize Constitution, s 38.
136 *Ibid*, s 54.
137 *Ibid*, s 54(12).
138 *Ibid*, s 55.
139 See Jamaica Constitution, s 34 (Her Majesty, Senate and House of Representatives).
140 See Barbados Constitution, s 35 (Her Majesty, Senate and House of Assembly).
141 See Bahamas Constitution, Art 38 (House of Assembly).
142 Belize Constitution, s 105.

(b) two, the *ex officio* Chief Justice and the judge appointed by him, are responsible for judicial and legal service matters;

(c) four, of whom the permanent secretary to the Ministry of Defence and the commandant of the Belize Defence Force are *ex officio* members, will look after military service matters; and

(d) two, of whom the commissioner of police is *ex officio* a member, will be responsible for the police force.

Dismissal of members of higher judiciary

In so far as the dismissal of a judge is concerned, the procedure varies from the regime prescribed in all the other monarchical systems in the Caribbean, whereby no such removal can take place unless there is a reference to the Judicial Committee of the Privy Council. In Belize, a justice of the Supreme Court or a judge of the Court of Appeal may be removed from office by the Governor General if the question of the removal of the justice has been referred to the Belize Advisory Council, which recommends dismissal for inability to perform (whether arising from infirmity of body or mind or any other cause), or for misbehaviour. The Advisory Council here converts itself into a tribunal under the chairmanship of a member 'who holds or has held high judicial office and who has been deputed to act in that capacity by the Governor General'.[144]

The Government of Belize is the first administration in the Commonwealth Caribbean (apart from Guyana) to localise the regime for the removal of judges. The people in this part of the world have matured sufficiently (after nearly 40 years of reference to the Privy Council in London for judicial disciplinary matters) to have local institutions to adjudicate on the removal of their judges. As will be pointed out in Chapter 13, it is now fair that we should deal with this matter ourselves without involving the hard-pressed members of the Judicial Committee of the Privy Council.

We must now in the next chapter address our attention to the all important matter of the judiciary.

---

144 Belize Consitution, s 98(4)–(7), dealing with the Supreme Court judges; and s 102(2)–(6) dealing with the judges of the Court of Appeal.

CHAPTER 13

THE JUDICIARY

A INTRODUCTION

One of the beneficial by-products of colonialism was that well trained and impartial judges were sent to the colonies by the Colonial Office in London as well paid members of the Colonial Legal Service. No political or other pressure could be exerted on them because they served under English Governors instructed to leave judicial business entirely up to those judges, who were subject to transfer from one part of the 'Empire' to another. This policy at the same time had its dangers and drawbacks since judges, to be effective in their work, should understand the social environment in which they serve. However, under that system judges could not be dismissed at pleasure: *quam diu se bene gesserint*, that is, so long as they behaved well. They could not be dismissed at all by local politicians. After independence following the end of the Second World War, things changed – as we shall see by an examination of the attitude of the executive to the judiciary in three newly independent countries.

B GHANA JUDICIAL COUP UNDER NKRUMAH

One of the first examples of the vulnerability of a judge of a superior court was seen in Ghana in 1964, seven years after independence.

In this connection, the author refers to what he wrote in 1978 in another book on this subject:[1]

> In that (Ghana) regime the President was prepared to stop at nothing to stamp out what was called subversion, and in 1964 a Special Criminal Division of the High Court was established to that end. Even though there was a Supreme Court which in its appellate jurisdiction was the final Court of Appeal in the country there was to be no appeal from this special division. The division, having been called upon to try five accused persons – including two former ministers and a former secretary of the Convention People's Party – acquitted the accused after hearing the evidence adduced against them. As a result of the acquittal, the President summarily dismissed or forced to resign the judges who had constituted the panel, including Sir Arku Korsah, the Chief Justice. The President was able to take this extraordinary step by virtue of a section in the 1960 Republican Constitution of Ghana providing that the Chief Justice's appointment could 'at any time be revoked by the President by Instrument under the Presidential Seal' ... It was clear that the Ghanaian law was intended to warn all judges that they were there to give effect to the President's behests, upon pain of dismissal.

---

1   See Phillips, 1978, pp 163–64.

C CONFRONTATION IN MALAYSIA BETWEEN THE EXECUTIVE AND THE JUDICIARY

Twenty-four years later, in 1988, the authorities in Malaysia staged a similar judicial coup in that country when they embarked upon the ruthless dismissal of the President of the Federal Supreme Court (Tun Salleh bin Abas) and two other Supreme Court Judges in what a very discerning writer has described as an event which does not seem likely to have ever occurred elsewhere in any common law jurisdiction.[2]

Article 127 of the Malaysia Constitution imposes a restriction on parliamentary discussion of the conduct of judges in either House except on a substantive motion of which notice has been given by not less than one-quarter of the total number of members of that House. Notwithstanding this stricture the Prime Minister (Dr Mahathir bin Mohamed) attacked the judiciary, during the second half of 1987. The President of the Federal Court considered he had no alternative, but to respond in the course of launching a book he had written on law, justice and the judiciary.

One of the judges wished to enter the fray, but the Lord President of the Supreme Court restrained him. Having called a meeting of the majority of his federal and State judges, it was agreed without dissent that individual judges would not reply, but that a letter would be despatched to the King expressing the concern of the judges about the criticisms. All the judges were given copies of the letter the day after it was sent and no objection was received – not even from the Supreme Court Judge who was not originally keen for the despatch of the letter.[3]

According to Trindale, the King having received the letter on 26 March 1988, summoned the Prime Minister on 1 May 1988 and showed him the letter about which he was displeased and instructed the Prime Minister to take steps to replace the Lord President.[4] After taking legal advice from the Attorney General, the Prime Minister advised the King that Art 125(3) of the Federal Constitution stipulated that the Lord President could only be removed on grounds of misbehaviour or inability from other causes properly to discharge the functions of his office. The Prime Minister, having undertaken to investigate whether there was evidence of misbehaviour, later addressed the King proposing that the Lord President should be removed on grounds of misbehaviour and other causes, 'which clearly show that he is no longer able to discharge his functions as Lord President properly'. The Lord President was promptly suspended from office and a tribunal appointed to enquire into the charges brought against him – shortly after having been received by the Prime Minister who informed him that the King had objected to the letter sent and had decided to dismiss him. (Immediately on his return to office, the Lord President had submitted a letter to the Prime Minister seeking early retirement, but the letter was withdrawn a day or two later – as the judge reasoned that such an application would be interpreted as an admission of guilt.)

The next step in the saga was the appointment of a tribunal, in respect of which the Prime Minister had made the nominations, although he was obviously a person

---

2   See a very enlightening article by Trindale, 1990, pp 51–56, from which the facts are drawn.
3   Tan Sri Hashim Sani.
4   The judges evidently felt they would receive protection from the King, but were mistaken.

'interested', since it was a result of the Prime Minister's criticism of the judiciary that the offending letter had been sent to the King. Article 145(2) of the Constitution of the federation envisages that, in circumstances such as this, the King should seek the advice of the Attorney General on the nominations, but such advice was not sought.

The composition of the tribunal was open to question on other grounds. For example, its chairman was to be Tan Sri Abdul Hamid Omar, the then Chief Justice of Malaysia, who as the most senior judge next to the Lord President was likely to be appointed as his successor, which in the event happened. The Chief Justice had also been one of the judges with whom the Lord President had discussed the letter to which there was no expression of dissent. A further objection to the composition of the Tribunal was that there were two retired High Court judges appointed to it, whereas there were available at the time three former Lord Presidents, two retired Chief Justices and five retired Supreme Court Judges – all carrying the same rank of Supreme Court Judge as the Lord President. And one would have expected that, in appointing members to such a body, care would have been taken to select judges of a rank not below that of a Supreme Court Judge. A still further problem with the tribunal was that there were no existing rules governing such an enquiry. However, some hurriedly drafted rules were sent to the Lord President, with a note that the tribunal would make any further rules *ambulando*, if necessary.

On the matter of the standard of proof, the tribunal arbitrarily decreed that this would be on the basis of a balance of probabilities rather than proof beyond reasonable doubt. The tribunal also decided not to hold public hearings, but to sit *in camera*. In the view of the Lord President, he was in several respects being tried as a criminal would be, instead of taking part in an inquiry, the standard of proof being in any case misconceived.

One must therefore applaud the Lord President for refusing to take part in the tribunal which proceeded to 'try' him *in absentia* and to recommend his removal.

When the Lord President, through his counsel, asked the tribunal to adjourn the hearing while he moved the High Court for a writ of prohibition to prevent the tribunal from continuing the investigation and reporting, the tribunal refused the request. The Lord President then petitioned the High Court and, as the tribunal had hurriedly completed the inquiry and were preparing to send their recommendation to the King, the Lord President asked the High Court Judge for a *limited* stay. This order was likewise refused.

The Lord President appealed to the Supreme Court against the refusal of the High Court to grant a stay.

Although obstacles were placed in the way of the Chief Registrar not to facilitate holding of the court session the judges succeeded in hearing the matter *and granted a stay*. Thereafter, the Acting Lord President made representations to the King that the judges who heard and granted the stay should also be removed from office for misbehaviour – the main allegation being that the court had no right to convene a session of the Supreme Court without his permission. Two of the judges, who were subsequently dismissed, were also charged with failure to attend a court session at a distant outpost without the Acting Lord President's permission: even though it was clear to the latter that, in the emergency, they had decided to adjourn the sitting to attend to a matter relative to the dismissal to the head of the judiciary – which they considered to be an occasion of national emergency.

A second tribunal was promptly set up to hear charges against the two judges who were suspended and subsequently also removed from office.

A few days later a new panel of the Supreme Court reheard the matter and refused a stay – whereafter the dismissal of the Lord President was duly finalised.

D ZIMBABWE HARASSES ITS CHIEF JUSTICE

Zimbabwe at the turn of the 21st century provided a classic example of the difficulties faced in some Third World countries by an independent judiciary endeavouring to operate under a regime without regard for the rights of others, especially members of the Opposition.

The Supreme Court, which was headed by Chief Justice Anthony Gubbay had, in February 2000 made a court order requiring the so called 'war veterans' to leave the white owned farms which they had occupied with the Government's support. The order was however largely ignored and the Supreme Court was criticised in Government circles for having made it.

In November 2000 there was an invasion by some 200 'veterans' – no doubt arising from the court's decision. In the course of the stampede, some 80 of the invaders clambered up on tables and demanded that the offending judges be killed.

When therefore the Chief Justice in January 2001 made a speech to mark the opening of the legal year he referred to the year 2000 as an *annus horribilis* for the Zimbabwe judiciary and remarked upon the position of judges having to operate in a climate of fear for their personal safety. He also quite understandably drew attention to the lack of official condemnation of the invading incident.

One month later – in February 2001 – the Chief Justice decided to take early retirement, that is, from 1 July 2001, although he was not constitutionally required to retire until April 2002 when he attained his 70th birthday. In the meantime, he agreed to proceed on four months pre-retirement leave from 1 March 2001.

Following a vitriolic attack upon the Chief Justice by certain parliamentarians, he subsequently decided to continue in harness until his normal retirement date and to forego the leave. On 27 February 2001, the Minister of Justice accused the Chief Justice of going back on his agreement to permit an Acting Chief Justice to assume full powers from 1 March 2001, and on 28 February he described the Chief Justice's behaviour as 'disgraceful, despicable and not worthy of a man in his position'. He accordingly ordered the Chief Justice to vacate his office by the end of that day.

The Chief Justice, however, returned on 1 March to his office without incident and on 2 March he had another visit from the war veterans led by a man who was on bail from a charge of attempted murder.

On that day, an agreement was signed between the Chief Justice and the Minister of Justice under which:

(a) the Chief Justice would raise no objection to the appointment of an Acting Chief Justice while he was on leave;

(b) the Chief Justice would be permitted to continue to use his chambers;

(c) the Minister of Justice withdrew his derogatory remarks and promised 'no steps (would) be taken to unlawfully cause the suspension, removal or resignation' of judges; and

(d) the Chief Justice would be permitted to remain in his official residence until the end of 2001 with his bodyguards and with the needs of his sick wife being met.[5]

The situation regarding the future manner of recruiting judges appears bleak, if one is to judge from a statement made by the Minister of Information in answer to a charge of political pressure against the judiciary. This is what he is alleged to have said (see Walsh, 2001):

> The Government has not put pressure on anyone. It has merely expressed its lack of confidence in some judges because of their lack of impartiality and independence. If we have to choose between a judge with a Rhodesian past and those from the liberation struggle, there is no question. We will choose the latter.

Chief Justice Gubbay was appointed as a judge in 1978 during the Ian Smith regime. But he was promoted to the office of Chief Justice by President Mugabe some years later.

E   JUDICIAL INSTITUTIONAL INDEPENDENCE IN AUSTRALIA, CANADA AND THE US

The attitude of the executive towards the judiciary in Australia, the United States and Canada has, by contrast to what has been happening in the last two decades in Zimbabwe and Malaysia, been to recognise the independence of the judiciary and to take careful steps to implement procedures to make such *independence* manifest. A brief analysis of the position follows.

Australia

In Australia there are three courts at the federal level – the High Court (the highest), the Federal Court (established in 1976) and the Family Court (established in 1975). Prior to 1979 all the courts in Australia were administered by the Ministry of Justice but, under the High Court of Australia Act 1979, the High Court 'shall administer its own affairs' subject to the Act (s 17). Under s 35 'there are payable to the High Court such moneys as are appropriated by the Parliament for the purposes of the Court'. The court is requested to prepare estimates of receipt and expenditure, to be approved by the Minister (the Attorney General) (s 36), but it is the court's responsibility (s 42) to keep proper accounts relating to the administration thereof: such accounts being, under s 43, subject to audit by the Auditor General. The change brought about by this enactment was, in fact, for the High Court to receive from the appropriate minister a 'one line budget' and for the court to assume full responsibility for the financial management of its affairs. There is a chief executive officer appointed by the Governor General upon the nomination of the court.

---

5   See Rozenberg, Joshua, 'How Mugabe undermined the rule of law' (2001) *Daily Telegraph*, 6 March, p 17 – from which most of the facts in this section are drawn.

For the other two federal courts referred to above, the arrangements are not quite so elaborate. Under the Federal Courts of Australia Act 1976 (s 18A), the Chief Justice, assisted by the registrar, is responsible for managing the administrative affairs of the court. The Chief Justice must each year prepare a report for the Attorney General with financial statements and an auditor's report.

Under the Family Laws Act 1975, the Chief Justice of the Family Court is likewise responsible for managing the affairs of the court, assisted by a chief executive officer (s 38A).

The position varies in the different Australian states. In South Australia, for instance, the administrator (who performs similar functions to the chief executive officer at the Family Court) is appointed with the consent of the Judicial Council.[6] This Act has transferred the administration of the courts in this State to a body known as the State Court Administration Council which comprises three members, viz, the Chief Justice of the Supreme Court, the Chief Justice of the District Court and the Chief Magistrate of the Magistrates' Court.[7] The council administers one budget for all levels of the court system and the Act provides that the council is 'responsible for providing, or arranging for the provision of, the administrative facilities and services for participating courts that are necessary to enable those courts properly to carry out their judicial functions'. Each court, however, remains responsible for its own internal administration. The council controls the physical plant of which it has the care and management and can even acquire and dispose of an interest in real property, with the Government's approval. The council submits estimates to the Attorney General who may approve them with or without modifications and no expenditure can be undertaken unless it is provided for in a budget so approved.

The Act also provides that a member of the council may appear before a parliamentary committee to answer questions pertaining to expenditure and the financial needs of the courts affecting their administration, but *not* in relation to adjudicative matters.

Previously, South Australia had in 1981 separated the administration of the courts from the Attorney General's Department by establishing a Court Services Department which was a separate department of Government.

In 1991, New South Wales took a similar step of establishing a separate Court Administration Department, but most of the other Australian States still follow the traditional arrangement whereby the Attorney General's Department runs the courts although it is felt by both sides to be an unsatisfactory arrangement.

The United States

In the United States, as far back as 1936, the American Bar Association advocated that the judiciary should be given administrative control over the courts. After Roosevelt threatened 'to pack' the Supreme Court during his Presidency, special impetus was given to the idea. Today, all the federal courts except the Supreme Court are administered by a

---

6   See the South Australian Court Administration Act 1993 (No 11 of 1993), s 16.
7   *Ibid*, s 17.

director of the Administrative Office: the Supreme Court having its own director. The office operates under the direction of the Judicial Conference which originally comprised the Chief Justice of the Supreme Court and the nine senior circuit judges, but which now has 27 members including chief (circuit) judges, district court judges and the chief judge of the Court of International Trade. The 1939 legislation provided for a judicial council in each circuit to which administration of the courts has been transferred from the Department of Justice, in which financial and administrative affairs were originally reposed.

Gradually, similar arrangements were made in the States: Connecticut in 1937; New Jersey in 1947; 12 more State Courts in the 1950s; 13 in the 1960s and the others in the 1970s.

Canada

The Canadians have, particularly since their Constitution was patriated in 1982, grappled with what has been referred to as an 'inherent conflict' when the chief litigator on Government's behalf (the Attorney General) has been the authority with a measure of financial control over the superior courts – especially, at a time when the judiciary has, under the human rights provisions in the Constitution, the power to strike down legislation and to declare unconstitutional executive acts that infringe those provisions.

The combination of the reports of commissions, pronouncements of senior judges and landmark cases, at the same time as the new Constitution was promulgated, provided the main stimulus for the clamour that the Ministry of Justice (headed by the Attorney General) should no longer run the financial and administrative affairs of the courts – even though the registrar acts as a chief executive officer.

In 1981, Quebec Chief Justice Jules Deschênes published on behalf of the Canadian Judicial Council a report[8] which was a study on the independent judicial administration of the courts. He recommended that the administration of the courts should be removed from the Attorney General's Department to the Courts Department.[9]

In a 1980 speech Chief Justice Bora Laskin of the Canadian Supreme Court argued for independence in budgeting and in expenditure from an approved budget and independence in administration. This was supported later by his successor, Chief Justice Dickson, who stressed that preparation of judicial budgets and distribution of allocated resources should be under the control of the Chief Justices of the various courts and removed from the control of the Attorney General.

Happily, there was already a clear indication that, even as far back as 1977, the then Minister of Justice was uneasy as to the extent to which his department was involved. In the second reading of the amendment to the Judges Act of 1977 to give the federal courts greater administrative autonomy, the minister made this admission:

> Since I became Minister of Justice I have been deeply concerned about the degree of my department's involvement in the administration of judicial affairs. I believe that since the

---

8   Deschênes Report, 1981.
9   Friedland, 1995, pp 188–90.

Department of Justice is responsible for the conduct of the government's litigation, it is preferable that the courts should not have to rely on the department for handling its administrative affairs ... It is a principle of independence of the judiciary.

Despite this very clear statement by the minister, it is still the case that the Ministry of Justice exercises an overview, although it is understood that today the Supreme Court's budgetary proposals are *in practice* submitted without change to the Treasury Board. The registrar does not *legally* have an independent role. He is appointed not by the court (as in Australia), but by the Cabinet. However, it is understood that he is chosen in practice by the court which will always be consulted if he had to be removed for any reason. The position with all provincial courts remains that they are all run by the departments of the Attorney General.

The essence of judicial independence

Then came the case of *Valente*[10] which brought the need for a clear definition between the judiciary and the executive very much to the fore. The courts in Ontario were called upon to decide the constitutional issue as to whether a *provincial* court was in fact an *independent* and impartial tribunal to try a person accused of having caused death by dangerous driving. The Ontario Court of Appeal having found that provincial court judges qualify as constitutionally *independent and impartial*, the applicant appealed to the Supreme Court of Canada. It was in rendering the unanimous opinion of this Court written by LeDain J, that the question arose of what constitutes independence for a judge. Whereas s 100 of the Constitution provides that the salaries of superior court judges are fixed by an Act of Parliament, provincial court judges have their salaries set by Cabinet order. The submission by counsel for Valente was that this distinction rendered the provincial court judge a not independent arbiter under the Constitution. In rendering this decision of the Supreme Court, LeDain J outlined three essential conditions for the existence of judicial independence, viz, security of tenure, financial security and institutional independence. In his view, so long as these were attained by legislative means, constitutional guarantees as set out in ss 99 and 100 of the Constitution were not imperative, especially if it was clear that the judge held his office during good behaviour and could not be dismissed at whim by the executive.

But it was left to Chief Justice Dickson of the Supreme Court in another case in 1986 to underscore the importance of separating the administration of the courts from external control, that is, of working towards institutional independence. Here is what he had to say:[11]

> The principle of judicial independence has grown and been transformed to respond to the modern needs and problems of free and democratic societies. The role of the courts as a resolver of disputes, interpreter of the law and defender of the Constitution requires that they be completely separate in authority and function from all other participants in the justice system.

So much for institutional and financial independence.

---

10 *Valente v The Queen* (1985) 2 SCR 673.
11 *Beauregard v Canada* (1986) 30 DLR 481, pp 491 and 494.

F IMPARTIALITY

There is no doubt that a further vital pre-requisite for the proper administration of justice is that the judiciary should also show total *impartiality*. But, is there a relation between independence and impartiality? According to Le Dain J, in *Valente*:[12]

> ... impartiality refers to a state of mind or attitude of the tribunal in relation to the issues and the parties in a particular case whereas the word 'independent' connotes not merely a state of mind or attitude in the actual exercise of judicial functions, but a status or relationship to others particularly the Executive Branch of the government, that rests on objective conditions or guarantees.

Friedland has pointed out[13] that it would have been better if the Supreme Court had not drawn (so) refined a distinction between the two concepts, since the section under consideration by the court only related to criminal matters where the Crown is almost always a party and 'if there is a reasonable apprehension of a lack of independence in a criminal case, there would at the same time surely be a reasonable apprehension of lack of impartiality'. Lamer CJC expressed the same sentiment in another way when he said, in *Lippe*:[14]

> Judicial independence is critical to the public perception of impartiality.

> Independence is the corner-stone, a necessary pre-requisite, for judicial impartiality.

G ETHICAL CODE FOR JUDGES

In the Canadian Judicial Council's Ethical Principles for Judges, the reader will find useful examples of the principles which are likely – if followed – to enable a judge to show his impartiality. Some of them are worth recording in a volume of this nature.

Judges should make every effort to ensure that what they do, both in and out of Court, instill confidence in their impartiality. To that end, they should conduct their personal affairs and business activities in such a manner that the occasions will be few when they will need to disqualify themselves from adjudicating matters.

The appearance of impartiality is to be judged by the standard of a reasonable, fair-minded and informed person.

Judges should, while demonstrating total control of their courts, treat all who come before them with unfailing courtesy.

They are at liberty to share the interest of the community and to take part in civic, religious and charitable activities, so long as their participation does not interfere with their judicial functions or compromise them in any way (as, for example, soliciting funds).

---

12 *Valente v The Queen* (1985) 2 SCR 673.
13 Friedland, 1995, p 9.
14 *Lippe* (1991) 2 SCR 114.

Judges should also avoid engaging in any organisation likely to be involved in litigation; nor should they give legal or investment advice.

Needless to say, judges should refrain from participating in politics in any way: they should not be members of political parties or take part in political meetings or contribute to parties or sign petitions seeking political favours or decisions. They should also monitor the political activities of members of their immediate families to ensure that those activities do not adversely affect the public perception of the judge's impartiality.

Judges should disqualify themselves where they consider their impartial judgment is open to question. No effort must be spared to avoid the appearance of a conflict of interest in the performance of their functions.

H   JUDICIAL INDEPENDENCE

Contemporaneously with the post-Second World War rights consciousness, which has progressively become more and more pronounced since 1945, judicial independence has become a matter of growing international concern. Where the legal profession and the judiciary are not independent, the fundamental rights of the individual cannot be preserved. But, in an area like the Caribbean, where political interference (when it exists) tends to be indirect and muted, many members of the profession do not fully realise how fierce the interference can be in some Central American and Asian countries.

As has been pointed out by an authority who has been at the centre of monitoring the problem,[15] although the principle of independence is widely acknowledged internationally, there have been in such countries as Chile, Uruguay, El Salvador, Guatemala, Syria, ante-democratic South Africa and Pakistan, widespread harassment and persecution of judges and lawyers: taking the forms of condemning individual judges; attacking their offices; assassination; banning orders; initiating tax investigations against judges shortly after the delivery of an unpopular judgement involving government decrees; dissolving the National Council of the Bar Association; arrest of magistrates shortly after releasing pre-trial detainees; and changing the jurisdiction of the court to prevent a judge from hearing a case he was previously competent to try.

I   THE STATE OF JUDICIAL ETHICS IN THE CARIBBEAN

Let us now look briefly at the state of judicial ethics in the Caribbean setting.

No doubt because it has not been bequeathed to us by our colonial masters, little or no attention has up till now been paid to this aspect of judicial life. However, in advocating it more than 20 years ago, the present writer was, like John the Baptist, a voice crying in the wilderness. This is what he had to say in a book written in 1978:[16]

We must now examine the feasibility of a Code of Judicial Ethics for those who as lawyers serve as members of the Judiciary.

---

15   See a useful article by Dolgopol (1984) 10(3) Commonwealth Law Bulletin, pp 1369–72.
16   See Phillips, 1978, pp 123–24.

There can be no doubt that more and more pressure will inevitably be brought to bear on the judicial department in the exercise of its functions in developing countries. The suggestion is not made because on any noticeable change or deterioration in the conduct of judges, but because the pressures of modern life may in time bring about such a deterioration ...

As the pressures increase, there are bound to be lapses and judges will, no less than the public, find it useful to have such a reminder of the principles which should govern their conduct. Such a code would in fact be supportive of the provisions in the various Constitutions purporting to proclaim the independence of the judiciary and the absence of political control.

At the time of writing, the judiciary in Trinidad and Tobago as well as the Law Association are engaged in drafting Codes of Judicial Ethics.

The writer is also aware that a task force,[17] appointed by the Chief Justice of the Eastern Caribbean Supreme Court, examined *inter alia* the structure and functions of the Judicial and Legal Services Commission. In the course of this work, the task force considered the ethical aspects of the judicial function and had discussions with many organisations and individuals with a view to recommending the introduction of a code of judicial ethics in the East Caribbean Supreme Court. The task force, in fact, recommended that enforceable codes of ethics for both the higher and lower judiciary should be introduced as soon as possible.[18] The writer was privileged in December 2000 to attend a meeting of Appeal Court and High Court judges in St Vincent at the invitation of the Chief Justice of the Organisation of Eastern Caribbean States (OECS) Supreme Court to discuss the matter of the introduction of a code and he was interested to observe that there was a strong group of those judges who were in favour of a code, though not one that will attract sanctions – an approach which is likely to conflict with the constitutional provisions relating to judicial discipline.

All Caribbean judges may now wish seriously to consider whether they should introduce such a code which would be a constant reminder to judges towards:

(a) upholding the integrity and independence of the judiciary;

(b) avoiding impropriety, and even the appearance of impropriety, in all their activities;

(c) performing their duties impartially and diligently;

(d) encouraging them to assume extra-judicial activities calculated to advance their legal knowledge, the legal system and the administration of justice;

(e) so organising extra-judicial activities as to minimise the risk of conflict with judicial functions;

(f) regularly filing reports of compensation received for non-judicial work; *and*

(g) maintaining strict abstinence from political activity of any kind.

Would it not be in their own interest and in that of the public for the judges in the United Kingdom and in the former colonial countries (now independent) in the Caribbean to be guided by codes of ethics such as exist in the United States of America or by the

---

17　The Eastern Caribbean Supreme Court (which serves the OECS). The Task Force of one was Mr Reginald Dumas.

18　*Report of the Task Force* (Dumas, 2000), pp 41–54.

Statement of Ethical Principles for Judges which is in operation in Canada? Or by a code similar to that which was promulgated in March 2000 for South African judges? The British have taken the consistent line that there is no need for such a code in the United Kingdom and one wonders whether what happened in the *Pinochet* case[19] (briefly discussed below) is not an indication that such a document is now past due and should be introduced.

J   THE *PINOCHET* CASE

In this case, which came before the House of Lords from the English Divisional Court, the question was as to the immunity – if any – enjoyed by Senator Augusto Pinochet of Chile, as a former Head of State, in respect of alleged crimes against humanity for which his extradition was sought by the Spanish authorities. The Divisional Court having unanimously quashed a provisional warrant issued by a stipendiary magistrate for the arrest of Senator Pinochet, the authorities appealed to the House of Lords in which, during November 1998, a committee comprising Lords Slynn, Lloyd, Nicholls, Steyn and Hoffman heard the appeal.

However, Amnesty International (AI) had, before the main hearing, petitioned with certain other bodies for leave to intervene in the appeal and had, in fact, been granted such leave. Lord Hoffman, although not himself a member of AI was a Director and Chairman of Amnesty International Charity Limited (AICL), a registered charity incorporated in England to undertake those aspects of AI's work which are charitable under United Kingdom law. Lady Hoffman (Lord Hoffman's wife) had been working at the AI Secretariat since 1977 and was at the time of the hearing programming assistant to the director of the media and audio-visual programme.

Judgment was given by the House of Lords on 25 November 1998: the appeal having been allowed by three Law Lords (including Lord Hoffman) to two.

At the time of the hearing in the House of Lords neither Senator Pinochet nor his legal advisers had knowledge of any connection between Lord Hoffman and AI. When the extent of this connection became known, Senator Pinochet's solicitors informed the Home Secretary and lodged a petition to the House of Lords asking that the order of 25 November 1998 should either be set aside completely or that the opinion of Lord Hoffman should be declared to be of no effect: the sole ground relied upon being that Lord Hoffman's links with AI were such as to give the appearance of possible bias.

The House of Lords was persuaded to set aside its own previous decision and did so on 17 December 1999. Since AI (as an intervener) thereby became a party to the appeal, Lord Hoffman was automatically disqualified, since he had an interest *in promoting the cause*, there being no good reason in principle for limiting automatic disqualification to cases where a pecuniary interest is shown.

In the words of Lord Browne-Wilkinson:

If the absolute impartiality of the judiciary is to be maintained, there must be a rule which automatically disqualifies a judge who is involved, whether personally or as a Director of a

---

19   Judgment of the House of Lords reported in [1999] 2 WLR 827; also reported in *Ex p Pinochet* [1999] 2 All ER 97.

company, in promoting the same causes in the same organisation as is a party to the suit. There is no room for fine distinctions if Lord Hewart's famous *dictum* is to be observed: it is of fundamental importance that justice should not only be done, but should manifestly and undoubtedly be seen to be done. (See *Rex v Sussex Justices ex p McCarthy* [1924] KB 256, 259.)

Judges need therefore to be excessively careful to avoid what may be even a semblance of a conflict of interest or of any bias in the course of their work. Already, counsel in England have begun to challenge judges on conflict of interest charges which would never have been raised before the *Pinochet* case.[20] In the small communities in the Caribbean, there are also bound to be numerous challenges, but when they prove frivolous they should be firmly resisted.

K   INTERNATIONAL RECOGNITION OF JUDICIAL INDEPENDENCE

International cognisance has been given to the need for judicial independence in several key instruments which we must now briefly consider.

There was, first, the Universal Declaration of Rights in 1948 setting the scene and declaring in Art 10:

> Everyone is entitled in full equality to a fair hearing from an independent and impartial tribunal in the determination of his rights and obligations and of any criminal charge brought against him.

Shortly thereafter came the European Convention on Human Rights of 1950, brought into force in 1953, Art 6 of which states:

> In the determination of his civil rights and obligations or of any criminal charge against him, everyone is entitled to a fair and *public* hearing *within a reasonable time* by an independent and impartial tribunal established by law.

Here the openness of the fair trial is established: it must be in public. Also a sense of timing comes into the picture: the hearing must take place 'within a reasonable time'.

Next came the Covenant for Civil and Political Rights (CCPR) and the Covenant for Economic, Social and Cultural Rights (CESCR), both of 1966 and both sponsored by the United Nations. The Universal Declaration of Human Rights is not a treaty but it carries considerable moral weight. On the other hand, the two covenants implement – as treaties – the relevant sections of the declaration: the CCPR (which came into effect in 1976) giving effect to Arts 1–21 and the CESCR to Arts 22–28. Article 14 of the CCPR is in part to the following effect:

> In the determination of a criminal charge against him, or of his rights and obligations in a suit at law, everyone shall be entitled to a *fair* and *public* hearing by a *competent, independent* and impartial tribunal established by law.

---

20   In the English *Times* of 31 August 1999 (Law Section), Martin Day and Russell Levy stated in an article captioned, 'Why judges must declare their interests', that City law firms have, since the *Pinochet* case, begun preparing files on High Court and Appeal Court Judges in England and will not hesitate in future to ask that judges should recuse themselves from hearing certain cases when counsel consider that conflicts of interest would arise. In other words, more and more lawyers are likely 'to play the Hoffman Card'.

Here one notes three elements, viz, a fair, public and competent tribunal. These three components also form part of the 1969 American Convention on Human Rights which was followed in 1981 by the African Charter on Human Rights – generally emphasising the need for an independent and impartial judiciary – although the African Charter only uses the word 'impartial'.

Meantime, the International Commission of Jurists (ICJ) had, since the 1960s, been active in advocating a strong and independent judiciary. In 1978, it created an umbrella organisation – the Geneva based Centre for the Independence of Judges and Lawyers (CIJL) – the main function of which is the promotion and elaboration of the concepts of judicial independence.

Together with its parent ICJ, the Centre has worked hard to collaborate with the United Nations sub-committee and the International Association of Penal Law in appointing a special rapporteur to make a study of the independence and impartiality of the judiciary, jurors and assessors and the independence of lawyers. Two meetings of experts were convened in 1981 and 1982: the first to prepare draft principles on the independence of judges and the second on the independence of the legal profession.

The International Bar Association has also been active in this field and, in 1982, at its meeting in New Delhi, it adopted Minimum Standards of Judicial Independence. In this effort it has been joined by the World Conference on the Independence of Judges which held a meeting organised in 1983 by Chief Justice Deschênes of Quebec[21] with the support of the Canadian Judges Conference, the Canadian Bar Association and the Canadian Judicial Council. This meeting produced a document – the Universal Declaration on the Independence of Judges. This move is said to have strongly influenced the 1985 document *Basic Principles on the Independence of the Judiciary*, embracing 20 principles which governments were invited to respect and to take 'into account within the framework of their national legislation and practice'.

The *Principles*, which were endorsed by the United Nations General Assembly in 1985, included the duty to provide adequate resources to enable the judiciary properly to perform its functions; as well as rules regarding the objective factors of ability, integrity and experience to be taken into consideration in appointing and promoting judges, adequate remuneration, conditions of service, pensions, age of retirement, personal immunity from civil suits for monetary damages for improper acts or omissions in the exercise of their judicial functions; and discipline, supervision and removal of judges on grounds of incapacity and misbehaviour rendering them unfit to discharge the duties of their office.

The United Nations monitoring is still underway: the Economic and Social Council having in 1994 approved a resolution of the United Nations Human Rights Commission to appoint a special rapporteur to keep the issue under constant review.

---

21 Chief Justice Deschênes has been active internationally in strongly advocating that court administration should be in the hands of the judiciary. See his report (Deschênes, 1981). Institutional independence is still very much on the cards in 2000 in Canada – though not yet fully achieved.

L APPLICATION OF INTERNATIONAL NORMS TO THE CARIBBEAN

How have these international norms affected the judiciary in the Commonwealth Caribbean? The Constitutions of Commonwealth Caribbean jurisdictions all make such provisions as to suggest that, apart from the post of Chief Justice, judicial appointments are not made on political grounds. In all the territories, the appointment of the head of the judiciary is usually made by the Head of State on the advice of the Prime Minister after he has consulted the Leader of the Opposition. On the other hand, except in Barbados and Belize, Justices of Appeal and Puisne Judges are appointed by the President or Governor General on the advice of the Judicial Service Commission.

There is no doubt that the judiciary in this region has made considerable progress in the matter of the executive recognising the independent status of the judiciary. Interference on political grounds takes place rarely and indirectly – one recent rare occasion being when a judge was refused by the heads of the OECS Authority an extension of two years after attaining retirement age. The authority's decision must be unanimous, but one Prime Minister was so annoyed about a decision given in his territory by the judge that he is said to have voted as a minority of one against the extension, even though the Judicial and Legal Services Commission had given its assent thereto. There is therefore still an urgent need in the Caribbean to educate some politicians (albeit a small minority) concerning the desirability of having a strong and independent judiciary if democratic governance is to thrive. This has special relevance to the appointment of magistrates.

In this connection, we must remember that the bulk of cases tried in our courts are heard by magistrates and that the higher courts would be unable to operate unless serviced by registrars. These two classes of officers must inevitably therefore be regarded as judicial officers and treated as such in terms of appointment and conditions of service. The ethical considerations which apply to the senior judiciary apply with equal force to them. It is on this account that the writer wishes to urge that Caribbean citizens must address afresh the position of magistrates and registrars in the society.

It is encouraging, therefore, to note that both the Forde Constitution Commission in Barbados[22] and the Dumas task force on the functioning of the OECS Judicial and Legal Services Commission[23] have made recommendations that the status of the magistracy should be the object of urgent and detailed study by the governments. In the case of the OECS, the task force (to which reference has already been made in this section when judicial ethics were being considered) has examined the matter in the light of useful previous studies carried out thereon by a distinguished legal practitioner (Mr JS Archibald QC) as far back as 1988 and later by two judges, and has recommended (p 35 of the report) that the idea of a regional magistracy should be accepted in principle, that there should be a similar detailed study of the matter including terms and conditions of service, and that, when that has been done, attention should be given to establishing a regional registry.

---

22 *Report of the Barbados Constitution Review Commission*, 1998, p 67.
23 Dumas Task Force, 2000.

Whatever is finally agreed, the fact is that all Caribbean jurisdictions need to grasp this nettle as a matter of urgency and provide for magistrates and registrars to be treated as a tier of the judiciary – making the necessary arrangements in the OECS for their appointment as already exist for discipline by the Judicial and Legal Services Commission – if the administration of justice is not to slide into disrepute. Codes of ethics should also apply to them in the same way as to the higher judiciary.

M COURT ADMINISTRATION IN THE CARIBBEAN

The matter of court administration discussed above has, in 2000, assumed special importance in the Caribbean region, having regard to certain developments in Trinidad and Tobago affecting the administration of justice which we must now outline.

In the course of his address at the opening of the 1999–2000 law term in the Supreme Court at the Hall of Justice in Port of Spain on 16 September 1999, the Chief Justice of Trinidad and Tobago made the following statement:

> Efforts are now being made to make the Judiciary's access to the funds voted to it by Parliament subject to the approval or disapproval of the Attorney General, even when the funds are required for such a mundane purpose as the payment of long outstanding bills from contractors who have been contracted by the Magistracy to transport dead bodies! If an Attorney General can control the flow of funds to the Judiciary, he will have a stranglehold on the Judiciary.

After expressing fears that the independence of the Bar was being compromised and suggesting that the President of the Law Association, Karl T Hudson-Phillips, had joined forces with the Attorney General to subvert the independence of the judiciary, the Chief Justice permitted himself – somewhat in desperation – to remark as follows:

> It would be foolish of me not to recognise, and cowardly not to acknowledge, that I am the target of much, if not all, of this. I assure you it is not a comfortable position, to be the target of a combination of such powerful forces. But I give you this assurance that I will not turn and run. My only regret is that those who wish to destroy me seem to be prepared to destroy, or at least damage, the institution of the Judiciary in the process. And who knows – they may succeed, but only if people, and lawyers in particular, let them. The Judiciary by itself is powerless to stop them. I have seriously considered whether I ought not to bow out in the interest of preserving the integrity of the institution. But I realise that by doing so, I may actually weaken it and make it more vulnerable to attack in the future.

This Chief Justice's address (and in particular the two excerpts quoted above) triggered a lengthy and acrimonious statement from the Attorney General supported by a caustic press statement from the President of the Law Association who concentrated mainly on what the Chief Justice had to say about the attitude of the President and some members of his Association to the New Rules of Court being considered for promulgation.

The Attorney General's Statement was made to Parliament on 29 October 1999 in a 13 page document which was captioned:

A Statement made by the Honourable Ramesh Lawrence Maharaj

at the Trinidad and Tobago Parliament on 29 October 1999 on

The Doctrine of Separation of Powers

The Independence of the Judiciary

The Obligation of Accountability

The Facts of the Matters Raised by the Chief Justice on 16 September 1999.

As regards the press statement made by the President of the Law Association, Mr Hudson Phillips was at pains to explain the reasons for the association's objections to the new rules which he contended would adversely affect the practice of new entrants to the profession. He accused the Chief Justice of being insensitive to their concerns and strongly urged that their point of view be taken into consideration in the interest of the administration of justice. In his view, the new rules would 'entrench the existing cartels and monopolies in the profession' and the Chief Justice's attack on him personally was because of attempts by the Chief Justice 'to ram [the new Rules] down the throats of a previously unsuspecting profession'.

The Attorney General's Statement to Parliament contained, *inter alia*, the following propositions:

1   The Attorney General has no say and cannot interfere with judicial functions, but *he is required to inquire about the operation and administration of Courts which are financed by Parliament, to which he, as a Minister, is responsible.*

2   In the discharge of his political responsibilities to the people, and to Parliament, *the Attorney General has a duty to require the Chief Justice, or the Court Administration Department, to provide a report or information at any time on any matter concerning the operations of the Court or their Administration if it is his view that the public interest requires him to get such a report or information* [emphasis supplied].

3   If he receives complaints from staff in the judicial department in relation to matters of administration he is entitled to hear and to communicate with the Chief Justice with a request for him to take action.

4   The Chief Justice is not and cannot be a member of the Executive or the Legislature.

N   INTERVENTION BY DISTINGUISHED JURIST

In his Report to the Law Association which had requested his intervention in settling the dispute, the Right Honourable Telford Georges – himself a former Chief Justice of Tanzania, Zimbabwe and The Bahamas – referred to the claim by the Attorney General that he 'is and has always been accountable to Cabinet and Parliament for the administration of law and justice in Trinidad and Tobago', and pointed out that there was no mention of law and justice in the list published in the *Trinidad and Tobago Gazette* of 1 June 1998, assigning responsibilities by the Prime Minister to the various ministers of Government. The learned judge also referred to several other claims in the Attorney General's statement and called attention to the flaws in his claims that he had responsibility for overseeing the judiciary.

Mr Justice Georges ended his report with a warning that highly placed judges should not lose their nerve and descend, or threaten to descend, into the arena when provoked. 'The case for the independence of the Judiciary and the separation of powers can be made on the basis of the logical analysis of constitutional principles.'

The Government of Trinidad and Tobago then proceeded to appoint a high level Commission of Inquiry presided over by Lord McKay, a former Lord Chancellor of Great Britain, to do a full investigation into the administration of justice in Trinidad and Tobago. The commission's terms of reference were as follows:

1   To enquire into and report and make recommendations on the machinery for the Administration of Justice in the Republic of Trinidad and Tobago with special reference to the following matters incidental thereto or connected therewith:

(a) the duties, functions, management and adequacy of the system of Courts and procedure to provide more efficient, accessible, affordable and expeditious justice for all;

(b) the qualifications which may be prescribed in the appointment and promotion of judicial officers and the manner of dealing with complaints by the legal profession and the public against judicial officers;

(c) the operation of the existing financial and administrative rules and procedure for the release and draw-down of funds allocated to the Judiciary by Parliament, for the approval of travel abroad by judicial and other officers for training and conferences, for the employment, on contract, of staff for the judiciary, for communication with the Cabinet and the Ministry of Finance by the judicial department and whether these rules and procedures impair or derogate from the independence of the judiciary and the rule of law;

(d) allegations that the Executive is attempting to undermine the independence of the judiciary.

2   To make such observations and recommendations pertaining to the findings of the Commission arising out of the enquiry as the Commissioners may deem appropriate.

The Commissioners reported in early October 2000.

They did not find well founded the allegations that the executive was endeavouring to undermine the independence of the judiciary and recommended that the channel of communication between the Chief Justice and the Cabinet should continue to be the Attorney General's Department. They made a number of other recommendations calculated to improve the administration of justice in the country including the introduction of a code of ethics for judges. The report was not particularly constructive.

O   REMOVAL OF JUDGES FROM OFFICE

All the Constitutions in the Caribbean provide a maximum age up to which a Justice of the Supreme Court should continue in office – it is usually up to the age of 62 years, although both Barbados and The Bahamas have recently extended the retirement age to 70. There is in the OECS, for example, a provision for a two year extension which is permitted by the Governor General, on the recommendation of the Judicial and Legal Service Commission to the OECS Authority (the Prime Ministers) who must agree unanimously, a most unsatisfactory provision in the area of political interference.

Removal from office is only permissible for inability to discharge the functions of office (whether arising from infirmity of body or mind or any other cause) *or* for misbehaviour.

The procedure for removal in all jurisdictions except Guyana and Belize is as follows:

If the Prime Minister (in the case of the Chief Justice) or the Chief Justice after consultation with the Prime Minister (in the case of any other Justice) represents to the Governor General or the President that the question of removing a Justice of the Supreme Court from office for inability to perform his duties or for misbehaviour ought to be investigated, then –

(a) the Governor General shall appoint a tribunal, which shall consist of a Chairman and not less than two other members, selected by the Governor General acting in accordance with the advice of the Prime Minister (in the case of the Chief Justice) or of the Chief Justice (in the case of any other Justice) from among persons who hold or have held high judicial office;

(b) that tribunal shall enquire into the matter and report on the facts thereof to the Governor General and recommend to the Governor General whether he should request that the question of the removal of that Justice should be referred by Her Majesty to the Judicial Committee; and

(c) if the tribunal so recommends, the Governor General shall request that the question should be referred accordingly.[24]

P   BELIZE BLAZES A NEW TRAIL

In Belize, a Justice of the Supreme Court or a judge of the Court of Appeal may be removed from office by the Governor General if the question of his removal has been referred to the Belize Advisory Council which recommends dismissal only on the grounds stated above. The Advisory Council converts itself into a tribunal under the chairmanship of a member 'who holds or has held high judicial office and who has been deputed to act in that capacity by the Governor General'.[25]

Under s 54 of the Belize Constitution, the Belize Advisory Council shall comprise not less than six persons of integrity and high national standing, of whom two shall be persons who, except for the judge on the council, are citizens who have held certain specified offices – for example, commissioner of police, commandant of the Defence Force, secretary to the Cabinet, permanent secretary, head of department, chief professional adviser, ambassador or high commissioner, or such senior office. At least one member shall be a member who has held office as a judge of a superior court and one member shall be a representative of a recognised profession in the country.

Two members are appointed on the recommendation of the Prime Minister, given with the concurrence of the Leader of the Opposition. The other members are all appointed on the advice of the Prime Minister after consultation with the Leader of the Opposition.

The members are appointed for a 10 year term of office.

---

24   See Jamaica, s 100; Bahamas, Art 96; Barbados, s 84.
25   Belize, s 98 (judges); s 102 (Court of Appeal judges).

Q GUYANA

In the case of Guyana,[26] the reference is to a tribunal appointed by the President comprising not less than three judges from among persons who hold or have held office as judges of a court having unlimited jurisdiction in civil and criminal matters in some part of the Commonwealth or a court having jurisdiction in appeals from any such court and who are qualified to be appointed as any such judge. The tribunal shall enquire into the matter and advise the President whether or not the judge ought to be removed from office.

Since independence, no judge has ever been removed from office in any of the Commonwealth Caribbean jurisdictions, although unsuccessful attempts were made to remove a Trinidad and Tobago judge and a Guyana judge in circumstances we must now consider. The case of the appointment of the Chief Justice of Belize which was declared a nullity is also worthy of notice and will also be examined.

R THE *CRANE* CASE

This was a case decided by the Privy Council in 1993.[27] It reached the Judicial Committee on an appeal from a judgment of the Trinidad and Tobago Court of Appeal of 20 November 1992. Crane J had been a judge since 1978 and since 1985 had been the senior *puisne* judge of the High Court of Trinidad and Tobago.

He moved the courts for judicial review of the decision of the Chief Justice and of the Judicial and Legal Service Commission (hereafter referred to simply as 'the commission') prohibiting him from presiding in court; and of the decision of the commission to represent to the President that the question of removing him from office should be investigated.

He petitioned by way of constitutional motion requesting that three persons be prohibited from proceeding as a tribunal to enquire into the question of removing him as a judge of the High Court.

He also asked the courts to find that there was bias on the part of the Chief Justice and that the commission was likewise biased in considering whether the question referred to above should be represented to the President for investigation.

Issues

The issues before their Lordships' board can briefly be summarised as follows:

1   Did the Chief Justice and/or the commission (of which the Chief Justice was chairman) have the constitutional right to suspend Crane J from presiding as a judge?

2   Did the commission – at the instance of the Chief Justice – have the constitutional right, in the particular circumstances, to represent to the President of the Republic that the question of removing Crane J from office ought to be investigated?

3   Was bias by the Chief Justice or the commission proved?

---

26 Guyana, Art 197(5).
27 *Rees v Crane* [1994] 1 All ER 833.

On point 1: the suspension

The Privy Council found that the Chief Justice's action in suspending the judge 'went beyond mere administrative arrangement (and) was in effect an indefinite suspension'. It was their Lordships' considered view that this 'was outwith the powers of the Chief Justice': the suspension being 'wrongful as long as it lasted'.

As for the commission, 'it had no power' either to endorse the Chief Justice's decision to suspend the judge or to suspend him itself.

The Privy Council therefore set aside both decisions against Crane J.

On point 2: breach of the rules of natural justice

Their Lordships held that since the judge had not been notified of any complaints against him and had not therefore been given an opportunity to tender a reply there was a clear breach of the rules of natural justice. They concluded with the statement that:

> Whatever standard of natural justice is used, one essential is that the person concerned should have a reasonable opportunity of presenting his case.

In all the circumstances, the board concluded that Crane J 'was not treated fairly. He ought to have been told of the allegations made to the Commission and given a chance to deal with them – not necessarily by oral hearing, but in whatever way was necessary for him reasonably to make his reply'.

On point 3: the issue of bias

On this point, readers should examine the actual words of the Privy Council:

> In the first place it is contended that there was personal animosity on the part of the Chief Justice which pre-disposed him against (Crane J). There *is certainly evidence of an acrimonious relationship between the two men and if the respondent's account (which was not challenged or answered) is accepted, the Chief Justice showed from time to time between 1986 and 1990 hostility towards the respondent.* It is indeed unsatisfactory that the respondent was not told by the Chief Justice of his decision to suspend the respondent and to raise with the Commission the question of referring the matter to a tribunal. *It is also curious to say the least that the respondent on his return had such difficulty in seeing the Chief Justice* [emphasis added].

The Privy Council nonetheless concluded that 'their Lordships are not satisfied that the allegation of bias is made out'.

On this issue of bias, the writer finds the reasoning of the Privy Council somewhat illogical, if not disturbing.

There are:

(a) Crane J's affidavit – unchallenged and unanswered – attesting to the Chief Justice's hostility towards him between 1986 and 1990;

(b) the inexplicable failure of the Chief Justice to advise him of the intention to put in train the regime for his dismissal; *and*

(c) the Chief Justice's refusal to see him (one of his own colleagues) for days after his return from leave, despite persistent requests for an audience!

The Chief Justice's attitude in these three respects must surely be sufficient to rebut any presumption of impartiality.

In the opinion of the writer, Davis JA in the Court of Appeal came to the right conclusion that bias had been established. As one reads the facts (as set out above on this aspect), bias leaps from the printed page.

The writer must also feel some sympathy for the view expressed in a local newspaper by one perceptive contributor[28] who asks the following question:

> If men such as the Chief Justice and members of the Commission have been found to have denied a fellow judge the basic principle of natural justice, what is the ordinary citizen to think of his or her chances for fair treatment in court?

The Privy Council's reasoning on this issue is even more puzzling when one notes that the board also found that there was 'some force' in the contention of Davis JA.

S   THE *BARNWELL* CASE

In several respects this case,[29] which was decided by the Guyana Court of Appeal (the court of last resort in that country), resembles the case of *Crane* discussed above: some of the issues involved being almost identical.

The appellant was a High Court judge. On two occasions preceding 1989 he was invited to appear before the Judicial Service Commission (hereafter simply 'the commission') in relation to allegations which had been made about his conduct. In an appropriate case, the commission was empowered under Art 197(5) of the Constitution to make a representation to the President that the question of removing a judge from office ought to be investigated by a tribunal appointed by the President. However, on each occasion, after the appellant had explained his conduct to that forum the issue was treated as closed and no further action was taken.

In September 1989, the appellant was summoned to the chambers of the Chancellor, who was *ex officio* the chairman of the commission. The Chancellor informed the appellant that a magistrate had made allegations against the appellant in a letter which she had sent to the Chancellor. The Chancellor read from the letter but did not show it directly to the appellant, nor provide him with a copy (until much later). The Chancellor reported to the commission on his discussion with the appellant and showed it the letter from the magistrate. A few days after the meeting between the appellant and the Chancellor, the commission (without having afforded the appellant an opportunity to appear before it or to comment in anyway), purporting to act in accordance with Art 197(5), made a representation to the President that the question of removing the appellant from office ought to be investigated. A few days later the appellant was suspended from office under Art 197(7). The appellant applied to the court for judicial review of the decision of the Commission. The declarations sought by him were refused by Perry J and he appealed to the Court of Appeal.

---

28   The contributor in the *Sunday Express* of 6 March 1994, is Mr Reginald Dumas, from whose erudite article some of the points in this section are drawn.

29   *Barnwell v AG of Guyana*, CA Guyana (No 84 of 1991).

Held, allowing the appeal, that the decision of the Commission to make representations to the President with regard to investigating the possible removal of the appellant from office under Art 197(5) was *ultra vires* and void.[30]

It was also held *a fortiori* that a judge is entitled as a matter of natural justice to be heard before the Chancellor offers advice to the President under Art 197(7) of the Constitution on the question of suspending the judge pending a disciplinary inquiry. It was further held that a judge had a legitimate expectation to put his side of the case to the Commission.

T   THE CASE OF THE FLAWED APPOINTMENT OF THE BELIZE CJ

A vacancy having arisen for the appointment of a Chief Justice in Belize, the Prime Minister of Belize decided to have the appointment of his nominee effected before a general election that was due to take place on 27 August 1998.

The Belize Constitution requires that the appointment of a Chief Justice be made by the Governor General on the advice of the Prime Minister after he has consulted with the Leader of the Opposition.[31]

To effect the appointment the following events were put in train.

On 19 August, the Cabinet Secretary addressed a letter to the Leader of the Opposition (who received it by fax on 20 August) inviting comments, on the Prime Minister's behalf, on the proposed appointment of Manuel Sosa as Chief Justice.

On 20 August, the Leader of the Opposition sent a reply to the Prime Minister pointing out that the communication from the Cabinet Secretary was despatched to him after the Attorney General had publicly announced the proposed appointment. The Leader of the Opposition invited the Prime Minister's attention to s 129(2) of the Belize Constitution which is to the following effect:

> 129(2) Where any person or authority is directed by this Constitution or any other law to consult any other person or authority, that other person or authority must be given a genuine opportunity to present his or its views before the decision or action, as the case may be, is taken.

The Leader of the Opposition ended his letter as follows:

> I stand ready to meet with you at your convenience so that I may present my views to you before you take any action or decision on the matter.

On 24 August, the file regarding the appointment was sent to the Governor General who signed and sealed the instrument appointing Mr Justice Sosa as Chief Justice to take effect from 26 August 1998 (which happened to be the day before the general election). On the same day as the Governor General signed the instrument (24 August), the secretary to the Cabinet despatched a further letter to the Leader of the Opposition inviting him to meet the Prime Minister the next day – 25 August.

---

30   Section 197(5) deals with the procedure for removing a judge from office, viz, if the Judicial Service Commission represents to the President that the question of removing a judge from office ought to be investigated, then the President shall appoint a tribunal consisting of a Chairman and not less than two other members to enquire into the matter and advise the President whether or not the judge ought to be removed from office.

31   See Belize Constitution, s 97(1).

On 24 August, the Leader of the Opposition replied to the Prime Minister by fax suggesting that the meeting take place instead on *26 August*. To this communication the Prime Minister replied on 25 August regretting his inability to accede to this further request of the Leader of the Opposition.

On 26 August 1998, the Chief Justice was sworn in by the Governor General.

In the general elections on 27 August 1998, the Government of Mr Manuel Esquivel (the Prime Minister up to that date) was defeated and the Leader of the Opposition (who had held that position before the elections) became the Prime Minister.

The next item in the saga took place on 16 February 1999 (six months later) when one James Jan Mohammed issued an Originating Summons in the High Court as Plaintiff against the Attorney General as defendant seeking the determination *inter alia* of the following questions:

Whether, in view of the provisions of sections 97(1) and 129(2) of the Belize Constitution the Hon Manuel Sosa was validly appointed as Chief Justice with effect from 26 August 1998; and

Whether a Writ of Prohibition should issue restraining the said Manuel Sosa from purporting to act or continuing to act as Chief Justice.

The terms of s 129(2) have already been recited above; s 97(1) states that: '[T]he Chief Justice shall be appointed by the Governor General, acting in accordance with the advice of the Prime Minister *given after consultation with the Leader of the Opposition* [emphasis added].'

Before Meerabux J the defendant submitted that the judge had no jurisdiction in the matter, praying in aid s 34(4) of the Constitution which refers to an ouster of jurisdiction in relation to consultation by the *Governor General* and suggesting that in principle the same ouster *should apply* to the Prime Minister – a submission which, not surprisingly, was rejected. He then addressed the issue of consultation and urged that, since consultation is a mere formality the Prime Minister being at liberty to ignore any contrary views – it did not matter whether or not the Leader of the Opposition had expressed his views. In any event, he was of the opinion that the Leader had been given adequate opportunity to express his views which need not have been in writing but could have been conveyed by telephone.

The judge, quite correctly, held the decision to appoint the Chief Justice void for failure to conform with s 129(2) and because 'it was vitiated by bad faith'.

In concluding his judgment the learned judge made use of the following *obiter*:

I take judicial notice of the fact that general elections of members of the House of Representatives were due to be held on 27 August 1998 and the proposed appointment of Mr. Sosa as Chief Justice became effective *a day before* the election, ie 26 August 1998. Such a course of action is unheard of in a parliamentary democracy based on the Westminster model where the government of the day after the issue of the Writ of Election acts merely in a caretaker capacity and refrains from taking any major decisions. To my mind to appoint a Chief Justice substantively just a day before the general elections makes a mockery of parliamentary democracy.

Did this pronouncement in any way form part of the *ratio decidendi* in this suit? It clearly did not. And why did the judge consider it necessary to embark gratuitously upon it? The writer can only direct the judge's attention to what Laskin CJ had to say concerning freedom of speech from the bench – a suggestion set out below when discussing the Canadian case of *Judge Sparks*.[32]

U   TWO LANDMARK CASES ALLEGING LOSS OF INDEPENDENCE AND JUDICIAL BIAS

Two recent Canadian cases involving members of the judiciary must now be considered. They underscore the extent to which (as occurred in the *Crane* and *Barnwell* cases considered above) members of the senior judiciary are prepared to go to impress upon the public what they deem to be a transparent rôle in the relation to fellow judges.

V   THE CASE OF CHIEF JUSTICE JULIAS ISAAC

The first case involved Mr Justice Julius Isaac, former Chief Justice of the Federal Court of Canada.

The Federal Government had been litigating in the Federal Court decertification matters affecting three alleged former Nazi war criminals. The cases seemed to be moving with painful slowness. The former Chief Justice had previously been working with some success with all concerned (including the Federal Ministry of Justice) on the administrative arrangements for speeding up delays in the administration of justice: this being within his statutory mandate.

On 1 March 1996, an assistant deputy Attorney General (Ted Thompson) telephoned the Chief Justice seeking his good offices in expediting the progress of the three cases. The Chief Justice saw the official in his chambers for about 20 minutes and asked him to put his representations in writing – which was done within hours.

The Chief Justice then conferred with Associate Chief Justice Jerome (who happened to be charged with the management of the cases) enquiring about the cases and informing him of his unhappiness that the Ministry of Justice was planning to short-circuit the Federal Court and to proceed by way of reference to the Supreme Court of Canada on the ground that the Federal Court was unable to deal with the cases in a timely manner a step the Chief Justice was anxious to avoid. As a result, the Chief Justice drafted a reply to the Ministry of Justice official with the help of the Associate Chief Justice promising to put arrangements in train for expediting the hearings.

As will be observed later, the meetings with the justice official and with the Associate Chief Justice were never intended to be a secret nor (in the opinion of the Chief Justice) was the letter from Mr Thompson regarded as a threat in any way.

Two months later the Associate Chief Justice, without informing the Chief Justice, recused himself from the cases and appointed another judge, Cullen J, to hear them. This was after the defendants in the matter had heard of the intervention of the Chief Justice and had made an application to the court for a stay of the proceedings on the ground of

---

32   See under the *Judge Sparks* case, later in this chapter.

judicial interference with the court's business which in their opinions was so grave as to negative the independence of the court.

After considering the cases on judicial independence and judicial impartiality, Cullen J came to the following conclusions:

(a) a reasonable person would believe there had been judicial interference and that the three respondents would not be coming before an independent court;

(b) the *influence* or *pressure* that was brought to bear on the Associate Chief Justice was especially egregious, given that the statements were conveyed by the Chief Justice of the Federal Court;

(c) a reasonable person would conclude that even if the Associate Chief Justice removed himself from these three cases, another judge of the Court would be perceived as responding to the *pressure that was brought to bear* by the Chief Justice and the *Assistant Deputy Attorney General*;

(d) *this affront to judicial* independence is the 'clearest of cases' and a stay of proceedings, in each of the three respondents cases, will be granted. (Emphasis added.)

This asperity of language was not followed in the Appeals Division of the Federal Court which reversed Cullen J and refused the stay on the ground that a stay was not a proper remedy in the peculiar circumstance of the case.

The matter was taken to the Supreme Court of Canada which likewise refused a stay but reverted to the language in which Cullen had condemned the Chief Justice's action. The Supreme Court only felt inclined to disagree with Cullen J on one other point, viz, the extent to which he considered all the judges in the entire Trial Division of the Federal Court would be influenced by the Chief Justice's intervention. They took a contrary view, at the same time praising the 'sturdy resolve that Cullen J had demonstrated' and stating that 'there [was] every reason to think that the example set by Cullen J would be followed by his successor'.

But as far as the Supreme Court was concerned, the appearance if not the fact of judicial independence had '*suffered a serious affront* as a result of the meeting of 1 March 1996'; and '*the affront seriously compromised the appearance of judicial independence*'. The court also referred to the '*improper behaviour*' of the Chief Justice and to his '*ill advised* intervention' while acknowledging in its judgment that the delay in processing the cases was 'inordinate and arguably inexcusable'. Nowhere in the record, however, does it appear that the Supreme Court heard the Chief Justice's side of the story.

The whole matter had by this time been referred to the Canadian Judicial Council operating through a three man panel consisting of Chief Justice Benjamin Hewak of the Court of Queen's Bench of Manitoba, Chief Justice Catherine Fraser of the Alberta Court of Appeal and Associate Chief Justice John Morden of the Ontario Court of Appeal.

On 24 May 1996, the council addressed a letter to the Chief Justice informing him that allegations had been made in proceedings pending in the Federal Court of Canada, Trial Division, that he, in his capacity as Chief Justice of the Federal Court of Canada, had entertained representations on behalf of one party in such proceedings and that such representations had led directly or indirectly to a decision of Associate Chief Justice Jerome to recuse himself as the presiding judge in those proceedings – the whole exercise constituting an interference with the independence of Associate Chief Justice Jerome contrary to the interest of the other parties to the proceedings.

In his reply of 14 June 1996, the Chief Justice defended these allegations with admirable clarity and candour. His reply may be encapsulated in the following seven points:

1   Immediately he became aware of the reported inordinate delay from his brief discussion with the Assistant Deputy Attorney General and from the letter, he summoned the Associate Chief Justice, showed him the letter and asked his help in drafting a reply to which the Associate Chief Justice readily assented, without expressing any disagreement with the terms of the letter; nor did he contest its contents.

2   The Associate Chief Justice not only assisted in preparing the letter but was given a copy thereof.

3   It was never intended that either the meetings with Mr Thompson and the Associate Chief Justice or the two letters would be secret. On Mr Thompson's directions and with the Chief Justice's concurrence copies were dispatched to all counsel concerned within a week.

4   The parties to the litigation were the Minister of Citizenship and Immigration as applicant, and the defendants, although counsel for the applicant was answerable to a lawyer in the Attorney General's Department who is a Senior Legal Adviser in the Department of Citizenship and Immigration.

5   If there was a real concern that a judge in the Federal Court was managing cases in a manner that could result in a failure of justice, it was for the Chief Justice (and no one else) to try and prevent that failure.

6   At no stage did Mr Jerome (the Associate Chief Justice) intimate to the Chief Justice or discuss with him his desire to recuse himself from hearing the cases and it was only when the defendants moved for a stay of the proceedings before him that on 6 May 1996 the Associate Chief Justice wrote to the Registry Officer of the Court recusing himself and assigning Cullen J to hear the cases in his stead.

7   The Chief Justice's actions on 1 March 1996 were motivated only by a conviction that he was performing his statutory administrative and supervisory role as Chief Justice and not by any desire to influence in any way the outcome of proceedings before the court.

The panel of the Judicial Council appointed to investigate the matter showed commendable balance and understanding of the Chief Justice's position and the commonsensical and pragmatic way they grappled with the issues contrasts sharply with the angry and condemnatory approach of the Supreme Court.

The panel made the following telling concessions, viz:

(a) The office of Chief Justice is often the first avenue of redress for lawyers and members of the public when problems are perceived in judicial administration or the conduct of judges. It is highly desirable that such problems be resolved informally, where possible, by the Chief Justice speaking to the judge involved.

(b) 'It follows that when a potential problem is brought to the attention of a Chief Justice concerning unwarranted court delay, it ought not to be ignored.'

(c) The panel 'recognized a number of broad considerations which form part of the background or context for the events of March 1st 1996'. In this regard they referred to a point made by Chief Justice Charles Dublin (who had investigated the matter from the Ministry of Justice aspect for the council) that a special societal interest existed in proceeding expeditiously with this class of case involving alleged war criminals.

The panel mentioned with obvious approval the success which the joint efforts of the Chief Justice, the Associate Chief Justice and Mr Thompson had met in resolving an earlier backlog of cases in relation to immigration applications as well as thousands of unemployment insurance appeals.

(d) The panel drew attention to the fact that the Information Commissioner had publicly criticized the delay by the Federal Court in his annual report prior to the problem being resolved in relation to access litigation. It also drew attention to a two year delay in giving judgment in a previous citizenship case (*Luitjens*) 'which had been the subject of justifiable public criticism'.

(e) Mr Thompson was not counsel in these cases but rather the 'manager' of civil litigation in the Justice Department.

(f) The meeting, which clearly was not meant to be a secret or clandestine, was held in good faith for the purpose of resolving a potential problem of undue delay by the court and without any intention to favour any party to the litigation.

(g) There was nothing improper in the Chief Justice's discussion with the Associate Chief Justice about timing concerns in the five cases before him. 'In these circumstances', wrote the panel, 'your relationship with him was comparable to that of a Chief Justice and a Puisne Judge of the same court. *The merits of these cases were never discussed. Nor were any of his previous adjudicative decisions in these cases (eg to require oral argument)*'.

The panel was however unhappy about the apparent deference to the executive implicit in the Chief Justice's phrase 'to avoid a reference' to the Supreme Court, but it went on to express satisfaction that, despite the wording, the Chief Justice's letter was not sent in response to a threat, 'nor was there any inappropriate deference in [his] conduct.'

The panel raised points about the manner the Chief Justice had dealt with correspondence from one of the defendants' lawyers – Mr Abols – and conceded that Mr Abols' complaint was made without realising the limited role played by the Chief Justice in respect of the cases. The panel also made the point that since Mr Abols' letter to the Chief Justice was copied to the Associate Chief Justice 'it was reasonable to assume that [the latter] would deal with that letter'.

The panel expressed the view that since the Chief Justice saw the justice official, and then corresponded with him, it would have been more appropriate for him to dispatch copies of the subject letters to all counsel *immediately*. No one can quarrel with this mild rebuke which clearly could not justify the intemperate and unjudicial language unleashed by the Supreme Court.

The Panel summarised as follows:

However the Panel does not consider this inadvertence on your part to have been serious for the following reasons:

(1) the reaction of the Associate Chief Justice to Mr Thompson's letter reasonably led you to conclude that there was scope to proceed more expeditiously without sacrificing fairness;

(2) the correspondence was actually circulated within one week of the discussions;

(3) the parties did have the opportunity to raise any potential concerns about undue expedition of the hearing when it subsequently resumed on 30 April 1996; and

(4) a review of the proceedings reveals no indication of any undue haste being experienced by the respondents. Indeed, counsel for the respondents were prepared to proceed as early as 12 December 1995.

When all these factors were taken into account, the panel found that the Chief Justice's failure to notify counsel for the respondents about the meeting was inappropriate *but not serious*.

The panel concluded that the enquiry into the complaint against the Chief Justice, as well as further enquiries conducted on the panel's behalf by Professor Ed Ratushny of the Faculty of Law, University of Ottawa, led to their decision that there should be no formal investigation pursuant to the relevant section of the Judges Act and felt that the Chief Justice's conduct '[did] not warrant even consideration of [his] removal from the office of judge'. They therefore closed the file.

When one examines the reasoned manner in which the panel studied the matter and contrasts it with the intemperate and strident way the Supreme Court dealt with the Chief Justice's well meant intervention in the cause of justice, it is difficult not to come to the conclusion that there was more to the judgment of the Supreme Court than meets the eye.

The result of the Chief Justice's action was intended to be expedition, but finalising the cases was eventually greatly prolonged by the bizarre turn of events. His well intentioned efforts were lamentably counter-productive, but his brethren in the Supreme Court were clearly not interested in minimising or arresting the delay which was ongoing.

In the case of *RDS v The Queen* (to which reference is made in the immediately following section) the Supreme Court went on record stating the following two propositions:

The onus of demonstrating bias lies with the person who is alleging its existence.[33]

Courts have rightly recognized that there is a presumption that judges will carry out their oath of office ... This is one of the reasons why the threshold for a successful allegation of perceived judicial bias is high.[34]

Was there some special reason why these two propositions were not applied in the *Isaac's* case, as they were in the *Sparks* case? They seem even more appropriate to the former than to the latter.

---

33   *R v RDS* [1977] 3 SCR 484, para 114.

34   *Ibid*, para 117.

W   THE *JUDGE SPARKS* CASE

This was a relatively minor criminal case, *RDS v The Queen*[35] which began in the Youth and Family Court in Nova Scotia and eventually reached the Supreme Court of Canada.

The facts of the case are set out in the following head note:

> A young accused was charged with two counts of assault on a peace officer and one count of resisting a peace officer in the execution of his duty. He had stumbled upon the scene of an incident involving his friend and a police officer in the course of which the friend was placed in handcuffs by the officer. The accused then inquired of his friend as to whether he wanted his mother to be notified that he was under arrest. Upon the accused making this inquiry, the police officer threatened to arrest him too and held him so tightly around the neck that he could hardly breathe. The police officer gave a totally different account and sought to present the young accused, a person of slight and slender build, as his attacker.

> He appeared very nervous while giving his evidence and never mentioned that he had handcuffed the accused's friend during the incident.

> It was HELD: Accused not guilty. The issue in this case was whether the officer and the accused's testimony was sufficiently credible so that the Crown had failed to prove all the elements of the three offences beyond a reasonable doubt.

In deciding to acquit, the trial judge made the following statement:

> In my view, in accepting the evidence, and I do not say that I accept everything that Mr S has said in court today, but certainly he has raised a doubt in my mind and, therefore based upon the evidentiary burden, which is squarely placed upon the Crown, that they must prove all the elements of the offence beyond a reasonable doubt, I have queries in my mind with respect to what actually transpired on the afternoon of 17 October.

The Youth Court Judge continued:

> The Crown says, well why would the officer say that events occurred the way in which he has relayed them to the court this morning. I am not saying that the constable has misled this court, although police officers have been known to do that in the past. And I am not saying that the officer overreacted but certainly police officers do overreact, particularly when they are dealing with non-white groups. That, to me, indicates a state of mind right there that is questionable.

> I believe that probably the situation in this particular case is the case of a young police officer who overreacted. And I do accept the evidence of Mr S that he was told to shut up or he would be under arrest. That seems to be in keeping with the prevalent attitude of the day.

> At any rate, based upon my comments and based upon all of the evidence before the court I have no other choice but to acquit.

This statement is quoted in full, because reference will hereafter be made to the second and third paragraphs of it, when consideration is being given to the question as to whether there wasa real likelihood of bias by the court of first instance.

The police appealed against the decision to acquit and this appeal was heard by Glube, Chief Justice of the Supreme Court of Nova Scotia, sitting as a summary

---

35   [1997] 3 SCR 484.

conviction appeal court judge. The Chief Justice ordered that a new trial be held before a different judge. She found that in spite of the thorough review of the facts and the finding of credibility, the second and third paragraphs referred to above 'lead to the conclusion that a reasonable apprehension of bias exists ... Having found that, I need go no further as such a finding requires that a new trial be ordered'.

Against that determination RDS (the young man) appealed to the Nova Scotia Court of Appeal which by a majority dismissed the appeal.

The matter was taken to the Supreme Court of Canada where the appeal was allowed by a 6:3 majority and the trial judge's acquittal ordered to be restored.

Three of the Supreme Court judges (Lamer CJ, Sopinka and Major JJ) took the view that the judge's comments stereotyped all police officers as liars and racists and were not based on the evidence before her. On this ground, they would have dismissed the appeal.

Four of the Judges (LaForest, Heureux-Dube, Gonthier and McLachlin) saw nothing wrong with the comments or with the judge using her experience as a member of the community – in particular the existence of racism – to evaluate the evidence.

Two of the judges (Cory and Jacobucci) concluded that the trial judge's comments concerning the propensity of police officers to lie and to over-react when dealing with non-whites (though 'unfortunate', 'worrisome' and 'close to the line') were not sufficient to demonstrate bias on her part when read in the context of the whole decision.

The four judges who gave very positive support to the impugned pronouncements of Judge Sparks had this to say:

> The impugned comments were not unfortunate, unnecessary, or too close to the line. They reflected an entirely appropriate recognition of the facts in evidence and of the context within which this case arose – a context known to the judge and to any well informed member of the community.

The writer commends the members of the Supreme Court who were willing to defend this 'contextualised judging' on the part of a family court judge.

The comments made by the judge in this case may not have been inappropriate but they were clearly unnecessary. The judge would have been well advised to be guided by some words of that wise Chief Justice of Canada (CJ Bora Laskin) in an address given by him at Lakehead University in 1974 in the course of which he had this to say about judicial pronouncements from the Bench:[36]

> Freedom of speech has a limited meaning for judges. They must confine themselves to such utterances as come from their reasons for judgment. They are not free to roam public assemblies and expatiate on public issues. This endangers their impartiality and their integrity, both of which must be preserved to maintain public confidence ... Judges, however bright, however knowledgeable on public affairs, cannot bring their judicial office into a public forum by participating in public affairs. Their choice of vocation has meant, in my view, a deliberate choice to leave public affairs alone and let others – and there are many others – deal with them.

All that the judge in giving judgment needed to say was that *on the evidence before her* the prosecution's case raised severe doubts in her mind as to the guilt of the accused – which doubts she had decided should be resolved in favour of the accused.

---

36   See the *Globe and Mail Newspaper*, Toronto, Canada, 28 March 1974.

X   CARIBBEAN COURT OF LAST RESORT

It is fashionable to criticise the draftsmen of our independence Constitutions on the ground that a Caribbean Court of Appeal should at the outset have been declared the final court for the determination of legal issues in the area. But in order to put the matter in proper perspective one must go back to the time and manner in which self-determination was achieved in the Caribbean. After the dissolution of the Federal Government in May 1962, Jamaica attained independence in a few months (by mid-August 1962), to be followed by Trinidad and Tobago on 31 August 1962. One can understand why they both could not at that time, with all the other problems they were then facing, consider establishing a final Court of Appeal in place of the Privy Council. Indeed, even when Trinidad and Tobago became a republic in 1976 it chose surprisingly to remain wedded to the Privy Council, unlike Guyana, which on changing to republicanism in 1980, immediately abolished appeals to the Privy Council.

What is odd is that although a high powered Committee of Caribbean jurists recommended that appeals to the Privy Council be abolished in 1972 in favour of a Caribbean Supreme Court,[37] up to the time of writing (July 2001) nothing has been achieved. So far the Attorneys General who have been drafting the Agreement establishing the court have produced eight drafts. The court was due to commence operation first in 1998, then in 1999, then in 2000: but, at the Heads of Government Conference of the Caribbean Community in July 2000, it was agreed, in deference to submissions from distinguished senior members of the Jamaican Bar, that further efforts should be made to involve the Caribbean public in the intended establishment of the Caribbean Court of Justice (hereafter referred to simply as 'the Court').

The agreement

The agreement establishing the Court (which was signed on 14 February 2001) provides, *inter alia*, for the following:

1   The abolition of appeals to the Privy Council.

2   The Court to have an original jurisdiction to hear and deliver judgments in disputes between the Contracting Parties; disputes between the community and the Contracting Parties; in respect of referrals from national Contracting Parties; and in respect of applications by nationals in accordance with Art IX of the agreement.

3   The Court's appellate jurisdiction to cover those powers conferred on it by the agreement or by the Constitutions of the Contracting Parties or any other law of a Contracting Party. Appeals to lie to the Court from:

(a) final decisions of Courts of Appeal in civil matters where the matter in dispute is of the value of EC$25,000 or if the appeal involves directly or indirectly a claim or a question respecting property or a right of the aforesaid value;

(b) final decisions in proceedings for dissolution or nullity of marriage;

---

37   See the Report of the Representative Committee of the Organisation of Commonwealth Caribbean Bar Associations (OCCBA) on the Establishment of a Caribbean Court of Appeal in substitution for the Judicial Committee of the Privy Council – June 1972. The Committee recommended the early establishment of a regional court, the only dissenting voice being that of Professor Keith Patchett in his Minority Report, pp 58–62.

(c) final decisions in any civil or other proceedings which involve a question as to the interpretation of the Constitution of a Contracting Party;

(d) final decisions given in the exercise of a jurisdiction conferred upon a superior court relating to redress for contravention of a constitutional provision for the protection of fundamental rights; and

(e) such other cases as may be prescribed by any law of a Contracting Party.

4   Appeals lie to the Court with the leave of the Court of Appeal of a Contracting Party in the case of final decisions in any civil proceedings where, in the opinion of the Court of Appeal, the question involved in the appeal is one that by reason of the great general or public importance or otherwise ought to be submitted to the Court. Appeals would also lie in such other cases as may be prescribed by any law of a Contracting Party.

There is provision for appeals to the Court by special leave in any civil or criminal matter.

5   *Rules*

Provision is made for the President and five other Judges of the Court to make rules of Court for regulating the practice and procedure of the Court; the selection of judges for any purpose; the period to be observed as a vacation in the Court; the transaction of business during such vacation; pleadings and practice; costs and taxation; forms and fees; and prescribing such matters as are required to be regulated.

The President of the Court is to be appointed by three-quarters of the signatory Member States on the recommendation of the Regional Judicial and Legal Services Commission which would be the administrative arm of the Court and would consist of:

(a) the President (Chair);

(b) two persons nominated jointly by OCCBA and the OECS Bar Associations;

(c) one Chairman of the Judicial Services Commission of a Contracting Party selected in rotation in the English alphabetical order for a period of three years;

(d) the Chairman of a Public Service Commission of a Contracting Party selected in rotation in the reverse English alphabetical order for a period of three years;

(e) two persons from civil society nominated jointly by the Secretary General of the Community and the director general of the OECS for a period of three years following consultations with regional non-governmental organisations;

(f) two distinguished jurists nominated jointly by the dean of the Faculty of Law of the University of the West Indies, the deans of the Faculties of Law of any of the Contracting Parties and the Chairman of the Council of Legal Education; and

(g) two persons nominated jointly by the Bar of Law Associations of the Contracting Parties.

It is this Commission too that will exercise disciplinary powers over the judges (excluding the President) and over officials and employees of the Court.

Availability of judges

When the time comes to select the nine members of the tribunal, the commission should bear in mind that this region has produced a highly distinguished former member of the International Court of Justice;[38] an outstanding former Chief Justice of the Federal Court of Canada;[39] two eminent serving members of the International Criminal Court[40] and two respected serving judges of the Law of the Sea Tribunal.[41] It seems only sensible therefore that a careful audit should be undertaken of the available judicial material on the Bench (wherever they are) or in other legal practice or public service in the Caribbean, as well as those whose domicile is in the area but who have found it expedient to live and work elsewhere. And such an audit should clearly be undertaken before recruiting judges from elsewhere in the Commonwealth.

It is hoped too that the selectors will not fail to select outstanding members of the practising Bar with the necessary qualifications of integrity, intellectual calibre and moral fibre. The Court's jurisdiction is extensive and multi-faceted. Not only will the judges have to be versed in constitutional law, international law and international trade law, but they will also have to be well acquainted with criminal law, equity, civil law and procedure while at the same time having arbitration skills.

It goes without saying that the Court will only attract the right calibre of judges if their salaries are adequate to enable them to live according to their independent station in life.

To those who doubt if we can still 'deliver the goods' judiciary-wise, as we did at the time of the Federal Supreme Court, the writer would point to such decisions as *LaSalle*[42] – a Trinidad and Tobago case in which, at the Court of Appeal level, the three presiding judges[43] gave judgments which were as brilliant as they were devastating to the Government, relative to the doctrine of condonation, thereby acquitting those accused of attempting to overthrow the Government. Reference can be made also to the judgments of Graham-Perkins and Swaby JJA in the Jamaica *Gun Court* cases, in which these judges declared the Gun Court Act unconstitutional[44] and to a number of cases in the OECS in which the judges of that court have shown much valour and fearlessness, thereby incurring the undying hostility of some Heads of Government. It would therefore be grossly unfair for a charge to be levelled against West Indian judges that on the whole they have displayed a lack of judicial valour or that many of them do not have the requisite level of competence.

Sometimes that valour has cost some of them promotion, but the facts do not often see the light of day, since no stranger can normally be privy to the activities of Judicial and Legal Services Commissions or the private discussions of Chief Justices with the

---

38 Judge Mohamed Shahabuddeen of Guyana.

39 Chief Justice Julius Isaac of Grenada and Canada.

40 Judge Patrick Robinson of Jamaica and Judge Mohamed Shahabuddeen.

41 Judges Edward Laing of Belize and Dolliver Nelson of Grenada. Judge Laing recently passed away.

42 *LaSalle v R* (1971) 20 WIR 361.

43 Fraser, Phillips and Georges, JJA.

44 See *Hinds v R* (1975) 24 WIR 339. The Privy Council subsequently held the legislation was *intra vires* the legislature but allowed the appeals in respect of sentence and to the extent that a jurisdiction was granted to the Full Court Division which belonged to the Supreme Court: such court comprising three resident magistrates.

executive. Sometimes that valour has prevented them even from obtaining an extension of their service, in cases where such extension requires the approval of the executive, for example, the OECS Authority, consisting of Heads of Govenment. For this reason it is certainly good to observe that the agreement creating the Court makes no provision for applications for extension beyond the prescribed retiring age.

Retiring age of judges

One is puzzled as to why the judges of this Court should retire at age 72. The United States Supreme Court has no retirement age for its judges. The Supreme Court of Canada and the House of Lords have a retirement age of 75. There is therefore certainly no reason why the Caribbean should not have a retiring age of 75.[45]

Should the Court travel?

There are those who feel the Court should *not* be itinerant on the ground, that justice should not be administered from a suitcase. That attitude is misconceived. If it is a regional Court, it should sit at various jurisdictions in the region. If it does not, the other territories will nurture a feeling (even if misguided) that the Court is there only to serve the litigants in the territory in which it is located – thus, defeating the regional nature of the Court. What is more, the expected reduction in the cost of accessing the Court will fail to materialise – thus, preventing financially disadvantaged litigants in other territories from having access to justice.

Financing the Court

One fear that has been voiced by well wishers and advocates of the Court is that, with their frail economies, Caribbean Governments would be unable sustainably to finance the Court on a permanent basis from their thin budgets.

Happily, from all appearances, all participating Governments have realised the need for the financial stability of the institution and have stated that the Court will not be launched unless they are satisfied that adequate funds are committed to guarantee that stability.[46] They have therefore arranged funding for the recruitment expenses of the Court for the first five years of its operation.

A trust fund – to be administered by the Caribbean Development Bank – has been established and is to be capitalised in an adequate amount so as to enable those expenses to be met by income from the Trust. This arrangement would obviate the possibility of judges' salaries and other emoluments being subject to any possible capricious disposition by a particular Government.

---

45 It is conceded that this age of 72 is an improvement on the prevailing retirement age of 65, as pointed out by Hugh Rawlins in his paper on the Caribbean Court to Justice (2000), p 36. (This is a paper commissioned by the Preparatory Committee on the Caribbean Court.)

46 *Ibid.*

Extra-regional international interests are likely to join participating Governments in capitalising the fund.

Without such a guaranteed arrangement, the judicial structure is likely to collapse and we cannot possibly allow our highest court to fall by the financial wayside.

Y   EDUCATING THE PUBLIC

The CARICOM (Caribbean Community) Secretariat must be highly commended for the steps it has taken to enlighten the Caribbean public on the benefits that will accrue from the establishment of the Caibbean Court of Justice and how those benefits can be accessed. Several vital questions have been answered in a monograph complied by Duke Pollard, the Secretariat's legal consultant, in the preface to which he speaks of the timeliness of the court in these terms:[47]

> At a time when the Caribbean Community is forging ahead with the creation of a Caribbean Single Market and Economy (CSME) as an answer to the aggressive pace of globalisation and configuration of international trade, the establishment of a Caribbean Court of Justice is a critical component in this effort, especially in its original jurisdiction.

The national debate on the court has gathered momentum and the concerns of individuals and organisations are being addressed.

At the regional level, the political directorate signed the agreement on 14 February 2001, but it is hoped that the court could be up and running by 2004. There are welcome signs that the area as a whole has at last become convinced, in Pollard's words that, 'an indigenous Court consisting of regional judges is best suited to pronounce on issues of regional importance and, in so doing, to contribute to the development of a regional jurisprudence'.

Z   ACCOUNTABILITY

To what extent are judges accountable, and to whom, in the discharge of their functions, especially in small Caribbean (or other similar) societies? As a judge in a Third World country recently wrote:[48]

> We live in an era of greater public demands for judicial accountability. The call for judicial accountability is gaining momentum in many parts of the world. The judiciary is no longer considered a sacrosanct and inviolable sanctuary of its occupants.

Theirs is a heavy duty of accountability in the adjudicative process. In order to understand their position one needs to go no further, but look at the section under

---

47   See Pollard 2000. See, also, a very useful article by the same author (Pollard, 1997).

48   See Tikeram, 1993, being an extract from a paper presented by the Hon Justice Sir Moti Tikeram, Vice President, Court of Appeal, Fiji, to the 10th South Pacific Conference held in Yanuca Island, Fiji, in May 1993.

'Provisions to secure protection of law', in the fundamental rights section of our respective Constitutions. This is what we find.

Every trial in court – civil or criminal – must normally be conducted in open court unless in a criminal case the accused so conducts himself/herself as to make the continuation of the proceedings in his/her presence impracticable.

A litigant must be accorded a fair hearing within a reasonable time before an independent and impartial tribunal established by law.

In a criminal cause or matter he/she is presumed innocent until proved guilty or until he/she has pleaded guilty. He/she must be informed in language he/she understands, and in detail, of the nature of the offence with which he/she is charged. Such an accused must always be given adequate time and facilities to enable him/her to prepare his or her defence and he/she must be permitted to defend himself/herself in person or by counsel of his/her choice and at his/her own expense.

The defendant or accused must also be given facilities to enable him/her to examine in person or through his/her legal representative any witness or witnesses called by the prosecution. He/she is also to be provided without charge with an interpreter if he/she is unable to understand the language used at the trial.

In some jurisdictions (for example, The Bahamas), he/she is entitled, when charged on information in the Supreme Court, to have the right of trial by jury. When tried for a criminal offence, the accused shall have the right, if he/she so requests and pays the prescribed fee, to be furnished, within a reasonable time after judgment, with a copy of the full record of proceedings.

A judge must give his or her decision in open court, usually in writing, in which case he or she is expected to furnish reasons for his or her decision. But even when he or she gives an 'off-the-cuff' oral decision, reasons must be provided.

If the litigant is dissatisfied with the judge's determination, he/she normally has a right of appeal to a higher court, unless the law prescribes otherwise.

Is the judge only concerned with interpreting the law as he or she finds it?

He or she has a more positive role than that. This is what the author has written in another book on that subject:[49]

> In a matter of family law in court, the judge may well, because of expert knowledge in that field, realise that a particular situation calls for some revision of the law – it may be in respect of rights in the matrimonial property or marriage contracts or the freedom to make special arrangements in respect of children of the union. The lawyer should not hesitate to put forward his view; it may be that his suggestion will be avidly adopted, in which case his submission will have served the public interest. As it was so felicitously put by a distinguished jurist, speaking on the law making process of a judge:
>
> > In sum, in the common law there is a general warrant for judicial law making; in statute law there is not. In the common law development is permitted, if not expected; in statute law there must be at least a presumption that Parliament has on the topic it is dealing with said all that it wants to say. (Lord Devlin in delivering the Fourth Chorley Lecture at the London School of Economics on June 25th, 1975.)

---

49   Phillips, 1978, p 147.

Z(i)   A LONELY EXISTENCE

In his treatise on the nature of the judicial process, Judge Benjamin Cardozo (a former Justice of the US Supreme Court) admitted to having been much 'troubled in spirit' in his early years upon the Bench 'to find how trackless was the ocean on which (he) had embarked'. He asserted that he sought for certainty but was oppressed and disheartened to discover that his quest for it was futile. He was trying, he said, to reach land, '... the solid land of fixed and settled rules, the paradise of a justice that would declare itself by tokens plainer and more commanding than its pale and glimmering reflections in my own vacillating mind and conscience'.[50] What Cardozo was emphasising was that judges are in 'a place apart' – as Senator Arthur Meighen of the Canadian Senate described them in 1932. At the same time, Cardozo was reflecting that, like other ordinary human beings, judges must sometimes be apprehensive as to whether in coming to a particular decision they are on the right track – or whether they are wide of the mark. Finally, we must let Cardozo's picturesque words speak for themselves[51] concerning the lonely place of judges in the scheme of things:

> They do not stand aloof on these chill and distant heights; and we shall not help the cause of truth by acting and speaking as if they do. The great tides and currents that engulf the rest of men do not turn aside and pass the judges by.

The position of a superior court judge is an almost impossible one. Such a person must be judicious, well read, restrained in manner and language, aloof without being grave, erudite, humane, learned, independent, impartial and humble – all rolled into one. Above all, such a judge must steadfastly heed the injunction of Socrates to hear courteously, answer wisely, consider soberly and decide impartially. He must in a word be as near super-human as any individual can ever be.

---

50   Cardozo, 1964, pp 166 and 167.
51   *Ibid*, p 167.

CHAPTER 14

THE PUBLIC SERVICE

HISTORICAL BACKGROUND OF DISMISSAL AT PLEASURE

Dismissal at pleasure was, at the time of colonial domination, a firm principle of British constitutional law which was applicable in the then British Empire. But (as we shall see in this chapter), there are still traces in the public service of present day independent States. The doctrine derives its origin from the *Stingsby* case[1] in which Stingsby, the Master of the Mint, having been accused of misdemeanour, was suspended by the Sovereign, even though he held office for life. The court upheld the suspension on the ground that it was within the King's prerogative to suspend a public officer. The doctrine was to reign supreme not only in Britain (as it still does) but in 'Her Majesty's Dominions and Realms' beyond the seas, where it is today very much on the wane, having been abolished in the Caribbean in the dramatic and abrupt manner that we shall show below.

Why did it linger so long?

It is hardly necessary to remind readers that the Caribbean territories were Colonies of Britain up to the second half of the 20th century and that, until that time, the civil service was manned especially in the smallest territories at the highest levels by expatriate British officers recruited by the then Colonial Office. They were all itinerant officials liable to be transferred from one territory to another serving as members of such Colonial Services as the administrative, educational, agricultural, legal and medical. They were servants of the Crown liable to dismissal at pleasure, as were (of course) also their local supporting clerical and administrative staff for whom rules and regulations were laid down by the expatriates who gave the orders and extracted compliance.

In respect of local junior staff in the colonies, the Governor promulgated administrative rules variously known as General Orders, Civil Service Staff Orders or Departmental Orders and these were at the time of independence to continue to operate in tandem with new Civil Service Acts of Parliament. In addition, there had in colonial times been what were called Colonial Regulations, with their origin in the Colonial Office in London, sent out as guides to Governors in their dealings mainly with the expatriate staff.

In general, the regulations, as they affected local civil servants, were draconian. A public officer was forbidden, for instance, from serving as an editor of a newspaper and a magazine, or from taking part in managing them either directly or indirectly.[2] Nor was a public officer permitted to contribute to journals or newspapers anonymously or to express opinions on matters of a political or administrative nature.[3] Nor may he

---

1   *Stingsby* [1680] 3 Swan 178.
2   St Vincent Public Service (Conditions of Employment) Act 1971 (No 16 of 1971), s 3(1)(a).
3   *Ibid*, s 3(1)(b) and (c).

broadcast or be interviewed on any matter which 'could reasonably' be regarded as political or administrative in nature.[4] Nor may he speak or preside or take any prominent part in a meeting which might be regarded as political.[5] Nor could a public officer summon a meeting to consider any action of the Government.[6] Nor was he permitted to serve as an agent or sub-agent of any political party or candidate during any local or national election.[7] All these restrictions were clearly intended to effect a total insulation of public officers from the political arm of Government. No one seems to have paid the slightest attention to the fact that most if not all of these restrictions were in breach of the fundamental rights and freedoms laid down by the Universal Declaration of Rights and the European Convention on Human Rights. The legislation affecting a civil servant's freedom of expression has already been successfully attacked in at least one jurisdiction[8] and is likely to be a further source of litigation in the years ahead.

A full and erudite exposition of the basis of the doctrine of dismissibility at pleasure has been given by Dr Kenny Anthony in one of his many writings on the subject.[9] He points out that it was Lord Hobhouse who in 1895 articulated the principle that dismissal at pleasure by the Crown was an implied term in the contract of every public servant.[10] The doctrine was, however, shortly afterwards qualified to the extent that it was then decided that the power of the Crown in dismissing at pleasure was limited by statute.[11]

Dr Anthony also stipulates that a further qualification attempted by Lord Atkin (relating to contractual fixed term and dismissal for cause) was not pursued.[12] In his own words:

> But this lead was never followed. Henceforth, the Courts retreated to assume vacillatory postures. Ironically, the defensive judicial posture developed in an environment in which there was a substantial increase in the legislation regulating the terms and conditions of employment of Crown servants.

In *Venata Rao v Secretary of State for India*,[13] the Privy Council held that, despite the existence of rules made under an Act of Parliament, a police inspector was liable to dismissal at pleasure where a provision in the rules had been breached requiring an inquiry before dismissal.

A second case which illustrates the attitude of Courts in this matter is *Malloch v Aberdeen Corp*.[14]

---

4 St Vincent Public Service (Conditions of Employment) Act 1971 (No 16 of 1971), s 3(1)(d).
5 *Ibid*, s 3(1)(e).
6 *Ibid*, s 3(1)(f).
7 *Ibid*, s 3(1)(h).
8 See the Antigua case *de Freitas v Ministry of Agriculture* (1998) 53 WIR 131.
9 See Dr Kenny Anthony's, 1983. The writer has, in this chapter, drawn heavily on the article and is much indebted to Dr Anthony, not only for recording in such a scholarly way his researches on this subject, but for the contribution in LLB Thesis (unpublished) entitled Legal Restraints and Disabilities of Caribbean Public Officers (1983). Dr Anthony is currently Prime Minister of St Lucia.
10 *Shenton v Smith* [1895] AC 229, pp 234–35.
11 *Gould v Stuart* [1896] AC 575.
12 See *RV Reilly* [1934] AC 176.
13 [1937] 2 AC 248.
14 [1971] 2 All ER 1278.

In this case, Malloch (a teacher) was dismissed without a hearing because he failed to place his name on a register when requested so to do under the provisions of the Teaching Council (Scotland) Act of 1965. The corporation contended that Malloch's appointment was at the pleasure of the Crown and that accordingly the rules of natural justice (that he should be heard) were not applicable. The House of Lords thought otherwise and held that Malloch should have been heard since 'the common law stands modified by statute'.

Thus, the law on the subject had in the space of 34 years come full circle: the *Malloch* decision being in full accord with *Gould v Stuart* in which the harsh rule was modified by a statutory limitation.

Public servants and Caribbean independence constitutions

Accordingly, one would have expected that, upon independence, there would have been a reversal of the dismissal at pleasure rule.

Nobrega v AG of Guyana

The first case in which a court in the Caribbean raised the possibility that the rule should be modified was *Nobrega v AG of Guyana*,[15] a case that came before the Guyana Court of Appeal shortly before Guyana became an independent country (in May 1966).

The facts of this case were as follows: in 1964 Ms Nobrega (the appellant) was offered and accepted employment by the Government as a Grade 1 Class 1 school teacher at a salary of $251 per month.

On 17 March 1965 she was asked by letter to submit her birth and academic certificates to the Ministry of Education, which she failed to do on that day. On 19 March 1965, she received a letter from the Ministry to the effect that *because of her failure to submit the documents requested* her appointment as a Grade 1 Class 1 teacher had been rescinded as from that date, and that she would thereafter be paid as an unqualified teacher; but that upon receipt of the documents her status would be reviewed and a new letter of appointment would be issued to her.

Upon receipt of the letter of 19 March 1965 the appellant promptly dispatched the documents, but she received no further communication from the Ministry until the time came at the end of the month to receive her salary when she discovered her salary had been reduced from $215 to $92 per month.

It was in these circumstances that the appellant brought an action asking the Court for a declaration that she was entitled to receive $215 per month and that the purported reduction of her salary to $92 per month was *ultra vires* and of no effect. Her action was dismissed by the High Court, but the Guyana Court of Appeal overturned the High Court's decision by a majority.

In the course of the Chancellor's judgment when the matter reached the Court of Appeal, Stoby (C) made a statement of the law which was to prove prophetic when the question of dismissal at pleasure was eventually abolished by the Privy Council in 1983 – a matter to be discussed later. Here is what the learned Chancellor had to say:[16]

15 (1967) 10 WIR 187.
16 *Ibid*, 192E.

In the light of these positive statements (concerning the Crown's right to dismiss at pleasure) and because *Shenton v Smith* is binding on this Court it is not open to us in a case occurring before the grant of Independence to express a different view. Suffice it to say that in a case occurring after 26 May 1966, having regard to Article 96(1) of the Constitution of Guyana the position of Crown servants may have to be re-examined and determined afresh ...

The Court did however consider that the case was *sui generis* in that not only was the appellant dismissed, but she had had her salary reduced. Citing Lord Atkin in *Reilly v the King*, the majority of the court ruled that since a contract existed in this instance the rights and liabilities thereunder subsisted. Accordingly, the appellant had a right under her contract to receive a specific salary for specific work. In other words, in the opinion of the Court of Appeal, while the Crown could dismiss at pleasure and no action lay for wrongful dismissal, the Crown was not at liberty unilaterally to alter the terms of a contract.[17]

The Attorney General appealed to the Privy Council who allowed the appeal on the ground that Ms Nobrega's appointment was rescinded on the basis of dismissal at pleasure and she was (by implication) offered a new contract at a lesser rate of salary, which she accepted.[18]

The Board did not review the line of cases, nor did they comment in any way upon the Chancellor's suggestion that with the introduction of the new Guyana Constitution the position of Crown Servants should be reconsidered as far as their dismissal was concerned.

A second opportunity to put the policy of dismissal at pleasure to rest was *AG of Trinidad and Tobago v Toby*.[19] This was a suit in which the Government of Trinidad and Tobago engaged the services of Toby, a barrister who had specialised in tax law. The contract was for a period of three years from 1 July 1970 with a fixed salary and certain allowances. The officer was to act in all respects according to the instructions given by the Government through the Minister and his duties were clearly defined. On 19 January 1972, he became a director of a private company whose principal business was the operation of cinemas. On 22 January 1972, his appointment was terminated, as his involvement with the cinema company was considered incompatible with his appointment as special fiscal adviser to the minister and in breach of the express and implied terms of the contract.

The officer brought an action in the High Court claiming damages for wrongful dismissal. The court held that the plaintiff was a servant of the Crown and was dismissible at pleasure; that in any event the nature of the business or trade in which he had become involved was likely to conflict with his duties under the contract and destroy the basis of trust essential to the proper relationship with the Government. The court, however, held that his gratuity provided under the contract was apportionable in respect of the period of his completed service.

---

17 *Ibid*, 193.
18 (1969) 15 WIR 51, p 55.
19 (1976) 28 WIR 277.

The Government appealed the matter to the Court of Appeal which agreed with the High Court on all aspects, except the decision to grant the officer a proportionate part of his gratuity.[20]

As we shall see when we consider the next case, a great deal of time was lost in the *Toby* case on the issue of whether Toby was dismissible at pleasure for, although not formally yet judicially declared, the doctrine was already dead – by virtue of the Trinidad and Tobago Constitution.

Thomas v AG of Trinidad and Tobago[21]

The next and decisive case to which reference must now be made is *Thomas v AG of Trinidad and Tobago* which has been described by Dr Francis Alexis as 'the most progressive decision given by a court in latter-day public law'[22] who has also picturesquely characterised the Privy Council decision in this case as having 'destroyed the dismissal at pleasure doctrine with a two-edged sword.'[23]

The facts of the case are as follows: Endell Thomas, an assistant superintendent of Police in the Trinidad and Tobago Police Force, was charged with three counts under Police Service Regulations. The commission acting under those regulations dismissed him from the force and he claimed declarations that the regulations were *ultra vires* the Constitution of Trinidad and Tobago, null and void and of no effect; that his purported interdiction on half pay and laying charges against him were *ultra vires* and of no effect; that the purported charges, enquiry and conviction were *ultra vires* the Police Service Regulations 1966, null and void and of no effect; that he was at all material times a public officer and a member of the police service holding the office of assistant superintendent of police; that he was and had at all material times been entitled to his full salary, emoluments, rights, leave and other benefits of that office and service. In the alternative, he claimed he had been wrongfully dismissed from the office and service and requested damages and costs.

The *Thomas* case is the *locus classicus* of the principle that where, in a constitution, the power to appoint and remove public officers is vested in a service commission, the doctrine of dismissal at pleasure ceases to have effect.

In this case, the Privy Council (speaking through Lord Diplock) held that the power of the commission to remove a police officer from office under s 99(1) of the Trinidad and Tobago 1962 Independence Constitution *embraced every means* by which a police officer's contract of employment could be terminated against his will but the power to remove had to be for reasonable cause of which the Commission was to be the sole judge. The Board accepted that reg 74 was *ultra vires* the Commission's power to regulate its own procedure, but was of the view that reference to that regulation in the charges made against assistant superintendent of police Thomas 'was mere surplusage' and could not be said to have misled the police officer or to invalidate the imposition of the penalty of his removal from the police service under s 99(1) (which was *intra vires* the commission's

---

20 (1976) 28 WIR 292–303, *per* Rees JA.
21 (1981) 32 WIR 375.
22 See Alexis, 1987, p 149.
23 See Alexis, 1982, p 41.

regulation making power) for disciplinary offences in the officer's contract of employment.[24]

It was also held that it was the duty of the court and not the Police Service Commission to determine the extent of the functions of the Commission in considering whether s 102(4) of the Constitution ousts the jurisdiction of the courts: 'Since, however, the removal of the plaintiff from the Police Service ... fell fairly and squarely within the Commission's functions ... the provisions of s 102(4) excluded any inquiry by the High Court into the validity of what had been done.'[25]

The Privy Council undoubtedly performed a useful service in this case in relegating the doctrine of dismissal at pleasure to the rubbish heap of constitutional irrationality and obsolescence. At the same time, it is difficult to escape the feeling that the Board should have been magnanimous enough to use its discretion *not* to award costs against Assistant Superintendent of Police Thomas. The point he raised was one of considerable public interest. It was because of his determination – albeit in his own interest – that the Privy Council was prevented, in the felicitous words of Adams J in a similar case,[26] from yielding to arguments which were calculated to:

> ... transfuse fresh life into the dying concept of dismissal at pleasure which, however much it may have thrived and clings to life in the wintry climes of the United Kingdom, must in the unyielding sun of the Eastern Caribbean receive little sustenance.

SPECIAL CONSTITUTIONAL PROTECTION TO CERTAIN PUBLIC OFFICERS

In Chapter 13, consideration was given to the way in which judges of the superior courts are insulated from the executive and the legislature. In this chapter, we now wish to consider the protection given – especially in matters of removal from office and discipline – to certain officials who support the higher judiciary and whose tenure it is deemed essential also to safeguard in our Constitutions.

The officials in question are *magistrates, registrars, assistant registrars* and other public officers in the *Departments of the Attorney General and the Director of Public Prosecutions*. The following s 83 from the St Kitts and Nevis Constitution[27] is the prototype of the provision found in all the Constitutions of the independent States in the Organisation of Eastern Caribbean States (OECS):

> 83(1)This section applies to the offices of magistrate, registrar of the High Court and assistant registrar of the High Court and to any public office in the department of the Attorney General (other than the public office of Attorney General) or the department of the Director of Public Prosecutions (other than the office of Director) for appointment to which persons are required to hold one or other of the specified qualifications.

---

24   Alexis, 1982, p 376.
25   *Ibid*, p 381.
26   See *Emanuel v AG of Dominica* (Suit No 194 of 1989) High Court of Dominica.
27   See the St Christopher and Nevis Constitution Order 1983 SI 1983/881.

(2) The power to appoint persons to hold or act in offices to which this section applies (including the power to confirm appointments) shall vest in the Governor General, acting in accordance with the recommendation of the Public Service Commission:

Provided that before making any recommendation as to the exercise of the powers conferred by this section in any case the Public Service Commission shall *consult the Judicial and Legal Services Commission.*

(3) The power to exercise disciplinary control over persons holding or acting in offices to which this sub-section applies and the power to remove such persons from office shall vest in the Governor General, acting in accordance with the recommendation of the Judicial and Legal Service Commission:

Provided that before making any recommendation as to the exercise of the powers conferred by this subsection in any case the Judicial and Legal Services Commission shall consult the Public Service Commission.

The Director of Public Prosecutions is assured even greater insulation in that his appointment is made in nearly all the Constitutions on the advice of the Judicial and Legal Services Commission, sometimes after consultation with the Public Service Commission. While in the case of magistrates and registrars, the appointments are made in most jurisdictions on the advice of the Judicial and Legal Services Commission.[28] In the removal of the Director of Public Prosecutions, the regime is strict, viz:[29]

(7) The Director of Public Prosecutions shall be removed from office by the Governor General if the question of his removal from office has been referred to a tribunal appointed under subsection (8) and the tribunal has recommended to the Governor General that he ought to be removed for inability as aforesaid or for misbehaviour.

(8) If the Prime Minister or the chairman of the Judicial and Legal Services Commission represents to the Governor General that the question of removing the Director of Public Prosecutions under this section ought to be investigated, then –

(a) the Governor General shall appoint a tribunal which shall consist of a chairman and not less than two other members, selected by the Chief Justice from among persons who hold or have held office as a judge of a court having unlimited jurisdiction in civil and criminal matters in some part of the Commonwealth or a court having jurisdiction in appeals from such a court; and

(b) the tribunal shall enquire into the matter and report on the facts thereof to the Governor General and recommend to him whether the Director ought to be removed under this section.

(9) If the question of removing the Director of Public Prosecutions has been referred to a tribunal under this section, the Governor General, acting in accordance with the advice of the Judicial and Legal Services Commission, may suspend the Director from the exercise of the functions of his office and any such suspension may at any time be revoked by the Governor General, acting in accordance with such advice as aforesaid, and shall in any case cease to have effect if the tribunal recommends to the Governor General that the Director should not be removed.

28 See the Grenada Constitution Order 1973, s 86(1), (2) and (3).
29 *Ibid*, s 86(6), (7), (8) and (9).

The *Director of Audit* holds a special position in the constitutional scheme of things and it should not be surprising that special arrangements govern his or her removal. The arrangements are found in the Grenada Constitution in the following terms:[30]

(6) A person holding the office of Director of Audit may be removed from office only for inability to exercise the functions of his office (whether arising from infirmity of body or mind or any other cause) or for misbehaviour and shall not be so removed except in accordance with the provisions of this section.

(7) The Director of Audit shall be removed from office by the Governor General if the question of his removal from office has been referred to a tribunal appointed under subsection (8) and the tribunal has recommended to the Governor General that he ought to be removed for inability as aforesaid or for misbehaviour.

(8) If the Prime Minister or the chairman of the Public Service Commission represents to the Governor General that the question of removing the Director of Audit under this section ought to be investigated–

(a) the Governor General shall appoint a tribunal which shall consist of a chairman and not less than two other members selected by the Chief Justice from among persons who hold or have held office as a judge of a court having unlimited jurisdiction in civil and criminal matters in some part of the Commonwealth or a court having jurisdiction in appeals from such a court; and

(b) the tribunal shall enquire into the matter and report on the facts thereof to the Governor General and recommend to him whether the Director ought to be removed under this section.

(9) If the question of removing the Director of Audit has been referred to a tribunal under this section, the Governor General, acting in accordance with the advice of the Public Service Commission, may suspend the Director of Audit from the exercise of the functions of his office and any such suspension may at any time be revoked by the Governor General, acting in accordance with such advice, and shall in any case cease to have effect if the tribunal recommends to the Governor General that the Director should not be removed.

COMMENTARY

Over the years 1989–2000, the courts in the Eastern Caribbean Supreme Court have had to grapple with cases involving a magistrate in Dominica, a registrar and additional magistrate in St Kitts and Nevis, and a Director of Public Prosecutions as well as a Director of Audit in Grenada. These issues have been the subject of some admirable judgments well worthy of study in their entirety.

1 The *Emanuel* case (magistrate)

The first case concerns a Chief Magistrate who was appointed under a three year contract in Dominica with effect from 15 July 1988. His appointment was purportedly made by the Public Service Commission as required by s 90 of the Dominica Constitution. However,

---

30 *Ibid*, s 87.

after serving only nine months of his three year contract, he received a very short letter dated 20 February 1989 and *signed by the Permanent Secretary to the Ministry of Legal Affairs* informing him that the Government of Dominica had decided to terminate his engagement 'with immediate effect' – no reason for such a termination being given. He moved the High Court for a declaration that the direction for his removal from the Government was in violation of his rights under s 90 of the Dominica Constitution:[31] this provision being in identical terms to the St Kitts and Nevis provision referred to above for the removal of magistrates and registrars.

The evidence at the trial revealed that the Judicial and Legal Services Commission had not, in fact, passed on the decision to remove the magistrate, after consulting the Public Service Commission, in terms of s 90. Indeed, the minutes of the latter body revealed that two months after transmission of the letter from the Ministry of Legal Affairs purporting to terminate his services the commission was just being brought into the picture and that happened only after the magistrate had represented to the Attorney General about the irregularity of his removal, and threatened legal action.

The judge quite properly found for the plaintiff, awarding him damages and costs.

This whole matter is a sorry comedy of errors. It illustrates bureaucratic bungling from start to finish – if not arbitrariness in the extreme. It shows how casual some governments can be about accepting their responsibilities in matters affecting dismissal of members of the lower judiciary and underscores the urgent need for protection of those officers from the vagaries of the executive. The future is bleak for the magistracy, if one of its officers can be dismissed with such indifference and irregularity.

Adams J, in the *Emanuel* case, discovered that contracts issued to magistrates and registrars in Antigua, Montserrat and Anguilla do, in fact, refer to the constitutional provisions. He did not advert to the position in Grenada, St Vincent, St Lucia or St Kitts, and one hesitates to believe that those territories would be prepared to ignore the Constitution and, instead, to pursue an illegal arrangement which would give the executive a free hand in removing such officers. If the proper action has not yet been taken, the defaulting governments may well take heed, 12 years after they were written, of these words of Adams J:

> Whatever contract the Chief Magistrate and Government may have entered into, neither he nor the Government was free to enter into such a contract that would violate the provisions of the Constitution, and that in so far as the contract under scrutiny does so, it is to the extent of such violation devoid of legal effect.

2 The *Holdip* (DPP) case

The next case to be dealt with is the matter of *an Application by the Grenada Bar Association for a Declaration that the provisions of ss 86(1), 86(5) and 86(6) of the Grenada Constitution Order 1973 had been contravened.*[32]

By an agreement expressed to be made between the Government of Grenada and Malcolm Holdip, the Grenada Government purported to enter into a contract with

---

31   *Emanuel v AG of Dominica* (Suit No 194 of 1989) High Court of Dominica.
32   The *Holdip* case, Supreme Court of Grenada (Suit No 650 of 1998, unreported).

Holdip for him to serve the said Government as the Director of Public Prosecutions for a two year period, the contract to be subject to renewal.

On 6 November 1998 (two months before the two year period expired), Holdip addressed a letter to the Minister of Legal Affairs requesting a renewal of his contract and, on 23 November 1998, the Permanent Secretary in the Ministry replied to him informing him that Government did *not* intend to renew the contract on its expiry.

On the above facts, the Grenada Bar Association, which claimed a relevant interest, applied to the High Court, by way of Originating Motion, for a declaration that the office of Director of Public Prosecutions enjoys security of tenure under s 86 of the Grenada Constitution Order 1973 and is not, therefore, subject to termination by effluxion of time in the manner set out in the Governor General's letter of appointment dated 29 November 1996 and the contract agreement to which reference is made above. The Bar Association also asked for a declaration that cl I of the said contract, that 'the Government shall employ the officer and the officer shall serve the Government: in the post of Director of Public Prosecutions for a period of two years effective 2 January 1997', is inconsistent with the provisions of ss 86(5) and 86(6) of the Constitution of Grenada, null and void and of no effect. Finally, the association asked the court to declare 'that the Director of Public Prosecutions of Grenada, Mr Malcolm Holdip, holds office subject to termination in accordance with the provisions of ss 85(5), (6), (7), (8), (9) and (10) of the Constitution of Grenada and not otherwise'.

In giving his judgment in the case, Alleyne J said:

> The Governor General, on the advice of the Judicial and Legal Services Commission had power to, and did, appoint Malcolm Holdip to the office of Director of Public Prosecutions. That appointment is valid. The Governor General, however, went on to prescribe an earlier time than the time prescribed by subsection (5) of section 86 for his retirement as one of the terms of his appointment.

> The Governor General has such a power in the case of a person appointed to *act* in that office. He does not have such a power in the case of an appointment to hold that office as in the instant case. In prescribing such a limitation the Governor General acted *ultra vires* the Constitution, and that provision of the instrument of appointment and the contract is void, null and of no effect in law.

The judge, in granting the declarations sought, suggested that that part of the instrument which reflected a lawful exercise of the Governor General's power on the advice of the Judicial and Legal Services Commission should be severed from the part which reflected the *ultra vires* exercise of a presumed power.

The judge continued: 'The substantial purpose of the Governor General on the advice of the Judicial and Legal Services Commission was, in my view, clearly to appoint a Director of Public Prosecutions for Grenada in accordance with the provisions of the Constitution. The limitation of the term was merely incidental.'

The case was taken by Government on appeal to the OECS Court of Appeal where Sir Dennis Byron CJ – in a characteristically masterly and scholarly judgment[33] – had this to say:

---

33   See Grenada Civil Appeal (No 8 of 1999).

In my view, the language of the section taken as a whole leads to the conclusion that the Constitution prescribes that the Governor General appoints during good behaviour and ability to perform; he does not appoint during pleasure. Consequently, the holder of the Office of Director of Public Prosecutions cannot be removed on any ground other than inability or misbehaviour before he attains the prescribed age. This leads inevitably to the ruling that he cannot be removed on the basis of the effluxion of time.

3 The *Angela Inniss* (registrar) case

The third case for our consideration is a case in which a registrar, who was purportedly also serving on a two year contract, had her appointment summarily terminated at what the judge who heard her case for wrongful dismissal called 'the fag end of her contractual term'.[34]

The facts of this case can be briefly stated: Miss Angela Inniss was by an agreement purportedly made between the Government of St Kitts and Nevis and herself, appointed as registrar and additional magistrate of Districts A, B and C for two years from 1 June 1996 which term could be extended by notice in writing (as provided in cl 4 of the said agreement).

It would appear that Miss Inniss exercised her undoubted right of freedom of expression to speak out robustly on a number of matters and, to quote Moore J, the authorities decided to rid themselves of 'this turbulent registrar' by summarily dismissing her. Accordingly, she brought an action for a breach of the constitutional provision which required that she could only be disciplined by the Judicial and Legal Services Commission after consultation with the Public Service Commission. It was clearly to insulate the holder of the office from executive disciplinary incursions of the kind she suffered that s 83 was entrenched in the Constitution. She had to be protected from what her counsel, Karl Hudson-Phillips QC, described as 'the capricious and whimsical exercise of executive power'.

The court had no difficulty in ordering and declaring;

(a) that a letter sent to the Registrar on 20 February 1998 by the Permanent Secretary, Establishments, was a contravention of section 83(3) of the Constitution which vests the power to discipline a registrar in the Judicial and Legal Services Commission;

(b) that that letter was null and void, purporting to usurp the power to remove the applicant from the office of Registrar and Additional Magistrate in an unconstitutional manner;

(c) that the Applicant should be paid damages amounting to $100,000 (to include an element of exemplary damages); and

(d) that costs should be paid by the Government of St Kitts and Nevis.

It may be that the time has come for the OECS to consider reviving the pre-independence regional service, which existed not only for magistrates (as now recommended by the

---

34 The case of *Angela Inniss v AG St Kitts and Nevis* (Misc Suit No 53 of 1998, judgment of 21 February 2000, unreported). On appeal to the OECS Supreme Court (August 2001).

Dumas Task Force),[35] but also for registrars, Directors of Public Prosecutions, solicitors general, chief parliamentary counsel and Crown solicitors. If the appointments of such legal and judicial officers are made subject to liability for transfers within the various jurisdictions of the sub-region, good career prospects will obviate the need for contract appointments and many of these officers can eventually look forward to elevation to the Bench.

4 The *Julia Lawrence* (Director of Audit) case

The fourth case concerns the attempted dismissal of the Grenada Director of Audit.[36]

The facts of this case can be summarised, thus: Julia Lawrence, Director of Audit, Grenada, pursuant to her responsibilities under the Constitution, submitted comments in her annual Reports to the Minister of Finance (Dr Keith Mitchell) who was also at the material time the Prime Minister of the country. Sometime thereafter, she was told by the clerk of Parliament that he had seen the reports which were 'mutilated' in that they contained a number of scratches and insertions.

At that stage, the director apparently addressed a letter to the Minister of Finance – to whom she had originally handed the reports – in which she stated *inter alia* as follows:

> I have been informed by the Clerk of Parliament that the Reports submitted to him for laying *were* mutilated: they contained a number of scratches and insertions. In effect the Reports of the Director of Audit *have been* doctored ... You also received comments from the Accountant General to lay therewith.

It would appear that when the Prime Minister read the letter from the Director of Audit he formed the impression that the director was accusing *him* of having altered her reports. In that frame of mind, he communicated with the chairman of the Public Service Commission advising the chairman that he considered the conduct of the Director of Audit as a gross act of misbehaviour. He apparently not only took strong exception to some of the director's statements in the letter, but to the fact that the letter was copied to the clerk of Parliament and the speaker of the House of Representatives.

The Prime Minister, accordingly, asked the chairman of the Public Service Commission to make arrangements for her removal from office and the chairman moved the Governor General to set up a tribunal for the purpose, as required by the Constitution.

Before taking this action the chairman communicated to the director, and asked her to set out her side of the story, which she did.

Although it was clear from the director's reply to the chairman of the Public Service Commission that the director at no time suggested that it was the Prime Minister and Minister of Finance who 'doctored' her reports, the tribunal chose to infer that it was the intention of the director to state that the Prime Minister and Minister of Finance

---

35 In the Dumas Task Force on the OECS Judicial and Legal Services Commission (Dumas Task Force, 2000), the recommendation is also made for a regional magistracy, p 35. Given the requisite political will and a properly staffed Judicial and Legal Services Commission or a properly financed Department of Court Administration, there is no reason why a regional service cannot work once again (as it did before independence).

36 High Court of Grenada (Civil Suit No 153 of 2000, unreported). On appeal to the OECS Supreme Court (August 2001).

personally made those alterations to her reports – thus, allowing itself to be guided by Dr Mitchell's subjective judgment in the matter.

The learned judge found as follows:

> The only act which the letter in fact states that the Minister did personally was to provide comments from the Accountant General to lay with the Reports, an act which the evidence discloses that at the least the Minister conceded that he informed the applicant that he intended to do in order to ensure that he did not 'interfere with due process'. In contrast, the other allegations were neutral in terms of the actual person or persons who might have offended. The assumption that the applicant intended to accuse the Prime Minister personally is no more than an inference which the Tribunal appears to have drawn from the following paragraphs of the letter, and the apparent incredulity of the Tribunal with regard to the 'unambiguous statement' of the applicant that she pointed out to him (the Prime Minister) that in her letter she was holding him constitutionally responsible and that he had the responsibility for protecting [her] reports until it (sic) reached Parliament seems somewhat strange.

The judge referred to the questions which the tribunal asked itself in reviewing the matter and drew attention to this statement:

> Clearly in our view, Julia Edwards, Director of Audit, could not have been in any doubt about how Keith C Mitchell, Prime Minister and Minister of Finance, felt when he read her letter, or that it was his intention to take the matter further, and it would not be unfair to her to say that knowing the constitution as well as she appeared to us to know it, she would have had an idea of what constitutional powers were open to the Prime Minister.

The judge found that the tribunal clearly adopted the Prime Minister's subjective interpretation of the letter as fact, rather than, as was its responsibility, objectively assessing the meaning and import of the letter. His Lordship concluded thus:

> It seems to me that the Tribunal in this respect abdicated its responsibility to independently and objectively evaluate the evidence, asked itself the wrong question and in that respect acted irregularly. The questions which the Tribunal asked itself were these:
>
> (a) Why would the Prime Minister and Minister of Finance accuse her subsequently, as he stated in his letter to her of 20 August 1999 and proceed further to bring the matter to this stage?
>
> (b) It is reasonable to ask these questions: Has she only now become aware of this interpretation which could have been put upon what she wrote, or of the interpretation which the Prime Minister actually put on her letter? Did she not understand what he was stating in his letter of 20 August 1999?

The judge accordingly ordered:

1   that the tribunal's recommendation, and the resulting decision of the Governor General to remove the applicant from office, be set aside;

2   that the applicant be re-instated without loss of pay or other benefits;

3   that the respondents pay the applicant's costs (fit for two counsel) to be taxed if not agreed.

5 The *de Freitas* case

The fifth and final case which illustrates the changed position of a public officer (post-independence) in this area is *de Freitas v Permanent Secretary of Ministry of Agriculture*.[37]

The facts of the case are as follows: the appellant (de Freitas) was a public officer in the Ministry of Agriculture of Antigua and Barbuda. In the course of an investigation by a Commission of Inquiry relating to the shipment into the country of a consignment of guns, there were allegations that implicated Mr Hilroy Humphreys, the Minister of Agriculture. Following the enquiry and while he was on vacation, the appellant took part in a peaceful picket of the Ministry Headquarters in which placards criticising the Minister were displayed. The first respondent, the permanent secretary in the Ministry, claimed that the appellant's action breached the restraints on political expression imposed by s 10(2)(a) of the Civil Service Act 1984 of the laws of Antigua and Barbuda which reads:

> A civil servant may not – (a) in any public place or in any document or any other medium of communication, whether within Antigua and Barbuda or not, publish any information or expression of opinion on matters of national or international political controversy.

As a result of the appellant's action the permanent secretary (the first respondent) interdicted him from the exercise of the powers and functions of his office.

The appellant issued an originating motion seeking redress for the breach of his constitutional rights and the judge at first instance, Redhead J made a declaration that s 10(2)(a) was unconstitutional.

The respondent appealed and the Court of Appeal held (applying the presumption of constitutionality) that by reading into s 10(2)(a) such words as:

> ... when his forbearance from such publication is reasonably required for the proper performance of his official functions,

the provision would be compatible with ss 12(1) and (4) and 13(1) and (2) of the Constitution. Section 12(1) provides a guarantee of freedom of expression and s 12(4), so far as material states:

> Nothing contained in or done under the authority of any law shall be held to be inconsistent with or in contravention of this section to the extent that the law in question makes provision that imposes restrictions upon public officers that are reasonably required for the proper performance of their functions and except so far as that provision or, as the case may be, the thing done under the authority thereof is shown not to be reasonably justifiable in a democratic society.

The matter was taken on appeal from the Court of Appeal to the Privy Council which allowed the appeal on the following grounds.

1   Any restrictions imposed on the freedom of expression and freedom of assembly of a public officer must be reasonably required for the proper performance of his functions and must be reasonably justifiable in a democratic society. The restrictions in s 10(2)(a)

---

37   [1998] 3 WLR 675 PC, (1998) 53 WIR 131.

of the Civil Service Act of 1984 without qualification did not satisfy the criterion of being reasonably required for the proper performance of a civil servant's functions.

2   That because s 10(2)(a) of the Act was free from ambiguity, it was not justifiable to imply words into that provision – especially as the legislature had enacted express exceptions in s 10(3) of the Act; and the words supplied by the Court of Appeal failed to take a form which Parliament would have intended.

3   That even if s 10(2)(a) had satisfied the criterion of being reasonably required for the proper performance of a civil servant's functions, it would not have satisfied the criterion of being reasonably justified in a democratic society: the quality of reasonableness in that criterion being infringed by arbitrary and excessive invasion of a guaranteed right.

4   Section 10(2)(a) was otiose on the ground of being disproportionate in not distinguishing between classes of civil servants as to the restraints imposed on freedom of expression and freedom of assembly and association.

This case could well become a public officer's charter for the future. We have indeed taken a quantum leap from dismissal at pleasure.

We turn now in our next chapter to the new approach to the English monarch as Head of State of the respective independent Caribbean monarchies in the area.

CHAPTER 15

HEADS OF STATE

MONARCHICAL V PRESIDENTIAL REGIMES

General historical introduction

In the Caribbean, the nomenclature of Heads of State depends on the constitutional system over which they preside. In colonial times, the Governor was the official representative of the British Sovereign in the colonies of Jamaica, Barbados, Trinidad and Tobago, Guyana, Grenada, St Vincent, St Lucia, Dominica, Antigua and Barbuda, St Kitts/Nevis, Bermuda, Cayman Islands, Turks and Caicos, Montserrat, and British Virgin Islands. In each colony, the Governor's deputy was styled 'Colonial Secretary', a designation which, in time, was changed to 'Chief Secretary' in the larger colonies and 'Administrator' in the smaller ones in an apparent attempt to avoid the increasing unpopularity of the words 'colony' and 'colonial'. Even at the present time the word 'colony' has become so odious that the British no longer speak of 'colonies' at all. Their colonies (wherever they still exist) are euphemistically referred to as 'overseas territories'[1]

Until the late 1950s, a Governor, in what was then the British Caribbean, usually presided over the larger territories and where that territory had 'dependencies', the dependency would be headed by a warden, district officer or commissioner who would, in effect, be the Governor's surrogate in the dependency. For example, warden was the term used to designate the Governor's representative in Anguilla and Nevis while the Colony of St Kitts itself – the parent territory – was presided over by an *administrator*. In the case of the Leeward Islands, for example, the term 'Governor' was, up to 1960, reserved for the Queen's representative of the group comprising St Kitts/Nevis/Anguilla, Antigua, Montserrat and the British Virgin Islands. His grandiloquent title was 'Governor and Commander-in-Chief in and over the Leeward Islands'.

The position was the same in the Windward Islands, the Governor and Commander-in-Chief of which would reside on the island where the 'seat of Government' was located'.

In the larger territories of British Guiana (as it then was), Trinidad and Tobago, Barbados, Jamaica and the Commonwealth of the Bahamas, the Queen's representative was called 'Governor'. As has been stated elsewhere, these Governors in colonial times (and those who still 'rule' today) derived their authority from Letters Patent and Royal Instructions. Letters Patent were 'passed under the Great Seal of the United Kingdom' while the Royal Instructions were given to the Governor 'under the Royal Sign Manual and Signet'.[2]

---

1   The remaining overseas territories in the Caribbean are Bermuda, Cayman Islands, Turks and Caicos, Montserrat, British Virgin Islands and Anguilla. See a discussion of these territories in Phillips, 1985, Chapter VII, pp 177–86.
2   See Phillips, 1977, p 107 and the Letters Patent and Royal Instructions at Apps I and II, respectively, pp 225–40.

PRESENT DAY POSITION REGARDING
CLASSIFICATION OF NOMENCLATURE

Today the hierarchy has, of course, changed dramatically. In the Commonwealth Caribbean, the Heads of State in 2001 comprise: three Presidents, nine Governors General and six Governors. We shall now have a look at the functions and the way they may be appointed and removed from office. In this section, Governors and Governors General will be referred to simply as Heads of State.

Functions and powers of Heads of State

Under the *Guyana* Republican Constitution of 1980 the President of Guyana is an executive President who is 'Head of State, the supreme executive authority and Commander-in-Chief of the armed forces of the Republic'.[3] He also presides over the Cabinet[4] and is empowered to address the National Assembly from time to time.[5] The Presidents of *Trinidad and Tobago* and *Dominica* perform neither of these functions, but are symbols of unity and perform such ceremonial functions as swearing in Chief Justices, receiving ambassadors and being present to deliver the Throne Speech at the opening of Parliament. Their method of appointment differs as well. The *Guyana* President is appointed at a general election by the people[6] whereas the *Trinidad* President is appointed by an electoral college comprising both Houses of Parliament.[7] In the case of the President of *Dominica*, if both the Prime Minister and the Leader of the Opposition agree on a nominee, the speaker of the House of Representatives simply declares the new President appointed. If they do not so agree, he (or she) is elected by a secret ballot of the House.[8]

But the Trinidad and Tobago President shares more functions with the Prime Minister than does his counterpart in *Dominica*. In the former case, he is the appointing authority in respect of a number of important officers who are appointed in his own discretion after consultation with the Prime Minister and the Leader of the Opposition, as well as such other persons as he considers fit. These appointments are:

(a) the Chief Justice;[9]

(b) the Acting Chief Justice;[10]

---

3   See Guyana Republican Constitution of 1980, Art 89 (hereafter 'the Guyana Constitution').
4   *Ibid*, Art 106(3).
5   *Ibid*, Art 67(1).
6   *Ibid*, Arts 91 and 177.
7   See Trinidad Constitution, ss 22 and 26.
8   See Dominica Constitution, s 19.
9   Trinidad and Tobago Constitution 1976, s 102.
10 *Ibid*, s 103.

(c) the ombudsman;[11]

(d) the chairman and members of the Elections and Boundaries Commission;[12]

(e) the three appointed members of the Judicial and Legal Service Commission;[13]

(f) the Auditor General;[14]

(g) the members of the Public Service Commission;[15]

(h) the members of the Police Service Commission;[16]

(i) the members of the Teaching Service Commission;[17]

(j) the members of the Salaries Review Commission;[18] and

(k) the chairman and two members of the Public Service Board of Appeal.[19]

By comparison with the previously restricted functions of the Governor General immediately before the introduction of republican status, it is true to say that the functions of the President of *Trinidad and Tobago* are no longer only ceremonial. However, that description can still be applied to the President of the Commonwealth of *Dominica*.

The Presidents of *Trinidad and Tobago* and *Dominica* can be regarded as symbols of national unity to whom the people of those territories owe due allegiance under their respective Constitutions. This allegiance is therefore constitutionally owed to the Queen only in those Commonwealth Caribbean countries which have retained a monarchical type of Constitution.

During the year 1999 and early in 2001, there developed two well publicised differences between the President of Trinidad and Tobago and the Prime Minister. The first was over the appointment of the two Tobago senators; the second involved the President's refusal to accept the nomination of seven of the 16 senators which, under s 40(2)(a) of the Constitution, the Prime Minister was empowered to make – the intention being to appoint them all ministers of Government. The seven persons had been unsuccessful at the general elections held in December 2000 and the President's argument was that it would be an insult to the electorate to put such persons in ministerial positions. Eventually, after a 'stand-off' of nearly two months the President relented and accepted the nominations – leaving the country confused and bewildered, and the relations between the Head of State and Head of Government severely strained.

---

11 Trinidad and Tobago Constitution 1976, s 91(2).

12 *Ibid*, s 71(3).

13 *Ibid*, s 110(3).

14 *Ibid*, s 117(1).

15 *Ibid*, s 120(2).

16 *Ibid*, s 122(2).

17 *Ibid*, s 124(2).

18 *Ibid*, s 140(1).

19 *Ibid*, s 130(2).

Discharge of functions in absence of Presidents

It is interesting to compare the different constitutional arrangements which have been made for the performance of presidential functions in the three jurisdictions referred to above.

In the case of Guyana, whenever the President is away from the country or considers it desirable to appoint someone to act for him because of illness or some other cause, he may direct by writing that any member of the Cabinet, *being an elected member* of the National Assembly, should discharge the functions of the office of President. If, however, the President is unable for whatever cause (including, presumably his sudden demise) to designate someone to act for him, succession devolves to the following persons:

(a) the Prime Minister; or

(b) if there is no Prime Minister, or if he is absent from Guyana, or is by physical or mental infirmity unable to perform the functions of his office, such other Minister as the Cabinet selects, being an elected member of the National Assembly; or

(c) the Chancellor,[20] if there is no Prime Minister and no Cabinet.

One can only speculate as to why at any given time there may be neither a President, a Prime Minister nor a Cabinet. However, no one who, in these circumstances, is temporarily called upon to assume the duties of the office of President has the right to dissolve Parliament or to revoke any appointment made by the President.[21]

In the case of Trinidad and Tobago, whenever the office of President is vacant or the President is incapable of performing his functions by reason of absence or illness, the President of the Senate shall act temporarily as President. Whenever the President of the Senate – for whatever reason – is unable so to act, the functions of the office of President of the Republic will be performed by the *speaker*. If the speaker is also unable to act, the succession then passes to the *vice president of the Senate*, in which case the deputy speaker of the House of Representatives shall, on giving 48 hours notice, summon the electoral college to meet within seven days after the vice president of the Senate has commenced to perform the functions of the office of President, for the purpose of electing a person to fill the vacancy (if one exists) or to appoint a person to act temporarily during such time as the substantive holder is unable to perform his duties.[22]

In the case of *Dominica*, the original 1978 Republican Constitution provided that where the President (because of absence or illness) is unable to perform his functions, it would be his responsibility to consult with the Prime Minister and the Leader of the Opposition (after receiving his nominee's consent) and to appoint an Acting President in writing. If the President fails to take this step, the Acting President must be designated by the House of Assembly in the same way as a substantive holder of the office is elected.[23] The previous discussion of constitutional developments in Dominica revealed what

---

20 Guyana Constitution, Art 96(1) and (2).
21 *Ibid.* See Proviso to Art 96.
22 The Trinidad Constitution, s 27.
23 Dominica Republican Constitution, s 28.

travail resulted when Parliament was, in very peculiar circumstances, actually on strike,[24] and the then President left the State without making a nomination in writing.

Immunities of Presidents and removal from office

Immunities

Under the Republican Constitution of *Guyana*, the President is granted complete immunity from suit in respect of the performance of the functions of his office or for any act done in the performance of those functions; and no proceedings, whether criminal or civil, shall be instituted against him in respect thereof either during his term of office or *thereafter*.[25]

The Trinidad[26] and Dominica[27] Presidents are equally not answerable in any court for the performance of the functions of their offices or for any acts done by them in the performance of those functions. But this immunity ceases when the President leaves office.

However, as far as *Trinidad and Tobago* is concerned, there are qualifications to the criminal and civil immunities of the President. Criminal proceedings may only be brought or continued against him *with the fiat of the Director of Public Prosecutions*; and no process for the President's arrest or imprisonment shall be issued from any court nor be executed during his term of office.[28] As regards civil proceedings, no such proceeding in which relief is claimed against the President can be instituted during his term of office in any court in respect of anything done by him in his personal capacity, whether before or after he assumed the office of President.[29] But this is subject to a peculiar condition which is worded as follows:

> The condition referred to in subsection (3) is that two months must elapse after a notice in writing has been served on him either by registered post or by being left at his office stating the nature of the proceedings, the cause of action, the name, description and address of the party instituting the proceedings and the relief claimed.[30]

This provision appears to make it mandatory for the solicitor of a client proposing to institute civil proceedings against the President to issue a notice, which is equivalent to the usual optional 'solicitor's letter before action', giving to the President two months' notice of intention to commence an action against him. However, it is expressly provided by sub-s 38(5) of the Constitution that the period of notice should not operate in favour of the President with respect to any relevant limitation period prescribed by law.

---

24 See Chapter 11, above, under the section dealing with Dominica.
25 See Guyana Republican Constitution, Arts 98 and 182(1).
26 See Trinidad Constitution, s 38.
27 See Dominica Constitution, s 27.
28 See Trinidad Constitution, s 38(2).
29 *Ibid*, s 38(3).
30 *Ibid*, s 38(4).

Removal from office of President – Guyana

Removal from office of the President of *Guyana* is based on two grounds only:

(a) he must be physically or mentally incapable of discharging the functions of his office;[31] or

(b) he must have committed a violation of the Constitution or be guilty of gross misconduct.[32]

In so far as removal on the ground of physical or mental incapacity is concerned, if the President's party colleagues in the National Assembly resolve, upon a motion supported by a majority of all of them, that the question of the physical or mental capacity of the President to discharge his functions ought to be investigated and the Prime Minister so informs the Chancellor, the Chancellor shall appoint a board consisting of not less than three persons selected from among persons who are qualified as medical practitioners under Guyana law, and the board will enquire into the matter and make a report to the Chancellor stating the opinion of the board whether or not the President is, by reason of infirmity of body or mind, incapable of performing the functions of his office.

If the board reports that the President is *incapable* of discharging the functions of his office, the Chancellor shall certify in writing accordingly and thereupon the President shall cease to hold office.[33]

Where it is sought to remove the President from office on the grounds that he has violated the Constitution or has been guilty of gross misconduct, the regime for dismissal is as follows:

Notice of a motion alleging that the President has committed a violation of the Constitution or is guilty of a gross misconduct, must be given in writing to the Speaker of the National Assembly. The Notice must be signed by not less than one-half of all the elected members of the Assembly, and must specify the particulars of the allegations and propose that a tribunal be established to investigate those allegations.

When such a motion is presented to Parliament, the National Assembly shall not debate it but shall proceed to take a vote. If the motion is supported by not less than two-thirds of all the members of the Assembly, the Speaker shall declare the motion passed.

Thereafter, the Chancellor is required to appoint a tribunal consisting of a chairman, and not less than two other members selected by the Chancellor from among persons who hold or have held high judicial office. The tribunal shall investigate the matter and shall report to the National Assembly whether it finds that the particulars of the allegations specified in the motion have been established. If the tribunal so finds, the Assembly may, on a motion supported by not less than three-quarters of all the elected members of the Assembly, resolve that the President has been guilty of such violation or gross misconduct as the case may be – whereupon the President shall cease to hold office upon the third day following the passage of the resolution unless he sooner dissolves Parliament.[34]

---

31 Guyana Constitution, Art 93.
32 *Ibid*, Art 94.
33 *Ibid*, Art 179.
34 *Ibid*, Art 180.

These provisions leave a great deal to be desired. In the absence of total estrangement between the President and his party colleagues, it is difficult to imagine the type of conduct which will be classified by the National Assembly as failing under either category as long as the President's party holds the majority of seats in the National Assembly. It must also be noted that two-thirds of the members of the assembly are first required to decide whether a *prima facie* case has been made out against the President, while not less than three-quarters of the assembly must support the motion on the question of whether the President has, in fact, been guilty of the acts alleged. The President also has a moratorium of three days between his being found guilty and his ceasing to hold office. During this time he can dissolve Parliament – presumably nullifying their decision!

Removal of Presidents of Trinidad and Tobago and Dominica

In the cases of *Trinidad and Tobago* and *Dominica*, the President may be removed from office if he willfully violates the Constitution; *or* he behaves in such a way as to bring his office into hatred, ridicule or contempt; or he behaves in a way that endangers the security of the State; or he is unable to perform the functions of his office because of mental or physical infirmity. The regime for removing the President in these two territories is as follows:

(a) the House of Representatives (or House of Assembly in the case of *Dominica*) passes a motion that his removal from office should be investigated;

(b) the motion must give full particulars of the grounds for the proposed removal and must be signed by not less than one-third of the total membership of the House;

(c) the motion must be adopted by not less than two-thirds of all the members of the House of Representatives (or Assembly) and the senators assembled together;

(d) a tribunal consisting of the Chief Justice and four other senior judges for Trinidad (two for Dominica) appointed by him must investigate the complaint and report on the facts to the House of Representatives (or assembly) and;

(e) the Senators and the members of the House assembled together must consider the report and if, by resolution supported by the votes of not less than two-thirds of the total membership of that assembled gathering, they declare that the President should be removed from office, he is so removed.[35]

There can be no doubt that this regime constitutes an eminently sensible, comprehensive and sound basis for dealing with a situation in which the President's behaviour calls for his removal from that high office. However, it lacks one ingredient: it does not set a time frame within which the procedure should be completed. A matter of this nature should not be permitted to drag on for an inordinate length of time and it would probably have been wiser if the Constitution had provided time limits to allow all these five stages to be completed within a period not exceeding three months. It should be pointed out that the recommendations for the procedures adopted were originally made by the Wooding Commission; and the section in the Constitution dealing with the removal from office of the President reproduces, *ipsissima verba*, the draft Constitution submitted by the said

---

35 Trinidad and Tobago Constitution, s 36.

Commission. In this respect, Dominica has already adopted these provisions verbatim[36] and they are, hereby, commended for adoption by any other governments which might, in the future, introduce a presidential Head of State, subject to the proviso proposed above, viz, that the whole matter should be concluded within a specified period of time.

Governors General: appointment and functions

Governors General of independent Commonwealth countries are appointed by the Queen on the advice of the Prime Minister of the particular territory. Associated statehood lasted from 1967–83. With the accession to independence of St Kitts/Nevis in 1983, that status is now a thing of the past. However, during that period, the appointment of the Governor of an associated State was also made by the Queen on the advice of the particular Premier. The Governors of all the present day 'dependent territories' are appointed by the Queen on the advice of UK ministers.

There is a widespread belief that a Governor General possesses executive powers under the Westminster model. Indeed, it is extremely difficult to persuade the uninitiated that when an Act states that:

It shall be lawful for the Governor General whenever deems it advisable...

what is intended is that the Governor General should act on the advice of the Cabinet.

In this connection we must examine, for example, the Antigua section which is found in identical terms in most of the other Constitutions in the area.

It reads as follows:[37]

In the exercise of his functions the Governor General shall act in accordance with the advice of the Cabinet or a Minister acting under the general authority of the Cabinet, except in cases where other provision is made by the Constitution or any other law.

There then follows certain specific examples of functions which he is at liberty to exercise in his own discretion, for example:

1   where a tribunal recommends to the Governor General the removal of a member of the Constituencies Boundaries Commission;[38]

2   where a similar tribunal recommends the removal of the supervisor of elections;[39]

3   where the House of Representatives passes a resolution of no-confidence in the Prime Minister who refuses within seven days to either resign or to advise a dissolution, the Governor General must act to remove the Prime Minister from office;[40]

4   where a tribunal recommends the removal of the Director of Public Prosecutions;[41]

---

36   See Dominica Constitution, ss 24 and 25.
37   Antigua Constitution, s 80(1).
38   *Ibid*, s 63(6).
39   *Ibid*, s 67(6).
40   *Ibid*, s 73(1).
41   *Ibid*, s 87(8).

5 where a similar body recommends the removal of the members of the Public Service Commission.[42]

The section, however, goes on to stipulate that a reference in the Constitution to the functions of the Governor General 'shall be construed as a reference to his powers and duties in the exercise of the executive authority of Antigua and Barbuda *and to any other powers and duties conferred on him as Governor General by or under the Constitution or any other law'.*[43] In other words, where a statute confers powers on the Governor General those powers cannot be exercised by him in his deliberate judgment, but upon the advice of Cabinet or a minister delegated by Cabinet. This is in keeping with the convention that the Sovereign acts on the advice of the Cabinet.

The Sovereign must not enter the political arena, with all that that implies for confrontation with the Cabinet and the members of the Opposition, not to mention the general public.

Failure to observe this convention can have dire consequences for the Governor General who is subject to dismissal by the Queen on the advice of the Prime Minister.[44] Such a failure can have the effect of bringing the Governor General into the political arena as a *player* instead of a *mediator*.

The Governor General does, however, have the right to appoint the Prime Minister,[45] and (in the circumstances mentioned above) to dismiss the Prime Minister.[46] He also has the power of appointing the Leader of the Opposition[47] and of dismissing him.[48]

The Governor General has the constitutional right to insist that he be furnished with any information concerning the government that he may request of the Prime Minister and that he be kept advised concerning the general conduct of government.[49]

It goes without saying that the Governor General is under a duty to offer to the Prime Minister advice and counsel and, if he considers his advice is being consistently ignored, to ask the Queen graciously to effect the withdrawal of his commission. If, however, the system is to work satisfactorily, there must be, at all time, collaboration between the Governor General and his Prime Minister. If, instead, confrontation ensues one must leave and that one must inevitably be the Governor General.

Removal of Governors General

Governors General may be removed by the same authority on whose recommendation they were appointed, viz, by the Prime Ministers of their respective countries. However, in any country where a Prime Minister may resort to dismissing the Governor General on

---

42 Antigua Constitution, s 99(5).
43 *Ibid*, s 80(6).
44 See below in this section.
45 Antigua Constitution, s 69(2).
46 *Ibid*, s 73(1).
47 *Ibid*, s 79(2).
48 *Ibid*, s 79(5).
49 *Ibid*, s 81.

a mere whim, a nominee for appointment to that high office should appreciate that his security of tenure in that position can, overnight, become tenuous in the extreme.

While Caribbean Constitutions of the Westminster model do not expressly afford to Governors General any immunities, whether during their term of office or otherwise, the relevant constitutional provisions which establish that office consistently declare that the Governor General 'shall be Her Majesty's representative' in the particular country.[50] In addition, these Constitutions[51] all vest the executive authority of the relevant country in Her Majesty and provide that it may be exercised on Her Majesty's behalf either directly by the Governor General or through officers subordinate to him. Accordingly, it is submitted that, at the very least, Governors General are not subject to personal liability for acts done in the lawful exercise of their constitutional functions.

Unique position of the Queen's representative in Grenada

From 1967, the position of Her Majesty's representative in Grenada was, in general, very stressful indeed, following the attainment of associated statehood in that year.

Mr Ian Turbott (later Sir Ian Turbott), who was the Administrator of Grenada, was appointed to the post of Governor. However, shortly after he was so appointed, differences arose between himself and the Premier and he was asked by Premier Gairy to make way for a new holder of the office. To succeed Sir Ian Turbott in the office of Governor, the Premier recommended the appointment of Dr Hilda Bynoe (later Dame Hilda Bynoe), a distinguished Grenadian medical practitioner who had been practising her profession in Trinidad and Tobago. For Gairy, this appointment conferred on Grenada the 'signal' honour of being the first British territory in the Caribbean to appoint a woman to this exalted office. True to form, he missed no opportunity in his attempt to make political capital, both locally and regionally, of this appointment which he then regarded to have been a unique achievement. In 1974, however, with the same facility of effort with which the Premier had secured the appointment of Dame Hilda as Governor of Grenada, he arranged for her removal from office in circumstances which will now be related.

There were, at that time, popular demonstrations of unprecedented proportions against the conduct of Gairy in particular and his Government in general; and the Governor, quite understandably, had shown some interest in the complaints being voiced by the demonstrators who had levelled a number of unjustifiable criticisms against her. In this state of turmoil, the Governor offered to resign her office by 14 January 1974, if the people so required. However, this appeared to be too great a jolt to Gairy's ego, for he is reported to have stated publicly that the Governor had been appointed on his specific recommendations and, therefore, could not demit office without his authority. Accordingly, on 12 January 1974, the Premier advised Her Majesty the Queen that the Governor's appointment should be terminated.[52] However, before the Palace could take action on this recommendation, Dame Hilda left the country hurriedly and unceremoniously on 21 January 1974. It was on that day that grave disturbances occurred

---

50 See constitutions of Antigua (s 22), Bahamas (Art 32), Barbados (s 28), Belize (s 30), Grenada (s 19), Jamaica (s 27), St Kitts (s 21), St Lucia (s 19), St Vincent (s 19).

51 *Ibid*, ss 68, 71, 63, 36, 57, 68, 51, 59 and 50 respectively.

52 See Duffus Commission, 1974, para 144.

in the capital, St George's, culminating in the murder of Rupert Bishop, the father of the late Maurice Bishop, to whom reference has been made in Chapter 10.

Shortly after Dame Hilda's departure, Grenada attained its independence on 7 February 1974, in circumstances which have been described in Chapter 10. She was succeeded in office by Sir Leo DeGale who, in consonance with Grenada's independent status, was appointed to be that country's first Governor General on the recommendation of the Prime Minister, Eric Gairy. Sir Leo also found it necessary before completing his term of office to leave Grenada to take up residence with his family in Australia. One can only guess the reasons for his migration, having regard to the fate of his two immediate predecessors in that post.

To succeed Sir Leo DeGale in the office of Governor General, Gairy recommended the appointment of his former Cabinet secretary, Mr Paul Scoon (later Sir Paul Scoon).

When on 13 March 1979, Maurice Bishop, then an elected member of Parliament, seized power as Prime Minister during the absence abroad of the substantive holder of that office (Sir Eric Gairy), it was stated in the 'Declaration of the Grenada Revolution' that constitutional government had 'been interrupted as a result of the violations and abuses of democracy committed by the administration of Eric Matthew Gairy', under the guise of constitutionality. Bishop, in his new role as Prime Minister, promised to return the country to constitutional rule 'at an early opportunity' and to appoint a 'Consultative Assembly' to consult with all the people for the purpose of the establishment of a new Constitution which would reflect the wishes and aspirations of all the people of Grenada. During this period of transition the People's Revolutionary Government (PRG) undertook to observe the fundamental rights and freedoms of the people subject to certain measures necessary to ensure stability, to eradicate 'Gairyism' and to protect the revolution.[53] This undertaking was not, however, to be honoured by Bishop's equally repressive regime.

One of the first acts of the new revolutionary regime was the suspension[54] of the 1973 Constitution of Grenada which provided, *inter alia*, for a Governor General 'who shall be appointed by Her Majesty and shall hold office during Her Majesty's pleasure'.

After issuing the further decree establishing the PRG[55] and vesting all executive and legislative powers therein, Mr Bishop proclaimed as follows:[56]

> The Head of State shall remain Her Majesty the Queen and her representative shall be the Governor General who shall perform such functions as the [PRG] may from time to time advise.

The section of the Constitution dealing with the executive authority of Grenada reads as follows:

> 57(1) The executive authority of Grenada is vested in Her Majesty.

---

53 Declaration of the Grenada Revolution on 13 March 1979; see *People's Laws of Grenada*, 1979, St Georges, Grenada: Government Printer, p 1.
54 People's Law (hereafter 'PL') No 1.
55 PL No 2.
56 PL No 3.

(2) Subject to the provisions of this Constitution, the executive authority of Grenada may be exercised on behalf of Her Majesty by the Governor General either directly or through officers subordinate to him.

(3) Nothing in this section shall prevent Parliament from conferring functions on persons or authorities other than the Governor General.

But, by virtue of the second decree passed by the PRG, all executive powers were transferred to the PRG. Accordingly, the ministers to whom the Queen's representative, the Governor General, had, pursuant to the relevant section of the Constitution, assigned responsibility for the administration of the government of Grenada, were forcibly prevented from performing their functions. For the most part, they were simply put in jail or permitted to leave the country. The Governor General (as well as the ministers) was rendered superfluous and their functions under the Constitution were effectively abrogated, although the regime purported to save the office of Head of State by a 'People's Law' which seems to have been accepted by the Queen and her advisers.

Traditionally, whenever a revolution occurs, such as took place in Grenada in March 1979, the revolutionary regime replaces the Head of State, quite often adopting a different nomenclature in place of the one in existence at the time of the triumph of the revolution. The new Head of State would normally be, or be appointed by, the person who presides over the 'Council of National Liberation' or (in the case of a military coup) 'the Revolutionary Military Council', or howsoever the new ruling body may be designated. However, in Grenada the tenure of the Head of State, the Governor General, was not interrupted by the revolution. To this extent, therefore, between 1979 and 1983 the position of the Governor General of Grenada was constitutionally anomalous, if not *sui generis*. During the four and a half years of rule by the PRG, the Governor General remained in almost the same position as he had occupied under the ousted regime; and it is perhaps ironic that this same Governor General from whom all executive functions were wrested in 1979, should become, after the unfortunate events of October 1983,[57] in reality the sole executive constitutional authority on the island.

Thus, in a tragic emergency, did a Governor General of an independent Commonwealth country find himself cast in a role of performing functions in a manner reminiscent of that in which early colonial governors, resplendent in their uniforms, plumes and scimitars, had been wont to execute their duties in the Caribbean. Needless to say, the Constitutions of the Commonwealth Caribbean countries never contemplated that Heads of State, be they Presidents or Governors General, would ever have been placed in a position in which they would be required, even from considerations of dire necessity, to rule by decree; or that if even they should unfortunately be so required, that they would usurp the functions of the cabinet and the legislature, under the guise that there is no lawful government in office.[58] But this is how things turned out after the revolution that overtook Grenada between 1979 and 1983.

---

57 These events have been fully described in Chapter 10, under Grenada, above.
58 See, generally, *Ref by His Excellency the Governor General (of Pakistan) No 1 of 1955*, reported in all Pakistan Legal Decisions (PLD) (Vol VII) 1955 Federal Court 435.

EXPERIENCES OF CERTAIN OTHER HEADS
OF STATE IN THE REGION

Apart from the incidents involving the Governors and Governors General of Grenada referred to above, there have been some unfortunate events affecting such dignitaries in other islands in the area, tending to indicate that, in some cases, the tenure of office of Head of State is becoming more and more coterminous with the term of office of the Prime Minister or Premier on whose recommendation they are respectively appointed. The recent experiences of the Heads of State of St Kitts and St Lucia, to which reference shall shortly be made, tend to underscore this point.

In November 1981, the Governor of the Associated State of St Kitts/Nevis (Sir Probyn Inniss) was relieved of his office by the Queen after unhappy differences had arisen between himself and the Premier of that State. The Governor had been appointed in 1975 on the recommendation of the former Premier. However, after a new Government, which won power in 1980, had been in office for about a year, severe friction developed as a result of the Governor's refusal to assent to a Bill that had been duly passed by Parliament, but which on the application of an Opposition member of Parliament, had been declared void by the High Court for having allegedly infringed the Constitution. Pending the hearing of the Government's appeal against the High Court's decision, the Bill was sent to the Governor for his assent on behalf, and in the name, of Her Majesty. Although the Attorney General, the principal legal adviser of the Government, had advised that the Bill was properly before the Governor for his assent, he nevertheless refused to signify his assent on the ground that in doing so he would be acting contrary to the Constitution.[59]

There appeared in the press at that time a particularly acrimonious exchange of correspondence between the Governor and the Premier.[60] The correspondence ended on 29 July 1981 with the following cryptic letter from the Premier to the Governor:[61]

Your Excellency,

I am in receipt of your letters of 11 June and 6 July, 1981.

I certainly have no intention of wasting more time on this fruitless acrimonious exchange of correspondence. Suffice it to say that I am certain that Her Majesty would not have written in such an offensive manner in the first place.

In all the circumstances I shall expect to be informed of your resignation shortly.

(Sgd) Kennedy A Simmonds,

Premier

When the Governor failed to submit his resignation as suggested, the Premier requested the withdrawal of his commission as Governor by Her Majesty the Queen. As a

---

59   See *The Labour Spokesman*, a newspaper published in St Kitts/Nevis, No 56, 2 December 1981, in which, on p 1, the ex-Governor, in an interview with Radio Antilles on 28 November 1981, is alleged to have said the government 'has been failing to comply with the laws and constitution'.

60   *Ibid.*

61   *Ibid*, p 7.

consequence, the Governor's commission was shortly thereafter withdrawn and he was given notice by Buckingham Palace to leave his official residence within three days.[62]

It is unfortunate that such an outstanding citizen of the country should have been subjected to treatment of this nature after such a long period of distinguished service.

The second point – the fact that Sir Probyn was a barrister – raises a fundamental question, viz, ought a governor who is legally trained (and who may be specially skilled in matters of constitutional law) to subordinate his own firmly held conviction on a vital issue affecting the exercise of his functions under the Constitution to the legal advice he receives from the principal legal adviser to the Government? The writer faced this very dilemma while he officiated as Governor of the same State. Indeed, there were occasions when he considered it expedient to summon the Attorney General to express his disagreement with legal advice tendered. Now, after a lapse of more than 30 years, he still considers that on all of the occasions such a course was desirable. He is, however, firmly of the view that if, after the necessary consultation, the official legal adviser persists in the advice tendered, the Governor or Governor General must be guided accordingly *if he wishes to retain his office as the Queen's representative in the particular State*.[63]

It is not without relevance to this discussion that the St Kitts/Nevis/Anguilla associated State Constitution of 1967[64] adopted a provision (which has been followed verbatim by the 1983 Independence Constitution) originally enacted in the 1966 Guyana Constitution[65] under which the Governor/Governor General is given the right once to question a recommendation made to him by the Cabinet or any other organ of government tendering advice. The provision in the 1983 St Kitts Independence Constitution reads as follows:[66]

> Provided that before the Governor General acts in accordance with a recommendation in any case he may, acting in his own deliberate judgment, once request the person or authority by whom it is made to reconsider the recommendation and, if upon any re-consideration of a recommendation, the person or authority makes a different recommendation, the Governor General, acting in his own deliberate judgment, may likewise once request the person or authority by whom it is made to reconsider that different recommendation.

Oddly enough, no such stricture is to be found in the Constitutions of the other former associated States and one is left to speculate as to the *raison d'être* therefor. The author, however, took full advantage of this clause during his tenure as Governor - in the interest of peace and national unity – but, regretfully, not with conspicuous success. It is for this reason he can write of Sir Probyn's difficulties with such understanding.

---

62 It is reliably stated that the document revoking the Governor's commission was delivered to him by a senior naval officer who landed with it on the grounds of the Governor's residence having been taken there by helicopter from a frigate of the Royal Navy then lying offshore.

63 The author considers he is in a unique position to make this point since, for reasons he has never made public, he found it necessary to ask the Queen to relieve him of his commission as Governor of the same state of St Kitts/Nevis/Anguilla. Her Majesty's approval was duly granted and the author retired with effect from 19 July 1969.

64 St Kitts/Nevis/Anguilla Associated State Constitution, s 55, sub-s (2) Proviso.

65 See Guyana Independence Order 1966 SI 1966/575, Sched 2, s 40.

66 St Kitts/Nevis Constitution, s 56, sub-s (2) Proviso.

ST LUCIA

A somewhat similar situation to the St Kitts issue arose in St Lucia in 1982, when the Head of State of that country found himself relieved of his commission as Governor General by the Queen in the following circumstances.

In 1979, shortly after the St Lucia Labour Party had won the general elections, with Allan Louisy as Prime Minister, pressure had apparently been brought upon the incumbent Governor General, Sir Allen Lewis, to retire from office: Sir Allen having been appointed by the outgoing Prime Minister, John Compton. At that point, the new Prime Minister had appointed as Acting Governor General a former secretary of the Labour Party, Boswell Williams, who was subsequently confirmed by the Queen in the office.

When in May 1982, John Compton's party was once more returned to office and as leader he again assumed the office of Prime Minister, he requested Boswell Williams to retire from the office with effect from 13 December 1982 – St Lucia's National Day. Despite repeated requests between May and December 1982 to surrender the office, Williams stubbornly refused, on the ground that he had been appointed to the office by the Queen and that he would not be pressured to relinquish it by what he termed 'political discrimination'. The Prime Minister therefore had no alternative, but to ask Her Majesty the Queen to revoke his commission, whereupon Her Majesty duly obliged with its withdrawal on a fixed day and re-appointed the retired Governor General (Sir Allen Lewis) with effect from the following day for a further term of office.[67]

DOMINICA

Reference has already been made when discussing constitutional developments in *Dominica* to the fact that the President of that country decamped rather unceremoniously when a state of rebellion threatened the country, without even appointing someone to act in his stead. The President subsequently tendered his resignation and never returned to Dominica. He also thereafter brought a suit against the Government in London, England, which he subsequently withdrew.[68] He died there shortly thereafter.

CONCLUSION

In the preceding pages of this chapter we have described in some detail the constitutional provisions relating to the appointment, functions and removal from office of Heads of State in the independent countries of the Commonwealth Caribbean. We have seen that, in three of these jurisdictions, a republican form of Constitution is in force, the Heads of State of these countries being styled Presidents. We have also shown that although these offices are similarly designated, the respective provisions applicable to each of them differ in several material particulars. In the remaining countries of this group, which all have

---

67   These details were kindly furnished to the writer when he interviewed the Prime Minister, the Rt Hon John Compton, on 17 April 1984, in St Lucia.

68   This information was kindly supplied to the author by the Prime Minister of Dominica.

monarchical-type Constitutions in force, there is greater similarity in the provisions with respect to the appointment, functions and removal from office of the respective Heads of State – Governors General.

Of course, the practical application of these provisions has been the primary focus of our attention; and we have described the somewhat bizarre experiences of some Heads of State in the region. Almost all of the incidents to which we have referred have occurred in the territories which became independent since 1974.[69] The Heads of State of the countries which became independent in the early or mid-1960s[70] appear to have been spared the travails of their counterparts in the former associated States.

Some of the events outlined above disclose an unfortunate, but perhaps unavoidable, tendency on the part of some Heads of Government to regard Heads of State as being required to fulfil a partisan role – a role for which they are ill-equipped and one which, it is fair to say, was never contemplated by the Constitutions which established the office of the Queen's representative. The genesis of this tendency lies in the fact that, in the selection of nominees for appointment to what must be regarded as a high, exalted office, Heads of Government appear in the main to have been motivated by narrow party political concerns. Thus, the successful appointee becomes less capable of symbolising the total unity of the nation. Moreover, the incidents involving Dame Hilda Bynoe and Sir Leo DeGale, respectively Governor and Governor General of Grenada, seem to expose the manner in which the constitutional provisions under which Governors General are appointed are applied in practice. The typical provision will be seen to contain four elements, namely:

(1) there shall be a Governor General;

(2) who shall be Her Majesty's representative;

(3) who shall be appointed by Her Majesty; and

(4) who shall hold office during Her Majesty's pleasure.

Of these four elements, only the first, viz, 'there shall be a Governor General', appears to square with the factual position. With respect to the appointment of the Governor General, the Prime Minister, on whose recommendation the appointment is made, regards himself as the appointing authority. The Governor General once appointed and installed in office becomes, in fact, the representative of the Government (which in the smaller territories is synonymous with being the representative of the Prime Minister or Premier). In this respect also, the peculiar position of the Governor General of Grenada immediately after the October 1983 troubles should be noted. It appeared from his conduct at that time that he was neither Her Majesty's representative nor the representative of the Prime Minister, there being no elected incumbent in that office.

Finally, the experiences of Sir Probyn Inniss of St Kitts and Nevis, Mr Boswell Williams of St Lucia and Dame Hilda Bynoe of Grenada, all illustrate that the tenure of office of a Governor General depends less upon Her Majesty's pleasure than on the displeasure of the person who, for the time being, holds the office of Premier or Prime Minister.

---

69 Grenada was the first former associated State to become independent in 1974.

70 These are Jamaica, Trinidad and Tobago, Barbados and Guyana.

The reason for the untenable situation in which some Heads of State in the newly independent countries of the Commonwealth Caribbean have been placed appears to lie in the fact the constitutional position of Her Majesty in Britain and of her Governors General in other parts of the Commonwealth depends on the observance of certain well established conventions, which regretfully have not been understood in the former associated States, or even in some of the independent jurisdictions. This is quite understandably so: these conventions took centuries to reach full development in Britain. Nevertheless, our Constitutions require their observance for the effective and satisfactory governance of the countries concerned. In addition, the relatively miniscule size of the political units for which the constitutions were tailored (or not tailored) and the concomitant absence of a significant body of public opinion, also contribute to the unfortunate experiences which our people and Heads of State alike must endure. It seems to have been assumed (quite falsely) by the Commonwealth Office draftsmen that a Constitution which works well for Jamaica or Trinidad, both with populations in excess of one million inhabitants, will, for example, work equally well for St Kitts which has a population of less than 100,000 persons: or for St Lucia and St Vincent with just over that number. And our politicians, anxious only to receive these dubious credentials of independence, have done nothing during the pre-independence 'negotiations' to dispel this false assumption. Hopefully, however, with the maturing of our politicians and heightening of the political consciousness of our electorates, these vitally necessary conventions will emerge.

In 1984–85, a Constitution Commission reviewing the Grenada Constitution found a groundswell of opinion in favour of a presidential system. Since then, three other commissions found public opinion strongly in favour of the Head of State being a citizen of the states in the case of Jamaica, St Kitts and Nevis and Barbados. Reports emanating from Antigua and Barbuda, St Lucia and St Vincent point in the same direction.

MYSTIQUE NO LONGER COMPELLING

Enlightened citizens no longer find the mystique of an absent Queen compelling. The Head of State is seen as one who is a symbol of unity in a polarised political context, who is a citizen of stature and who can use his influence and good offices in time of need.

His term of office would be prescribed by the Constitution and everyone, including the appointee, will realise that he is to demit office at the end of a five year term or whatever else may be the length of the term.

Governors General are appointed by commission during Her Majesty's pleasure. Although, they know at the relevant time it is the Prime Minister who makes the appointment, once in office they tend to feel they cannot be removed by the Prime Minister and the Queen will not remove them unless the Prime Minister so directs. The result is that there is almost always a degree of bitterness between the Prime Minister and the Governor General when the latter's time is up. All this will disappear when the Head of State is appointed for a time certain, even if there is provision for his re-appointment for a further term. When that time will come is not easy to predict since, in the smaller territories comprising the OECS, the procedure for amending this particular section of the

Constitution requires the votes of a 2:3 majority on a referendum. Unless there is bi-partisan agreement on the issue (which is hard to come by), the change will be well nigh impossible. But our politicians may one day surprise the rest of us.

CHAPTER 16

EPILOGUE

OUR POST-INDEPENDENCE CONSTITUTIONS

In these pages, we have expressed the view that, from the end of the Second World War in 1945 to the beginning of the 21st century, the Commonwealth Caribbean witnessed much constitution making as one of its incidents of decolonisation.[1]

We have looked at the sources of the relevant constitutional provisions.[2]

We have examined in some depth the changing functions and responsibilities of the judiciary, in the course of which we have suggested changes in court administration to underscore the institutional independence of the judges in both the superior and lower courts.[3]

We have drawn attention to a variety of problems encountered throughout the area in the operation of all the Constitutions which have been the objects of our study.[4]

We have critically reviewed a number of Bills of Rights cases decided by different judiciaries throughout the region. This work has been a tribute to the industry and single-mindedness of our judges who have on the whole displayed much judicial valour in the process.[5]

In the interest of students-at-law and others interested in the subject, we have also examined in brief compass a number of broad themes such as the rule of law,[6] the sovereignty of Parliament,[7] the separation of powers[8] and the conventions of the Constitution.[9]

Implicit in our study of the broad themes, we have shown that the theory of the indivisibility of the Crown has undergone considerable change since decolonisation began. In those countries where the Queen remains Head of State, there is still a constitutional fiction that all official acts are done in Her Majesty's name, that the assent given to legislation is 'the royal assent'. The name of the Queen appears upon all writs in the civil courts and criminal indictments are framed against accused persons in the Sovereign's name, viz, 'R v John James'. Public officers are sometimes described as servants of the Crown. In most Caribbean jurisdictions, the local police force is styled, the ... Royal Police Force. Even the prison is referred to as Her Majesty's Prison.

---

1   See Wolf-Phillips (1970), p 18. See, also, a useful discussion of criteria of statehood by Judge Edward Laing in an article entitled 'Independence and islands' (Laing, 1978, pp 302–06).
2   See Chapter 1.
3   See Chapter 13.
4   Chapters 7–12.
5   Chapter 6.
6   Chapter 2.
7   Chapter 3.
8   Chapter 4.
9   Chapter 5.

In the three republics, the position is entirely different. The Queen is no longer their Head of State, although honorifically she is, in relation to these territories, still Head of the Commonwealth. But loyal toasts are, in those jurisdictions, made to the President. Crown counsel is replaced by State counsel, Queen's counsel by senior counsel, 'the State' appears on legal documents *vice* the Queen (R). The citizens of the three countries no longer owe allegiance, for purposes of the law of treason, to the Queen, but to the President.

The *sovereignty of Parliament* (as has been shown) in its old form has given way to a new concept providing for Parliament in certain prescribed circumstances to yield to referenda and other constraints as a condition precedent to constitutional amendment. Thus, in the Caribbean, only the Parliaments of Trinidad and Tobago, Barbados and Belize can be truly referred to as sovereign, since those Parliaments are competent to change all laws, including the Constitution, without recourse to the type of deeply entrenched clauses provided in the Constitutions of the other States, under which alteration cannot occur unless approved by a referendum, as well as by Parliament itself. And even this statement is subject to the qualification that Parliament in these three countries, in amending the Constitution, is compelled to comply with the provisions of the instrument itself.

The *separation of powers* is no longer the absolute doctrine it at one time seemed to be. Ministers of Government as instruments of the executive daily make inroads into the arena of the legislature by the many rules, regulations and orders they are empowered to make, as has been illustrated in the text. In the course of this work, we have also seen that there was a time before the separation of powers became more pronounced when the Governor was actively part and parcel of the legislative process in that, not only did he physically preside over the legislative council with an original and a casting vote in all the territories of the Caribbean, but he was even empowered (as he still is in the ones that remain Colonies) to veto legislation passed by the legislative chamber, whenever he considered such legislation repugnant to the interest of the United Kingdom. Generally speaking, there is today much in common between the *legislature* and the *executive* in the sense that all the legislative measures must first be passed upon by the executive in Cabinet. Accordingly, the separation of powers currently operates mainly as between the judiciary on the one hand and the other two organs of government (the executive and legislature) on the other; and that is as it should be. Accordingly, we have throughout this work highlighted how essential it is that the judiciary should continue to be impartial and independent, if the rule of law is to be maintained and a proper balance struck between the individual and the State in the multifarious activities of government.

CONSTITUTIONS TO BE KEPT UNDER CONSTANT REVIEW

It is hoped that as a result of the spate of Constitutional Commissions which have spawned the jurisdictions in the two decades before the end the 20th century, the political directorate will be convinced that they cannot let up in their efforts to remodel their constitutional instruments. The public has of late been showing a keen interest in governance.

In this connection, we have referred with qualified approval to the achievement of Guyana in framing the Constitution that was at the time (1970–80) considered suited to the ethos and aspirations of its people. But Communism has, since 1989, become an unpopular ideology and the Guyana Constitution Commission of 1999 made a valiant attempt to distance itself from some of the concepts informing the 1980 Co-operative Republic which provided for such bodies as the Supreme Organs of Democratic Power, the National Congress of Local Democratic Organs and the Supreme Congress of the People. To this end, we have outlined the efforts of the commission and of Parliament in trying to fashion a new Constitution in keeping with the 21st century. From all appearances, the Opposition is actively collaborating in that venture.[10]

We have adverted to the carefully crafted Republican Constitution of Trinidad and Tobago introduced in 1976 following a local rebellion by 'Black Power' elements against the status quo which triggered the appointment of the Wooding Commission.[11] We have also drawn attention to a follow-up Commission appointed in 1987 by the Prime Minister (ANR Robinson) who, at the time of writing, is the President of the republic. The events which occurred in late 2000 and early 2001, at the time this section was being written, send a warning signal as to the basis on which a President, as Head of State, should be given a share of executive powers together with the Prime Minister. The clashes between the President and the Prime Minister also set off alarm bells as to whether active politicians should not be debarred from holding the office of President, if the latter is to be pre-dominantly a figurehead. The alternative is to have an Executive President.

WHAT OBJECTIVES SHOULD A CONSTITUTION SERVE?

We hope that in the preceding pages we have shown that a Constitution is not an end in itself. In the ultimate analysis, it is how a constitutional instrument is permitted to work that matters. The most well intentioned instrument may easily become entirely counter-productive, if it only enures to the benefit of the political arm or even one section of the people of the country it is designed to serve. For, we must never forget that in small communities such as the Caribbean States, it is easy for a Prime Minister, wielding an all pervasive influence, to manipulate almost everything and everybody, especially since, in most territories, he (or she) is the appointing authority in respect of almost every person or board operating in the public domain.

A further matter which has been carefully examined in this book is the present plight of small, poor Caribbean nations which – as a result of the pressures from the Committee on Decolonisation at the United Nations – have exercised their undoubted right to self-determination and become independent.[12] They dwell in a cruel, polarised, selfish world. Those countries which nature has placed geographically in the Caribbean Sea and, therefore, like the rest of Latin America find themselves subject to the political doctrine which has shaped American policy of continental hegemony over weaker neighbours, must not be surprised if Washington sooner or later acts towards them as it did to Santo Domingo and to Grenada, viz, employs military might to knock them into shape

---

10 See Chapter 8.
11 See Chapter 9.
12 See Laing, 1978, pp 302–06.

whenever any of them attempts to fall out of line with the stronger neighbour to the North. Thus, we find ourselves living in what David Green has so rightly characterised as 'a closed hemisphere in an open world'.[13]

CARICOM'S INTERVENTION IN GUYANA, ST KITTS/NEVIS AND ST VINCENT

The attempts at concilation performed by CARICOM in Guyana, St Kitts and Nevis and St Vincent, at the end of the last century and at the turn of this century, in settling political differences are worthy of praise. Care should, however, be taken that senior politicians sent on conciliation missions do not personally undermine the process by unfairly sabotaging the central government or others trying to assist. Politicians from one territory have their secret political allegiances in other jurisdictions and it would be more transparent and desirable for CARICOM to utilise in the future the more objective services of retired senior officials of the rank of ex-Presidents, ex-Governor Generals, senior ex-judges, ex-heads of international organisations, top university personalities and top executives from the private sector – although this list is by no means exhaustive.

THE IMPACT OF THE UNITED NATIONS AND THE ORGANISATION OF AMERICAN STATES

The developments which have been considered in this volume emphasise not only that most of the countries reviewed have succeeded in being de-colonised but they demonstrate the part which the United Nations has played in effecting that de-colonisation. In this connection, the attention of the reader is directed to a detailed discussion in the previous work[14] of how effective the UN Committee on Decolonisation was in bringing about both self-determination in the Caribbean area and the status of associated Statehood, a process which inevitably gave the islands of Grenada, St Vincent, St Lucia, Dominica, Antigua and St Kitts and Nevis valuable experience in the internal operations of their governments in preparation for their later independence. The United Nations Organisation through its development programmes has also been most supportive of the territories by way of capacity building in the spheres of public administration and constitutional change.

In so far as the Organisation of American States is concerned that body, while not taking an active part in the matter of de-colonisation, has played the role of an interested bystander, ready to assist where necessary. In 1973, in connection with the study of provisions of the charter of that organisation on the admission of new members, the General Assembly adopted a resolution asking the General Secretariat to prepare a background information report on the status of the non-independent countries in the western hemisphere and other countries in the Americas having ties with countries

---

13 Green, 1971, p 230.
14 See Phillips, 1977, Chapter VIII.

outside the hemisphere. Since that time, a yearly updated version of the report has been presented to the General Assembly.

The Organisation of American States has therefore come to regard the independent Caribbean States as truly integrated into that body, as witness the fact that a former Assistant Secretary General is a national of Barbados, and another a national of Trinidad and Tobago. It is also significant that the organisation, in 1983, held in Barbados a seminar on 'Comparison of Law and Legal Systems of the Commonwealth Caribbean States and the other Members of the Organisation of American States'. There is no doubt whatever, too, that the organisation has increasingly shown deep concern for the social, cultural and economic interests of the Caribbean in many ways and in no greater way than in the Declaration of La Paz, adopted at the ninth regular session of the General Assembly in 1979,[15] para 4 of which:

> ... expresses its satisfaction with the progress the nations of this hemisphere have made in achieving independence, and re-affirms its determination to aid in the continuing process of decolonisation of the region so as not to defer the exercise of the legitimate right of the peoples to forge their own destiny.

THE POLITICS OF FRAGMENTATION

As we begin the 21st century, it is clear from the foregoing that the strides we have made in the Caribbean in governing ourselves have been accompanied by hideous fragmentation and proliferation. Independent jurisdictions: national honours: national flags: national anthems: even national airlines: all these abound. Is it not time to draw the curtain down on fragmentation in these many spheres?

WHITHER THE CARIBBEAN?

Where do we go from here?

As the author brings this study to a close, he feels bound to underscore what he has already submitted in a previous work,[16] viz, that the forces of divisiveness are today more actively at work that at any other period of our history and that the surest route to persistent poverty and economic deterioration and catastrophe is by way of the continued insistence on trying to operate the present multiplicity of jurisdictions as separate independent States on the world scene. Surely, our politicians are wise enough to take a hard look at the United States and Canada, from both of which they so often request aid and technical assistance, and to observe how each of these two vast countries has come together as one nation to further the interests of its citizens.

The leaders in the Caribbean have deemed it fit in the space of 38 years since 1962 to install three Presidents, nine Governors General, six Governors, as well as 12 Prime

---

15 OAS – AG/RES 429 (IXO/79) Declaration of La Paz Resolution adopted at the 12th plenary session held on 31 October 1979.
16 See Phillips, 1977, pp 78, 79 and 201–02.

Ministers, one Premier, four Chief Ministers and between 150 and 200 ministers of government, as the top administrative machinery for a population of about five million, that is, less than one-half of the population of the City of Shanghai in China, the administrative machine of which the writer was privileged to observe on visits in 1983, 1986 and 1988. The duplication of ambassadorial establishments in such capitals as London, Brussels, Ottawa, New York and Washington boggles the mind and can only result in further depriving these pauperised States of the already scarce financial resources at their disposal. Despite the existence of CARICOM, there is little rationalisation of industry – as a result of which oil refineries, beer factories, flour mills, cement factories, rum distilleries, are duplicated in various territories – sometimes within 100 miles of each other. Is it therefore any wonder that there existed, by the year 2002, in this area political confusion, attempts at secession, revolution and human suffering? The political upheavals taking place in Guyana and St Vincent at the dawn of the new century did not engender optimism. However, we commend the steps initiated by OECS Heads who seem to have agreed in July 2001 that, with effect from 1 January 2002, there should be freedom of movement of people, a common passport, an identification card and an Economic Union of Eastern Caribbean States (ECUIS) in place. If these developments do materialise, they will give a clear indication that our leaders have begun to work again towards political and economic union.

To the extent that politicians fail to discern that unity is strength, a thick chauvinistic darkness continues to engulf our leaders and we must look to a new generation to dispel the encircling gloom. When that time comes, sooner or later, we can only earnestly hope that our benighted people – after having endured the weeping of a long night – will share in that joy which cometh in the morning. The global village which is our world becomes smaller and smaller. The sooner we realise that, the better.

BIBLIOGRAPHY

SECTION I

General works

Alexis, Francis, *Changing Caribbean Constitutions*, 1987, Bridgetown, Barbados: Carib Research and Publications

Alexis, Francis, *The Labour Movement and the Law of Barbados*, 1982, Commonwealth Caribbean Legal Essays, Faculty of Law, Cave Hill, Barbados

Barnett, LG, *Constitutional Law of Jamaica* , 1977, Oxford: OUP

Blackstone's Commentaries on the Laws of England, Books I–IV, 1803, London: printed by A Strahan, Law Printers to the King's Most Excellent Majesty for T Cadell and W Davies, The Strand

Cardozo, Benjamin N, *The Nature of the Judicial Process*, 1964, New Haven and London: Yale UP

Chaskalson, A, 'Annex I', *Developing Human Rights Jurisprudence*, Vol 2, *A Second Judicial Colloquium on the Domestic Application of International Human Rights Norms*, 1989, London: Comm Secretariat

Dale, Sir William, The Modern Commonwealth, 1983, London: Butterworths

Demerieux, Margaret, *Fundamental Rights in the Commonwealth Caribbean*, 1992, Faculty of Law, University of the West Indies

Denning, Lord, *The Due Process of Law*, 1980, London: Butterworths

de Smith, Stanley, *The New Commonwealth and its Constitutions*, 1964, London: Stevens and Sons

Dicey, AV, *The Law of the Constitution*, 10th edn, 1959, London: Macmillan

Eaton, George E, *Alexander Bustamante and Modern Jamaica*, 1975, Kingston: Kingston Publishers

Emanuel, Patrick, *Crown Colony Politics in Grenada 1917–1951*, 1978, ISER, University of the West Indies

Erskine May, T, *Treatise on the Law, Privileges, Procedures and Usages of Parliament*, 20th edn, 1983, London: Butterworths

Fiadjoe, Albert K, *Commonwealth Caribbean Public Law*, 1999, London: Cavendish Publishing

Frankfurter, Mr Justice F, 'Discussions of current developments in administrative law' (1938) 47 Yale LJ 515

Friedland, Martin L, *A Place Apart: Judicial Independence and Accountability*, a report prepared by the Canadian Judicial Council, 1995

Green, David, *The Containment of Latin America: A History of the Myths and Realities of the Good Neighbour Policy*, 1971, Chicago: Quadrangle

Hailsham, Lord, *The Dilemma of Democracy, Diagnosis and Prescription*, 1978, London: Collins

Hart, HLA, *The Concept of Law*, 1961, Oxford: Clarendon

Hayek, FA, *The Road to Serfdom*, 1944, Chicago: Chicago UP

Hogg, PW, *Constitutional Law of Canada*, 2nd edn, 1985, Toronto: Carswell

Jagan, Cheddi, *The West on Trial: The Fight for Guyana's Freedom*, 1966, Berlin: Seven Seas Publishers

Jennings, Sir Ivor, *The Law and the Constitution*, 5th edn, 1933, London: University of London

Jennings, Sir Ivor, *Constitutional Laws of the Commonwealth – Vol I: The Monarchies*, 1961, Oxford: Clarendon

Jowell, J, 'The rule of law today', in Jowell, J and Oliver, D, *The Changing Constitution*, 2nd edn, 1989, Oxford: Clarendon

Jowell, J and Oliver, D, *The Changing Constitution*, 2nd edn, 1989, Oxford: Clarendon

Kerr, Sir John, *Matters for Judgment*, 1979, London: Macmillan

Lawson, FH and Bentley, DJ, *Constitutional and Administrative Law*, 1961, London: Butterworths

Lester, A, 'The constitution: decline and renewal in the changing constitution', in Howell, J and Oliver, D, *The Changing Constitution*, 2nd edn, 1989, Oxford: Clarendon

Lester, Lord and Pannick, David (eds), *Human Rights Law and Practice*, 1995, London: Butterworths

Lewis, Gordon K, *The Growth of the Modern West Indies*, 1968, New York and London: Monthly Review Press/Modern Reader Paper Backs

Lutchman, Harold, *From Colonialism to Co-operative Republic: Aspects of Political Development in Guyana*, 1974, Institute of Caribbean Studies, University of Puerto Rico

Maitland, FW, *Constitutional History of England*, 1959, Cambridge: CUP

Marshall, Gregory, *Parliamentary Sovereignty and the Commonwealth*, 1957, Oxford: Clarendon

Montesquieu, C de, *L'Esprit des Lois* (1748), 1989, Cambridge: CUP

Munroe, Trevor, *The Politics of Constitutional Decolonisation: Jamaica 1944–1962*, 1972, Surrey: Unwin Bros/Gresham Press

Nettleford, Rex, *Manley and the New Jamaica*, 1971, Jamaica: Longman, Caribbean

Phillips, Sir Fred, *Freedom in the Caribbean: A Study in Constitutional Change*, 1977, Dobbs Ferry, New York: Oceana

Phillips, Sir Fred, *The Evolving Legal Profession in the Commonwealth*, 1978, Dobbs Ferry, New York: Oceana

Phillips, Sir Fred, *West Indian Constitutions – Post Independence Reform*, 1985, Dobbs Ferry, New York: Oceana

Robson, WA, *Justice and Administrative Law*, 2nd edn, 1947, London: Stevens

Ryan, Selwyn D, *Race and Nationalism in Trinidad and Tobago: A study of Decolonisation in a Multi-racial Society*, 1974, Institute of Social and Economic Research, University of the West Indies, Mona, Jamaica

Salmond, Sir John, *Jurisprudence*, 12th edn, 1966, London: Sweet and Maxwell

Scarman, Lord, 'English law: the new dimension', Hamlyn Lecture, 1974

Shahabuddeen, Mohamed, *The Legal System of Guyana*, 1973, Georgetown: Guyana Printery

Tarnopolsky, WS, *The Canadian Bill of Rights*, 2nd revised edn, 1975, Toronto: McClelland and Stewart

Trudeau, Pierre Elliott, *Memoirs*, 1993, Toronto: McClelland and Stewart

Westlake, Donald, *Under an English Heaven*, 1973, London: Hodder and Stoughton

Wheare, KC, *Modern Constitutions*, 1951, London: OUP

Williams, Eric, *Inward Hunger: The Education of a Prime Minister*, 1969, London: André Deutsch

Williams, Eric, *Capitalism and Slavery*, 1964, London: André Deutsch

Williams, Eric, *The History of the People of Trinidad and Tobago*, 1961, Port of Spain, Trinidada: PNM Publishing House

Wilson, Roy and Galpin, Brian (eds), *Interpretation of Statutes*, 11th edn, 1961, London: Sweet & Maxwell

Wolf-Phillips, Leslie, *Constitutions of Modern States*, 1968, London, Pall Mall

SECTION II

Official publications, articles and other documents

Anguilla (Appointed Day) Order 1980 SI 1980/1953

Anguilla (Consequential Provisions) Act 1981 SI 1981/603

Anguilla Constitution Order 1982 SI 1982/334

Anguilla (Constitution) Order 1976 SI 1976/50

Anthony, Dr Kenny, 'Dismissal at pleasure: the history and consequences of its abolition' (1983) 7 WILJ 56

Antigua and Barbuda Constitution Order 1981 SI 1981/1106

Antoine, Rose Marie, 'The re-introduction of the cat-o'-nine tails: a tale of woe' (1991) 1(1) (June) Caribbean Law Rev 26–35

Alexis, Dr Francis, 'When is an existing law saved? (1976) Public Law 256

Arthurs, HW, 'Re-thinking administrative law – a slightly Dicey business' (1979) 17 Osgoode Hall LJ Pt 1

Barbados Constitution Review Commission Report, 1979

Barbados Independence Order 1966 SI 1966/1455

Belize Constitution, Gazetted, 15 August 1981

Bermuda Constitution Order 1968 SI 1968/182

Bermuda Constitution (Amendment) (No 2) Order 1979 SI 1979/1310

Bermuda Constitution (Amendment) Order 1979 SI 1979/452

Brazier, R and Robbillard, St J, 'Constitutional conventions: the Canadian Supreme Court's view reviewed' (1982) PL 28

British Foreign Affairs Committee, *Fifth Report*, Session 1981–82 (HC (1981–82) 47

British Guiana (Constitution) Order in Council 1961 SI 1961/1188

Cayman Islands Constitution Order 1972 SI 1972/1101

CO 7/116 1861 January No 2

Commonwealth of Dominica Constitution Order 1978 SI 1978/1027

Constitution of the Republic of Guyana Act 1980 (No 2 of 1980)

Demerieux, Margaret, 'The codification of constitutional conventions in the Commonwealth Caribbean' (1982) 31 ICLQ 263

Denning, Lord, 'The individual, the State and the law' (1964) 6 The Lawyer

Deschênes, J, *Masters in their Own House: A Study on the Independent Administration of the Courts*, Ottawa, Canadian Judicial Council, 1981

Dolgopol, Ustinia, 'Protecting the independence of judges and lawyers' (1984) 10(3) Commonwealth Law Bulletin 1369–72 (the author is secretary for the Centre for the Independence of Judges and Lawyers (CIJL))

Dominica Termination of Association – Miscellaneous No 20, Cmd 7279, 1978 London: HMSO

Duffus Commission, *Report of the Commission of Enquiry under the Chairmanship of Sir Herbert Duffus*, submitted to the Governor General on 27 February 1975

Dumas Task Force, *Report of the Task Force on the Judicial and Legal Services Commission of the Eastern Caribbean Supreme Court* (Mr Reginald Dumas), 2000

Eastern Caribbean Supreme Court Agreement, 1982

European Convention on Human Rights, Cmd 8969, 1953, London: HMSO

Forde Commission Report, Report of the Constitution Review Commission into the Barbados Constitution (Chairman: Sir Henry Forde) 1998

Foreign Affairs Committee, Second Report from the Session 1983–84 'Grenada', London: HMSO

Grenada Constitution Order 1973 SI 1973/2155

Hansard, House of Commons Debate on the Antigua (Termination of Association) Order, 1981

Hansard, State Opening and First Meeting of the 1983 Session of the Legislative Assembly, 17 February 1983 (Cayman Islands)

Hansard, Trinidad House of Representatives, 4 February 1977

Hughes, Alister, *Violation of Human Rights in Grenada*, 1977, Human Rights Research Project of the Caribbean Conference of Churches

Hyatali, Sir Isaac, 'The protection of judicial independence' (1983) Civil Justice Quarterly 276 (Address delivered at the Sixth Commonwealth Law Conference in Lagos, Nigeria, 1980)

Jamaica (Constitution) Order in Council 1962 SI 1962/1550

James, RW, 'Address' (1983) Guyana Bar Association Review, NS Vol 5, 1 December

James, RW, 'The state of human rights enforcement in the Co-operative Republic of Guyana' (1983) (May) West Indian Law Journal 14–35

Johnson, P, 'No Law without order, no freedom without law' (1999) *Sunday Telegraph*, 26 December

Joint Select Committee Final Report, 1995, Joint Select Committee of Jamaican Houses of Parliament on Constitutional and Electoral Reform, Gordon House

Laing, Edward A, 'Independence and islands: the decolonisation of the British Caribbean' (1978) 12 International Law and Politics 281–312

Leeward Islands (Emergency Powers) Order in Council 1959 SI 1959/2286

Lewis, Sir Allen, 'The separation of powers: its relevance for parliamentary government in the Caribbean' (1979) WILJ 4

Liverpool, NJO, *A Study in Peaceful Extra-constitutional Change on the Caribbean Island of Dominica: An Application of the Legal Doctrine of Necessity*, 1978, University of the West Indies, Cave Hill, Barbados: Faculty of Law

Lowenthal, David and Clarke, Colin G, 'Common ands, common aims: the distinctive Barbudan community', in Cross, Malcolm and Marks, Arnand (eds), *Peasants, Plantations and Rural Communities*, 1979, Department of Sociology, University of Surrey, Department of Caribbean Studies, Royal Institute of Linguistics and Anthropology

Lowenthal, David and Clarke, Colin G, 'Slave breeding in Barbuda: the past of a negro myth', (1977), from *Annals of New York Academy of Sciences*, Vol 292 (June) pp 510–35

Montserrat Letters Patent, 1959

Montserrat Royal Instructions, 1959

Phillips Commission Report, Report of the Constitutional Commission into the St Kitts and Nevis Constitution (Chairman: Sir Fred Phillips), 1998

Phillips, Sir Fred, 'Politics and the administration of justice in newly independent countries' (1966) 16(2) University of Toronto LJ 401

Pollard, Duke, 'Revisiting Chaguaramus: Institutional development in CARICOM since 1973', (1997) 67 (June) Caricom Perspective, pp 223–28

Pollard, Duke, 'The Caribbean Court of Justice: What it is and what it does' (2000) pamphlet, the Caribbean Community Secretariat, 8 April

Rawlins, Hugh, *The Caribbean Court of Justice: The History and Analysis of the Debate*, Report Commissioned by the Preparatory Committee of the Caribbean Court of Justice, 2000

Report of the Antigua Constitutional Conference, December 1980

Report of Bermuda Commission under the Chairmanship of Sir Hugh Wooding, 1968

Report of the Closer Union Commission of 1932

Report of Commonwealth of Dominica Constitution Review Commission (Chairman: Right Hon PT Georges), February 1999

Report of the Constitution Commission of Trinidad and Tobago (Chairman, Sir Isaac Hyatali), June 1990

Report of Constitution Task Force appointed by the Government of St Kitts and Nevis (Chairman: Sir Fred Phillips), July 1999

Report of the Dominica Constitutional Conference, Cmd 6901, 1977 (May), London: HMSO

Report of the Grenada Constitutional Review Commission (Chairman, Sir Fred Phillips), November 1985

Report of the Hosea Riots Commission, 1884

Report of the Major Wood Commission of 1921

Report of the Royal Commission into the 1977 Disturbances, Bermuda, under the Chairmanship of the Rt Hon Lord Pitt of Hampstead, 1977

Report of the Royal Commission on Public Revenues, 1882

Report of the Royal Franchise Commission of 1888

Report of the Special Select Committee on the Report of the Constitution Reform Commission, Guyana (Chairman: Hon RD Persaud), November 1999

Report of the Sugar Commission of 1929

Report of the Tobago House of Assembly for the year ended 31 December 1982, 1983

Report of the Trinidad and Tobago Constitution Commission, presented to the Governor General, 22 January 1974

Report of the Trinidad Disturbances Commission of 1937

Report of the West Indian Royal Commission of 1897

Report of the Water Riots Commission of 1903

St Christopher, Nevis and Anguilla Constitution Order 1967 SI 1967/228

St Christopher and Nevis Constitution Order 1983 SI 1983/881

St Lucia Constitution Order 1978 SI 1978/1901

St Vincent Constitution Order 1979 SI 1979/916

Tikeram, Sir Moti, 'Who judges the judges?' (1993) 19(3) (July) Commonwealth Law Bulletin 1231

Treaty establishing the Organisation of Eastern Caribbean States, signed 18 June 1981

Trindale, FA, 'The removal of the Malayan judges' (1990) 106 LQR 51–56.

UN General Assembly, Distr General A/AC 109/722, 27 October 1982

Walsh, Declan, 'Mugabe to force chief justice out of court' (2001) *The Independent*, 1 March, p 18

West Indies Associated States Supreme Court Order 1967 SI 1967/223

Whitson, Agnes, *The Constitutional Development of Jamaica, 1660–1729*, 1929, Manchester

Wolf-Phillips, Leslie, 'Post-independence change in the Commonwealth' (1970) 18 Political Studies 18

Wolf-Phillips, Leslie, 'Constitutional legitimacy: a study of the doctrine of necessity' (1979) (October) 1(4) Third World Quarterly, pp 97–133

INDEX